Doing Criminological Research

Doing Criminological Research

Pamela Davies | Peter Francis | Victor Jupp

Second
edition

Los Angeles | London | New Delhi
Singapore | Washington DC

SAGE Publications Ltd
1 Oliver's Yard
55 City Road
London EC1Y 1S

SAGE Publications Inc.
2455 Teller Road
Thousand Oaks, California 91320

SAGE Publications India Pvt Ltd
B 1/I 1 Mohan Cooperative Industrial Area
Mathura Road, New Delhi 110 044
India

SAGE Publications Asia-Pacific Pte Ltd
3 Church Street
#10-04 Samsung Hub
Singapore 049483

Library of Congress Control Number: 2009938436

British Library Cataloguing in Publication data

A catalogue record for this book is available from the British Library

ISBN 978-1-84860-652-4
ISBN 978-1-84860-653-1 (pbk)

Typeset by C&M Digitals (P) Ltd, Chennai, India
Printed and bound in Great Britain by the MPG Books Group
Printed on paper from sustainable resources

MIX
Paper from
responsible sources
FSC
www.fsc.org   FSC® C018575

BRIEF CONTENTS

DETAILED CONTENTS

ACKNOWLEDGEMENTS

In drawing up the list of contributors for this fully revised second edition, we were very keen to work with a number of respected academics whose work has influenced our own research and teaching over recent years. We are therefore very grateful to each of the contributors for agreeing to be involved in this edition of *Doing Criminological Research* and for delivering their draft chapters and subsequent revised versions speedily and as requested. We are also grateful to Caroline Porter at Sage whose commitment to and support for this book has never wavered despite our regular attempts at testing her patience. We have had the pleasure of working with Caroline for over a decade now, and hope that we can continue to develop our relationship with her in the years to come. Finally, we would like to acknowledge the contribution of Victor Jupp, a colleague whose reputation for research methods brought us to Northumbria University some 17 years ago, and whose work continues to influence our own thinking about and practice of doing criminological research today.

Pamela Davies and Peter Francis, Newcastle upon Tyne, May 2010

CONTRIBUTORS

Faye Cosgrove is a Teaching Fellow in Criminology in the School of Applied Sciences, Durham University. Before joining Durham University, Faye was a Researcher at the Community Safety Research Unit (CSRU) and a Graduate Tutor within the Department of Sociology and Criminology at Northumbria University. Her research interests include contemporary policing, police culture and the fragmentation of public policing. She has recently completed a PhD on the occupational culture of Police Community Support Officers (PCSOs), their socialization within the police organization and the development of the craft of reassurance policing.

Pamela Davies is Programme Director and Principal Lecturer in the School of Arts and Social Sciences at Northumbria University where she has worked alongside Peter Francis since the early 1990s. Her main research and teaching interests are gender related and connect to doing crime - in particular women who commit crimes for economic gain - and experiencing victimization. She has published on the subjects of doing criminological research, crime and victim policy and on gender issues connected to crime, victimisation and community safety. Her new book *Gender, Crime and Victimisation* (2011) is also published by Sage.

Jo Deakin is a Lecturer in Criminology and Criminal Justice in the School of Law, University of Manchester. She is also a Research Fellow in the Criminal Justice Research Unit within the school. Her research interests lie principally around the reintegration of offenders, including criminal justice interventions with female offenders, social networks and informal social support for offenders. She has carried out qualitative and quantitative research on a range of other issues including child victimization, offenders' experiences of committing street robbery and barriers to employment for a range of offenders.

Peter Francis is Associate Dean in the School of Arts and Social Sciences at Northumbria University where he has worked alongside Pamela Davies since 1994. His last book was *Victims, Crime and Society*, with Pamela Davies and Chris Greer (Sage 2008). He is currently writing a book on contemporary criminological theory for Sage. He is a council member and trustee of the independent charity the Centre for Crime and Justice Studies.

Alex Hirschfield is Professor of Criminology and Director of the Applied Criminology Centre (ACC) at the University of Huddersfield. His research interests include environmental criminology, situational crime prevention, crime mapping and the analysis and evaluation of crime reduction policies. He has undertaken academic research for bodies such as the ESRC (Crime and Social Order Programme, Regional Research Laboratory Initiative, the Social Context of Pathways in Crime – SCoPic Research Programme), Department of Health (crime and health impacts), Department for Transport (crime on public transport) and the EPSRC (surveillance technologies and crime reduction). He has directed several major national policy evaluations, including the Reducing Burglary Initiative (Home Office), New Deal for Communities Crime Theme (Office of the Deputy Prime Minister) and is currently leading a process evaluation of the Youth Justice Board's Preventing Violent Extremism Programme for the Home Office.

Barbara Hudson is Emeritus Professor in Law at the University of Central Lancashire, and Visiting Professor at the Faculty of Law, State University of Parana, Jacarezinho, Brazil. Her research and teaching interests are in theories and models of justice; justice, inequality and diversity; human rights in the contexts of the war on terror and migration, and she has published many chapters and journal articles on these topics. Her most recent book is *Justice in the Risk Society* (Sage 2003) and she is currently working on theories and models of cosmopolitan justice.

Gordon Hughes is Professor of Criminology and Director of the Centre for Crime, Law and Justice at Cardiff University. He is co-editor of the journal *Criminology and Criminal Justice*. His research interests lie in crime prevention, the governance of safety and expertise in late modern societies. His most recent monogaph is *The Politics of Crime and Community* (Palgrave, 2007). His next monograph will explore the new criminological imagination and is entitled *Sociology and Crime* (Sage, 2011).

Yvonne Jewkes is Professor of Criminology at the University of Leicester. She has published many books on media and crime, including, most recently, *Media and Crime* (2nd revised edition, Sage, 2010) and *Crime and Media* (3-Volume Set, Sage, 2009). She is Associate Editor of *Crime, Media, Culture: An International Journal*, and Series Editor of both the Sage Key Approaches to Criminology series and (with Katja Franko Aas) the Ashgate Crime, Technology & Society series. Yvonne has also published extensively on prisons and imprisonment and is especially interested in the role of emotion and empathy in prison research.

Robert MacDonald is Professor of Sociology at Teesside University. His work bridges sociology, criminology, social policy and youth studies, and he has researched and written about young people and youth questions for many years. Currently his main research and teaching interests focus on: social exclusion, inclusion and poverty; criminal careers, drug use and desistance from crime; and work, worklessness and changing local economies.

Rob C. Mawby is a Senior Lecturer in criminology at the University of Leicester. He teaches undergraduate modules on criminal justice, policing and crime and the media. A criminal justice researcher since 1993, Rob has published widely on police–media issues.

Linda Moore is a Lecturer in criminology in the School of Criminology, Social Policy and Politics at the University of Ulster. Linda's main research interests are youth justice, children's rights and imprisonment. She is currently a principal researcher on a European comparative project, co-ordinated by the Danish Institute for Human Rights, on meeting the rights of children with imprisoned parents. Linda was previously investigations worker with the Northern Ireland Human Rights Commission where she co-authored investigation reports into the rights of children and women in custody in Northern Ireland. She is on the board of VOYPIC (Voice of Young People in Care).

Natasha Semmens is a Lecturer in Law and Criminology at the University of Sheffield. Her research interests include fear of crime, white-collar crime and neighbourhood policing, and she is an experienced fieldworker and project manager. She also has extensive experience of teaching research methods to under-graduates, postgraduates and practitioners. She co-authored a key text on *Researching Criminology* (with Iain Crow) in 2008 (McGraw-Hill).

Jon Spencer is Senior Lecturer in Criminal Justice and Director of the Criminal Justice Research Unit, School of Law, University of Manchester. Jon's recent research has investigated ethnic minority prisoners' experiences of race relations in English prisons, the process of sentence planning and the illegal movement of people across borders. Jon's research explores the day-to-day experiences of people who do not regularly have their voices heard and these experiences are applied to the process of policy implementation and formulation.

Azrini Wahidin is a Reader in the School of Sociology, Social Policy and Social Research at Queen's University, Belfast and a visiting Professor in the Faculty of Law, at the University of Malaya. She has written on the subject of women in prison, managing the needs of older people in prison, prison architecture, alterna-tives to custody, ethics and prison research. Her research interests primarily focus on female offenders. Azrini is a trustee for the Howard League for Penal Reform, a member of the Irish Criminology Research Network and was on the Executive Committee of the British Society of Criminology.

Alison Wakefield is a Senior Lecturer in the Institute of Criminal Justice Studies, University of Portsmouth where she specializes in security and policing, having recently moved back to the UK after working at the University of New South Wales, Sydney. Alison's publications include *Selling Security: The Private Policing of Public Space* (Willan Publishing, 2003), which was shortlisted for the British Society of Criminology Book Prize 2003, *The Sage Dictionary of Policing*, edited with Jenny Fleming (Sage, 2009) and *Ethical and Social Perspectives on Situational Crime Prevention*, edited with Andrew von Hirsch and David Garland (Hart Publishing, 2000). She is currently working on a textbook for Sage entitled *Security and Crime*, and is undertaking research projects on corporate and commercial security, and community-based security organizations.

David S. Wall is Professor of Criminology at Durham University where he conducts research and teaches in the fields of cybercrime, policing and intellectual property crime. He has published a wide range of articles and many books on these subjects which include: *Cybercrime: the Transformation of Crime in the Information Age* (Polity, 2007). He is an Academician of the Academy of Social Sciences (AcSS) and a member of the ESRC Research Grants Board. He was formerly Head of the School of Law (2005–2007) and Director of the Centre for Criminal Justice (2000–2005) at the University of Leeds.

Matthew Williams is a Senior Lecturer in Criminology and Criminal Justice at the School of Social Sciences, Cardiff University. His main research and teaching interests are cybercrime, digital and online qualitative methodology and policing, diversity and equal opportunities. He has published a range of articles and books on these subjects which include his 2006 book: *Virtually Criminal: Crime, Deviance and Regulation Online* (Routledge).

INTRODUCTION

PAMELA DAVIES AND PETER FRANCIS

The purpose of this textbook is to cement the relationship between criminological study and research practice. The intended audience for the book includes students pursuing research methods courses on criminology and related social science programmes. As part of any degree-level study, students will engage in research of a primary or secondary nature. They may undertake research for an essay or examination, or as part of a structured piece of independent learning including a dissertation or thesis.

While there are many general research methods textbooks that describe the core features of types of research design, often they do not contextualize discussions and analysis within actual studies of crime and criminal justice. Similarly, while there are many accounts of criminological research, the processes involved in its planning and doing are often neglected or confined to a short preface or appendix, while critical reflection upon the experience of doing it is nowhere to be found. It was in response to this that the first edition of this textbook was originally compiled (Jupp et al. 2000). Since its publication, new textbooks have been written that either focus upon criminological research (see King and Wincup 2000, 2007; Crowe and Semmens 2008) or include a chapter on doing criminological research (see Hale et al. 2009; Newburn 2008).

This second edition builds upon the strengths of the first edition with the aim of bringing together issues regarding the practices, strategies and principles of criminological research within the context of a range of research studies.

Research is a word heard more and more during everyday life, although it means quite different things to different people. The word is often used simply to mean finding out about something. Given this definition, nearly every person has been engaged in some form of research, and many of the skills used are commonplace and everyday. They include the ability to ask questions, to listen, to observe and to make notes. For example, buying a car, a computer or a piece of household furniture is a task more often than not associated with visiting a variety of stores, reading catalogues and inquiring about the possibilities of special offers, discounts and additional goods as part of the deal. When we do so, however, it does not matter much whether mistakes are made, or that the wrong information is collected, or that information is incorrectly interpreted (apart from to our own pocket or household enjoyment, recreation and comfort).

One of the ways of distinguishing scientific inquiry from such everyday inquiry is by the systematic manner in which data are collected and analyzed to reach conclusions about the problem which is at the centre of the research. Research inquiry is likely to conform to specific standards, will be pursued through the use of appropriate research methods and will invariably culminate in a report of some kind, which will also conform to accepted standards. Whether 'systematic' is the same as 'scientific' in the traditional sense of the word and whether criminology can be viewed as equivalent to one of the so-called 'hard' physical sciences, however, is a matter of dispute and debate. There are lots of different ways in which criminologists go about their work. Indeed, by bringing together different criminologists within this volume, it was our intention to demonstrate the plurality of types of criminological research. In many respects, the variety and form reflect the range of disciplines which comprise the social sciences. For example, the development of psychology has been influenced by the use of the experimental method to generate findings against which to test ideas. Sociology has been much more closely associated with the use of official statistics, such as published statistics on crime, as indicators of features of society and also with the use of social surveys to study large populations and social groups. Social anthropology has contributed certain types of observational method, detailed interviews and case studies as means of producing detailed descriptions of cultures. Sometimes such methods, which are typically non-quantitative in emphasis, and which seek to understand the social world from the point of view of participants, are known as ethnographic methods. Ethnography, as applied to modern society, is used to study small-scale contexts such as the courtroom or to analyze subcultures in society, such as police 'canteen' culture or youth drug culture. The study of politics has many strands to it and one of the most influential involves the analysis of social structures, power and the political ideas which underpin these. This has been coupled with reflection not just on 'what is', but more especially on 'what should be' (for example, in the search for a just society).

In exploring the practice of criminological research within this volume, there is an emphasis on the following four questions: How is criminological research planned in relation to what have come to be defined as important research questions? How is criminological research accomplished? What is the experience of doing criminological research in the field? What are the institutional constraints and impediments to criminological research? These questions provide the main organizing structure for the volume, and are explored in greater depth within the three main sections of the book:

- Part I. Preparing Criminological Research
- Part II. Doing Criminological Research
- Part III. Reflecting on Criminological Research

Part I, Preparing Criminological Research, explores the differing ways in which research problems are formulated alongside the factors which influence such formulation. It also considers the specifics of taking decisions regarding constructing research problems, the writing of proposals and the operationalization of strategies. The chapters in Part I are geared towards getting students to start preparing to undertake criminological research, and are focused on the various stages associated with getting criminological research started. As a result, each chapter in this section is rich in illustrative and boxed materials and the focus is on supporting the developing practice of the researcher. In Chapter 1, Peter Francis illustrates the core decision-making processes associated with planning criminological research. The chapter outlines the various aspects of the planning process, including research initiation, formulating research questions, reviewing the literature, project design and proposal development and presentation. These stages of decision-making are subsequently discussed in depth in the chapters that follow. Pamela Davies in Chapter 2 examines the interchange between problems, theories and methods in criminological research. In doing so, she examines the role of theory in problem formulation and also as an influence on the specificity with which problems are formulated. These first two chapters introduce the important first stages of research design: planning the research and formulating the research questions. Once these stages have been completed, the researcher will then move on to make decisions about the kinds of methods to use and the sorts of data to collect. These decisions will be taken in the context of the purpose of the research and the time and resources available. Chapter 3, by Natasha Semmens, examines the different methodological approaches in criminological research, and in particular the decision-making involved in choosing the methods to use and the sorts of data to collect. Alongside these decisions, as Alison Wakefield notes in Chapter 4, getting to know the literature is an essential element of defining the topic, formulating the research question and doing the research. Indeed, there are several types of literature review. The key differences relate to the level of systematization of the process, and range from systematic reviews that follow a set of procedures, to narrative reviews that, while still involving a series of stages and procedures, are fluid and iterative.

Part II, Doing Criminological Research, explores the many ways in which criminological research is carried out. Throughout the chapters in this section a range of themes and issues recur, including the different styles of criminological research (policy-related, action-based, critical, etc.); the different types of research design (survey, evaluative, ethnographic); and the use of different forms of data (primary and secondary; qualitative and quantitative). Each of the chapters is contextualized in differing criminological issues and they are written from a variety of criminological perspectives. Several include comparative dimensions and all stress the ways in which comparison is an essential part of research methodology and that comparison permeates different stages of doing research. In addition, each of these chapters explores the many difficulties associated with using particular methods of research in specific contexts. They also express the need for innovation and reflexivity in the way in which criminologists approach data collection and analysis. In Chapter 5, Alex Hirschfield focuses upon the mapping and use of crime data, and in doing so explores the importance of scale in crime analysis and the use of Geographical Information Systems (GIS) in mapping crime, while Jo Deakin and Jon Spencer in Chapter 6 explore the potential of collecting sensitive crime data from the use of large-scale survey research. In both of these chapters the importance of getting to grips with the principles and processes of working with large crime data sets are highlighted, as is the importance of asking the right questions and ensuring the approach fits the purpose of the research.

The next three chapters are concerned more specifically with qualitative data collection approaches. In each, the focus is on using small sample sizes drawn from particular locations (such as a prison, a community or an organization) to explore specific experiences and issues. In Chapter 7, Pamela Davies examines the use of interviews with offenders and the use of their words as sources of data in conducting criminological research. Drawing upon her own experience of doing qualitative research with women prisoners, female offenders on probation and women ex-offenders, she highlights how, despite the array of methodological problems associated with the interview method, it can generate effective and reliable data, if conducted in a reflective manner. In Chapter 8, Robert MacDonald examines the way in which qualitative data collection methods can be used to examine the experiences of young people in specific marginalized communities. Using the work of Charles Murray as a departure point, MacDonald demonstrates the way in which data findings can be used to refute previous thinking and to develop a more robust theoretical understanding of the relationship between young people and the existence of an underclass. In Chapter 9, Faye Cosgrove and Peter Francis discuss the use of ethnography in policing research. In particular, they examine the benefits of using ethnographic approaches to the study of police culture, and describe their use of an appreciative ethnographic approach to researching Police Community Support Officers.

The final three chapters in Part II focus upon the importance of the media and the internet in much criminological research. In Chapters 10 and 11, Rob C. Mawby and Yvonne Jewkes, respectively, examine the importance of studying media representations of crime. While having a long tradition within criminology, arguably it can be suggested that criminology is only now fully realizing the importance of media analysis to understanding crime, and the necessity for interdisciplinary practices. The development of digital media through the expansion of the internet has introduced a further new social landscape of crime and criminality, and one that requires careful regulation and monitoring. However, it has also opened up new possibilities for research, and in Chapter 12, by David Wall and Matthew Williams, the different ways that the internet, digital technologies and environments have changed the ways that research in criminology and criminal justice can be undertaken are explored and illustrated.

Part III, Reflecting on Criminological Research, offers critical reflection upon the practice of doing and experiencing research. It acknowledges the issues that arise, including the relations and interactions between the researcher and the researched; those involving emotions, subjectivity and objectivity; and the many constraints on research.

In Chapters 13 and 14, Azrini Wahidin and Linda Moore, and Gordon Hughes respectively, examine the ways in which ethics and politics not only impact upon criminological research, but also play a key role in the form criminological research agendas take. The aim of both chapters is to help the reader gain an informed and systematically sceptical understanding of the varying political, ethical and moral factors which impact on and inform contemporary criminological research. The final chapter of Part III, and of the book, by Barbara Hudson, explores critical reflection as research methodology. Drawing upon a critical social theory perspective, she argues that reflection on crime and criminal justice may be viewed not solely as a personal endeavour but as a valid form of research in its own right. The chapter explores some of the research problems and issues to which such an approach might be applicable.

In putting together the second edition of this book, we have provided a number of devices to facilitate the reader's learning and reflection. First, we have included at the front of each part of the book a commentary within which general thematics, specific issues and questions and conceptual definitions are 'sign-posted' and discussed. These commentaries direct the reader to issues which recur in different parts of the book. To develop understanding, the commentary should be read prior to the specific chapters within each part. Second, at the end of each of the commentaries and chapters we have included a number of study questions and activities. The purpose of these is to help the reader make linkages between chapters, and to develop understanding of the key issues discussed within each chapter. Third, at the end of each chapter a list of suggested readings and resources is highlighted. The purpose of these is to allow the reader to explore further and in greater depth the issues and points raised within each chapter. Fourth, a comprehensive **glossary** is provided at the end of the book. This has been **compiled from key terms and concepts highlighted in bold throughout the book**. Fifth, in order to facilitate the overall aim of the volume – to bring together issues regarding the practices, strategies and principles of criminological research within the context of a range of research studies – we have ensured that each of the contributors has based his or her writing on actual criminological research that they have delivered in the field. While not doing so in a way which is too context-specific, each chapter carefully, yet concisely, explores methodological issues within a criminological context.

We are keen to stress the need to contextualize the practices, strategies and principles of criminological research within actual experiences in the field. Each chapter emphasizes critical reflection on the planning, doing and experiencing of criminological research. The volume provides discussion of the core aspects of research design and practice, together with exemplification from real research of the many issues, problems (both theoretical and practical) and questions which arise as a result of doing it. Acknowledgement of these is central to the successful doing of criminological research.

REFERENCES

Crowe, I. and Semmens, N. (2008) *Researching Criminology*. London: McGraw Hill.

Hale, C., Hayward, K., Wincup, E., Wahidin, A. (eds) (2009) *Criminology*, 2nd Edn. Oxford: Oxford University Press.

Jupp, V., Davies, P. and Francis, P. (eds) (2000) *Doing Criminological Research*. London: Sage.

King, R. and Wincup, E. (2000) *Doing Research on Crime and Justice*. Oxford: Oxford University Press.

King, R. and Wincup, E. (2007) *Doing Research on Crime and Justice*, 2nd Edn. Oxford: Oxford University Press.

Newburn, T. (2009) *Criminology*. Abingdon: Willan.

PART ONE

PREPARING CRIMINOLOGICAL RESEARCH

PAMELA DAVIES AND PETER FRANCIS

Part Contents

DECISION-MAKING

The first part of this book is concerned with preparing criminological research. A central theme which runs throughout is that doing research involves engaging in a process of **decision-making**. One key decision concerns the choice of subject matter of research, or what is sometimes referred to as the research problem. This decision is pivotal because the research subject or problem provides the main focus for the project and is a major influence on subsequent decisions about the ways in which the project is to be accomplished. Another key decision concerns the kinds of methods to use and the sorts of data to collect. Crucially, each decision must be properly reasoned and justified to ensure that the research is as valid, reliable and robust as it can be. Chapters 1 to 4 are all concerned with decisions which need to be taken in relation to preparing criminological research.

DEFINING THE TOPIC

One obvious starting point is deciding 'what to study'. Even though a project may take many paths before its conclusion, there must be some initial statement of the territory to be examined. This acts as a benchmark against which progress is measured. It also acts as a reminder to the researcher that he or she should not wander off down a fruitless cul-de-sac. One of the hallmarks of effective research is the clear formulation of **research questions**. These guide the project by encouraging the researcher to constantly return to key issues, while not acting as straitjackets to inhibit creative inquiry (and possibly reformulation of the research problem) as the project progresses. One of the hallmarks of ineffective research is a research problem which allows an investigator to lose his or her way, with the outcome that conclusions do not address what was intended. A key decision, then, concerns *topic* – what to study? For most criminologists, the starting point for a research topic is an idea or a topic that is of interest to them, the source of which may be many and varied and can include personal interest, the research literature, social problems or a new development in society.

TOPICS, CASES, CONTEXT AND TIME

Criminology is diverse, wide-ranging and, in places, fragmented. It is carried out by a variety of researchers (for example, academics, policy analysts and practitioners) who work within a variety of institutions (for example, universities, central and local government, criminal justice agencies) and from a variety of different discipline bases (sociology, politics, psychology, geography, history). If one wants to draw rough boundaries around a territory within which research topics and problems can be located, then it can be said that criminology asks questions about the following: the nature of crime and its extent; the perpetrators of crime; victims of crime; institutions of the criminal justice system and their workings; and how each of these interacts with wider social structural dimensions such as power, inequality, age, social class, gender and ethnicity. Typical questions might include 'How much crime is there and how is it geographically and socially distributed?'; 'What kinds of people commit crimes?'; 'Are there any patterns to victimization in society?'; 'In what ways does the criminal justice system discriminate against categories of people?' Such questions are necessarily broad but are an essential element in the decisions about what to study. What is more, they form a platform for taking decisions about who to study, where and when, that is decisions not just about *topic* but also about *cases*, *contexts* and *time*. Broad research questions can be refined and reformulated to be more incisive and penetrative to take the form, for example, 'How do urban and rural areas (context) differ in terms of victimization of racially motivated crimes (cases) in the period between 1980 and 2010 (time)?' In this way decisions are taken to open up some dimensions of a broad topic to inquiry and not others.

END PURPOSE OF RESEARCH

Many factors influence such decisions, one of the most important of which is the end purpose of research. For example, where an investigator is commissioned to evaluate the introduction of some aspect of crime prevention policy, the selection of topic, cases, context and time will typically be specified in advance by the sponsor. Even where there is a commitment to a broad academic aim of making some contribution to knowledge and to theory, it will be necessary to ground empirical inquiry in specific cases, contexts and time periods. The significance of decisions about such 'grounding' lies in the limits of generalizability. That is, all research takes *place* in particular contexts, studying particular cases at specific times and yet aims to make broad claims beyond the particularistic scope of inquiry. The extent to which it can do so depends upon the representativeness and typicality of the contexts, cases and times which have been chosen.

ANTICIPATING CONCLUSIONS

When formulating research problems the researcher must not just consider what to study, where and when, but must also anticipate the answer to the question, 'What do I want to say?' This is not to suggest that researchers can write a final report before carrying out research (although that is a possibility in some cases). Rather it is to indicate that there needs to be some anticipation of the kind of conclusion that may be reached and the kind of evidence required to support it. For example, where the aim is to evaluate the effectiveness of the introduction of some form of criminal justice policy, it is necessary to formulate research problems and questions in such a way that a conclusion can be reached about such effectiveness. There are other ways in which researchers anticipate outcomes when formulating research questions. In a more radical and critical vein, what is sometimes termed standpoint research seeks to pose problems and address them from a particular standpoint (for example, a feminist perspective) and anticipates reaching conclusions which reflect that standpoint. Such research is less likely to be concerned with questions about the effectiveness of specific policies and more concerned with addressing fundamental issues such as discrimination, inequality, oppression and justice.

AUDIENCES OF RESEARCH

Researchers need to pose not just the question 'What do I want to say?' but also 'To whom do I want to say it?' The audiences of research findings include academic peers, policy-makers who have commissioned research, practitioners who are interested in applying findings in their work, pressure groups who want to put forward a particular viewpoint and politicians who want to formulate or justify policies. The nature of the intended audience should be anticipated when formulating research problems. This is because of the strong connection between the way in which a research problem is expressed and the types of findings and conclusions which are eventually presented. Different audiences give credibility to evidence and arguments presented in certain ways. For example, most articles in academic journals are expected to be presented in a very formal way. Further, there is a wealth of experience which indicates that policy-makers give greater credence to statistical as opposed to non-quantitative evidence, whereas pressure groups often favour detailed case studies of 'deviant' cases or *causes célèbres* so as to make maximum impact. The ways in which arguments and conclusions emerge and are presented are very much influenced by earlier decisions about the nature of the research problem and how it is expressed.

THE RESEARCH LITERATURE

Researchers also need to be aware of what has been said before, by whom and in what ways. Preparing an area for research involves making sense of that which has been undertaken before, how, why and with what results. In making decisions about what to study, the investigator will draw upon an initial review of the academic and scholarly literature. After all, the objective here is to discover relevant material published on the topic area in order to help support the framing of the research questions. The purpose of reviewing the literature is to identify the key issues and problems and controversies surrounding the proposed research area. This may be by identifying a gap in existing knowledge, articulating the weakness of argument of a particular approach, or assessing the evidence against competing perspectives. Thus a literature review allows the investigator to locate their research within the work of others. In doing so, the researcher will explore the conceptual literature on the topic area, written by the leading thinkers in the field and which gives insight into theories, concepts and ideas, as well as the research literature, offering specific accounts and findings of other research projects carried out in the field.

METHODOLOGICAL APPROACHES

The formulation of a research question also underpins the design of research as a whole and implies what form the research project will take. That is, in preparing criminological research, the researcher will also make decisions about the kinds of methods to use and the sorts of data to collect. First, the investigator will need to develop a **research strategy** and **research design**. Second, the research will need to identify what data to collect and how to collect it. Third, s/he will have to make a number of decisions regarding the **operationalization** of the approach and methods chosen, and include **sampling**, access and ethical issues. These decisions will be taken in the context of the purpose of the research and the time and resources available. Crucially, each decision must be properly reasoned and justified to ensure that the research is valid, reliable and robust as it can be. Green (2008:

58–59) asks the following in relation to the connections between research questions and research design:

- Are your approaches and research strategies commensurate with the question you are asking?
- Is your proposed sample consistent with the groups, organizations, relationships or processes specified in the question?
- What methodological strategies are implied by the purposes and objectives of your research question?
- What methods of data collection are most consistent with the objectives of the research, as they are embedded in the question?
- Does the question need adjusting in light of your proposed research design, or could you rework your research design on the basis of your reconsidered question?

RESEARCH PROPOSALS

Ultimately, the aim of research is to bring forward evidence to make an argument in relation to the research problem(s). The means by which this is to be accomplished is stipulated in a **research proposal**, which is a statement of preliminary decisions about the ways in which such evidence will be collected, analysed and presented. A research proposal can have varying degrees of formality. In the Appendix to his classic book *The Sociological Imagination* (1970), C. Wright Mills describes the early stages of research as involving the collecting of notes, cuttings, extracts and personal thoughts. These are organized and categorized to formulate research ideas and plans, but in a manner which is constantly under review and reformation. For Mills, the writing of research proposals is a continuous process of reflection and of stimulating the 'sociological imagination'. However, at the more formal end of the spectrum, grant-awarding bodies and other sponsors of research require precise written statements which address specific headings and must be submitted by a stipulated deadline. There are variations in the context of a proposal, but typically it will address the following. First, there will be a statement about the mechanisms by which cases will be selected. Such cases may be individuals selected to be interviewed as part of a survey but they may also be documents to analyze or interactions to be observed. Second, the means by which data will be collected should be outlined. This may be, for example, by **interviews**, observational methods or by the use of secondary sources such as documents or official governmental statistics. Third, it is necessary to detail the ways in which data will be analyzed, for example by using one or more of the computer packages which are available for this purpose. Other issues also need to be addressed, for instance timescale and budget, anticipated problems, such as gaining access to data, ethical dilemmas, confidentiality issues and policy implications. A research proposal is a statement of intent about the ways in which it is anticipated that the research will progress, although, as most researchers will attest, the reality of how the project is actually accomplished is often somewhat different. Part III of this volume provides a discussion of the problems that researchers can face 'in the field'.

VALIDITY

A primary factor in determining the content of a proposal is the research problem: an investigator will seek to design a strategy of research that will reach conclusions which are as valid as possible to the research problem. There are two aspects of **validity** which need to be emphasized. The first concerns whether the conclusions a researcher reaches are credible for the particular cases, context and time period under investigation. Conclusions are neither 'right' nor 'wrong'; they are more or less credible. The extent to which they are credible is the extent to which they are said to be internally valid. For example, if a researcher is investigating the effects of CCTV on levels of crime in a particular area, the strength of validity will depend on whether there is evidence that a drop in crime levels followed the introduction of cameras and also evidence that no other factor could have produced or affected the change (such as the introduction of police beat patrols).

A second aspect of validity concerns whether it is possible to generalize the conclusions to other cases, contexts and time periods. The extent to which this is possible is the extent to which conclusions are said to be externally valid. External validity is very much dependent upon the cases, contexts and time periods which form part of the research design having representativeness and typicality. The hallmark of a sound proposal is the extent to which the research decisions which comprise it anticipate the potential threats to validity.

Typically, research proposals are sent to reviewers for some recommendation. Reviewers will be concerned with the degree of 'fit' between a research problem and the strategy proposed to investigate it. A key question concerns whether the proposed design is likely to produce valid conclusions in relation to the research problem as stated. So a clearly formulated research problem, which is capable of being investigated by social scientific methods of inquiry, in a way which is as valid as possible, is pivotal in any research.

Several factors are likely to influence the degree of fit between research problem and research design and are therefore likely to affect validity. For example, decisions about research design have to be taken in the context of constraints imposed by cost and time, and there are many forms of research which cannot be justified on the grounds of ethics. Also, it is not possible to anticipate threats to validity which may occur unexpectedly and when research is under way. So all research, whether in the planning stage or in the operational stage, is a compromise between what is desirable in pursuit of validity and what is practicable in terms of cost, time, politics and ethics. This can be termed the validity 'trade-off'.

In all of this lies the value of viewing research as a form of decision-making. Focusing on decision-making at the planning stage encourages us to take decisions to rule out, as far as possible, potential threats to the validity of our conclusions. This is vital to the 'doing' of research. Focusing on decisions taken when research is under way helps us evaluate the ways in which the validity of conclusions has been affected in ways which were not – and, perhaps could not be – anticipated. This is vital to the evaluation of research which has already been completed.

1 Read Chapters 1 and 2 and then write a sentence describing each of the following terms: research proposal; research focus; research problem; research question; research hypothesis.

2 Read Chapters 3 and 4 and then write a sentence describing each of the following terms: research strategy; research design; quantitative research; qualitative research; systematic literature review; narrative review.

3 Choose a topic of criminological interest and express it in terms of research focus; research problem or question; research hypothesis.

4 Build up a very short research proposal of your own by considering how each component (research question, literature review, data collection and analysis, and politics and ethics of research) could address your chosen research topic.

5 Reflect on your short proposal and ask yourself the question, 'Are there any threats to validity?'

REFERENCES

Green, N. (2008) 'Formulating and refining a research question', in Gilbert, N. (ed.) *Researching Social Life* (3rd edn). London: Sage.

Mills, C. Wright (1970) *The Sociological Imagination*. Hammondsworth: Penguin.

ONE
PLANNING CRIMINOLOGICAL RESEARCH

PETER FRANCIS

Chapter Contents

KEY POINTS

This chapter:

- Outlines the key decisions involved in planning criminological research
- Introduces the processes involved in defining a topic and formulating research questions
- Explores the interconnection between research questions, the literature review and developing an approach to data collection and analysis
- Outlines the importance of a research proposal for the purpose of structuring and formalizing your ideas on planning criminological research
- Highlights the importance of supervision, peer review and time management to planning successful criminological research

INTRODUCTION

My chapter in the first edition of this book drew upon my experience of undertaking evaluative research in Newcastle upon Tyne. Specifically, the chapter discussed the process of getting a particular piece of research started. It described the key decisions that I had to make and illustrated the processes involved, including responding to the tender document and writing a **research proposal**. The proposed research aimed to evaluate the implementation and impact of a range of local community projects funded by Newcastle City Council, including initiatives focusing on home security, the prevention of racism, trader security, CCTV surveillance, youth work, support for victims of racist harassment, truancy and exclusion, and anti-social behaviour and dumping. The proposal was successful and I carried out the research with a colleague towards the end of the 1990s.

As part of the process of developing this second edition, I received feedback on the structure, content and layout of the original chapter in much the same way students receive feedback on their work from tutors, supervisors and peers. While the feedback was generally positive, it suggested that some of the coverage was too wide and too detailed for a predominantly undergraduate student audience. Specifically, it noted that although students should become familiar with the ways in which research is planned, organized and conducted on the larger scale, a chapter primarily aimed at an undergraduate audience should be pitched at the level at which they themselves will be working. The feedback went on to suggest that the chapter could better address the needs and experiences of students undertaking criminological research at undergraduate level, and then illustrate these through supporting materials and relevant exercises with appropriate signposts to the more substantive chapters in the book.

This chapter therefore examines the key decisions that a student will have to make in planning to undertake a piece of criminological research. It introduces the process through which research ideas arise and notes the context within which they are developed, discusses the necessity of formulating feasible **research questions** and reviewing the literature, and impresses upon the reader the importance of **research design** and data collection and analysis.

DISSERTATION RESEARCH

Students are given a variety of opportunities to make decisions about doing criminological research. Sometimes this occurs in specific modules where they may be tasked with formulating a research question, delivering a data collection method, analyzing a particular data set or developing a research proposal, with the key decisions undertaken being assessed as part of the final summative assignment. However, the nearest that many students get to actually undertaking a piece of criminological research is for their final-year project or dissertation. A dissertation may involve a critical review of the literature. In some cases,

TYPES OF DISSERTATION

Literature-based dissertation

- Involves analyzing existing literature and developing an argument about it
- Will not consist of a separate literature review but rather the literature will be embedded throughout the dissertation in a series of chapters
- Does not have a separate methodology chapter but a discussion of how you searched and reviewed the literature will be contained within the introduction

Primary research-based dissertation

- Involves undertaking a primary piece of research on your chosen topic area, ensuring the validity and ethical nature of the work undertaken
- By the very nature of the small sample sizes used, your findings will be illustrative only, and the focus is on your ability to operationalize data collection methods and data analysis
- Will involve a separate literature review chapter that critically reviews the literature on your chosen topic
- Contains a separate methodology chapter that details what you did, how you did it and any issues and developments along the way

students opt to undertake primary research. Box 1.1 identifies the key elements of each.

Whatever type of dissertation is undertaken, students are often fearful of doing such a large piece of research. Often they feel as though everything they have learned about doing criminological research drains away from them. They complain of being unable to think of a topic, or that they don't know how to formulate a focused research question. They also complain of not knowing what literature to review or in some cases where to start searching for it. It is as though the knowledge and skills learned over the previous three years vanish at the very mention of the word dissertation. Yet while doing a dissertation is time consuming and certainly requires intellectual and physical stamina, it can also be a very rewarding experience. It supports the development and application of in-depth knowledge and understanding. It offers specialisation and secures opportunities for students to immerse themselves in a particular topic area. It should be the most rewarding and interesting assignment undertaken since it is very much the student's own work. To help you cope with the pressures of planning a criminological dissertation, this chapter describes and illustrates the key decision-making processes relevant to getting your research started, including:

- defining the topic
- reviewing the literature
- proposing data collection methods
- writing and presenting a research proposal

Alongside reading this chapter, you may also wish to consult the sources of guidance on dissertation preparation and academic writing detailed in Box 1.2.

Defining the topic

Perhaps the most important decision concerns the choice of topic as it not only provides the main focus for the dissertation but it is also a major influence on the subsequent decisions taken about the ways in which the project is to be accomplished (Jupp 2000). For Bryman (2008: 70), researchers usually start out with a research topic that is of interest to them, which may derive from one of many sources:

- personal interest or experience
- the research literature
- a wish to test or explore the validity of a particular theoretical perspective or model
- an ambition to 'solve' a puzzle
- new developments in policy, legislation or practice
- specific social problems

For example, Pamela Davies in Chapter 7 describes how the research she undertook for her PhD arose from an interest in women's criminality and feminist methodologies. Often, the source of an idea derives from a combination of these factors, as Robert Reiner (1991: 39–40) makes clear in his research on Chief Constables:

> A number of factors … made it an attractive and interesting project. Above all, there was the growing prominence of some Chief Constables as vocal and controversial public figures. … At the same time, a study of Chief Constables seemed a logical progression to plug a gap in the burgeoning field of police studies. … Having previously published a study of the backgrounds, careers and occupational perspectives of the federated

ranks of the police (Reiner 1978), it seemed a logical step to attempt to conduct similar research on the elite levels.

It is worth noting at this point that criminological research develops within a context where values, politics and ethics influence what is proposed, by whom, and with what intention (Hughes 2000; Morgan 2000; Hughes in Chapter 14 of this book). Acknowledgement of this for May (1997: 45–46) 'enables an understanding of the context in which research takes place and the influences upon it, as well as countering the tendency to see the production and design of research as a technical issue uncontaminated by political and ethical questions'.

For undergraduate criminology students, the topic is usually derived from a subject area or issue that has captured their imagination over the course of their studies and which lends itself to being researched (Davies 2007). It is often the case that students identify more than one topic and the problem is deciding which one to research for their dissertation. However, when the identification of a topic area is a problem, the best way to overcome this is to look back at what you have studied in specific modules, or read in particular textbooks or journal articles and talk to your guidance tutor or module tutors for inspiration. Think about what has excited or interested you during the course of your studies. In addition, look back at some of the previous year's dissertations to get a feel for the work that other students have carried out. It is worth noting that some of the best dissertations derive from some of the simplest topic areas and you should not get caught up in trying to be the most original or unique. Davies (2007: 26) suggests that you should approach defining the topic logically by thinking about:

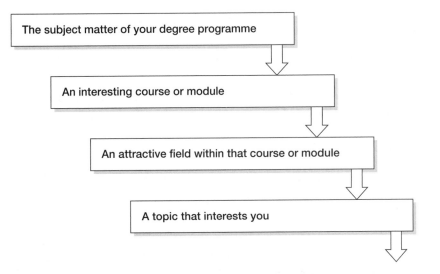

The subject matter of your degree programme

An interesting course or module

An attractive field within that course or module

A topic that interests you

Once a topic has been identified, the more taxing aspect of the process is defining the research question (Davies 2007). While, for example, 'women and law enforcement', 'mental illness and crime', 'Asian men and prison', 'violence in the media', 'globalization of criminal justice', 'transnational crime', 'the mafia' and 'youth crime' might well be useful initial ideas they are far too broad as dissertation topics. You need to be more specific about the aspect of such topic areas that you will be considering and from what angle. As Jupp (2000: 14–15) notes:

> The conclusions of research will be credible and plausible only to the extent to which the questions and problems they address are clearly formulated and expressed and followed through in a consistent manner during the inquiry. Above all, research problems and questions should be capable of being answered by some form of social inquiry.

This is not always that easy. Once you have managed to identify a topic, you then need to develop the specificity of a research question, so that the proposed research is both feasible and manageable (Bryman 2008; Green 2008; Jupp 2000; and Davies in Chapter 2 of this book). Your research must be achievable in the time constraints available and be able to produce valid conclusions. Failure to do so will leave you with a question that is too broad, lacks depth or is too hard to manage within the confines of time and resources. Hopefully you will already have experience of undertaking a not dissimilar process in your research methods modules, which involves subjecting your research topic to a rigorous process of interrogation (Davies 2007). Throughout the process you should ask yourself what it is you want to find out. What is it that really excites you about this topic? Has it been researched before? If so, who by and how will your proposed research differ? Are there gaps in the literature? What will your proposed research contribute? What insights do you hope to gain from doing the dissertation? There is no easy

---

BOX 1.3

MOVING FROM TOPIC AREA TO A RESEARCH QUESTION

1 Go large – think of all of the possible research questions about the research topic, and test the questions against what you know and what the discipline knows.
   - Think about broad themes and questions

2 Narrow the list – iterative process, thematically cluster, exclude sub-questions or peripheral ones, through a critical reflexivity.
   - Think of different 'players', types of people, structural features, gender, etc., specific area of focus

3 Refine the list – attention to wording, the assumptions that underpin them.
   - Think about research objectives; terms, assumptions, conceptualization

4 Reflect upon the question(s) – at all stages of the research process.
   - Think about literature review, data collection methods

Adapted from Green (2008)

way of defining and specifying the research question and it involves trial and error, as Pamela Davies highlights in Chapter 2 of this book. Also, too often what is missing is the explicit criminological problem – an understanding of what it is you want to do in the dissertation. Thus, interrogating your topic involves teasing out the criminological problem, the perspective from which you want to approach it and the research questions that you wish to answer as part of doing the research. Some students like to capture their thoughts in a mind map, in which they visualize both the overall picture and the fine detail. This can be a great help when you are planning the structure of your dissertation. Box 1.3 offers some guidance on moving from a topic area to a research question.

Reviewing the literature

In the early stages of planning criminological research it is important that you focus your energies on reading around your chosen topic as much as possible. Immersing yourself in the literature is an essential aspect of defining and interrogating the topic and formulating the research questions, although the literature review is an activity that continues well into the period of fieldwork itself (Walliman 2004; Wakefield in Chapter 4 of this book). In some cases the **literature review** will form the substantive basis upon which the dissertation will be based, while in dissertations that propose primary research, the literature review will be used to support the development of the research strategy, will act as your springboard into the field and will be drawn upon when making sense of the data collected. As Alison Wakefield details in Chapter 4 of this book, the process of doing a literature review enables the criminologist to identify relevant questions to ask, themes to include, methodologies to follow, as well as allowing for the development of conceptual or theoretical frameworks, and the framing of empirical research findings.

Literature reviews can take several forms. These can include a **systematic review**, a rapid evidence assessment and a **narrative review** (Bryman 2008; Hart 2001), and the choice of review that students adopt is determined by their research questions and overall ambitions for the dissertation. During the course of doing your research you will be interested in gathering together and critically reviewing everything of relevance to your chosen topic area. This is in part to demonstrate that you are aware of and understand the work of others, and that you are able to interpret it in relation to your chosen study.

However, at this early stage of planning your dissertation, your approach to reviewing the literature will most likely resemble that of a narrative review. Narrative reviews are used much more to develop understanding of a topic area and can involve more of a developmental and uncertain process. By that is meant that while narrative literature reviews may have a starting point, they do not always have an identifiable end point, and the student often journeys to places that they had not anticipated at the outset. They offer less specific criteria for the inclusion and exclusion of studies and are, by their very nature, much more wide-ranging and fluid pieces of work.

Most students start by reading textbook overviews and summary articles on the particular chosen area and scanning the bibliography for relevant further sources. This in itself is not a particularly bad place to begin your search of the literature, but remember that summary and textbook overviews will have been written with a particular emphasis in mind, and that an author's take on a particular research study may differ from someone else, so it is important to read the original studies. Nevertheless, overviews and summaries will allow you to get started quickly. After all, the objective here is to discover relevant material published on the topic area and help support the framing of the research questions. Thus the purpose of the literature review is to allow you to locate your research within that of others. After a while you will start to build up a succinct overview of the proposed subject area, detailing what the literature has to say, identifying gaps, key themes, areas of informed debate and specific research studies.

As part of your degree programme you will already have developed skills in critical reading, a process which is much slower than reading for pleasure and involves a questioning frame of mind, together with absorption and reflection of the material being read to ensure that you understand what you are reading and how it relates to your topic. A critical reading of the research should begin with an acknowledgement that different perspectives will exist on a given topic and will have influenced the research you are reading about. It should also ensure a questioning of the evidence, bias and authority of the author(s) of the research paper that you are reading, reflection on the connection and relevance between one particular piece of work and the work of others on the topic, as identification of the strengths and limitations of the research presented, together with an assessment of its implications and significance.

In doing so, it is essential that you take good notes. Remember, you will come back to these at some point in the future. Your notes must therefore be succinct and detail the page number of any quotes listed. Don't just copy, but summarize and critically evaluate the text that you have read. In addition, always note the full bibliographical details of all the sources you use. You may wish to teach yourself how to use Endnote bibliographic software. Endnote can help you to manage your references, insert citations into your text, and at the same time create a reference list in your selected reference style, e.g. Harvard.

PROPOSING DATA COLLECTION METHODS

While some students choose to undertake a critical literature review for their dissertation, many of you, either because you are drawn to the excitement of entering the field, or because it is stipulated in the dissertation or project guidelines you are working towards, will engage in a process of data collection and analysis. You may decide to use data that is already available. Much of this data will be **secondary data** in that it has been collected and collated by someone else. For Jupp et al. (2000: 62), secondary data and analysis:

> Refers to a form of inquiry and analysis based entirely on pre-existing data sources. ...
> A secondary source is an existing source of information which has been collected by

someone other than the researcher and with some purpose other than the current research problem in mind.

Negotiating access to the data may prove difficult and it may also involve negotiating access to it in a format that is suitable and appropriate. In proposing the collection of secondary data, it is important to be aware of issues relating to its **reliability**, accuracy and availability. Just because it is already collected does not mean that it will be accurate or reliable, or that it will be made available. In proposing this form of data, you will have to think about how you will ensure the reliability and **validity** of the data that you wish to use.

Data that is not available from a secondary source will have to be collected using **primary research** techniques. This is often called primary data collection and refers to the process whereby the researcher collects the data. Primary data can be collected in many ways, including questionnaires, activity diaries, interviews, focus groups and observation. The key decisions that you will be faced with at this stage of planning are what type of data you will need to collect. The **quantitative approach** to collecting data is about counting, ranking and ordering in a systematic way (Denscome 2007). It is used to answer predetermined questions, such as the percentage of people who are satisfied with the police or fearful of crime (see, for example, Deakin and Spencer in Chapter 6 of this book). Quantitative data collection generally involves statistics and seeks to be reliable (that is, the same results would be produced if the data was collected again). **Qualitative data** is about people's attitudes, motives and behaviours. If you have focused your research topic and have developed a degree of specificity (see, for example, Davies, and Cosgrove and Francis in Chapters 7 and 9 respectively in this book), the questions that you have already identified should help inform the selection of the most appropriate data that you need and point towards the methodological tools relevant for data collection and analysis. For example, Brett Davies (2007: 26) suggests that for dissertations that aim to:

- describe, monitor and investigate – both qualitative and quantitative research can provide evidence, although with different descriptions
- explore – it depends on the form of exploration, but both quantitative and qualitative research can be used, but will produce different exploratory material
- interpret – qualitative research is especially strong here
- look behind the surface – is usually undertaken using qualitative research
- evaluate – if it concerns replication and quantification, then quantitative research is appropriate, although if the aim is to evaluate perspectives, then qualitative forms can be used
- explain – both quantitative and qualitative approaches can be used
- prove – is mostly a quantitative approach, but can involve qualitative approaches

Quantitative and qualitative data is available from many sources. Box 1.4 sets out the data collection approaches.

Each source of data and collection method that you may consider using has particular strengths and weaknesses (see Box 1.5). See Chapter 6 for a discussion of the strengths and weaknesses of the survey method.

BOX 1.4

WAYS OF COLLECTING DATA

- **Observation**: indirect, covert observing and participant observation where the researcher is implicit in the activity being observed. While observation may seem casual, informal observation is often a structured activity where the researcher will usually have a plan or tick sheet that enables the observations to be recorded and annotated
- **Interviewing**: face to face, by email, questionnaire, telephone and can take the form of structured and semi-structured questions. Conversations with a purpose discovering information from the individual's own interpretation (Lauder 1993)
- **Questionnaires**: can be completed en masse as a survey at a distance or one-to-one with the researcher present
- **Documents and artefacts**: internal to an organization, individual or in the public domain
- **Content analysis**: extracting content from web pages, radio, television programmes, texts within books, visual images

Adapted from Robson (1993)

In planning criminological research, it is also important that you give consideration to:

- the process of negotiating access to respondents or documents
- the data processing and analysis procedures
- the ethical issues that may arise
- the time it will take to do the research

Each of these is now discussed.

Access and sampling

Blaxter et al. (2006) identify that in planning all research consideration must be given to the issue of access to:

- people: in the community, their place of work, the home, particular groups
- organizations or institutions: government/public departments, public institutions, private organizations
- documents: held in public or private institutions, libraries and archives

Decisions about selecting a **sample** will be dependent on your research approach as sampling is relevant in both qualitative and quantitative research:

- A quantitative approach determines that a statistical confidence is required. It is crucial in maintaining confidence and rigour in the findings and you should think of between 50 and 100 respondents.
- If your approach is qualitative, then a richer understanding of the issue is required and a smaller number of respondents is acceptable. In qualitative studies a relatively small

BOX 1.5

STRENGTHS AND WEAKNESSES OF DATA COLLECTION METHODS

Data source	Strength	Weakness
Documentation	• Stable repeated review • Unobtrusive existence prior to case study • Exact names etc. • Broad coverage – extended time span	• Retrievability difficult • Biased selectivity • Reporting bias, author bias • Access may be blocked
Archival records	• As above, precise	• As above • Privacy may inhibit access
Interviews	• Targeted • Insightful – provides perceived casual inferences	• Bias due to poor questions • Response bias • Incomplete recollection • Reflexivity – interviewee expresses what interviewer wants to hear
Direct observation	• Reality – covers events in real time • Contextual – covers event context	• Time consuming • Selectivity, might miss facts • Reflexivity – observer's presence might cause change
Participant observation	• As above • Insightful into interpersonal behaviour	• As above • Bias due to researcher's actions
Physical artefacts	• Insightful into cultural features • Insightful into technical operations	• Selectivity, availability

Adapted from Yin (1994), in Tellis (1997)

sample can produce great diversity, detailed information and rich descriptions. Lincoln and Guba (1985) estimate that a relatively small sample can reach saturation point (the greatest possible amount of data or information is obtained). You may wish to think about between four and ten respondents.

There are various types of sampling, some more appropriate to a quantitative or to a qualitative approach. Kumar (2005: 169) considers the aims of selecting a sample to be:

• to achieve maximum precision within a given sample size
• to avoid bias

Sampling strategies can be identified in two broad categories: probability sampling, which involves *randomization*; and non-probability sampling, which does not involve randomization. Box 1.6 identifies some of the more familiar sampling strategies.

Data processing and analysis

Data, particularly that collected specifically for the dissertation, will need to be analyzed and it is important from the outset that you make yourself aware of the analytical facilities available to you. Quantitative and qualitative data have particular characteristics in the approach taken, the form the data takes and the analysis methods used. Quantitative data analysis can involve inputting the data into a spreadsheet or IT statistical package that will allow for calculations and their presentation in the form of tables and charts. Qualitative data is undertaken in a different way. Although there are IT packages that can help in the analysis of qualitative data, such as NUD*IST, NVivo or ATLAS*IT, many students analyze qualitative data derived from interviews or observations by identifying themes, patterns and trends, and then illustrating them with quotations drawn from the transcripts or field notes. Thinking carefully about how the data will be analyzed, whether you have the knowledge and skills to do it, and how long it will take are three key decisions to take. Box 1.7 provides detail on approaches to data analysis.

BOX 1.6

TYPES OF SAMPLING STRATEGIES

Type of sample	Definition
Probability sample – randomized	
Random	Selection is random, each individual has an equal chance of selection
Stratified	Sampling within groups of the population, e.g. by gender, social class, education level, religion, etc. and then the population is randomly sampled *within* each category
Systematic	Selecting every *xth* case from a list
Cluster	Selecting whole clusters of population at random
Non-probability sample – non-randomized	
Convenience	Sampling those most convenient
Quota	Convenience sampling within groups of, for example, 100 females between the ages of 18 and 25 years
Purposive	Handpicked sample constructed to serve a very specific case and/or issue
Snowball or Chain	Identifies respondents who are information-rich, relying on one respondent leading to another
Self-selecting	Sample is voluntary and selects itself

Adapted from Blaxter et al. (2006), Neill (2003), Trochim (2006)

Ethical considerations

Ethical considerations also influence the planning of a dissertation, particularly if the research proposed involves human participants or data on individuals (see Wahidin and Moore in Chapter 13 of this book). Often ethical considerations are formalized as guidelines (see the British Sociological Association's statement of ethical practice at www.britsoc.co.uk/equality/statement+ethical+practice.htm as well as the British Society of Criminology's statement at www.britsoccrim.org/codeofethics.htm). Ethical implications usually occur around five main areas:

1 Agreement about the use and storage of the data.

2 Working with vulnerable groups, for example young children, asylum seekers and those unable to give informed consent.

3 Confidentiality must be honoured and material collected should remain in confidence.

4 Anonymity: participants or organizations may request and seek assurance that they will not be identifiable in the dissertation. You will need to give consideration as to how this will be achieved, for example by removing names and referring to participants as participant 1, removing biographical or some contextual information.

5 Informed consent: this process confirms that the participant has been supplied with sufficient information regarding the research and has had time to decide whether or not to participate.

Undertaking research for your dissertation requires that you work within your own university's guidelines and ethical regulations. As with every aspect of your dissertation, it is very important that you consult your supervisor about the proposed research that you plan to undertake.

Time management and practicalities

The dissertation is a significant piece of work and a culmination of your studies. As an extended piece of work it requires good time and organizational management. It will feel as though you have lots of time to begin working on it as a dissertation tends to have a long lead-in time with the hand-in date a considerable way off. This time should be used well to plan the things covered in this chapter, including thinking about the topic, reviewing the literature and exploring access, sampling and data collection approaches. It is essential to get into good habits from the beginning, for example by keeping a research diary.

A research diary can be used to record your first thoughts, day-to-day activities, insights, decision-making and anxieties as the research unfolds and progresses. The diary can also be used as a reflective tool and a source of data, filling in elements of the research context, reminding you of particular incidents and aspects of fieldwork, sampling and data collection (Bowen 1997; Meloy 1994).

Setting yourself a timetable is also useful in providing an overall understanding of what it is you need to do week by week or month by month. It will allow you

BOX 1.7

APPROACHES TO DATA ANALYSIS

Quantitative data

In taking a quantitative approach, you will know in advance what you are looking for (hypothesis), you will remain objective and distinct from the focus of the research and will use the data to count, classify or construct statistical models to explain your observations. What does the data look like? How is it explored and analyzed?

Data:
- Numbers and statistics
- Efficient in testing hypothesis
- Misses contextual detail

Exploring the data:
- Graphs and charts
- Cross-tabulations
- Seeking patterns and relationships in the data
- Comparing means, exploring correlations

Steps in analysis method:

1 Identifying a data entry and analysis manager (e.g. SPSS, www.spss.com, MS Excel)
2 Reviewing data (e.g. working with surveys, questionnaires, etc.)
3 Coding data
4 Data entry
5 Analyzing data (e.g. descriptive statistics, statistical tests)

Qualitative data

In taking a qualitative approach, the aim is understanding and the creation of a holistic, rich picture. You may know only roughly in advance what you are looking for. The design emerges as the study unfolds, enabling a responsive approach to data collection and analysis. As the researcher, you play a subjective role in data collection and analysis. What does the data look like? How is it explored and analyzed?

Data:
- Words, pictures, objects
- Activities, behaviour, attitudes
- In-depth interviews
- Direct observation
- Documentation
- Artefacts
- Time consuming
- Less able to generalize

Exploring the data:
- Seek relationships between identified and emerging themes
- Relate behaviour or ideas to biographical characteristics of respondents

Steps in analysis method:

1 Familiarization with the data through repeated reading, listening, etc.
2 Transcription of interview, etc. material
3 Organization and indexing of data for easy retrieval and identification (e.g. by hand or computerized programs such as ATLAS*TI, NUD*IST, NVivo)
4 Anonymizing of sensitive data
5 Coding (may be called indexing)
6 Identification of themes
7 Development of provisional categories
8 Exploration of relationships between categories
9 Refinement of themes and categories
10 Development of theory and incorporation of pre-existing knowledge

Adapted from Charmaz (2003), Blaxter et al. (2006), Neil (2003)

Month	S	O	N	D	J	F	M	A	M
Define topic/formulate research questions	█	█							
Undertake literature search and review	█	█		█					
Develop data collection tools and data analysis approaches			█	█					
Identify and contact participants for research purposes				█	█				
Undertake data write-up (transcription of interviews, etc.)				█	█	█			
Analyze data and further search the literature				█	█	█			
Write up the dissertation and ensure university guidelines are met							█	█	
Hand in the dissertation with time for it to be printed and bound									█

FIGURE 1.1   Research Timetable

to identify the key tasks that need doing and by when. You will need to allow for slippage by identifying periods of extra time in your planning.

Figure 1.1 provides an example of a research plan.

WRITING AND PRESENTING A RESEARCH PROPOSAL

A good way of presenting your ideas is to write a short proposal that describes the research that you wish to undertake. A **research proposal** is a written document which describes the proposed research, including what it aims to do, how it will be undertaken, and the anticipated outcome(s). A proposal also outlines why the proposed research is important and justifies the research design, including how it connects research questions to data. In combining description and argument, a research proposal must emphasize internal cohesiveness and consistency in the planning of the research.

In some dissertation modules, the proposal is the first of two summative assessment points. Even when a proposal is not a formal requirement, its usefulness outweighs the time it takes to write it. It offers an opportunity to structure and formalize what it is you want to do. In writing the proposal you will be able to identify all those areas that you will encounter without exploring them in depth at this initial stage of the research process. Finally, if done well, the proposal can act as a sound foundation upon which to prepare and implement the research activity, a stage-by-stage guide to carrying out your research.

A good proposal should answer a series of interrelated questions about the research that you are proposing, and these are detailed in the left-hand column of Box 1.8. In writing it, you should also consider a series of further questions detailed in the right-hand column of Box 1.8 that should allow you to continue to reflect upon, interrogate and refine what you have proposed.

In presenting the proposal, take care to identify a series of headings that allow you to build up your proposed research idea. Box 1.9 (see Francis 2000) details the key elements of a research proposal.

What follows is a description of the key elements outlined in Box 1.9.

- *Title page, title and your name.* The front page provides the title of the study along with your name and course.

- *Introduction and statement of purpose.* The aim of the section is to outline the topic area, highlight the importance of the study, identify its relation to what is already known about the topic area, and provide a concise statement of purpose. The discussion may also detail the general research strategy and whether a tightly structured or more evolving piece of research is proposed.

- *Topic area, research aims and objectives.* Under this section conceptual frameworks are identified, together with the specific aims of the proposed research and the means by which they are to be secured – the objectives.

- *Background literature review.* In writing up your review, ensure that it does not become a description of what others have done in the area, but rather use it to develop your own research questions and demonstrate their importance. This may be by identifying a gap in existing knowledge, articulating the weakness of a particular approach, or assessing the evidence against competing perspectives.

- *Theoretical and practical significance.* It is essential to address the questions of how and why the proposed research aims to contribute and in what way.

- *Research strategy and data collection methods.* Discussion of the rationale for the research design, together with a description of the particular methods chosen, is an essential part of any research proposal. It is important to show how the research methodology is appropriate and to ensure that the research design connects questions to data.

- *Sampling, data processing and analysis.* The proposed sampling frame must be described, along with a discussion of how it relates to the research strategies and methods. Additionally, a description and justification of procedures for data processing and analysis must be detailed, including the use of computer-assisted mechanisms.

- *Political, ethical and practical issues.* Any limitations to the study which are foreseen, or any issues that have been overcome should be dealt with in this section. The proposal should show how all ethical issues have been given due consideration and reflection.

- *Timetable.* A detailed research timetable or timeline must be outlined.

BOX 1.8

THE RESEARCH PROPOSAL

A proposal must answer the following questions:

- What is the topic area under review and why is it important?
- What is your research question or what are your research questions?

- What does the research literature have to say about the topic and how does your proposed research 'fit' with that which has already been done?

- How do you intend to carry out the research?
- What data collection and analysis techniques do you propose using?

- What is your timetable and what resources do you need to carry it out?

- What political and ethical issues, if any, may arise during your proposed research?

Ask yourself the following questions when writing the proposal:

- Why are you interested in this topic?
- Will your interest last over the length of the dissertation?
- Is it a topical question and if so why?
- Are the research questions focused and does it/do they offer a feasible, manageable piece of work?

- Is there enough literature on your chosen topic?
- Have you managed to read all the relevant material contained in books, journals, ebooks and ejournals?
- Have you reflected upon your research question(s) as a result of what you have read so far?
- Do you still need to access some literature via inter-library loan and online?
- Do you have the time left to access it?
- Have you kept records of what you have read?

- Have you given due consideration to the design of the dissertation?
- Are the methods that you have chosen appropriate for the research questions asked?
- Are you comfortable in designing and delivering the methods chosen or do you need to undertake some more reading and piloting of them?
- How will you analyze the data? How do you intend to handle the dissertation?

- Have you left yourself enough time to undertake the fieldwork and write up the results?

- Are there likely to be any political or ethical issues that you will need to address as part of your dissertation?

SUPERVISION AND PEER SUPPORT

Supervision and peer support are essential aspects of planning research, no matter whether the person involved is an undergraduate student, a postdoctoral researcher or an experienced academic. Part of the process of research planning involves sharing ideas with others. This allows an opportunity for the researcher to outline the topic and his/her question(s) and for feedback to be received on the feasibility,

BOX 1.9

ELEMENTS OF A RESEARCH PROPOSAL

1 Title page, title and your name

2 Introduction and statement of purpose

3 Topic area, research aims and objectives

4 Background literature review

5 Theoretical and practical significance

6 Research strategy and data collection methods

7 Sampling, data processing and analysis

8 Political, ethical and practical issues

9 Timetable

manageability and validity of what is proposed. More formally, peer review on research proposals is expected at every level of submission and offers an important opportunity for effective feedback and dialogue about a proposed piece of research at an early stage.

As an undergraduate student, supervision is an essential ingredient in doing a dissertation, and you should draw upon the expertise and knowledge of your supervisor regularly. This is particularly so when planning what to do. Your supervisor will support your search for a topic area and help you focus the research question, and will constantly prompt you to think about the context and consequences of what you are planning to do. They will raise questions about the manageability and feasibility of what you have proposed, and offer constructive advice regarding your research questions. Meeting your supervisor also allows an opportunity for an early discussion about the politics and ethics of that which is proposed (if this is appropriate).

When consulting your supervisor, remember that the dissertation is your piece of work based on your independent study, and responsibility for searching out and reviewing appropriate literature is properly yours. Your supervisor will not tell you how to do your dissertation or what to put in it. The role of the supervisor is to give advice and guidance on the generic skills required for the writing of the dissertation.

In addition to formal supervision, peer support is also a useful mechanism through which to gain feedback on your proposed research. Sharing ideas with friends, talking through each other's plans and reading each other's proposals are all useful in helping structure and focus your proposed research activity as well as your proposal.

SUMMARY

This chapter has described the key decision-making stages involved in planning research for a dissertation. You will need to identify a topic that interests you and one that is suitable in terms of ethics and in terms of getting it done in the time and with the resources you have available to you. Of particular importance is formulating a research question that focuses your ideas and demonstrates specificity. The process of formulating research questions is ongoing. It will be informed by an initial search and review of the research literature and will continue through the process of identifying the data to collect and the methods to be used. To help formalize and structure your planning of criminological research, it is useful to write a research proposal that structures what it is you wish to study, why, how and with what resources and in what time frame.

■ Study Questions/Activities for Students

1 Think about a criminological topic that you are interested in undertaking research on. Write down what it is and where the idea came from.

2 Think again about the research you would like to undertake and brainstorm the various areas of interest that relate to the broad topic.

3 Begin to formulate a research question that you would like to study (think of the process – the funnelling of ideas (large to narrow)). Is it interesting, relevant, feasible, ethical, concise, answerable?

4 Identify the core characteristics of qualitative and quantitative research design. Make a list of the key methods relating to quantitative and qualitative research. Against each method, identify the key strengths and key weaknesses and how these connect to the broader approaches (qualitative/qualitative).

5 Think about how you would go about researching the topic that you have identified. What data collection methods would you choose? Qualitative? Quantitative? Which of the following is the most appropriate in answering your research question?

   (a) A statistical confidence

   (b) A rich understanding

6 How do you propose to secure access to the data? Are there key individuals or a gatekeeper who will assist you in accessing documents, people and places (for example, accessing an organization)?

RESOURCES

Crowe, I. and Semmens, N. (2008) *Researching Criminology*. London: McGraw-Hill

Davies, M.D. (2007) *Doing a Successful Research Project Using Qualitative and Quantitative Methods*. Basingstoke: Palgrave

Gilbert, N. (ed.) (2008) *Researching Social Life* (Third Edition). London: Sage

REFERENCES

Blaxter, L. et al. (1996) *How to Research*. Buckingham: Open University Press

Blaxter, L., Hughes, C. and Tight, M. (2006) *How to Research.* Buckingham: Open University Press

Bonnett, A. (2001) *How to Argue: A Student's Guide*. Upper Saddle River, NJ: Prentice Hall

Bowen, T.J. (1997) 'Understanding Qualitative Research: A Review of Judith Meloy's *Writing the Qualitative Dissertation: Understanding by Doing*'. *The Qualitative Report*, 3 (3), September. Available at: www.nova.edu/ssss/QR/QR3-3/bowen.html [accessed 25/09/10]

Bryman, A. (2008) *Social Research Methods*. Oxford: Oxford University Press

Charmaz, K. (2003) 'Grounded theory', in Gibbs, G.R. and Taylor, C. (2005) *Qualitative Data Analysis*. Available online at: onlineqda.hud.ac.uk/Intro_QDA/how_what_to_code.php [accessed 25/09/10]

Cottrell, S. (2003) *The Study Skills Handbook*. Basingstoke: Palgrave

Davies, M.D. (2007) *Doing a Successful Research Project Using Qualitative and Quantitative Methods*. Basingstoke: Palgrave

Green, N. (2008) 'Formulating and refining a research question', in Gilbert, N. (ed.), *Researching Social Life* (Third Edition). London: Sage

Hart, C. (1998) *Doing a Literature Review: Releasing the Social Science Research Imagination*. London: Sage

Hay, C. (2002) *Political Analysis: A Critical Introduction*. Basingstoke: Palgrave

Hughes, G. (2000) 'Understanding the politics of criminological research', in Jupp, V., Davies, P. and Francis, P. (eds), *Doing Criminological Research*. London: Sage

Jupp, V. (2000) 'Formulating research problems', in Jupp, V., Davies, P. and Francis, P. (eds), *Doing Criminological Research*. London: Sage

Jupp, V., Davies, P. and Francis, P. (eds) (2000) *Doing Criminological Research*. London: Sage

King, R. and Wincup, E. (2007) *Doing Research on Crime and Justice*. Oxford: Oxford University Press

Kumar, R. (2005) *Research Methodology: A Step-by-step Guide for Beginners*. London: Sage

Levin, P. (2007) *Excellent Dissertations*. Maidenhead: Open University Press

Lincoln, Y. and Guba, E. (1985) *Naturalistic Inquiry*. London: Sage

Marsh, D. and Stoker, G. (2002) *Theory and Methods in Political Science*. Basingstoke: Palgrave

May, T. (1997) *Social Research Issues, Methods and Processes* (Second Edition). Buckingham: Open University Press

Maykut, P. and Moorhouse, P.R. (1994) *Beginning Qualitative Research: A Philosophic and Practical Guide*. London: Falmer

Meloy, J.M. (1994) *Writing the Qualitative Dissertation: Understanding by Doing*. Hillsdale, NJ: Lawrence Erlbaum Associates

Morgan, R. (2000) 'The politics of criminological research', in King, R.D. and Wincup, E. (eds), *Doing Research on Crime and Justice*. Oxford: Oxford University Press

Neill, J. (2003) *Quantitative Research Design: Sampling and Measurement.* Available at: wilderdom.com/OEcourses/PROFLIT/Class5QuantitativeResearchDesignSamplingMeasurement.htm [accessed 25/09/10]

Punch, K. (2006) *Developing Effective Research Proposals* (Second Edition). London: Sage

Redman, P. (2006) *Good Essay Writing*. London: Sage

Reiner, R. (1991) *Chief Constables*. Oxford: Oxford University Press

Robson, C. (1993) *Real World Research*. Oxford: Blackwell

Silverman, D. (2010) *Doing Qualitative Research*. London: Sage

Tellis, W. (1997) *Introduction to Case Study*. Available at: www.nova.edu/ssss/QR/QR3-2/tellis1.html [accessed 25/09/10]

Trochim, W. (2006) *The Research Methods Knowledge Base*. Available at: www.socialresearchmethods.net/kb/sampling.php [accessed 25/09/10]

Walliman, N. (2004) *Your Undergraduate Dissertation: The Essential Guide for Success*. London: Sage

Yin, R.K. (1984) *Case Study Research: Design Methods*. Thousand Oaks, CA: Sage

Yin, R.K. (1993) *Applications of Case Study Research*. Thousand Oaks, CA: Sage

TWO
FORMULATING CRIMINOLOGICAL RESEARCH QUESTIONS

PAMELA DAVIES

Chapter Contents

KEY POINTS

This chapter:

- Explains the importance of establishing and articulating clear research questions and the role they play in effective criminological research

- Outlines some key principles in designing social and criminological research questions

- Examines how social scientists' research ideas can be framed as researchable criminological questions

- Notes some techniques and strategies for formulating and refining your research question

- Provides guidance on how to turn a research topic/area into a research question

INTRODUCTION

Research inquiries that have a criminological bent to them have a head start in terms of attracting popular and political interest and generating topical debate and controversy. If criminological research is to be taken seriously by popular, academic, policy and practitioner audiences, however, it must strive to be valid, ethical, relevant, effective and rigorous. One of the easiest ways to denigrate criminological research is to point out poorly formulated and expressed research questions. One of the hallmarks of effective criminological research, therefore, is the clear formulation of the research questions flowing on from the choice of subject matter. 'What to study', the research question, provides the main focus or a 'blueprint' for the project (O'Leary 2004). A **research question** has been described as 'the overarching question that defines the scope, scale and conduct of a research project'. It is the research question that 'focuses research design and methods towards the provision of evidenced answers' (Gilbert 2008: 512). Sometimes 'research question' and 'research problem' are used interchangeably. Here we mainly use the words 'research question' as research problems conjures up all manner of problems which are associated with the practicalities of doing criminological research in addition to those of determining a good research question.

This chapter is primarily concerned with the fundamentals of formulating criminological research questions. While this is inseparable from some other fundamental criminological research considerations, such as planning criminological research (see Chapter 1), methodological approaches to criminological research (Chapter 3), the politics and ethics of criminological research (Chapters 13, 14) and conducting sensitive research (Chapter 6), these key issues are specifically foregrounded in other chapters. This chapter characterizes how research questions of a criminological nature might be formulated to best effect. This is done to provide the would-be researcher – whether student, practitioner or academic – with prompts to assist in the formulation of future research ideas and how they can be firmed up, by narrowing the focus, from research topic to research question. This chapter therefore explores how clear and effective criminological research questions are formulated and expressed.

The specific aims of this particular chapter are fivefold. They are: to explain the importance of establishing and articulating clear research questions and the role they play in effective criminological research; to establish some key principles in designing social and criminological research questions; to explain and illustrate how social scientists' research ideas can be framed as researchable criminological questions; to point out some useful techniques and strategies for formulating and refining your research question; to provide you with guidance on how to turn a research topic/area into a valid, ethical, relevant, effective and rigorous research question.

The chapter is divided into three sections. In the first section, criminological research questions are contextualized. Here a distinction is made between inductive and deductive approaches and a discussion of purposes of research and types of research also draws out a distinction between a descriptive and explanatory type of research question. Second, the problems of devising effective and researchable criminological research questions are addressed. The third section concerns the move from topic to question and narrowing the focus through a select number of ways. It considers units of analysis; levels of specificity and complexity; research products and conclusions; and the importance of attending to meaning. Each of these sections refers to real criminological research examples.

CONTEXTUALIZING RESEARCH QUESTIONS

Effective social research requires a clearly formulated research problem at its heart, one that asks the questions to which the investigator wants an answer and one that acts as the main 'signpost' for the researcher and audience (Creswell 2009) from the inception of a project through to the writing of a final research report, dissertation or thesis. Your research question is a guide and a focus for your research. The research focus specifies the general type or set of social phenomena about which the research is designed to provide information and about which the investigator will reach conclusions. All research begins with a research problem – an initial statement of the territory to be examined – although this may shift and be reformulated and refined as research unfolds. Indeed, it should be developed into a well-articulated research question, a written formulation which narrows the research focus by posing questions about the topics or object of inquiry. A research question should be capable of being answered in such a way as to allow conclusions to be drawn about the question or questions. Research questions therefore imply what kinds of data need to be collected, the units of analysis about which data needs to be collected and the contexts in which they need to be collected.

Social science research encompasses a wide variety of methodological approaches, styles of research and practices. This variety means that we can draw distinctions between different approaches to research and different types of research question. This variety can often be a source of dispute with regard to fundamental issues such as whether social science should adopt a natural scientific model, as used in physics or chemistry; whether or not the social world can be expressed in terms of statistical models rather than qualitative descriptions; or whether social science should aim to be value-free and neutral or be committed to particular social and political standpoints. As a consequence, some research questions can be very narrow and explicit in terms of units of analysis and contexts, perhaps grounding questions in particular contexts and in relation to particular kinds of people. Other social research questions are broad, merely acting as 'signposts' to the direction in which an inquiry might proceed. Such research questions – as signposts – tend to typify qualitative, ethnographic-type research. Some of these latter issues are returned to below.

Within the variety of methodological approaches, the distinction between inductive and deductive approaches to social research is one of the most obvious. Different reasoning applies to each of these approaches. Induction is the basic technique for moving from a set of observations to drawing out a theory from the observations. Once a theory has been formulated it can be used to develop explanations. Theory-testing differs in that it starts with a theory – which involves deducing or predicting – and uses it to explain particular observations. This type of approach is deductive. Induction is the technique for generating theories whereas deduction is the technique for applying them (De Vaus 2002). While these are neat distinctions, much social and criminological research falls between the two and there is, in practice, an intertwining of theory construction and testing.

For the purposes of this chapter, a further broad distinction is worth pointing out early on too – the difference between **descriptive** and more complex **explanatory**-type research questions. For descriptive type research, you must be clear and specific about what you want to describe. This might include a clear time frame, geographical location and comparative details. For explanatory-type research questions, what you are trying to explain is key, together with the possible causes, which you will explore (De Vaus 2002). Box 2.1 shows a checklist of questions to help focus descriptive and explanatory-type research questions.

While original criminological research studies exhibit differences, at least two commonalities distinguish social science research from everyday inquiry. First, observations are collected and assembled in a systematic way in order to reach conclusions and to put forward an argument. Second, observations are collected and assembled, and the arguments are presented, not in a vacuum, but in relation to some research focus, problem or question. A key feature of social scientific and criminological inquiry is the centrality given to a research problems or research question. Conclusions of research will be credible and plausible only to the extent

---

BOX 2.1

DESCRIPTIVE AND EXPLANATORY TYPE RESEARCH QUESTIONS

Descriptive research and research questions

- What is the time frame of interest?
- What is the geographical location of interest?
- Is your interest in broad description or in comparing and specifying patterns for subgroups?
- What aspect of the topic are you interested in?
- How abstract is your interest?

Explanatory research and research questions

- What are you trying to explain?
- What are the possible causes?
- Which causes will you explore?
- What are the possible mechanisms?

Adapted from De Vaus (2002: 23 and 25)

to which the questions and problems they address are clearly formulated and expressed and followed through in a consistent manner during the inquiry.

Your research question is then hugely important because it defines your research, sets boundaries, provides direction and acts as a frame of reference for assessing your work (O'Leary 2005). Sometimes one problem or central question may be broken down into sub-questions (Creswell 2009) or subsidiary problems (Blaikie 2000). Research problems vary in explicitness and breadth. They can comprise questions about *topic, cases, contexts* and *time periods* so that the question leads beyond descriptive conclusions towards analytical ones. For example:

> How do urban and rural areas (context) differ in terms of victimization of racially motivated crimes (cases) in the period between 2000 and 2010 (time)?

In this way decisions are taken to open up some dimensions of a broad topic to inquiry and not others. Before these 'narrowing of focus' issues are considered in further detail, however, it is worth pausing to explore what the purpose of your research is and what types of research are common to criminological inquiry.

Purposes of and types of research

Asking questions from the outset about the intended purpose of research is important to the would-be researcher in terms of clarifying the objectives of the research. This is because research questions which address different purposes need to be expressed in different ways.

To illustrate, we can make distinctions between **policy-related** research, **intervention**-based research, **theoretical** research and **critical research**, although these distinctions are over-tidy since there can be overlaps between such types of research.

Policy-related research is concerned with the collection of data and the presentation of conclusions and arguments as aids to the formulation of social policies. In criminology it has been associated with the development of criminal justice policies and therefore tends to be commissioned and sponsored by central government, especially the Home Office, and by the major institutions of criminal justice, such as the police or the prison service. Sometimes it is referred to as mainstream or conventional criminology and by others as administrative criminology. The research focus of policy-related investigations is largely determined by the sponsor of the research, with a particular emphasis on the customer–contractor relationship, that is, a relationship within which the researcher is a contractor who is required to produce certain 'deliverables' for the customer, the sponsor of the research. The deliverables will usually be specified outputs which it is thought will be an aid to decision-making about social or criminal justice policy. Examples of policy-related research questions include the following:

- How much crime is there and how is it geographically and socially distributed?
- Who are the perpetrators of crime and why do they do it?

- Are there any patterns to victimization in society?
- Who are the victims of crime and how are they socially and geographically distributed?
- In what ways does the criminal justice system discriminate against categories of people?
- To what extent do courts discriminate against categories of people?
- What role does the state play in the formulation of criminal justice policies and practices?

Intervention-based research is very close to policy research in so far as it is often concerned with evaluating the effectiveness, or otherwise, of interventions in producing intended outcomes. This form of research is sometimes also known as evaluation research. Research questions are usually framed in such a way as to direct the investigations to 'test' the effectiveness of policy interventions. Sponsors of research are often looking for conclusions that are expressed in terms of either success or failure of policies. This zero-sum formulation is popularly known as the 'what works' approach. Such research should be sensitive to the possibility that there may be different levels of effectiveness (short-term, intermediate and long-term), and also that policies may work in different ways in different contexts with different types of people. This is a case for 'narrowing the focus' by producing a cluster of interrelated and more specific research questions rather than one that is expressed purely in terms of 'success' or 'failure' of policy interventions. In the area of penal policy there have been several imaginative interventions, including forms of behavioural therapy, group therapy and counselling alongside other educational and training programmes. There has also been a strong tradition of evaluating these to discover what works, if anything, and, more precisely, what works where, when and with whom.

Matthews and Pitts (2000) provide a useful overview of the issues that are raised in connection with evaluating programmes related to rehabilitation and recidivism. In the specific context of evaluating violence reduction programmes in prison, they usefully dwell upon the problems of: **evaluation** generally and of evaluating cognitive skills programmes in particular; using recidivism as a measure of success and of developing realistic intermediate measures of success; and, finally, explaining why programmes work. Their conclusions suggest that it would be highly useful to develop a range of realistic intermediate measures which combine qualitative and quantitative data through 'intensive' and 'extensive' forms of research (Matthews and Pitts 2000: 140).

The emphasis in *theoretical research* is on understanding and explaining human behaviour and social action, the workings of social institutions and how all of these connect with the different dimensions of social structure. Such understandings and explanations may have policy relevance, but the primary aim is knowledge accumulation and ideas about future research often result from bringing together different theoretical strands or from empirical inquiry. The specific research questions that are typically asked in theoretical research vary. However, they are most likely to be expressed in ways which encourage the search for patterns in social life and for understandings and explanations of these patterns in general terms rather than in a way which addresses the effectiveness of specific policies or interventions. This may involve exploring dominant world views and unpacking problems perhaps by exploring your own perspectives or stakeholder perspectives in a way which opens up assumptions (O'Leary 2005: 28–29). The tradition of **ethnographic** research includes a strand which is concerned with formulating research ideas as a result of being immersed and grounded 'in the field', perhaps by carrying out participant observation.

Critical research is both theoretical and policy-related. It is theoretical in so far as it draws upon abstract concepts, such as ideology, power and discourse, and also on bodies of ideas which are expressed in terms of these. In addition, it often addresses criminal justice policies but in a critical vein rather than as a form of evaluative research which will act as an aid to management. Critical research works on the 'outside' rather than on the 'inside'. It is important to distinguish 'criticism', in its everyday usage, and 'critical analysis', as used in this context. 'Criticism' usually refers to an evaluation that is negative, censorious or fault-finding, whereas 'critical research' refers to an analysis of forms of behaviour, of policies or of practices in terms of underlying social structural issues and theories about these. It may result in criticism of such behaviour, policies or practices, but that is not an essential requirement.

The hallmark of critical research is the movement between different levels of analysis. The research focus of critical research varies, but it starts with an interest in specific actions, practices, policies or documents. It then poses research questions about the connections between these specifics and the wider and more fundamental underpinnings. Essentially, critical research questions whether there can be objectively produced knowledge or whether such 'knowledge' represents the world as the ruling classes, men, white, able-bodied people want it to be seen. A fuller articulation and illustration of critical research can be found in Chapter 15 of this volume.

EFFECTIVE AND RESEARCHABLE CRIMINOLOGICAL QUESTIONS

Examples of criminological research exist within the broach 'church' of social science research. The enterprise comprising criminology is diverse, wide-ranging and, in places, fragmented. It is carried out by a variety of researchers (for example, academics, policy analysts and practitioners) who work in a variety of institutions (universities, central and local government, criminal justice agencies). However, in broad terms, research questions of a criminological nature typically focus on the following: the nature of crime and its extent; the perpetrators of crime; the victims of crime; punishment and penology; the role of the state; the institutions of criminal justice and their workings; and how each of these interacts with wider social structural dimensions such as power, inequality, social class, gender and ethnicity. Such topics give a rough idea for a research study and simply delineate broad terrains for research which can then be refined and reformulated to be more incisive and penetrative. They form a platform for taking decisions about 'who to study', where and when, that is decisions not just about *topic*, but also about *cases*, *contexts* and *time*.

The examples of topics noted above show that criminological research is nearly always '**sensitive research**'. There are many ethical issues to consider in any social science research, but within criminological inquiry these concerns are especially significant. Highly controversial topics and questions, and especially vulnerable populations, are often thrown together. You as the research instigator and potential researcher should always be mindful of the question 'Can the research be justified?' Other questions which help determine whether research is justified are also helpful and you should ask yourself: Is my research likely to harm anyone or put the respondent and/or researcher in danger or at risk at any stage of the inquiry? For further details on sensitive and ethical research, see Chapters 6 and 13 in this volume.

A first stage in formulating criminological research problems involves deciding what to study. A central theme which runs throughout this book is that the doing of criminological research involves engaging in a process of **decision-making**. Essentially there are three key questions that demand clear decisions at the stage of formulating researchable questions. These three key questions are listed in Box 2.2, together with helpful subsidiary questions that will help make your research focus firm and clear and your criminological inquiry more effective.

Out of the three key questions in Box 2.2 – *what, why* and *how* – the first question is the most important – what are you doing? This decision is pivotal. It is the fulcrum around which all other research decisions are made (Green 2008) and a major influence on subsequent decisions about the ways in which the research project is to be accomplished. One of the most common problems is that proposed topics for criminological research are often far too broad or unfocused. While 'The Fear of Crime', 'Women and the Police', 'Mass Media and Violence', 'Juvenile Crime', 'Corporate Crime', or 'Drugs and Crime' might be general areas within which you wish to study, they are far too broad as dissertation topics. If unrefined, such broad topic areas are likely to lead to the 'kitchen-sink' approach to conducting research (Silverman 2007) and will fail on the 'how' question as they are not feasible to research. All too often the crucial element that is missing, especially from undergraduate dissertations, is an explicit theme or criminological problem, an understanding of what you want to 'do' in the dissertation. This is the first and most important *what?* question. *What do I want to know?* You need to be specific about the aspect of the broad topic area that you will be considering and from what angle. You need to think about how to ensure that you have a set of 'researchable foci', a series of research aims (Berg 2007: 24–25). For example, within a broad topic area such as 'Women and Imprisonment' there are a host of relevant and contemporarily interesting and provocative questions that can be posed. A research project on 'Women's Imprisonment' must identify the particular facets of women's experiences that the research will address. A series of research questions that stimulate a comparative inquiry might be formulated. For example:

- Are women treated fairly/unfairly in prison?
- Are women treated more leniently/harshly than men in prison?
- Are women treated differently from men in prison?

BOX 2.2

EFFECTIVE RESEARCH QUESTIONS

1 *What* are you doing?

- What do you want to explain/find out about?
- Can you define your research question?
- Can you articulate your research 'angle' clearly?

2 *Why* are you doing it?

- Why is this question criminologically significant, important and worthwhile?
- How will it be different from what has already been done before?
- Why are you curious about this?
- What are the gaps in existing knowledge?
- What is your rationale?
- Who will be interested in your research?

3 *How* you will do it?

- Is your question doable?
- How will you operationalize the research?
- How will you go about conducting the research and collecting information in order to answer your research question?
- How will you design your research?
- What is your research methodology?
- How will you collect your data and from which people, organizations, newspapers ...?
- How will you ensure the research is ethical and valid?
- Is your research feasible and practical?
- Are there any time constraints?
- Do you have the skills?
- Is the project affordable?
- Is ethical approval likely?

- Are any gender differences justifiable?
- Do women suffer double doses of punishment?

In Chapter 7 of this volume, 'Doing Interviews in Prison', Pamela Davies discusses using detailed semi-structured interviews with informants. This research inquiry was driven by a concern about theoretical knowledge and understanding around women's motives for doing economic crime. Some of the main and subsidiary problems as well as categories of analysis are outlined in Box 2.3.

BOX 2.3

THE MAIN AND SUBSIDIARY RESEARCH PROBLEMS FOR A STUDY ON WOMEN'S MOTIVATIONS FOR DOING ECONOMIC CRIME

Main research problem:

Women's motives for doing economic crime

Subsidiary research problems:

- defining economic crime
- the variety and extent of women's criminality
- women's initial and post hoc reasons and justifications for specific instances of criminality
- women's means and methods of carrying out crimes
- women's views of themselves as offenders
- explored and compared in the light of the empirical data, existing theoretical connections and debates about women's experiences and motivations for doing economic crime

The analysis of the interview data identified key themes, including those related to:

- motivations
- allusions to the economic
- ways of representing the notion of the economic
- degrees of rationalism

The research ultimately provided the theoretical basis for a more comprehensive explanatory framework of the behaviour of women who commit crime for economic gain.

Drawing upon Pat Carlen's research (1998) on women's imprisonment at the millennium, the following questions remain relevant to the twenty-first century and women's imprisonment:

- Why has there been a steep increase in women's imprisonment since the 1990s?
- Over the last twenty years have women been committing more serious and violent crimes?
- Have the last two decades seen increased punitiveness towards lawbreaking women?
- Is racism the key to increases in the female prison population?

Further examples of interesting and pertinent criminological research questions covering different topic areas can be illustrated:

- How many health and safety crimes are committed in the UK in any given year?
- What are the levels of crime and disorder in different areas of a large urban conurbation?
- How many people in the community under investigation express feelings of fear of crime?

Research questions such as these are not fixed and immutable. Indeed, they often shift and change as a project unfolds and as new dimensions open up. An inductive approach allows themes and questions for analysis to emerge from the early data. For this reason, researchers should be aware that their research question may need revisiting and adjustment (Noaks and Wincup 2004). For example, a project that starts out investigating the number of health and safety crimes may move into a consideration of the mechanisms by which employers and other interested parties manage to make a good number of these crimes invisible. Initial decisions on your primary research question are a powerful starting point and may prompt a further set of research questions. For example, the decision to ask the question, 'How many people in the community under investigation express feelings of fear of crime?' may lead to further subsidiary questions such as: 'Are there variations according to categories of people (for example, male and female, old and young)?', and 'What is the relationship between people's fear of crime and the likelihood that they will become victims of crime?'

So far we have seen how important finding a topic area is and how within that broad topic area there is a need to specify more precisely the nature of the research question and/or questions, and indeed the research aims and objectives. **Research objectives** are the purposes for which the research is being carried out. As noted earlier in this chapter, research objectives can be basic, for example couched in terms of exploration, description, understanding, explanation or prediction. Or, research objectives can be of an applied nature, for example to change, to evaluate or to assess social impacts (Blaikie 2000; Gilbert 2008). Sometimes a set of subsidiary questions help to break down the bigger question into more manageable pieces of the research jigsaw. I now turn to explain *how* this is done. There are several ways in which you can *find* a researchable criminological question.

Researchable criminological questions

Green (2008: 44) argues that 'the formulation of the research question is intellectual *work*, and a task that is continually revisited throughout the research project', and further suggests that in order to be sufficiently systematic, clearly defined and specific, questions must 'first and foremost, be *researchable*' (2008: 47). It must be possible to do the research, that is, to interrogate the problem. As stressed above, questions should be capable of being answered by the criminological inquiry. Problems suitable for criminological research are problems where you can make a difference (O'Leary 2005). Green proposes a useful checklist for refining research inquiry that has a broad focus or topic into researchable questions. She suggests six properties that a research question or problem should have. These are summarized in Box 2.4.

These are all issues that have been addressed in Chapter 1 and upon which, to various degrees, other chapters in this volume elaborate.

BOX 2.4

SIX PROPERTIES OF RESEARCHABLE QUESTIONS

Criminological research questions should be:

1 Interesting – to the curious, passionate and enthusiastic researcher.

2 Relevant – and make a contribution, through being significant, novel or original, to the research community of which the research forms a part, while maintaining a balance between the specific research interests of the researcher and the interests of the research community as a whole.

3 Feasible – with specific and limited boundaries which are mindful of practicalities and resources, including costs, time frames, skills, access and safety.

4 Ethical – ethical issues and considerations should be embedded from the outset in the research planning and formulation stages and thereafter should inform obligations and procedures in the doing of the research.

5 Concise – well articulated, with terms, concepts and objects of research clearly, specifically and precisely defined.

6 Answerable – interrogative questions that ask who, what, when, where, how, which and why tend to make a question answerable.

Adapted from Green (2008: 47–50)

FROM TOPIC (ROUGH NOTION) TO QUESTION (CLEAR AIMS) – NARROWING THE FOCUS

There are lots of different ways in which a topic area, which might also serve as a working title, such as 'crime victims', can lead to a narrower focus. One way of finding an 'angle' is to ask questions about how the different 'players' in the criminal justice system relate to each other. For example, 'How do the police deal with victims of crime?' Another way is to introduce types of crime, perhaps by considering how the police deal with victims of rape in comparison with how they deal with victims of burglary. Other dimensions can be introduced to make your research angle more precise. These include types of people, types of context and a consideration of different time periods. As we have seen, critical criminology seeks to introduce wider structural dimensions, such as power, inequality, social class, gender and ethnicity, into research questions.

So, to summarize, there are various considerations, techniques and strategies that can be called upon to refine and hone down your research idea into a manageable and doable criminological research inquiry. The remainder of this chapter focuses on a few key issues the would-be researcher might consider when narrowing the focus in order to formulate researchable criminological questions. These are: the *units of analysis, end-products of research, levels of specificity, levels of complexity* and *'meaning'*.

Units of analysis

All research questions are framed in terms of units of analysis or cases. As already noted, data might be specifically collected on *individuals*, social groupings, contexts, events, geographical areas and institutions. In terms of units of analysis being broken down by individuals, this might relate to crime victims or particular types of crime victim, such as victims of domestic violence. This can be narrowed further still by choosing to focus only on male victims of domestic violence and further still to male victims of domestic violence perpetrated by women. Units selected according to social groupings might include the young, whereby age groups might be specified. Another type of social grouping could relate to criminological research with 'the homeless'. Units of analysis specified by context or geography might distinguish, as we have noted, between urban and rural areas. Units specified by events might focus on numbers of specified crimes, such as domestic violence or health and safety crimes. Specific institutions might provide the unit of analysis in some types of criminological research and here we have mentioned the prison as one such example. Units of analysis are likely to be most explicitly specified in your explanation of *how* you will operationalize your research question. Research questions, such as those in the preceding sections, raise important issues regarding the unit of analysis which should be used. Most significantly, the scope of any conclusions which emerge from an investigation should be limited to the units of analysis as defined in research questions. So, as an example, findings about male victims of domestic violence are not necessarily true for female victims.

Levels of specificity and complexity

Research questions, then, can take the form of propositions or questions. Another form they may take is **hypotheses** (Denscombe 2006). Each of these is very much within the deductive approach to conducting criminological inquiry. A hypothesis is a logical conjecture about the possible relationship between two or more variables expressed in the form of a testable statement (O'Leary 2004). Hypotheses narrow your focus by turning research questions into testable propositions. The role of data analysis is to assist in the formation of judgements about the degree of 'fit' between data and hypothesis. This is known as hypothesis testing. In some projects a single research question may generate many hypotheses for testing. For example, a research focus on fear of crime in the United Kingdom may lead to the research question, 'How is fear of crime socially distributed?' In turn, an investigator may generate a number of research hypotheses which suggest conjectures about the relationship between membership of social categories and expressing fear of crime. Such hypotheses are plausible implications of the research questions, based on an understanding of existing research findings and also on what sensibly might be expected.

Hypotheses provide a much sharper focus than general research questions and a much firmer guide to the direction a project should take in terms of the following: from whom to collect data and what to collect data about. Hypotheses also imply certain forms of data analysis. Yet despite providing a sharper focus, they can remain basic in so far as they offer conjectures simply about relationships but say nothing about the *strength* or *direction* of the relationship. There are ways, however, in which hypotheses can be made more specific and complex. Hypotheses might put forward conjectures about the character of relationships, for example, that there are distinctive connections between the *values* of one variable and the values of another. Hypotheses that characterize interdependence or interrelationships include the following:

- Women are more likely to express fear of crime than men
- The more times a person has been a victim of crime the higher his/her level of fear of crime

Hypotheses such as these can be made more complex by hypothesizing about the relationships between several variables and their combined and independent effects on the fear of crime.

Research products and conclusions

Criminological and victimological research questions have different purposes which gives rise to different types of research, as we have seen above. They will also lead to different types of end-product or conclusions. Here we can distinguish between conclusions that are intended to be *descriptions*, conclusions that are put forward as *explanations*, and conclusions that *evaluate* policies.

Descriptions provide information about the unit of analysis at the centre of the research question. Some descriptions are qualitative. For example, a study of decision-making in magistrates' courts typically would describe the physical layout of the court, the different roles which are played (solicitor, defendant, witness, magistrate), the type of proceedings (committal, sentencing) and the nature of decisions (legal, administrative and so on). Such qualitative descriptions are very much within the ethnographic tradition in criminological research. Descriptions may also be numerical, for instance where a police area is characterized in terms of the number of offences recorded by the police. Thus areas may be described on several variables at one and the same time.

Typical research questions which point the way to descriptive conclusions are as follows:

- What roles are played in the courtroom?
- What kinds of decisions are taken by the magistrates?
- What is the level of crime in an area?
- How many children truant from school in an area?
- How can we describe the area in terms of crime and disorder, employment, health and education?

Research questions geared towards reaching conclusions that offer explanations are much more likely to be expressed in terms of patterns and relationships between variables (especially in quantitative research). Research questions cast in explanatory terms, then, are more likely to be expressed in the following ways:

- What is the *relationship* between crime levels and levels of unemployment, income and housing standards?

Or,

- To what extent can changes in crime levels be *explained* by changes in levels of unemployment, income and housing standards?

The sponsors of policy-related, especially intervention-based, research are likely to expect conclusions to be expressed in evaluative terms, that is making a judgement that the policy achieved its aims. Therefore, at their simplest, evaluative research questions are usually expressed in terms of inputs and outputs, with subsequent analysis geared towards before-and-after measurements of the output variable to see if there has been a significant change as a result of the input of policy. Typically, they take the form: 'Does the introduction of input X result in a change in output Y?' In some cases a research question may be more specific, hypothesizing about the degree of change in output variables. For example, asking: 'To what extent does the introduction of input X result in a change in output Y?' In this example we can expect that conclusions will very specifically report upon the extent to which the introduction of X results in a change in Y. We might also expect information to be forthcoming upon the nature of the change. For an illustration see Hood's *Race and Sentencing: A Study in the Crown Court* (1992). Hood's study of the courts is an example of a factorial research question, where he tried to eliminate the influence of all independent variables except ethnicity on sentencing.

Attending to meaning

Some of the more complex ways of narrowing the research focus can inhibit what should be an iterative process and stifle formulation of new yet highly relevant ideas as a project develops. Going too far down the line of statistical modelling, for example, as might arise from an overly sophisticated hypothesis, can mean that the models do not correspond with social reality in a meaningful way. In a similar way, hypothesis testing can sometimes be inappropriate or inapplicable for many types of research. Modelling and hypothesis formation tend to impose preconceived ideas, which are not necessarily the same as those of the people being studied. Also, for some researchers, it is the viewpoint of the people who are the subject of the research that is paramount. For these reasons, research questions should pay particular attention to social meanings to ensure that the research does not become divorced from social reality. Prioritizing social meaning will safeguard the research question so that it is capable of producing conclusions that will be grounded in such meanings and expressed in terms which would be used by the subjects of inquiry themselves. This reminds us of the importance of the interplay between inductive and deductive approaches where one approach is often tempered by the other in effective and rigorous criminological inquiry.

SUMMARY

This chapter has explored a range of key issues concerning formulating criminological research questions. Criminological research is about a series and range of important decisions for the researcher, decisions that can impact upon the effectiveness of the research project as a whole. Among these decisions, those concerning your research question are perhaps the most significant. A good question, 'What to study?', provides the main focus for the project. We have stressed how a good research question is researchable and supports an effective research design and methods towards the provision of evidenced answers and conclusions. The chapter has provided examples and illustrations that indicate how to move from a research idea and a general topic to a question by narrowing the focus. Various influences on how this 'angle' or narrower scope and refined scale can be achieved have been outlined. This has included a look at the purposes of research, units of analysis, levels of specificity and complexity, end-products and conclusions to research and the importance of attending to meaning.

In doing so, the chapter has explained the importance of establishing and articulating clear research questions and the role they play in effective criminological research. It has covered the principles in designing social and criminological research questions. It has offered guidance on how social scientists' research ideas can be framed as researchable criminological questions and has explored techniques and strategies for formulating and refining your research question. Finally, some tips about formulating criminological research questions are outlined in Box 2.5.

BOX 2.5

BASIC GUIDELINES ABOUT FORMULATING CRIMINOLOGICAL RESEARCH QUESTIONS: DO'S AND DON'TS

Do	Avoid...
Be realistic	pure and simple inductivism
'Say a lot about a little (problem)'	'the "kitchen-sink" gambit' (Silverman 2007)
Take account of practicalities – timescales, finances, resources	reductionism
Be mindful throughout of ethical issues	'grand theorizing' (Silverman 2007)
Be flexible and allow for a change of focus	being too ambitious
Write out your research question separately from your project title	over-complex modelling and hypotheses that do not attend to social meaning
Practise verbally articulating your research question in simple terms	over-complicating and embellishing your research ambitions

---

Study Questions/Activities for Students

Consider your own research ambitions and work through the following questions:

1 What are your research ideas? How do you broadly define your research topic? Practise talking about these to others (friends, family, students, colleagues, tutors).

2 What is your primary research question? Write this/these down as clearly as you can.

3 What are your subquestions? Write these down and link them clearly to your primary research question.

4 What 'type' of research question have you arrived at?

5 Is your research question researchable – by you?

6 Are your research questions ethical and justifiable?

7 Revisit and rewrite your research question and subquestions after one week and then again after one month.

8 How have your questions changed and why?

RESOURCES

There are several social science resources which are easily adapted for criminological research purposes. These include the following:

Booth, W.C. (2003) 'From topic to questions', Chapter 3 in *The Craft of Research* (2nd edition). Chicago: University of Chicago Press. This chapter includes lots of examples of ways to find the makings of a problem and how to turn it into a problem that guides your research.

De Vaus, D. (2002) 'Formulating and clarifying research questions', Chapter 3 in *Surveys in Social Research* (5th edition). London: Routledge. The first half of this chapter is especially useful for considering the type of research question that you are formulating and the scope of your research.

O'Leary, Z. (2004) 'Developing your research question', Chapter 3 in *The Essential Guide to Doing Research*. London: Sage. See especially the section on moving from ideas to researchable question using insights from personal experience, theory, observations, contemporary issues and engagement with the literature. See also the section on narrowing, clarifying and redefining your research question.

Tashakkori, A. and Creswell, J.W. (2007) 'Exploring the nature of research questions in mixed method research', Editorial in *Journal of Mixed Methods Research*, 1(3): 207–11. Concerned with exploring how to frame a research question in a mixed methods study, this editorial reviews three models and practices the authors have observed in the literature.

REFERENCES

Berg, B.L. (2007) *Qualitative Research Methods for the Social Sciences* (6th edition). London: Pearson

Blaikie, N. (2000) *Designing Social Research: The Logic of Anticipation*. Cambridge: Polity Press

Carlen, P. (1998) *Sledgehammer: Women's Imprisonment at the Millennium.* Basingstoke: Macmillan

Creswell, J.W. (2009) *Research Design: Qualitative, Quantitative, and Mixed Methods Approaches* (3rd edition). London: Sage

Denscombe, M. (2006) in V. Jupp (ed.), *The Sage Dictionary of Social Research Methods.* London: Sage

De Vaus, D. (2002) *Surveys in Social Research* (5th edition). London: Routledge

Gilbert, N. (ed.) (2008) *Researching Social Life* (3rd edition). London: Sage

Green, N. (2008) 'Formulating and Refining a Research Question', in N. Gilbert (ed.), *Researching Social Life* (3rd edition). London: Sage

Hood, R. (1992) *Race and Sentencing*: *A Study in the Crown Court.* Oxford: Clarendon Press

Matthews, R. and Pitts, J. (2000) 'Rehabilitation, Recidivism and Realism: Evaluating Violence Reduction Programmes in Prison', in V. Jupp, P. Davies and P. Francis (eds), *Doing Criminological Research.* London: Sage

Noaks, L. and Wincup, E. (2004) *Criminological Research*: *Understanding Qualitative Methods.* London: Sage

O'Leary, Z. (2004) *The Essential Guide to Doing Research.* London: Sage

O'Leary, Z. (2005) *Researching Real-World Problems*: *A Guide to Methods of Inquiry.* London: Sage

Silverman, D. (2007) *Doing Qualitative Research.* London: Sage

THREE
METHODOLOGICAL APPROACHES
TO CRIMINOLOGICAL RESEARCH

NATASHA SEMMENS

Chapter Contents

KEY POINTS

This chapter:

- Outlines the different methodological approaches in criminological research
- Explores a range of methodological decisions that must be taken in the context of your research as well as the time and resources available to you
- Explores choices in relation to your research strategy and design
- Explores choices regarding types of data, data collection and data analysis
- Considers how to operationalise your research design

INTRODUCTION

This chapter is about the different methodological approaches in criminological research. Chapters 1 and 2 have introduced you to the important first stages of **research design**: planning the research and formulating the research questions. Once these stages have been completed, you will move on to make decisions about the kinds of methods to use and the sorts of data to collect. These decisions will be taken in the context of the purpose of the research and the time and resources available. The aim of this chapter is to explore some of the options which are available to the criminological researcher and to explore the appropriateness of different methods in different contexts.

The chapter is structured in four main sections, as illustrated in Figure 3.1. The first is concerned with the process of developing a **research strategy** and research

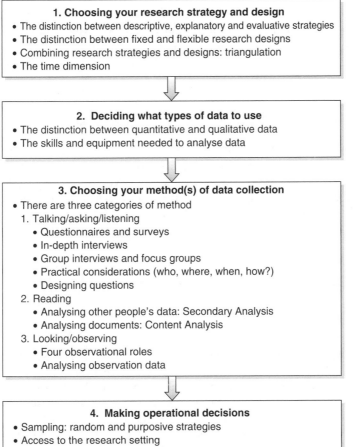

FIGURE 3.1 Chapter Outline

design. There are different strategies or designs available and whichever one you adopt will influence the decisions which need to be made subsequently. The second set of choices to be made relates to data collection and analysis. A distinction is made between **quantitative** and **qualitative** data and issues concerning the processes of storing and analysing different types of data are discussed. The third section deals with the question of choosing the most appropriate method of data collection. This section covers in detail the main methods available to the researcher, grouping them into three categories: methods involving talking/listening, reading/analysing other people's data and looking/observing. The fourth section is concerned with a series of operational choices once the research methods have been chosen. These include decisions about sampling, access, the role of the researcher and ethical/legal issues.

By helping you to understand the process of decision-making which takes place when a research study is designed, this chapter achieves two things. First, it gives you the basic knowledge and confidence to make these decisions yourself. Many of the points raised within the chapter can be linked directly to chapters later in this book which expand on the points made and serve as detailed practical examples of the decisions 'in action'. Second, it enables you to evaluate the methodological decisions made by other researchers and to view criminological research critically.

CHOOSING YOUR RESEARCH STRATEGY AND DESIGN

In Chapter 2 three different types of strategy were introduced: **descriptive**, **explanatory** and **evaluative** strategies (a summary is provided in Box 3.1). Once the initial 'vision' of the project has been established, the next stage is for you to refine the research design. If you recall, the choice of strategy will be influenced by the purpose of the research, the nature of the research question and the theoretical framework underpinning it.

BOX 3.1

THREE STRATEGIES FOR RESEARCH

Descriptive strategies focus on uncovering information about the unit of analysis at the centre of the investigation. The aim is to paint a picture of a phenomenon, identifying the key characteristics and examining any patterns which occur. Although the aim of the research is not to look for causal relationships (see explanatory research), it is possible for descriptive research to be deeply analytical. Research of this kind often incorporates some kind of comparison, either across categories or over time. So, you might compare the *rates* of different crime types (burglary, mugging, vehicle theft) to assess which is the most prevalent. You might also make comparisons over time to get a picture of any *trends*.

(Continued)

Example: Soothill et al. (2008) studied the offending behaviour of young adults (aged 16–20) across different generations using The Offenders Index, a court-based database of criminal convictions in England and Wales since 1963. They examined crime data from the 1970s, the 1980s and the 1990s, focusing on the types of offence committed by male and female offenders. They found that patterns of offending have shifted over time. In the past, offenders tended to specialise in one offence. The most recent generation of offenders are more versatile, exhibiting a range of offences. The researchers discuss how their analysis might be used to inform policy and practice in the courts.

Explanatory strategies focus on looking for a cause of something. This means that concepts have to be defined and operationalised into variables before the research is actually carried out. There are three types of variable in causal relationship – the dependent variable(s), the independent variable(s) and the intervening variable(s). Criminological research cannot always expect to be able to predict every possible (and unlikely) intervening variable, but you must take care to ensure (as far as possible) that the relationship between the dependent and independent variable is logical and true.

Example: Harris and Murphy (2007) conducted an empirical test of Braithwaite's theory of reintegrative shaming in the white-collar context. They interviewed a group of people who had committed and been punished for tax offences with a view to testing the relationships between disapproval, shame-related emotions and recidivism. They wanted to find out whether different forms of disapproval (reintegrative vs. stigmatising shaming) are related to different shame-related responses, and whether these shame emotions are related to reoffending behaviour. The variables used were grouped in five categories: shame acknowledgement (where the offender expressed feelings of shame), feelings towards the authorities, reformed behaviour, shame displacement (where the offender feels angry and wants to get even with the authorities) and desire to put things right. The results showed a clear relationship between reintegration and reoffending: offenders who perceived the authority's treatment of them as more reintegrative, and consequently as less stigmatising, were less likely to reoffend. The relationship between reintegration and shame emotions was more complex. Reintegration predicted less shame acknowledgement, not more, as was hypothesised, and did not predict reoffending. On the other hand, more stigmatisation resulted in more shame displacement and higher rates of reoffending. The authors concluded that the relationships between disapproval, shame-related emotions and recidivism are complex and need further conceptual exploration before we can draw solid conclusions about causal links.

Evaluation strategies assess the impact of interventions, initiatives, laws or policies. There are two types of evaluation study. **Outcome-oriented evaluations** adopt a strict scientific approach, using pure experiments to look for direct causal relationships between the initiative and the outcome. **Realistic evaluations** place more of an emphasis on understanding why an initiative does or does not work. They also utilise experimental methods, but they examine the processes, mechanisms and contexts which have an influence on the success of an initiative.

Example: In a large-scale project, Shapland et al. (2004, 2006a, 2006b, 2007, 2008) conducted an evaluation of three restorative justice schemes. They focused on how the schemes were implemented, the participants' expectations and take-up rates, victims' and offenders' views of the processes and outcomes and, finally, whether restorative justice 'works' (in the sense of reducing the likelihood of reoffending and for whom it 'works' in this way). They also asked whether the schemes were value for money.

Once the strategy has been selected, you can move on to build the research design. There are different research designs which can be adopted and you will see them referred to in different ways in the research methods literature (for example, you will see reference to **positivistic** vs. **interpretivistic** designs, quantitative vs. qualitative designs, etc.). However, Robson (2002) introduces two categories of design which I find useful because they effectively capture the theoretical and practical features of the research design: these are **fixed** and **flexible** designs. The key features of both designs are summarised in Box 3.2.

BOX 3.2

FIXED AND FLEXIBLE RESEARCH DESIGNS (ROBSON 2002)

Fixed designs

The distinguishing feature of the fixed design is the large amount of prespecification which must be carried out before the research begins. This includes the development of concepts and operationalisation of those concepts into measures which can be used to test hypotheses. Often these measures are used as part of a research tool, for example a questionnaire or observation schedule. In a fixed design, the researcher seeks to maintain as much control as possible over the research setting, controlling and manipulating variables. There is a heavy emphasis on carrying out the research in a subjective, professional way using a series of rules/procedures. Often, fixed designs involve the collection of quantitative data, but it is also possible for qualitative data to be used.

Example: Semmens et al. (2002) conducted a survey to measure the effect of seasonality on fear of crime. The hypothesis was that fear of crime would be higher in the winter months than in the summer months. Great care was taken to ensure that the research setting was controlled. The survey was conducted in two cities (Sheffield and Glasgow) using a quota sample approach (see below). It was carried out on a series of prespecified dates in the winter, spring, summer and autumn. The questionnaire was structured and contained several different measures of fear of crime. Notes were taken of the light and weather conditions at the time of each interview. The results showed that fear of crime was, indeed, higher in the winter months. This was an important finding because the British Crime Survey (BCS) was at that time conducted only in the winter. The authors suggested that future sweeps should be carried out at other times of the year in order to build a more accurate picture of crime and fear of crime. Subsequently, the BCS moved to a continuous sampling design.

Flexible designs

Flexible designs often use methods that collect qualitative data, but quantitative data can also feature in flexible designs. The key feature is that the research design evolves as the research progresses and therefore involves little prespecification. The researcher is not obsessed with procedures, although questions of validity are important and care must be taken when interpreting data and drawing conclusions from the research. Importantly, the researcher does not seek to control the setting. Instead, s/he allows the concepts to emerge naturally and examines them as they manifest, looking for themes and relationships to develop.

Example: Sandberg (2008) carried out an ethnographic study to explore the world of ethnic minority drug dealers at a street drug market in Oslo. He lived close to the market and spent a lot of time there, walking, sitting and speaking to people when he felt it was appropriate. He observed what was going on around him and immersed himself in the culture. Interviews were carried out in whatever location the offender felt comfortable in – a café or bar or his/her apartment. Interviews took the form of life histories which involved very little prompting from the interviewer and allowed the interviewee to tell his/her own story. This means that the interviewees highlighted the issues which were most important to them.

It is important that the design you opt for is consistent with the strategy you have selected. Explanatory strategies tend to incorporate fixed designs, but for descriptive and evaluative studies there is more scope to adopt either a fixed or flexible approach. Sometimes, the nature of the research question may require a hybrid design which incorporates some elements of both fixed and flexible approaches (Green and Preston 2005). A good example of this can be found in Box 3.3.

BOX 3.3

NEIGHBOURHOOD POLICING IN SOUTH YORKSHIRE: COMBINING FIXED AND FLEXIBLE APPROACHES IN RESEARCH

I recently conducted some research for South Yorkshire Police which explored and evaluated the implementation of the national Neighbourhood Policing Programme in 2008. In South Yorkshire, the implementation process involved an extensive training programme which sought to equip Safer Neighbourhood Teams (SNTs) with the knowledge and skills needed to embark upon effective partnership working and community engagement. The project, then, required a two-stage research design.

1 An evaluation of the training programme itself. A fixed design at this stage, using a combination of observational work, focus groups and evaluation questionnaires, enabled us to measure the learning outcomes of the training programme.

2 An investigation into how the knowledge/skills delivered in the training were subsequently implemented into the everyday work of the SNT. This was done using a case study approach. Two student researchers were posted with separate Safer Neighbourhood Teams. They spent time immersed in the setting, talking to staff and observing meetings and interactions with the public. Their objective was to explore how the SNTs utilised the skills learned during training and to identify the enablers and barriers to the implementation of Neighbourhood Policing principles. The design for this part of the research, then, was very flexible and the emphasis was on letting themes emerge. As a result, two separate themes emerged as being important to the different teams. In one, the issue of partnership working was paramount. In the other, the challenges associated with identifying and responding to community priorities was more important. This enabled us to draw some interesting conclusions about the different experiences in different contexts – something we would not have been able to achieve had we adopted a fully fixed design throughout.

Combining research strategies and designs: triangulation

The research project described in Box 3.3 is an example of **triangulation**. Triangulation is an approach to research design that places a heavy emphasis on improving **validity** through the combination of different research methods. There are four types of triangulation. These are summarised in Box 3.4.

BOX 3.4

FOUR TYPES OF TRIANGULATION (DENZIN 1988)

1 Theoretical

Looking at the phenomenon under investigation through a combination of different theoretical perspectives. This can involve both the explanatory and epistemological frameworks of a research project.

2 Data

The combination of different types of data, to include both quantitative and qualitative data collected from different sources (across different times, spaces and people).

3 Method

A combination of different methods to measure the same thing.

4 Investigator

Multiple investigators are used in the collection of data (perhaps several interviewers or observers).

Research design: the time dimension

One final thing to consider as part of the research design is the time dimension. There are two important distinctions to be drawn here: the first is between **prospective** and **retrospective** research designs and the second is between **cross-sectional** and **longitudinal** research designs.

Where your research subjects are going through a process (say, a court case or a rehabilitation course), you need to decide whether to conduct a prospective and/or a retrospective study. Prospective studies involve waiting for subjects to enter the process and studying them throughout their journey. These studies tend to be time-consuming and resource-intensive, but give the researcher a great deal of control over the data collection process. Retrospective studies involve the examination of subjects at the end of the process. They are quicker and easier to conduct, but the researcher must make do with the data that is available (usually collected by the administrators of the process under study).

Cross-sectional studies involve the collection of data at one specific point in time. So, for example, if I were to conduct a victimisation survey of my first-year students, this would be a cross-sectional study. Because cross-sectional research provides a snapshot of a situation, it is vulnerable to claims of non-generalisability and criticisms of a lack of spatial–temporal perspective. Some studies, then, are conducted in a series of different places and at different times (for example, Semmens et al. 2002). Longitudinal studies are different in that they involve the re-examination of the same group over time. So, they record snapshots of the same people over time. Often these are called cohort studies. Longitudinal studies are difficult to administer because people tend to drop out of the research study for various reasons (for a good discussion, see Farrington 2006).

DECIDING WHAT TYPE OF DATA TO USE

Once the research strategy is in place and the research design established, the process of designing the research methodology begins. One of the most important things to decide at this point is what type of data to collect. There are different kinds of data available to the researcher, including numbers, words, pictures and sounds, and a distinction is made in research between two main categories: quantitative and qualitative data. Quantitative data consists of numbers; qualitative data consists of non-numerical data such as words, images and sounds.

The decision about the type of data to collect will be shaped to a large extent by the kind of research strategy adopted. However, sometimes researchers make the mistake of pigeon-holing quantitative data with fixed, positivistic research designs and qualitative data with flexible, interpretivistic research designs. While there is a tendency for explanatory studies to draw heavily on quantitative data and for exploratory studies (searching for meaning) to involve the collection of qualitative data, the rules are not that simple. It is common for studies to utilise a combination of data types and therefore it is important to be clear from the outset whether a triangulation approach can and should be adopted.

Crucially, the analysis of both quantitative and qualitative data requires the researcher to have specific skills and equipment. Quantitative data are usually analysed using a dedicated statistical package on a PC (see Box 3.5). Therefore, the researcher needs to know how to create data sets, how to input data and how to conduct (and interpret) statistical tests. An example of quantitative analysis can be found in Chapter 6 by Jo Deakin and Jon Spencer. Qualitative data are also sometimes analysed using special computer packages (see Box 3.5), but some researchers prefer to use more traditional methods (literally cutting and pasting sections of text!). Either way, the analysis process involves the coding and categorisation of the data so that patterns and relationships can be identified and explored. A good example of research using this approach can be found in Chapter 10 by Rob C. Mawby. We will not spend time discussing these approaches in depth in this chapter, but you are referred to the sources listed in the Resources section.

EXAMPLES OF SOFTWARE USED FOR DATA ANALYSIS

SPSS

Statistical Package for the Social Sciences (SPSS) is the most widely used package for statistical analysis in criminological research. It can be used to conduct a wide range of statistical tests on data, outputting results in both tabular and chart form. SPSS is most useful when you are dealing with quantitative data.

NVivo

NVivo is a package designed for analysis of qualitative data (transcripts, audio or video data). It helps researchers to organise and analyse non-numerical data by providing functions for coding and grouping data. It also has a search engine that allows the researcher to find common concepts or phrases occurring in large numbers of documents. The researcher is also able to explore relationships between different concepts/people.

CHOOSING THE METHOD(S) OF DATA COLLECTION

Once you are clear about the types of data you wish to collect, you can move on to decide on your method of data collection. There are many different methods available to the criminological researcher. It is not unusual to see references to quantitative and qualitative research methods in the literature, but these labels can be misleading. In my own teaching (and indeed my research) I have found it easier to group methods according to the three sets of skills that the researcher uses to gather the data:

- Talking/asking/listening
- Reading
- Looking/observing

Talking/asking/listening

Much criminological research involves asking people questions about their attitudes and experiences. Questions can be asked using a range of methods and the key feature that unites these methods is that they require an interaction or conversation between the researcher and the subject.

It is important that you choose a method that is appropriate to the aims and objectives of the research. Where the aims are to describe or explain a phenomenon by testing a series of predetermined **hypotheses**, a formal structured questionnaire is likely to be of most use. Conversely, where the aim of the research is to explore a phenomenon or uncover the meanings which underlie a social situation, an in-depth **interview** which is loosely structured is more suitable. It is important that all decisions are made with the issues of validity, **reliability** and **replicability** in mind, and there are situations when a combination of methods is appropriate. An example would be where a self-completion questionnaire is followed up by a series of in-depth interviews (for a good example, see Semmens 2001).

Questionnaires and surveys

Questionnaires are commonly associated with surveys and can be distributed for self-completion or administered by an interviewer. Questionnaires are structured, encouraging the respondent to answer questions by ticking boxes, selecting words or inserting short (one or two word) answers. Every respondent is asked the same set of questions in the same way. Questionnaires can collect both quantitative and qualitative data, depending on the kinds of question used.

The main benefit of questionnaires is that it is possible to collect information from a large sample of people relatively easily and cheaply. Responses can be gathered immediately where a group of people are already assembled or over a short amount of time where questionnaires are posted or distributed electronically. The data analysis process is also quite efficient. Inputting the data into a data set (which must be pre-prepared) can be time-consuming but it is not a difficult job. Responses are given numerical codes and these are inputted into the database. Great care is needed, though, to ensure that the data are inputted accurately. Sometimes problems arise because people may not have answered the question in the way in which they were instructed. The inputter may, then, have to make a judgement about whether/how to code the data, ensuring that all queries are dealt with as consistently as possible. This is known as 'cleaning' the data. It is important that the analysis strategy is devised in advance, preferably when the questions are designed.

There are some disadvantages to questionnaires. Sometimes they are received negatively by respondents – most of us routinely discard invitations to take part in email surveys or walk past surveyors in the street, avoiding eye contact! This can create real problems with poor response rates and skewed samples (Marshall 1994). Respondents can also suffer from 'questionnaire fatigue', especially where the questionnaire is lengthy (Schuman and Presser 1996).

In-depth interviews

Interviews can be one of three types (Denzin 1988):

1 *Schedule standardised or structured* interview

   A detailed plan of the interview is used. This contains all of the questions to be asked. All respondents are asked the same questions, in the same order.

   Example: The British Crime Survey is a good example of a structured interview. Interviews are conducted using a laptop computer in an approach known as CAPI (computer-assisted personal interviewing). The computer program controls the order in which questions are asked and responses are inputted and saved in situ.

2 *Non-schedule standardised or semi-structured* interview

This is a list of the information that needs to be drawn from the respondent, but the questions used can be changed by the interviewer to fit in with the conversation.

Example: Pamela Davies conducted semi-structured interviews with female offenders in prison (see Chapter 7). This method was selected because one of the aims of the research was to explore the different types of crime the women engaged in and to gain an insight into the criminal methods they used. Although it was important to steer the interviews in the direction of these topics (using key concepts and issues that had emerged from the pilot interviews), it was felt to be important to maintain respect for the narratives of the individual women. Thus, a semi-structured interview was the best approach in this instance.

3 *Non-standardised or unstructured* interview

The interviewer simply has a broad topic to discuss with no specific pieces of information to seek out. There are no predetermined questions and the conversation is allowed to take whichever route is suitable.

Example: An important study carried out by Hollway and Jefferson (1997) made use of life histories to explore the relationship between fear of crime and risk. Their main hypothesis was that fear of crime is not a direct response to risk of victimisation but is mediated by anxiety and defences against it. They sought to understand how some people have rational or realistic responses to the threat of criminal victimisation and some have irrational or unrealistic responses. They used techniques from psychoanalysis to examine anxiety in the interviewees' accounts. These included eliciting narratives structured by free association and interpreting the significance of avoidance, contradiction, error and changes in emotional tone. The interviews started with the invitation 'tell me your life story'. As the respondent told the story, the interviewer took notes, ensuring that s/he recorded the themes (as labelled by the respondent) in order. Probing was used (only in an open form) to encourage the respondent to build a fuller picture.

The main advantage of interviewing is that the interviewer can encourage the respondent to open up and probe for further explanations where a response is unclear or, in the case of unstructured interviews, to uncover new themes. There are, though, some potential disadvantages. It can be difficult for the interviewer to build a trusting rapport with the respondent and there is a chance that the respondent will not answer honestly, giving a response that is socially desirable or that will satisfy the interviewer in some way. Also, there is a danger of the interviewer misinterpreting the things people say, so it is important to assign the right meaning in the right contexts.

Group interviews and focus groups

There is a difference between **group interviews** and **focus groups**. Group interviews involve interviewing a group of people at the same time; the researcher poses questions and records and analyses the responses of individuals just as if each one had been interviewed separately. Focus groups, on the other hand, are used when the researcher wants to explore a topic in detail. The group is given a topic to discuss and the researcher takes more of a 'facilitator' role. There is also an emphasis on studying the interactions between the group members and, for this reason, focus groups are often video-taped for analysis (Crow and Semmens 2008).

Focus groups are useful because they take us beyond the 'snapshot' view that we often get from questionnaires and interviews. You can see how people interpret and manage their experiences, and how these interpretations mould their perceptions is a process which occurs in a social context. The focus group approach allows people to discuss their views and compare their decision-making processes with others, in a social dynamic. The researcher can therefore gain more of an insight into how meaning is attached to certain phenomena (Morgan 2006). The success of the focus group does, though, rest on the assumption that all group members will feel comfortable expressing themselves and disagreeing with others. As with all methods of research, there are also some issues of validity which need addressing. It is not usually acceptable for only one or two focus groups to be conducted; ideally the researcher would continue to run new group sessions until no new topics emerge. This is known as '**category saturation**' (Morgan 1992).

Interviews: practical decisions

Whatever approach is used, the researcher has to make a series of practical decisions relating to the conduct of the interviews themselves. One of the first decisions to be made is where the interview will take place – the respondent's workplace, home or on neutral ground? Next, how to record the interview? In the case of questionnaires, a recording method will be predetermined. For in-depth and group interviews, it is often a good idea to use a voice recorder (tape or MP3) but this should only be done where the respondent has given consent. The interview will need to be transcribed afterwards and this can be a lengthy process which produces a lot of data. An alternative to recording is note-taking. This approach has the disadvantage that concentration on the notepad can disrupt the flow of the conversation.

Designing questions

The process of designing questions is more complex than many people think. There are a number of different question formats that can be used.

One of the main distinctions to be drawn is that between *open* and *closed* questions. Closed questions are questions which require the respondent to select a single response from a predetermined list. For example:

How safe do you feel walking alone in your neighbourhood at night?

☐ *Very unsafe (1)*

☐ *Fairly unsafe (2)*

☐ *Quite safe (3)*

☐ *Very safe (4)*

Note how each of the responses is given a numerical code which is used to enter the response into the database. There are a range of different responses which can be offered in closed questions. These are summarised in Box 3.6.

BOX 3.6

DIFFERENT TYPES OF RESPONSE FOR CLOSED QUESTIONS

- **Factual quantities**
  What age were you on your last birthday? ………

- **Categories**
  What is your gender? *Tick one only*.

  ☐ Male
  ☐ Female

- **Multiple choice**
  Have you experienced any of the following problems in your neighbourhood in the last 12 months? *Tick all that apply*.

  ☐ Young people hanging around in groups
  ☐ Graffiti
  ☐ Litter
  ☐ Drug dealing
  ☐ Noisy neighbours

- **Ranking**
  Which of the following do you think are the most serious problems in your neighbourhood? *Rank the three most serious problems, where '1' is the most serious problem*.

  ☐ Young people hanging around in groups
  ☐ Graffiti
  ☐ Litter
  ☐ Drug dealing
  ☐ Noisy neighbours

- **Scales**
  How worried are you about someone breaking into your house and stealing something? *Tick one*.

  ☐ Very worried
  ☐ Fairly worried
  ☐ Not very worried
  ☐ Not at all worried

- **Grids**
  Do you agree or disagree with the following statements? *Put one tick in each row*.

	Agree	Neutral	Disagree
People on my street help each other			
People on my street keep their properties tidy			
People on my street are noisy and inconsiderate			

Open questions are questions that do not provide a list of responses and instead allow the respondent to answer in his/her own words in the space provided. For example:

How do you feel when you are walking alone in your neighbourhood at night?

Where open questions are used, the data has to be coded at the stage of analysis. The coding frame has not been predetermined, as is the case for closed questions. Instead, the coding frame emerges from the open responses. This involves the creation of categories based on recurrent themes. So, to use the example just given, my respondents might fall into three groups: the fearful, the nervous or those who feel completely safe. Sometimes, this qualitative data can be transformed into quantitative data through the assignment of numerical codes or where frequencies of responses are calculated (for example, 55% of respondents discussed feelings of fear).

Finally, it is important to think very carefully about the wording of questions and the order in which they are placed. In particular, great care must be taken to:

- Avoid leading questions
- Use only one idea per question
- Avoid complicated, technical or ambiguous terms
- Avoid questions that invite a socially desirable answer
- Ensure that response categories do not overlap

Research by reading

This section describes a range of methods which involve the analysis of documents or data that have been produced by other people. What unites these methods is the fact that they are 'reading-based'. They are likely to involve the collection and analysis of written data/information, activities that are inherently desk-based. This data may be data that has been collected as part of another research project or it may be documentary material, such as policy documents or media articles. The two main methods covered here are the analysis of other people's data (known as **secondary analysis**) and the analysis of documents (**content analysis**).

Of course, all research will involve *some* reading! One of the most important parts of any research project is the **literature review**. It is important that you have a good, in-depth understanding of the literature in an area so that you can design your research. Most research either seeks to fill a gap in knowledge or replicate findings from other studies in new contexts. Both of these objectives would be impossible to set unless the researcher had a good understanding of the literature in that area.

Analysing other people's data (secondary analysis)

Secondary analysis is conducted using data that has been collected by another party. In criminological research, this is most likely to be a government department, a criminal justice agency or an academic researcher. Both quantitative and qualitative data are available from a range of sources and are provided in 'raw' form (i.e. the original data set). Often, some personal data will be removed or altered so as to preserve the anonymity of the research subjects.

For the criminological researcher in the UK, official data relating to crime (as well as the economy, society and government more generally) are available at the national level via the Office for National Statistics. The official statistics most commonly used in criminology include:

- Criminal statistics – produced for more than 150 years, a national compilation of police and court records relating to notifiable offences, cautions issued and the number of offenders found guilty of specific offences
- Recorded Crime statistics – produced since 1876, a national compilation of crimes recorded by the police
- British Crime Survey – produced since 1982, a national household survey that collects data about experiences of and attitudes towards crime

There are also some major survey series that can be very useful, including the General Social Survey and the British Social Attitudes Survey.

It is also increasingly common for data from funded academic projects to be made available to researchers for secondary analysis. In the UK, the major hub for such data is the UK Data Archive (UKDA) hosted by Essex University. The UKDA acts as a curator of the largest collection of digital data in the social sciences and humanities in the UK.

Secondary analysis is an attractive research method for a number of reasons. First, because research can be an expensive and arduous process, it is a great advantage if the data you are interested in is already available. Second, many of the data sets that are available are large-scale and therefore much more substantial than the average researcher could achieve alone or working in a small team. Third, the data sets that are available have usually been produced by professional research agencies/consultants and therefore have been subject to high standards of validity and quality control. Finally, it involves a new interpretation of data and can give rise to novel findings, thus making the most out of data that would otherwise lay underexploited (Arber 2001).

There are, though, disadvantages. The major problem is that when you have not been closely involved in the research design and the production of research tools such as questionnaires and interview schedules, it can be very difficult to get to grips with the data. Another issue is the need for permission to use data and publish from it. This is especially true where the data is made available by government departments. An example of my own experiences with these problems can be found in Crow and Semmens (2008: Chapter 12). This chapter describes in-depth my personal experience of contributing to and analysing data from the British Crime Survey in 2000.

Analysing documents

The final method considered here is the analysis of documents, often referred to as content analysis. In criminology, content analysis has most commonly been conducted on printed news media, witness statements, court judgments and official policy documents. This approach to analysis can produce quantitative data (for example, the number of times a word is used) and/or qualitative data (the nature of language or layout of the text) and is often used as part of a multi-method strategy.

The development of categories for analysis (Holsti 1969) can be manifest (physically present) or latent (inferred) (Robson 2002). So, for example, if I were seeking to analyse the ways in which knife crimes are reported in the press, manifest categories would include the actual descriptions of the event and the characteristics of the victim and latent categories would include sympathy towards the victim (judged by interpreting the tone of the language used) and any incitement of moral panic. The next stage is to establish the recording units and devise a coding schedule. In the case of a newspaper analysis, this might include the number of times words/phrases are used, column inches, number of stories, size of headline, colour of text and position on page. Bryman (2004) gives an excellent example of a coding schedule, together with sample news items to illustrate how the schedule is used.

There are a number of advantages and disadvantages associated with content analysis. On the plus side, documents are readily available and comprise a rich source of information about the way in which crime stories and crime policies are communicated and developed, helping us to better understand the context in which crime problems are socially constructed. The documents have been produced for a purpose – to entertain, to sensationalise, to inform or to make proposals/recommendations – and this gives the researcher the opportunity to conduct research from a non-obtrusive and non-participant position. The main disadvantage, though, is that the material can be very hard to organise and analyse. Also, there is always a danger of mixing 'witting' and 'unwitting' evidence (Robson 2002). Research of this kind is always vulnerable to the question: did the author intend to convey information or is the researcher misreading between the lines? (Bryman 2004).

Research through observation

Observation is a method that has been used extensively in criminology, particularly where the research question focuses on finding out what happens in previously unexplored social situations. There are two different ways of approaching an observation study: a structured or an unstructured observation. Where a fixed, structured approach is adopted, the observer is detached from the situation under observation and contact with the subjects is kept to an absolute minimum. The observation process involves the use of an observation schedule or pro-forma which sets out what the observer should record, rather like a questionnaire does. The criteria to be observed will have been carefully defined and operationalised and will be designed to test specific hypotheses. The data collected may be quantitative and/or qualitative. A good example of this approach being used in the context of the Youth Court (together with an example of an observation schedule) can be found in Crow and Semmens (2008: Chapter 10).

In contrast, an unstructured observation will involve much more participation on the part of the observer. S/he will immerse him/herself in the social setting and may interact with the subjects. The criteria to be observed and hypotheses are not predefined and a formal schedule is not used. Instead, the observer will look for commonalities and themes to emerge and record events, conversations and relationships using extensive field notes. Again, the data collected may be quantitative and/or qualitative. A good example of this kind of approach is Tomsen's ethnographic study of drinking behaviour among males (1997). **Ethnography** is an approach to research that involves the immersion of the researcher into the social setting for a long period of time. The emphasis is on describing and understanding the social processes that are observed and experienced. This involved Tomsen spending a lot of time in pubs and clubs, informally (and secretly) interviewing the people around him and observing their behaviour. He collected both quantitative and qualitative data and his analysis allowed him to explore in great detail the nature of the relationship between drinking, violence and social disorder.

The researcher needs to make a series of important decisions about his/her role in the observation process. A distinction is drawn in the methods literature between four different types of role, which are summarised in Box 3.7.

The process of analysis in unstructured observation is not a distinct stage in the research process. Instead, it takes place as the research progresses. Robson (2002) says that all observation studies should start with a 'painting the picture' exercise. Then, this is followed by a deeper analysis of emergent concepts and the construction of a theoretical framework. Once concepts have been identified, they can be examined for frequency/distribution and linked together to form hypotheses. These hypotheses are then tested and, if necessary, reformulated and retested. The final analysis involves the construction of relationships and the relationships between relationships, moving the researcher towards a deep understanding of the social setting and the people within it.

The biggest drawback of observational work is that it involves a large input in terms of time and resources. In addition to the time spent in the social setting, observational work generates a lot of data and the process of data management and analysis can be very demanding. Another criticism of observation is that it can be overly subjective. It is therefore important that validity checks are built into the methodology. For a structured observation, this could involve piloting the schedule with a range of different observers to test how they interpret the concepts they are observing. Bryman (2004) even suggests that a period of unstructured observation prior to the design of the schedule can help eliminate subjectivity.

MAKING OPERATIONAL DECISIONS

In this final section, three main decisions are considered: the sampling strategy, how access will be negotiated/achieved and ethical/legal considerations.

BOX 3.7

THE FOUR OBSERVER ROLES (GOLD 1958)

Role	Description	Advantage	Disadvantage	Example
Complete participant	A fully participating member of the setting and his/her role is not known to other group members.	Full immersion in the setting allows for an in-depth understanding of the social interactions. Subjects are not going to change their behaviour because they do not know they are being observed.	There is a danger of becoming so emotionally involved that objectivity is lost. This is known as 'going native' (Hobbs 1988). This is a deceptive role, raising a number of significant ethical questions.	Holdaway (1983) conducted a study on 'cop culture'. He was a serving police officer and was able to conduct his observations on his colleagues without them knowing about it.
Participant as observer	Full participation in the setting (as for the complete participant) but the group members are aware of his/her dual role as a researcher.	Direct questioning can be easier and less deception is involved.	Subjects may be wary of the researcher, wondering what s/he is researching and thus change their behaviour as a result.	Ditton (1977) got a job in a bakery to study the fiddling and pilfering carried out by his co-workers. They knew he was a student but they did not know that he was studying their behaviour.
Observer as participant	Does not actually participate in group activities but can be present in the setting. Bryman (2004) states that this role focused on the 'interviewing' element – the researcher asks questions about the way people do things and the decisions they make.	More of a detached role which can make the process of setting up and recording interviews less awkward.	It is assumed that people can explain why they do things and how they make decisions. Robson (2002) argues that being present in the setting can have an impact on the way people behave.	Punch (1979) conducted research on police work in Amsterdam. Since he was not a trained officer, he was not able to participate fully in police activities. Instead he was able to accompany officers on patrol and ask them questions.
Complete observer	The observer is completely detached from the setting and does not interact with the group members in any way.	The researcher can observe a social setting without intruding on it or influencing people.	The researcher cannot talk to people and ask them why they are acting in a specific way.	Sampson and Raudenbush (1999) observed disorder on the streets of Chicago by discretely driving through the streets, filming their surroundings.

Sampling

In the vast majority of research designs, a sample will be used. Sometimes, the **sampling** strategy will be complex, including elements of time, location, people and events. We refer to these as *sampling units*. There are two types of sample: **random** (sometimes called **probability**) samples and **purposive** (**non-probability**) samples. Random samples are intended to be representative of the population from which they are drawn, and therefore the characteristics of the sample are assumed to be generalisable across the whole population. Members of the sample are drawn randomly and everyone in the population stands the same chance of being included in the sample. Purposive samples are not intended to be generalisable to the population as a whole. Instead, they are used to focus on specific groups or categories and select units based on predefined characteristics (such as gender or victim status). Some examples of sampling methods are given in Box 3.8.

BOX 3.8

DIFFERENT TYPES OF SAMPLING METHODS

Random samples are drawn using a *sampling frame*. This usually takes the form of a list of all the units in a population (examples include the electoral role or a list of all students enrolled on a university course). There are three ways of drawing a random sample:

1 A *simple random sample* is drawn by simply selecting units at regular intervals. So, for example, I might select every tenth person from my sampling frame.

2 A *stratified random sample* is drawn by dividing the population into groups or strata and then sampling randomly within those strata. So, for example, I could organise my list of students enrolled on a university course into Level 1, Level 2 and Level 3 students. As for the simple random sample, I would select units from each level at regular intervals.

3 A *multi-stage* or *cluster sample* is a more complicated form of random sampling. First, a sample of large units is drawn, then samples of smaller units contained within the larger units are drawn. So, for example, I might begin by sampling a series of districts in a city. Then, within each of the districts I selected, I would draw a random sample of streets. Then, for each street I would draw a sample from the houses on the street.

Purposive sampling takes a different approach. A sampling frame is not needed. There are three main types of purposive sample:

1 A *quota sample* is used to ensure a certain distribution of demographic variables. Subjects are recruited on the basis of their characteristics (demographic groups or physical appearance). When the quota for a given demographic group is filled, the researcher will stop recruiting subjects from that particular group.

2 A *snowball sample* is used when access to members of a population is particularly difficult. Once the researcher has identified one subject, s/he will ask that subject to suggest other possible participants.

3 *Availability* or *accidental samples* are drawn simply using participants who are at hand. So, this could be the first ten people to walk into a room regardless of their characteristics.

All sampling strategies have potential weaknesses. The researcher should always consider potential bias that might occur as a result of the sampling strategy and, where possible, make attempts to eliminate or ease bias. Importantly, when research is published the researcher ought to provide information about the sample and discuss the question of validity in a transparent way.

Access

Getting access to a research setting can be difficult for the criminological researcher, especially if that setting is a closed one. If the population you are sampling is open/public, then access is easy because you are stopping people in the street, delivering surveys to the home, using a publically accessible sampling frame or observing a public place. However, if you are interested in studying people working in an organisation or those contained in a secure environment (such as prisoners), access can be a much trickier issue.

Access is a particular problem for observational work. Having an observer invade a working environment or social group can be a threatening prospect. It is important, therefore, to gain access to a setting via a 'gatekeeper' – someone who is responsible for the setting and who can vouch for your legitimate presence. Even when access is secured, difficulties can occur in becoming accepted by the people within the setting.

Ethical and legal considerations

Awareness of ethical issues in criminological research is of huge import and it is essential that the researcher addresses any ethical or legal issues as part of the research design process. All university-based projects have to go through a process of ethical approval which involves the scrutiny of a project methodology by a panel of experts. Similarly, bodies which fund research, such as the Economic and Social Research Council, require researchers to demonstrate adherence to a set of ethical principles. It is important, therefore, that you build a strong ethical framework for your research design. The framework devised by Beauchamp and Childress (2001) has been useful in my own research and it is worth keeping these principles in mind as you progress through the rest of the book:

1 People have the right to decide whether or not to take part in research (informed consent).

2 We should not knowingly cause harm or expose people to unacceptable risks.

3 We should not put people at a disadvantage. Our research should be governed by fairness and equality.

4 We should be honest and truthful. We should not deceive people.

5 We should avoid fraud and plagiarism.

6 We should preserve confidentiality.

SUMMARY

This chapter has introduced you to the key methodological approaches in criminological research. You should now have the basic knowledge and confidence to design your own research study. In addition, you should feel able to evaluate the methodological decisions made by other researchers and to view criminological research critically.

In order to help you understand the research design process, the chapter was structured as a series of decisions to be made, in the order in which they usually come in real life:

1. What type of research design is appropriate?
2. What type of data shall I use?
3. What methods shall I use?
4. How will I operationalise my research design?

However, you have hopefully realised that many of the decisions are inextricably linked and therefore will often need to be approached in a holistic, rather than purely linear, way. Your decisions should be justifiable in the context of your original research strategy.

Throughout the chapter, I have drawn distinctions between different methodological approaches and highlighted their various strengths and weaknesses in different contexts. However, you should also have come to appreciate that the quality of research can be enhanced through the combination of different methods and data. Ultimately, good research requires creativity and innovation, and you should use this chapter as a starting point. A lot can be learned through reading about the experiences of others, something that you will be doing as you work your way through the rest of the book.

■ Study Questions/Activities for Students

1. Read a published research study such as:

   Cammiss, S. and Stride, C. (2008) 'Modelling mode of trial', *British Journal of Criminology*, 48 (7): 482–501.

   Identify and evaluate the decisions that were made by the researchers using the analytic framework in Box 3.9.

2. Imagine you have been asked to design a research project to investigate the experiences of, and attitudes towards, crime among first-year university students in the UK. Work through the series of decisions you would need to make (use the framework in Box 3.9 as a template). Note down the reason for each decision, including any difficult dilemmas.

BOX 3.9

ANALYTIC FRAMEWORK

1 What is the research strategy?

   (a) What is the point of the study? Identify the research question and the aims and objectives.

   (b) Is the study descriptive, exploratory or an evaluation?

   (c) Has the researcher chosen a fixed or flexible design? Why?

   (d) What theory underpins the study?

2 What kind of data is used?

   (a) Quantitative and/or qualitative data?

   (b) What are the key concepts? How have they been defined?

   (c) How have the data been analysed?

3 What method(s) has/have been used?

   (a) Identify the method(s) used.

   (b) Why was/were the method(s) selected?

   (c) What are the strengths/weaknesses of the selected method(s)?

4 Operational decisions

   (a) What sampling procedures were used? Is there any bias in the sample?

   (b) How was access gained?

   (c) What ethical/legal considerations were involved?

5 Conclusions

   (a) What are the conclusions to the study?

   (b) Do the conclusions fit the results (are there unjustified leaps of guesswork)?

   (c) Do the conclusions reflect the original aims and objectives?

RESOURCES

The following texts cover all topics discussed here in great detail:

Bryman, A. (2004) *Social Research Methods* (2nd edition), Oxford: Oxford University Press.

Robson, C. (2002) *Real World Research* (2nd edition), Oxford: Blackwell Publishing.

The following websites are also useful:

British Society of Criminology (ethics): www.britsoccrim.org/ethical.htm

Office of National Statistics: www.ons.gov.uk

UK Data Archive: www.data-archive.ac.uk/

REFERENCES

Arber, S. (2001) 'Secondary analysis of survey data', in Gilbert, N. (ed.), *Researching Social Life*, London: Sage.

Beauchamp, T.L. and Childress, J.F. (2001) *Principles of Biomedical Ethics* (5th edition), Oxford: Oxford University Press.

Bryman, A. (2004) *Social Research Methods* (2nd edition), Oxford: Oxford University Press.

Crow, I. and Semmens, N. (2008) *Researching Criminology*, Maidenhead: McGraw-Hill.

Denzin, N.K. (1988) *The Research Act: A Theoretical Introduction to Sociological Methods*, Englewood Cliffs, NJ: Prentice-Hall.

Ditton, J. (1977) *Part Time Crime: An Ethnography of Fiddling and Pilfering*, London: Macmillan.

Farrington, D.P. (2006) 'Key longitudinal-experimental studies in criminology', *Journal of Experimental Criminology*, 2(2): 121–141.

Gold, R.L. (1958) 'Roles in sociological fieldwork', *Social Forces*, 36: 217–223.

Green, A. and Preston, J. (2005) 'Speaking in tongues: diversity in mixed methods research', *International Journal of Social Research Methodology*, 8(3): 167–171.

Harris, N. and Murphy, K. (2007) 'Shaming, shame and recidivism: a test of reintegrative shaming theory in the white-collar crime context', *British Journal of Criminology*, 47(6): 900–917.

Hobbs, D. (1988) *Doing the Business*: *Entrepreneurship, the Working Class and Detectives in the East End of London*, Oxford: Oxford University Press.

Holdaway, S. (1983) *Inside the British Police*: *A Force at Work*, Oxford: Blackwell.

Hollway, W. and Jefferson, T. (1997) 'Eliciting narrative through the in-depth interview', *Qualitative Inquiry*, 3(1): 53–70.

Holsti, O. (1969) *Content Analysis for the Social Sciences and Humanities*, Reading, MA: Addison-Wesley.

Marshall, G. (ed.) (1994) *The Concise Oxford Dictionary of Sociology*, Oxford: Oxford University Press.

Morgan, D.L. (1992) 'Designing focus group research', in Stewart, M. (ed.), *Tools for Primary Care Research*, Thousand Oaks, CA: Sage.

Morgan, D.L. (2006) 'Focus groups', in Jupp, V. (ed.), *The Sage Dictionary of Social Research Methods*, London: Sage.

Punch, M. (1979) *Policing the Inner City*: *A Study of Amsterdam's Warmoesstraat*, London: Macmillan.

Robson, C. (2002) *Real World Research* (2nd edition), Oxford: Blackwell.

Sampson, R. and Raudenbush, S. (1999) 'Systematic social observation of public spaces: a new look at disorder in urban neighbourhoods', *American Journal of Sociology*, 105(3): 603–651.

Sandberg, S. (2008) 'Black drug dealers in a white welfare state: cannabis dealing and street capital in Norway', *British Journal of Criminology*, 48(5): 604–619.

Schuman, H. and Presser, S. (1996) *Questions and Answers in Attitude Surveys*: *Experiments on Question Form, Wording and Context*, London: Sage.

Semmens, N. (2001) 'The relationship between accuracy and confidence in survey-based research: findings from a pilot study on the fear of crime', *International Journal of Social Research Methodology*, 4(3): 173–182.

Semmens, N., Dilane, J. and Ditton, J. (2002) 'Preliminary findings on seasonality and the fear of crime', *British Journal of Criminology*, 42: 798–806.

Shapland, J., Atkinson, A., Colledge, E., Dignan, J., Howes, M., Johnstone, J., Pennant, R., Robinson, G. and Sorsby, A. (2004) *Implementing Restorative Justice Schemes (Crime Reduction Programme): A Report on the First Year.* Home Office Online Report 32/04. London: Home Office. Available at www.homeoffice.gov.uk/rds/pdfs04/rdsolr3204.pdf.

Shapland, J., Atkinson, A., Atkinson, H., Chapman, B., Colledge, E., Dignan, J., Howes, M., Johnstone, J., Robinson, G. and Sorsby, A. (2006a) *Restorative Justice in Practice: Findings from the Second Stage of the Evaluation of Three Schemes.* Home Office Research Findings 274. London: Home Office.

Shapland, J., Atkinson, A., Atkinson, H., Chapman, B., Colledge, E., Dignan, J., Howes, M., Johnstone, J., Robinson, G. and Sorsby, A. (2006b) *Restorative Justice in Practice: The Second Report from the Evaluation of Three Schemes.* The University of Sheffield Centre for Criminological Research Occasional Paper 2. Sheffield: Faculty of Law. Available at: ccr.group.shef.ac.uk/papers/pdfs/Restorative_Justice_Report.pdf and from the Faculty of Law.

Shapland, J., Atkinson, A., Atkinson, H., Colledge, E., Dignan, J., Howes, M., Johnstone, J., Robinson, G. and Sorsby, A. (2007) *Restorative Justice: The Views of Victims and Offenders. The Third Report from the Evaluation of Three Schemes.* Ministry of Justice Research Series 3/07. London: Ministry of Justice. Available at www.justice.gov.uk/docs/Restorative-Justice.pdf.

Shapland, J., Atkinson, A., Atkinson, H., Dignan, J., Edwards, L., Hibbert, J., Howes, M., Johnstone, J., Robinson, G. and Sorsby, A. (2008) *Does Restorative Justice Affect Reconviction? The Fourth Report from the Evaluation of Three Schemes.* Ministry of Justice Research Series 10/08. London: Ministry of Justice. Available at: www.justice.gov.uk/publications/docs/restorative-justice-report_06-08.pdf.

Soothill, K., Francis, B., Ackerley, E. and Humphreys, L. (2008) 'Changing patterns of offending behaviour among young adults', *British Journal of Criminology*, 48: 75–95.

Tomsen, S. (1997) 'A top night: social protest, masculinity and the culture of drinking violence', *British Journal of Criminology*, 37: 90–102.

FOUR
UNDERTAKING A CRIMINOLOGICAL LITERATURE REVIEW

ALISON WAKEFIELD

Chapter Contents

KEY POINTS

This chapter:

- Details the nature and purpose of a literature review
- Examines the difference between narrative and systematic reviews
- Describes how to locate your sources
- Examines the various ways to review your sources
- Evidences how to write the review

INTRODUCTION

A literature review is an evaluative overview of the state of academic knowledge on a research topic. It is often the first stage in a research project because the researcher needs to establish the nature and extent of what is already known in order to justify and contextualise any empirical work, although there is likely to be a continuing engagement with the research literature right through the research process.

The chapter is a detailed guide to doing a criminological literature review. It begins with a definition and explanation, and then goes on to describe the two main types of literature review and how they are applied within criminology. The steps in doing a literature review are then outlined, with guidance on each and criminological examples provided. Breaking the task down in this way should reassure any inexperienced researcher that an apparently daunting task is actually quite straightforward and, with the right choice of topic, can be a fascinating and illuminating undertaking, generating valuable new ideas and knowledge.

WHAT IS A LITERATURE REVIEW?

A **literature review** provides a survey and discussion of the main published work in a given topic or field. It is a key element of an empirical research project which conveys to the reader that you have:

- read widely around the chosen topic
- gained a good command of the issues
- acknowledged the work of others
- set your study in the context of the existing body of literature, highlighting gaps in research

The process of doing your literature review enables you to identify relevant questions to ask, themes to include and methodologies to follow within your study. It also informs the development of your conceptual or theoretical framework and, when presented as a chapter in a student project, dissertation or thesis, should frame the empirical research findings.

A literature review is much more than an **annotated bibliography** or set of descriptive summaries of previous work. It provides a critical, evaluative synthesis of the research literature on a given topic set out according to a number of organising themes. Different models can be used, most notably the **narrative literature review** and the **systematic review**. Unlike an academic essay providing a general discussion on a particular subject, the literature review provides a synthesis of others' findings, arguments and ideas in your field of study, and in doing so it asks a number of different questions, some of which are summarised in Figure 4.1.

Two types of literature normally feature in such a review: theoretical literature and substantive literature. The theoretical literature is employed by the criminologist for the purpose of devising a theoretical framework to anchor the research

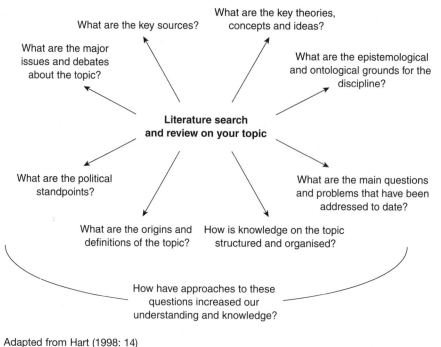

What are the key theories,
concepts and ideas?

What are the key sources?

What are the major
issues and debates
about the topic?

What are the epistemological
and ontological grounds for the
discipline?

**Literature search
and review on your topic**

What are the political
standpoints?

What are the main questions
and problems that have been
addressed to date?

What are the origins and
definitions of the topic?

How is knowledge on the topic
structured and organised?

How have approaches to these
questions increased our
understanding and knowledge?

Adapted from Hart (1998: 14)

FIGURE 4.1   Some of the Questions the Literature Review can Answer

within the discipline, give direction to the study and make explicit the *ontological* and *epistemological* assumptions that the researcher brings to the research. These latter concepts relate to how one sees the nature of society, institutions and relationships (ontology), and whether these can be assessed objectively or are socially constructed; and how human actors may go about making sense of the social world (epistemology), including the question as to whether its existence can be proven, or whether it can only be described and interpreted. Different perspectives, such as **positivism** and **interactionism**, support more objective or more subjective views of the world and its interpretation, and thus favour different methods of research. In devising your theoretical framework, it is also important to note how the various criminological (and other) theories falling into these or other schools of thought operate at different levels of analysis. They may be divided into the following categories, and used separately or in combination:

- *Micro theories* – concerned with types of people, individual agency and interpersonal interactions, such as biological or rational choice perspectives
- *Meso theories* – relating to communities, social movements or organisations, and to collective agency and organisational processes, such as ecological or subcultural perspectives
- *Macro theories* – regarding social institutions, cultural systems and societies, such as critical criminology or feminist perspectives (adapted from Einstadter and Henry, 2006: 319).

Certain perspectives span more than one category, such as labelling or control theories (which, arguably, bridge the micro and meso levels), while others integrate theories either at the same level of analysis or across levels, such as cultural criminology's fusion of a number of perspectives, including labelling, subcultural theories and postmodernism. Criminological research should also look beyond criminology to engage with social, political or cultural theories, in order to consider crime and criminal justice topics in a broader context of political economy, social stratification, social capital or cultural change, for example.

Two main routes to theorising are open to you. Research may be *theory-generating* or *inductive*, where theories are derived from the data collected, in which case the literature review will normally critically discuss previous theoretical and empirical works to highlight the lack of knowledge that is used to justify the study. Alternatively, it may be *theory-testing* or *deductive*, with the literature review outlining the concepts and propositions of theory to be tested (Fawcett, 1999; see also May, 2003). The importance of theory to the research process cannot be overstated: May (2003: 29) stresses 'the constant relationship that exists between social research and social theory' with each influencing the other. He further points out that, 'Data are not collected, but produced', and 'Facts do not exist independently of the medium through which they are interpreted, whether that is an explicit theoretical model, a set of assumptions, or interests that have led to the data being collected in the first instance' (2003: 28). In deciding your theoretical perspective, you will need to reflect carefully on your values, beliefs and assumptions to establish which theory will best represent these in your research.

The substantive literature is the general literature on the specific topic you are studying, including theory and research in similar or related areas. Most of this literature is published in academic books and peer-reviewed journals, but there is also what is known as 'grey literature' – information sources that are not controlled by commercial publishers. These include reports published directly by the organisations producing them, such as government agencies, as well as conference papers, student theses and newspaper articles.

In an ideal world, you would complete the literature review prior to the planning of the research, in order to establish whether the study is needed, to differentiate your work from past studies and add to the body of knowledge, and to build on the concepts, theories and methodologies that have already been created. Such a review may establish that the **research questions** can be answered from the existing body of knowledge, and that a research synthesis by means of systematic review, rather than an empirical study, would be the most appropriate strategy. For these reasons, the literature review is typically perceived as one of the first stages in the research process. But in practice, the criminological researcher has to be alert to new research as it is published, and the completion of empirical research and comparison of findings with the extant literature may lead you into further avenues of reading. This is particularly the case when adopting a **grounded theory** methodology (Glaser and Strauss, 1967), an **inductive approach** that operates more or less in a reverse direction to traditional research by starting with data collection, and as data emerge, making constant comparisons between data and theory and accessing literature only as it becomes relevant.

BOX 4.1

TYPICAL STRUCTURE OF A STUDENT DISSERTATION

- Introduction
- Literature review
- Research methods
- Findings and discussion (sometimes separated into two chapters)
- Conclusion

What is the purpose of a literature review?

There are different purposes for writing a literature review. The most common are:

- a *stand-alone literature review article* or assignment and hence a project in itself, giving an overview of the literature on a particular topic

- part of a *research proposal*. This could be a proposal for an undergraduate or postgraduate dissertation or research project, or an application for a grant. It should include a section summarising the key issues and existing findings on a given topic in order to demonstrate how the proposed research will contribute to the field of study

- part of a *research report*. It may be an early chapter in an undergraduate or postgraduate dissertation or research project, providing the context to which an empirical study has contributed.

For the purposes of a student project, dissertation or thesis, it normally takes the form of a literature review chapter, although many students are required to submit a research proposal for assessment at an early stage in their studies. In a typical student dissertation, as shown in Box 4.1, a literature review is preceded by the introductory chapter, and followed by a methods chapter in which the empirical **research design** is explained and justified. In the social sciences, it might normally comprise 20–25% of the available words. Yet references to the academic literature should not be confined to the literature review chapter: they will help to introduce the topic in the introductory chapter, illustrate methodological issues in the methods chapter, and form a basis for comparison and discussion in the latter chapters.

WHAT DOES A LITERATURE REVIEW LOOK LIKE?

It is always helpful to find models to follow when undertaking an unfamiliar task. Other literature reviews in your topic area or discipline may reveal the sorts of themes you might explore in your own research, or show you ways of organising your review. Numerous criminological examples are available online, or can be found by browsing libraries for bodies of literature such as those outlined in Box 4.2.

SOURCES OF EXAMPLE LITERATURE REVIEWS

- *Websites*, such as those of the Research, Development and Statistics Directorate of the British Home Office, the Australian Institute of Criminology, the Swedish National Council for Crime Prevention and the US National Institute of Justice
- *Dissertations* and theses by past students
- *Research monographs* (as opposed to student textbooks), many of which are based on doctoral research, including Wakefield (2003) on private security, Piacentini (2004) on prison labour and Brown (2005) on sex offender treatment programmes
- *Journal articles* based on reviews of literature, such as those published in the prestigious annual series of commissioned reviews, *Crime and Justice: A Review of Research*, Gresswell and Hollin (1994) on multiple homicide or Waddington (1999) on police culture.

Two types of literature review are introduced in this section: the narrative review and the systematic review.

Narrative reviews

A 'traditional' literature review is increasingly known as a narrative literature review, particularly among those who seek to distinguish it from the systematic review, of which more shortly. Narrative reviews are well suited to broad fields of study, being comprehensive in nature and covering a wide range of issues. They enable the researcher to contribute to the body of knowledge by bringing together disparate contributions to an emerging field, or updating an established field with new research findings and theoretical perspectives.

In preparing this type of review, criminological researchers need to be careful to go beyond providing a series of descriptions of past studies, offering an overarching **critical perspective** of the field. The researcher must identify categories for structuring the discussion, allowing the literature to be broken down into sections. Examples include a thematic or chronological approach, outlined in more detail later in the chapter.

Box 4.3 reproduces part of the table of contents of a thematic narrative review on police corruption, carried out by Newburn (1999) as a stand-alone report for the British Home Office. The table of contents offers an overview of the key themes identified in the literature: definitions of police corruption (Chapter 2), its causes (Chapter 3) and control strategies (Chapter 4). These in turn are divided into sub-themes to sort and categorise the literature still further. The stated purpose of this report was 'to identify key issues in police integrity and corruption, with a specific emphasis on the causes of corruption and the efficacy of different

WHAT DOES A NARRATIVE REVIEW ON POLICE CORRUPTION LOOK LIKE?

1 **Introduction**

Corruption in various jurisdictions

Aim and methodology

The report

2 **What is police corruption?**

Corrupt activities

The problem of definition

A question of ethics?

The 'slippery slope' to 'becoming bent'

Summary

3 **The causes of police corruption**

A few bad apples?

The causes of corruption

Drug-related police corruption

4 **Corruption control**

Human resource management

Anti-corruption policies

Internal controls

The external environment and external controls

Possible unintended consequences of corruption control

5 **Conclusion: Toward 'ethical policing'**

Extract from Newburn (1999)

prevention strategies' (Newburn, 1999: 2), providing a comprehensive overview of the topic at a time when, as the report states, a series of recent scandals had brought the matter into the political spotlight.

In the first chapter Newburn provides a brief outline of his methodology, reported to cover 'the main English language literature on the issues of police corruption and police ethics over the last 20 years', drawn from sociology, criminology and 'official inquiries from the US and Australia' (1999: 2). More recent literature reviews published by the Home Office, such as Myhill's (2006) study of community engagement in policing, tend to have more detailed methodology sections, particularly with respect to **sampling**, setting out the literature search strategies, number of sources included and the inclusion criteria.

The main weakness of narrative reviews is their inability to demonstrate an absence of reviewer subjectivity or bias. In other words, because of their breadth, they do not necessarily state how sources have been identified, how fully the literature has been appraised or how sources have been included or excluded.

Systematic reviews and meta-analysis

A type of review that became popular in medical and health services research in the 1990s, taking hold in the social sciences in the new millennium, is the systematic review. Now preferred in some areas of criminology, it is typically used for the purpose of evaluating the effectiveness of an intervention as evidenced in past studies in order to support future evidence-based policy-making. Such reviews address common failures of social science and other disciplines to produce cumulative knowledge on given **hypotheses**, since studies carried out into a similar issue have frequently provided differing results, and literature reviews taking account of a range of separate studies have not always been systematic in their approach. According to Pawson (2006: 18), systematic reviews have also come to be favoured over evaluation studies as a means of feeding into policy-making, on the basis that 'in order to inform policy, the research must come before the policy'. Systematic reviews are intended to bring together the most directly relevant and rigorous **evaluations** that have been conducted on a particular topic, employing transparent and systematic criteria for searching the available literature, evaluating the suitability of each source for inclusion in the review, and synthesising the results. Such reviews are designed to offer a rigorous and replicable approach to reviewing the literature, for the purpose of eliminating the subjectivities of reviewer bias, and addressing the uncertainty as to whether all the evidence has been identified and evaluated. The approach followed in the systematic review is described as fully and systematically as would be any empirical research.

The Campbell Collaboration is an international research network that produces systematic reviews of social interventions in order to inform policy-making, including criminal justice interventions, and which has been instrumental in raising the status of the approach within criminology. It is a sibling organisation to the longer-established and healthcare-focused Cochrane Collaboration. On its website, the Campbell Collaboration outlines four components of a systematic review:

1 Clear inclusion/exclusion criteria
2 An explicit search strategy
3 Systematic coding and analysis of included studies
4 Meta-analysis (where possible)

Box 4.4 provides a second extract from the contents page of a literature review, in this case a systematic review by Farrington and Welsh (2002) of research evaluating the effects of street lighting on crime, once again conducted for the British Home Office. In this example, the parameters of the literature were much narrower than those employed by Newburn (1999). Rather than interrogating a general literature on street lighting and crime, the focus was on establishing the combined results of 13 American and British studies, selected by means of an exhaustive literature search process and the application of explicit and rigorous inclusion criteria. All of the chosen studies adopted the same general strategy of evaluating the direct relationship between interventions to improve street lighting in the study areas and crime levels in those areas, for the purpose of informing crime prevention policy-making. Aggregating the statistical results by means of a

---

BOX 4.4

WHAT DOES A SYSTEMATIC REVIEW OF THE EFFECTS OF IMPROVED STREET LIGHTING ON CRIME LOOK LIKE?

1 **Background**

Research on street lighting and crime

How might improved street lighting reduce crime?

Causal links between street lighting and crime

Determining what works to reduce crime

Characteristics of systematic reviews

Aims of this report

2 **Methods**

Criteria for inclusion of evaluation studies

Search strategies

Programmes not meeting inclusion criteria

3 **Results**

Key features of evaluations

Results of American studies

Results of British studies

4 **Conclusions**

Summary of main findings

Priorities for research

Policy implications

Extract from Farrington and Welsh (2002)

meta-analysis, Farrington and Welsh were able to draw the conclusion that 'improved street lighting was followed by a decrease in crime' (2002: 39).

The structure of this systematic review differs markedly from Newburn's (1999) narrative review. The general literature is briefly summarised in the introductory 'Background' chapter (Chapter 1) to provide a mini narrative review, and then the review methods are explained in much greater detail in a distinct 'Methods' chapter (Chapter 2). The findings in this much more focused study are set out in a single chapter (Chapter 3) and, like the Newburn review, it ends with a 'Conclusion' chapter (Chapter 4).

The strengths of the systematic review are also its limitations, emphasising the very different purposes of the two types of literature review. The prescriptive approach required of a systematic review precludes the comprehensive coverage of the literature that, in the case of the Farrington and Welsh (2002) study, would include a detailed exposition of the relevant theoretical explanations, such as environmental and situational theories of crime, and a discussion of the causal links between street lighting and crime that are proposed within the literature. Both topics are discussed briefly by Farrington and Welsh in their introductory chapter, whereas a narrative review would give these themes far more weighting and serve as a more general appraisal of the topic area.

A systematic review can be a huge undertaking, generating tens of thousands of sources that need to be filtered, depending on the scope of the topic. Joliffe (2008) describes using the approach in his doctoral research, which sought to establish whether there was empirical support for the relationship between empathy and offending. The field of study can of course be narrowed. Lösel (2008) gives the example of a broad definition (sex offender treatment) versus a narrow one (hormonal treatment of adult child molesters), the former of which will generate a large body of results and perhaps one that is *too* large. Yet, he argues, the latter approach may produce only a limited number of studies and present dilemmas of inclusion and exclusion of those identified, some of which may be limited in their methodological rigour. An alternative approach based on similar principles is a rapid evidence assessment, as employed by Joliffe and Farrington (2007) in relation to the impact of mentoring on re-offending, in which the methods used in a systematic review are applied within a restricted time frame.

Petrosino et al. (2003) and Farrington and Welsh (2005) offer guidance on the systematic review as applied to criminology. Examples of systematic reviews can be found on the websites of the British Home Office Research, Development and Statistics Directorate, and the Swedish National Council for Crime Prevention (*Brottsförebyggande rådet – Brå*), on such topics as closed-circuit television, street lighting, drug treatment and bullying.

A 'meta-analysis' (a term coined by Glass in 1976) is an optional component of a systematic review, and comprises a statistical synthesis of the findings. This is achieved by identifying a common measure of effect size, such as a standardised mean difference (a way of standardising a range of outcomes measured on different scales) or correlation coefficient (showing the relationship between variables demonstrated by the combined results). Criminological examples are provided by Andrews et al. (1990) on the effectiveness of correctional treatment and Gore and Drugs Survey Investigators' Consortium (1999) on young people's illicit drug use.

Finally, a related movement is the emergence of the 'qualitative meta-synthesis' (including its subgenre, 'meta-ethnography'), advocating synoptic interrogations of literature according to systematic methods to ensure comprehensiveness and eliminate researcher bias. Like the systematic review, its origins are in health services research, with the objective of enhancing evidence-based decision-making.

Can the two approaches influence each other?

There is no doubt that the systematic review is starting to have a wider influence. Within the British Home Office, for example, an increasing proportion of the literature reviews published online are systematic reviews. Those that are not badged as such nonetheless now incorporate distinct methodology sections, outlining the search methods used, the bodies of literature consulted and the approaches to synthesis that have been employed. While the formulaic approach of systematic reviews can militate against the richness of language and creativity of style often found in narrative reviews, this does not have to be so. There is scope to bring some of these linguistic techniques into the systematic review. There is currently a sense of debate within the social sciences over which method is 'best', with a proliferation of papers coming particularly from the natural sciences encouraging researchers to implement more systematic approaches to reviewing the literature. The most biting critiques of this approach have pointed to the broader limitations of the policy context into which research findings are received, such as the fact that no policy 'happens from scratch' since other provisions will always be present and that 'synthetic recommendations cannot match the complexity of the policy systems that will host them' (Pawson, 2006: 12–13), and to the danger that political preference for 'evidence-based' research legitimates a targeting of government research objectives on narrowly focused and short-termist studies that support partisan objectives (Hope and Walters, 2008; Morgan and Hough, 2008). Further, Pawson criticises the meta-analytic orientation of the Campbell Collaboration systematic reviews, questioning the assumption that past studies are directly relevant to future interventions and arguing that 'a more adaptive mode of knowledge management is required to cope with the vicissitudes of complex systems' (Pawson, 2006: 171). He provides an alternative model of 'realist review', incorporating analyses of the contexts in which interventions take place, including the staffing and implementation arrangements, institutional culture and political climate.

A summary of the strengths and weaknesses of both approaches is presented in Box 4.5.

BOX 4.5

NARRATIVE VERSUS SYSTEMATIC REVIEWS

Narrative reviews

Strengths

1 Suit broad fields of study

2 Provide holistic interpretations

3 Cover topics comprehensively

4 Bring together diverse perspectives

5 Can accommodate a richness of language and creativity of style

6 Are flexible to different epistemological frameworks

Systematic reviews

Strengths

1 Identify the cumulative knowledge on a given hypothesis

2 Support evidence-based policy-making

3 Employ systematic and transparent literature search criteria

4 Seek to include only high-quality research

5 Provide a rigorous and replicable approach to reviewing the literature

6 Seek to eliminate reviewer bias

7 Address uncertainties as to whether all the evidence has been identified and evaluated

Weaknesses

1 Do not always clearly specify the review methodology

2 May not explicitly differentiate low- and high-quality research

3 May have little practical application

Weaknesses

1 The prescriptive approach precludes comprehensive coverage of the literature

2 Can generate an excess of sources requiring extensive filtering

3 Can be formulaic and dry in style

4 Interventions' relevance and effectiveness may be undermined by the complexities of the policy process

5 Are not impervious to political agendas despite claimed methodological rigour

HOW DO I GO ABOUT DOING A LITERATURE REVIEW?

The process of reviewing the literature begins as soon as you have a provisional research topic, and before you finally decide on the precise scope of your research. At this stage you need to establish how much has already been written on your topic, what has been said – and not said – and the sorts of questions others have asked. Such a review will help you determine the feasibility of your own ideas, identify knowledge gaps and decide the scope and parameters of your research, research questions and research methods.

As a preliminary measure, it is best to skim the surface of the literature rather than undertake a full-scale literature search. Online facilities – library catalogues, databases and the internet – offer the best starting point.

Searching the literature

A literature strategy involves the following steps:

Deciding what you are looking for

List your subject keywords, thinking about your topic and the key concepts associated with it.

- What alternative terms are used to describe it?
- Are there alternative spellings, such as British and American variants of a term?
- Are common acronyms used?
- Can a word be truncated to incorporate different words with the same stem (e.g. *rehabilit** to find *rehabilitate*, *rehabilitation* or *rehabilitative*)?
- Are there any specific themes, cases or examples you are interested in?
- Are there any terms that you should exclude?

Group these keywords using Boolean operators:

1 OR to group alternative terms (e.g. *police OR policing*).
2 AND to link words together (e.g. *crime AND prevention*).
3 Brackets to clarify a combination of terms (e.g. *(police OR policing) AND (crime AND prevention))*.
4 NOT to exclude terms (e.g. *police AND violence NOT domestic*).

Boolean operators should be expressed in capital letters because this is required by some search tools.

Deciding where to look

A number of different electronic sources are available to help you search the literature:

- Many university libraries have *subject-specific guides* which provide a helpful starting point for literature searches in a given discipline.
- You can use *library catalogues* to find books and journals held within those libraries, but not their content. Use keywords to identify books and journals relevant to your topic.
- *Bibliographic databases* allow you to search the academic literature in more detail, some covering a wide range of disciplines and others being more focused. You can search these not only by subject but also by author, publication date and other features. Often the search results will include short summaries or abstracts of the articles identified to help you assess their relevance, and some services are 'full text', providing you with the full document.
- *Subject gateways* function like internet search engines, but websites in particular subject areas are assessed for quality and relevance, and sources are organised to allow for

subject browsing. In Britain, those available include SOSIG, the Social Science Information Gateway, and the British Education Internet Resource catalogue.

- *Google Scholar* functions in a similar way to commercial databases, its main advantage being its accessibility to all internet users.

Limiting or expanding your search

Make sure you are focused when choosing your sources, considering each in terms of its relevance to your research questions. If your search produces too many sources, perhaps including many which seem irrelevant, you will need to narrow your search by including more search terms. If the amount of literature still seems infinite, it may be sensible to limit yourself to research published within a certain time frame or jurisdiction, or to identify other parameters for narrowing your scope.

On the other hand, for some emerging topics there may appear to be little literature or even none at all. If your search identifies too few sources, you will need to broaden your search by using more general words. For example, if your study is about criminal justice responses to adolescent violence towards parents, on which there is a limited but emerging literature, you may find it helpful to draw on the broader literatures on responses to domestic violence in general, and on juvenile justice. In turn, it may then be necessary to limit the literature search to work published in your own country in the past ten years.

Reading and note-taking

An initial appraisal of the literature will help clarify the key issues, controversies and debates and provide a basis for future readings. What are the main theoretical perspectives, major research studies and their methods and results? If there is an up-to-date student textbook or chapter among your sources that is directly relevant to your topic, start here for a comprehensive overview of the field, key texts and further readings.

In this initial phase, researchers can waste a lot of time reading in too much detail. Rather than reading a whole book, why not look for book reviews which summarise and evaluate the content for you? You should be able to get the measure of a book with thoughtful use of the contents and index pages and from the summaries provided in the introductory and concluding chapters, or of an article by reviewing the abstract (summary). Different reading techniques include *skimming*, where you look quickly through the text focusing only on these elements; *scanning*, which is searching rapidly for specific information, such as a key word, and ignoring everything else; and *reading to understand*, which involves more detailed study of a key source (Freeman and Meed, 1993).

Once this initial appraisal is complete, you need to make a decision about which aspect of the topic on which to focus. Hopefully, certain themes within the literature will have intrigued you, and you will find it helpful at this stage to discuss your findings with your supervisor and agree a feasible research problem and specific research questions. Following this, a more extensive and thorough literature review is needed for the purpose of obtaining a detailed knowledge of the specialist area being studied, in order to refine the research aims and objectives and devise an appropriate research design. As outlined earlier in the chapter, the approach to this will differ depending on whether you are carrying out a narrative review, a systematic review or a rapid evidence assessment.

As you conduct your detailed review, be sure to record the full bibliographic details of any texts you think will be relevant, using a consistent format. It is usual in the social sciences to employ the Harvard system of referencing, and adopt a consistent approach to the recording of bibliographic information. Specialist bibliographic software such as EndNote is a useful aid in this process. Box 4.6 reproduces the instructions provided by Sage Publications to authors submitting their work to the journal *Criminology and Criminal Justice*, the official journal of the British Society of Criminology.

It is also critical that you make sure any phrases copied directly into your notes are placed in quotation marks and page referenced, to avoid the risks of inadvertent plagiarism.

Annotated bibliographies

A useful way both of organising your material and of making notes is to put together an annotated bibliography. Numerous online examples are available,

---

BOX 4.6

GUIDE TO REFERENCING IN THE SAGE JOURNAL *CRIMINOLOGY AND CRIMINAL JUSTICE*

Use the Harvard-style system: surname and date cited in the text; with an alphabetically ordered end list, headed References, and typed double-spaced for ease of editing. Use the following style:

(a) Downes, David (1988) *Contrasts in Tolerance: Post-War Penal Policy in the Netherlands and England and Wales*. Oxford: Oxford University Press.

(b) Baron, Stephen and Timothy Hartnagel (1997) 'Attributions, Affect and Crime: Street Youths' Reaction to Unemployment', *Criminology* 35(3): 409–434.

(c) Andrews, David A. (1995) 'The Psychology of Criminal Conduct and Effective Treatment', pp. 88–103 in J. McGuire (ed.), *What Works: Reducing Reoffending*. Chichester: John Wiley.

When citing a new edition of a previously published work, include both dates, e.g. Durkheim (1912/1976), in text and references.

Source: Sage Journals Online, at crj.sagepub.com/

---

many of which can be accessed via the bibliographies section of the World Criminal Justice Library Network website, although the quality and recency of the bibliographies is variable.

Box 4.7 provides an example of an annotation, which should include at the very least the full bibliographic citation; a brief summary of the content, including theoretical frameworks and methodological approaches; and a short evaluation or analysis. Other elements may include the background of the author, the target audience, the reliability of the text, and any special features (such as tables, diagrams or graphs) that are particularly useful. For each source, it is also a good idea to note how the material will contribute to the objectives of your literature review and, if applicable, your wider empirical study.

BOX 4.7

WHAT DOES AN ANNOTATION LOOK LIKE?

Annotation

(1) Hayward, K. (2004) *City Limits: Crime, Consumer Culture and the Urban Experience*, London: Routledge-Cavendish.

(2) This book explores the 'crime–city nexus' within a cultural criminology framework. (3) Its aim is 'identifying the myriad forms of relationships that exist between the contemporary "urban experience", certain forms of criminal behaviour, and the particular social forces and cultural dynamics that one associates with '*late modern consumer culture*' (p. 1, emphasis in original), drawing on a multidisciplinary range of theoretical and cultural sources, including art and literature. (4) The article is useful to my research because of its application of theory to contemporary youth crime in the city.

(5) Hayward builds on strain theory and the relative deprivation thesis to build a picture of the distinctive needs and desires of late modern youth, focusing on the insatiability of contemporary consumption, the risk-taking behaviours characteristic of today's urban lifestyles (from binge-drinking to adventure holidaying), and the construction of crime in popular culture as cool and exciting. (6) Criminologists will debate whether Hayward's thesis really offers important new insights or simply a synthesis of old perspectives on crime, but it is useful in its application of established sociological perspectives to the analysis of late modern social change and urban crime. (7) The cultural criminological framework used by Hayward will help inform the theoretical framework I plan to develop in my study.

Based on guidance provided by the University of New South Wales (2009). Extracts from Wakefield (2005: 671–673)

Key

(1) Citation

(2) Introduction

(3) Aims and research methods

(4) Usefulness to your research

(5) Summary

(6) Evaluation

(7) Reflection (how the work illuminates your topic or will add to your research)

Writing the review

Writing a literature review is an iterative process – you will find yourself going back to the literature many times. It is important, however, to begin with a plan setting out the progression of your review, and indicating the depth of content required for each section in accordance with the overall word limit you have assigned to it. The following guidance is focused on how to write a narrative review, as opposed to the more specialised techniques and purpose of a systematic review.

The literature review should be written in such a way that no expert knowledge is assumed on the part of the reader. As with any essay or research paper, it needs to start with a clear introduction, outlining the structure of the review. The introduction may also give a general outline of the key features of the literature.

Your literature review should follow a coherent structure, engaging analytically with the assembled sources to group related items together and draw out key issues and trends. You may find it useful to consult others' work for examples as to how this can be done. Some make the mistake of doing little more than an annotated bibliography, which focuses on one source at a time. The most common ways of organising the literature are as follows:

- *Thematically*, grouped according to the main trends and categories in the field of scholarship, as shown in Newburn's (1999) corruption study (see Box 4.4)

- *Chronologically* or historically, divided into historical or developmental phases, if the topic has a historical background or there have been discernable shifts in thinking over time

- *Methodologically*, organised according to the research methods used across the field of literature, if the field is characterised by several main methodological approaches

It may sometimes be appropriate to use more than one of these strategies, for example dividing the literature by themes and then chronologically within each section. Such groupings will help you move from reading and note-taking to producing a structured analysis of the literature, making it easier to compare and contrast different theoretical approaches, findings and methodologies and analyse the strengths and weaknesses as well as the gaps in previous research.

In the process of writing, your review ought to engage critically with the literature, rather than simply summarising what others have said. The research questions should frame the review and may, in a thematic structure, each relate directly to the respective sections into which the review is divided. Your task is to show how the literature addresses your research questions, supporting or extending existing knowledge. It is also important to ensure that your 'voice' or position is clearly identifiable, and use language that clarifies your position or that of others on a particular issue. Some examples relating to the subject of policing are provided in Box 4.8, drawn from Wakefield (2003).

The literature review should end with a conclusion, summarising the main points, identifying the limitations and gaps in the literature, and making recommendations for future research (your empirical research). It should be noted that the review will only be finalised when your whole project is close to completion,

BOX 4.8

SAMPLE TEXT FROM A LITERATURE REVIEW

The sociology of policing has persistently entertained the debate as to what constitutes 'policing'. Johnston argued that one of the major limitations of this area of criminology has been its tendency 'to conflate policing (a social function) with police (a specific body of personnel)' (1999: 176–7), leading to a preoccupation with the role and functions of the state police forces as opposed to the wide range of bodies engaged in policing activities …

relational marker indicating the writer's relationship to the audience or scholarly community in which they are writing

… Definitions of 'policing' have abounded in recent years, highlighting the difficulty in encapsulating in a few words the diversity of objectives it might encompass, and the range of agencies engaged in their pursuit.

attitude marker indicating the writer's assessment of an issue. An alternative would be to include 'Johnston **perceptively** argued'

… The first interpretation of policing as a 'regulatory process', formalised in the nineteenth century in Britain through the establishment of a public police force, encompasses the activities of multiple agencies, in common with the more recent conceptions of policing as 'governance' (Shearing, 1992), 'networked nodal governance' (Kempa et al., 1999) and the 'governance of security' (Johnston and Shearing, 2002). It may be argued … that as policing is becoming increasingly 'segmented', it is taking a form that appears less and less as an explicit and unified 'process' of regulation, in a reversal of nineteenth-century developments.

For the same reason, the usefulness of the interpretation of 'policing' as 'the work of the police' must also be called into question.

hedging expression making a statement about the degree of certainty of a question, as contrasted with an **emphatic expression** relating to the strength of the claim or the writer's level of confidence in it

Based on guidance provided by the University of New South Wales (2009). Extracts from Wakefield (2003: 3, 4, 15).

because new research is constantly being published and any relevant studies will need to be added to the literature review throughout the research process.

SUMMARY

A literature review is an evaluative overview of the state of knowledge on a research topic. In broad terms its purpose is to show that the researcher has read widely around the chosen topic, gained a good command of the issues, acknowledged the work of others, and set their study in the context of the existing body of literature, highlighting gaps in research. It provides a critical, evaluative synthesis of the research literature on the topic at hand set out according to a number of organising themes. Examples of literature reviews include narrative reviews, in which the researcher seeks to identify trends and categories in a broad field of scholarship, and systematic reviews, used for the purpose of evaluating the effectiveness of an intervention in order to support evidence-based policy-making.

The literature review process begins with the devising of an appropriate search strategy. Once gathered, a useful way both of organising your research material and of making notes is to put together an annotated bibliography. In the process of writing, your literature review needs to engage critically with the literature, speaking directly to the research questions. Your task is to show how the literature addresses these questions, supporting or extending existing knowledge.

■ Study Questions/Activities for Students

1 When might it be most appropriate to conduct a systematic review or rapid evidence assessment, as opposed to a narrative review?

2 What is the purpose of a theoretical framework for your research?

3 Contact a subject specialist librarian for assistance in researching your topic and register for any courses that are available.

4 Search the website of your university library for subject-specific resources, and practise using the search tools (e.g. the library catalogue, online databases and the search tools on the website of key subject journals) and exploring the types of resources available.

5 Compose a 'search string' using your subject keywords and Boolean operators. Type it into Google and Google Scholar, and note the number and quality of results returned. Widen or narrow your search as appropriate.

6 Analyse your approach to reading – are you managing your time effectively, employing techniques of skimming and scanning as much as possible? Are you being selective in your note-taking, noting only the information that is relevant to your needs?

7 Devise a plan for your literature review, assigning a word limit to each of the main sections. Add to the sections of the plan as you develop your ideas until you and your supervisor are happy with the structure.

RESOURCES

The definitive textbook on literature reviews is Hart's *Doing a Literature Review* (1998). *Your Research Project* (Walliman, 2005) is a great companion text for novice researchers, and it includes a very good chapter both on searching and reviewing the literature. Criminological researchers should also consult the annual journal *Crime and Justice: A Review of Research* for examples of authoritative literature reviews on a range of criminological topics.

Many examples of literature reviews carried out by and for government agencies can be found online, on such sites as:

- The Research, Development and Statistics Directorate of the British Home Office (www.homeoffice.gov.uk/rds)
- The Australian Institute of Criminology (www.aic.gov.au)
- The Swedish National Council for Crime Prevention (www.bra.se/english)
- The US National Institute of Justice (www.ojp.usdoj.gov/nij)

The World Criminal Justice Library Network is an excellent starting point for identifying annotated bibliographies and other subject reading lists, but they are of varying age and quality (andromeda.rutgers.edu/~wcjlen).

Detailed information on systematic reviews can be found on the websites of the Campbell Collaboration (www.campbellcollaboration.org) and the Cochrane Collaboration (www.cochrane.org), and guidance on rapid evidence assessments is provided by Britain's Government Social Research Unit (www.civilservice.gov.ukmy-civilservice/networks/professional/gsr/index.aspx). Pawson provides details of his realist synthesis model at www.leeds.ac.uk/realistsynthesis/.

Finally, there is a host of online guidance on literature reviews and annotated bibliographies provided on university websites. The University of New South Wales, Sydney, provides excellent resources on both www.lc.unsw.edu.au/onlib/litrev.html and www.lc.unsw.edu.au/onlib/annotated_bib.html.

REFERENCES

Andrews, D.A., Zinger, I., Hoge, R.D., Bonta, J., Gendreau, P. and Cullen, F.T. (1990) 'Does correctional treatment work: a clinically relevant and psychologically informed meta-analysis', *Criminology*, 28(3): 369–404.

Brown, S. (2005) *Treating Sex Offenders*: *An Introduction to Sex Offender Treatment Programmes*, Cullompton: Willan Publishing.

Einstadter, W.J. and Henry, S. (2006) *Criminological Theory: An Analysis of Its Underlying Assumptions* (2nd edn), New York: Rowman and Littlefield.

Farrington, D.P. and Welsh, B.C. (2002) *Effects of Improved Street Lighting on Crime*: *A Systematic Review*, Home Office Research Study 251, London: Home Office, www.homeoffice.gov.uk/rds/pdfs2/hors251.pdf (accessed 2/4/09).

Farrington, D.P. and Welsh, B.C. (2005) *What Works in Preventing Crime: Systematic Reviews of Experimental and Quasi-Experimental Research,* London: Sage.

Freeman, R. and Meed, J. (1993) *How to Study Effectively*, London: Collins Educational.

Glaser, B.G. and Strauss, A.L. (1967) *The Discovery of Grounded Theory*: *Strategies for Qualitative Research*, Chicago: Aldine.

Glass, G. (1976) 'Primary, secondary, and meta-analysis of research', *Educational Researcher*, 5(10): 3–8.

Gore, S. and Drugs Survey Investigators' Consortium (1999) 'Effective monitoring of young people's use of illegal drugs', *British Journal of Criminology*, 39(4): 575–603.

Gresswell, D.M. and Hollin, C.R. (1994) 'Multiple murder: a review', *British Journal of Criminology*, 34(1): 1–14.

Hart, C. (1998) *Doing a Literature Review*, London: Sage.

Hayward, K. (2004) *City Limits: Crime, Consumer Culture and the Urban Experience*, London: Routledge-Cavendish.

Hope, T. and Walters, R. (2008) *Critical Thinking about the Uses of Research*, London: Centre for Crime and Justice Studies, available at: www.crimeandjustice.org.uk/opus557/Evidencebasedpolicyfinal.pdf (accessed 1/4/09).

Joliffe, D. (2008) 'Researching bullying in the classroom', in R. King and E. Wincup (eds), *Doing Research on Crime and Justice* (2nd edn), Oxford: Oxford University Press.

Jolliffe, D. and Farrington, D.P. (2007) *A Rapid Evidence Assessment of Mentoring*, London: Home Office.

Lösel, F. (2008) 'Doing evaluation research in criminology', in R. King and E. Wincup (eds), *Doing Research on Crime and Justice* (2nd edn), Oxford: Oxford University Press.

Morgan, R. and Hough, M. (2008) 'The politics of criminological research', in R. King and E. Wincup (eds), *Doing Research on Crime and Justice* (2nd edn), Oxford: Oxford University Press.

Myhill, A. (2006) *Community Engagement in Policing: Lessons from the Literature*, London: Home Office, available at: www.crimereduction.homeoffice.gov.uk/policing18.htm (accessed 1/11/09).

Newburn, T. (1999) *Understanding and Preventing Police Corruption: Lessons from the Literature*, Police Research Series Paper 110, London: Home Office, available at: www.homeoffice.gov.uk/rds/prgpdfs/fprs110.pdf (accessed 1/4/09).

Petrosino, A., Boruch, R., Farrington, D., Sherman, L. and Weisburd, D. (2003) 'Towards evidence-based criminology and criminal justice: systematic reviews and the Campbell Collaboration Crime and Justice Group', *The International Journal of Comparative Criminology*, 3(1): 18–41.

Piacentini, L. (2004) *Surviving Russian Prisons: Punishment, Economy and Politics in Transition,* Cullompton: Willan Publishing.

University of New South Wales (2009) *Getting Started on Your Literature Review*, Sydney: The Learning Centre, University of New South Wales, available at: www.lc.unsw.edu.au/onlib/litrev3.html (accessed 11/4/09).

Waddington, P.A.J. (1999) 'Police (canteen) sub-culture: an appreciation', *British Journal of Criminology*, 39(2): 286–308.

Wakefield, A. (2003) *Selling Security*: *The Private Policing of Public Space*, Cullompton: Willan Publishing.

Wakefield, A. (2005) 'Review of *City Limits: Crime, Consumer Culture and the Urban Experience* by Keith Hayward', *British Journal of Sociology*, 56(4): 671–673.

Wilson, J.Q. and Herrnstein, R.J. (1985) *Crime and Human Nature*, New York: Simon & Schuster.

PART TWO

DOING CRIMINOLOGICAL RESEARCH

PAMELA DAVIES AND PETER FRANCIS

Part Contents

DOING RESEARCH

The second part of this volume explores the many ways in which criminological research is carried out in the field. Throughout, the contributors demonstrate the many exciting and innovative ways in which criminologists do research. This includes undertaking interviews with women in prison, observing police community support officers on patrol, researching vulnerable young people in deprived neighbourhoods, doing survey research on sensitive topics, analysing crime data using geographical information systems (GIS), analysing the media and using the internet.

Each of the contributors, however, also acknowledge that the practice and experience of research often differs to that which was originally planned and proposed. Criminological research, like any social research, is unable to escape the reality that even the best laid plans are actualised in social, institutional and political contexts which can have a profound effect on what is done, when, how and with what outcomes. Evidence of the influence of context on research practice is not new. Feminist scholars, for example, have long argued that 'methodology matters' (Stanley 1993; Stanley and Wise 1993) yet it remains usual for these messy aspects of research to be sanitized, de-emotionalized and glossed over in reports of findings in journal articles, book chapters and monographs, and even in some research methods textbooks. Yet, as Letherby reminds us, there is always a "dirtiness" of so-called "hygienic" research' (2003: 79) and it is important to stress that the untold hours of personal, ethical and reflexive pondering that goes on in preparing, planning and doing research offer important lessons for any student of criminology embarking on a piece of research themselves.

Essentially this part of the volume focuses upon how criminological research is accomplished – that is how it is carried out and the factors that influence its operationalization and completion. It does so through illustration and exemplification offered by those who have experienced doing criminological research in the field. Each of the contributors describe and reflect upon the decisions and the methodological choices they made during the course of their research.

Criminologists often collect data from existing resources, including using other people's data. This is generally known as **secondary research** or **secondary analysis.** Sometimes they collect data from subjects of research first hand. This is generally known as **primary research** or **primary analysis**. These categories overlap and criminologists often **triangulate** methods to ensure **validity** of measurement and that valid conclusions are arrived at. Criminologists also draw upon the media and the internet for research purposes. Here we follow these broad distinctions and the discussion that follows is divided into three sections: secondary data collection, primary data collection and using the media and internet for research.

SECONDARY DATA COLLECTION AND ANALYSIS

There are several ways in which existing resources are used by criminologists. Typically advice and guidance in textbooks refer to the use of secondary analysis of official statistics and in this part of the volume we too discuss the use of crime data in criminological research. Secondary analysis is a form of investigation which is based upon existing sources of data. A secondary source refers to any existing source of information which has been collected by someone other than the researcher and with some purpose other than the current research question. There is a wide range of secondary sources available to criminological researchers, such as those collected by criminal justice organizations including reports, institutional records, diaries and letters as well as other documentary resources. One form of data that is routinely used for criminological research is official statistics on crime.

Crime in England and Wales has for a decade now been annually reported in a form that combines police recorded crime data and the British Crime Survey

(BCS). Police recorded crime data reports on a financial year basis (for example, 2009/10 and 2010/11) and is governed by the Home Office Counting Rules and the National Crime Recording Standard (NCRS) as introduced in all police forces in April 2002 to make all crime recording more consistent. There are three key stages:

1 Reporting a crime – someone reports a crime to the police or the police discover a crime. The police register these reports as a crime-related incident and then decide whether or not it is a 'notifiable' (recorded crime) offence and therefore whether or not to record it as a crime.

2 Recording a crime – the police decide to record the report or their discovery of a crime and need to determine how many crimes to record and what the offence type/s is/are.

3 Detecting a crime – once a crime is recorded and investigated, and evidence is collected to link the crime to a suspect, it can be detected.

Thus 'counting rules' need to be thoroughly understood together with changes in the counting of crime over time as this affects comparisons and trends. The discrepancy in some areas and for some crimes remains worryingly disparate. Nevertheless, these statistics provide a good measure of trends, particularly for crimes that are well reported. They are an important indicator of police workload and can be used for local crime pattern analysis. However, despite there being more consistency and better quality of crime recording over time, there is still the problem of 'attrition' and the mis-match between what people report to victim surveys and what is recorded by the police.

The BCS measures crime in England and Wales and the data collected draws upon a sample of interviews with members of the population. Given that it is based on interviews with individuals, it captures experiences and thus reports data on crime which is not necessarily reported to the police. Collecting information on victims of crime, the circumstances in which incidents occur and the behaviour of offenders in committing crime, it is an important and complementary source of information about levels of and attitudes to crime, as well as related issues including fear of crime, and perceptions of the criminal justice system and its agencies.

Despite their accessibility, there are numerous complexities involved in using crime data for criminological research not least because crime is a complex and multifaceted phenomenon. Police recorded crimes are offences that are known to the authorities and classified accordingly. However, there are many dimensions to crime not captured in police statistics. How one person experiences an incident may differ from how someone else and thus how they define it and report it (or not). In Chapter 5, Alex Hirschfield examines various forms of crime analysis, including the use of GIS in criminological research. As he is at pains to stress, explaining and understanding crime requires more than just possessing and analysing crime data.

PRIMARY DATA COLLECTION AND ANALYSIS

Primary data collection and analysis can be conducted in several ways by criminologists. Here we note a number of common methodological issues that relate to obtaining data from subjects first hand. We focus on data collection using surveys, interviews and observations.

Surveys

One important method of collecting data is the social survey. Social surveys have been used extensively in criminological research and **crime/victim surveys**, for example the BCS typically use structured questions as a means of collecting data from individual respondents first hand. This can be done by interviewing them or by requesting that respondents fill in a self-completion questionnaire. Survey research can lend itself towards the collection of both **quantitative** and **qualitative** data. A primary purpose is often the collection of quantitative data so as to allow for the generation of generalizable findings across a population. Whilst questions posed are typically structured, allowing the researcher to collect the same kinds of data from a large number of people, quickly, cheaply and with comparability of response, such questions in surveys run the risk of being too structured.

It is very rare to collect data from the whole of the population: this would be a very costly and time-consuming exercise. For this reason social surveys are usually sample surveys. A sample survey is a form of research design which involves collecting data from, or about, a subset of the population with a view to making inferences from, and drawing conclusions about, the population as a whole (the term 'census' is generally used when all members of a population are included in a study). There are skills in selecting a sample which is representative of the wider population and several chapters in this volume refer to **sampling** issues, some in the context of gathering data from respondents first hand.

The BCS selects a random sample of men and women of all ages (extended to children aged 10 to 15 since January 2009) and all backgrounds in order to reflect the experiences, attitudes and concerns about crime. Since the first survey was carried out in 1982, there is now an extensive and rich database of information on levels, trends and attitudes to crime resulting from this and similar survey-based research studies. The BCS has paved the way for a number of additional surveys that are useful to criminological researchers. These include:

- The Northern Ireland Crime Survey
- Scottish and Justice Survey
- Offending, Crime and Justice Survey (OCJS)
- Commercial Victimisation Survey (CVS)

The nature of the BCS and other victim-oriented surveys are often such that they deal with sensitive issues. Respondents, for example, are asked to discuss harmful topics and emotional experiences that they may not have disclosed previously either by talking to strangers or by keying in data to a computer, albeit in a confidential manner. However, the extent to which surveys are an appropriate method for researching sensitive topics is a contested subject. In Chapter 6, Jo Deakin and Jon Spencer discuss whether it is possible to deal with difficult subjects and gather sensitive data with vulnerable populations through large-scale surveys. They explore criticisms of large-scale surveys and illustrate issues with reference to the BCS. They go on to consider ways of generating ethically sound survey data collection on sensitive topics with hard to reach and vulnerable groups. A children and young people's safety survey is used as an example as is a survey on public attitudes to sex offenders. Open, closed and loaded questions, **vignettes** – alternatives to traditional questions where the main element is a description of a scenario – are all featured in this chapter as examples of delivering surveys on sensitive topics.

Interviews

Interviews can be defined as a method of data collection, information or opinion gathering that specifically involves asking a series of questions. Typically, interviews represent a formal meeting or dialogue between people where personal and social interaction occur (Davies 2006). Interviews are typically associated with qualitative social research and are often used alongside other methods. They can vary enormously in terms of the context or setting in which they are carried out, the purpose they serve as well as how they are structured and conducted. This means that interviews are a flexible and adaptable tool and as a result there are many different types of interview. Interviews can take the form of informal, unstructured, naturalistic and in-depth discussions in which the individual respondent largely determines the shape of the interview. They can also be very structured discussions delivered in a format with answers offered from a prescribed list in a questionnaire or ideal standardized interview schedule.

Most commonly, interviews are conducted face-to-face and can include one or more interviewers who are normally in control of the direction of the questions that are put to one or more interviewees or respondents. Sometimes interviews may be conducted by telephone or by way of electronic communication such as e-mail. An example of an interview with little interaction between the researcher and the researched is Computer Assisted Personal Interviewing (CAPI) where interviewers enter responses into a laptop computer, self-keying, to answer questions themselves. Since 1994 this mode of interviewing has been used in the British Crime Survey (BCS) for more sensitive topics. Interviews of this nature are popular for reasons due to cost-effectiveness and for the speed of data collection. Telephone interviews are routinely used for the conduct of opinion polls by market researchers. Political opinion polls are some of the most well-known types of interview conducted by this method.

As a means of collecting data, interviews can be an invaluable source of information and opinions that generate valid, representative and reliable data. They enable the interviewer to follow up and probe responses, motives and feelings and in many of their forms non-verbal communications, facial expressions and gestures, for example, can enrich the qualitative aspects of the data. However, assuming the use of the interview as the obvious method of choice for qualitative research can generate inappropriate or unmanageable data unfit for specific contexts and for specific purposes. In addition to this, there are skills associated with interviewing.

Different types of interviews are associated with distinct advantages and disadvantages. Unstructured interviews where the respondent talks freely around a topic can produce rich grounded data but can be very time-consuming to analyse and the potential for bias on behalf of the interviewer might be increased. The more guided or focused the interview, generally speaking, the less time-consuming and less problematic is the analysis due to the more standardized nature of the responses. In opting for the latter form of interview, there is generally an increased likelihood that the researcher might not be asking the most significant questions.

In Chapter 7 Pamela Davies discusses how she collected data from women offenders in prison using semi-structured interviews. She highlights how she accomplished this despite an array of methodological, ethical and practical problems, and provides a stage-by-stage discussion of how, if conducted reflexively, criminological research in a closed women's prison is doable. This and other chapters demonstrate how by devising appropriate operational rules, research dilemmas can be overcome and innovative and original research can be achieved.

In Chapter 8 Rob MacDonald discusses the use of loosely structured interviews as part of longitudinal research. Spurred on by a range of criticisms directed at the lack of rigour associated with Charles Murray's work on the underclass, MacDonald argues that Murray provides no evidence for his claims, ignores British research evidence from the preceding decade, and suggests that if we are to engage properly with **underclass** theory, what is needed is research which is able to explore in depth the values, activities and outlooks of the most likely members, in the most likely places and during the most likely periods in which the underclass phenomena might arise. MacDonald goes on to demonstrate how his focused, qualitative, extensive and critical **case study** research with hard to reach and vulnerable populations – working-class young people (aged 15 to 25 years) – shed new light on how these young people made transitions to adulthood in contexts of multiple deprivation. The chapter illuminates 'participation/observation', biographical interviews, sample, purposive, theoretical, convenience and snowball sampling in the context of social inquiry.

Observations

Research observations can be used in various criminal justice settings, including the prison, and might well be used in conjunction with other methods such as interviews. In the pilot stages of research it is desirable and often necessary to spend some time among the populations being studied and/or in the institutional setting, particularly if this happens to be a prison, before embarking upon interviews or survey work (Martin 2000). The ethnographic researcher will enter the field as soon as possible and is likely to undertake other tasks such as a literature review and conceptualization during and on completion of fieldwork (Silverman 2007). **Participant observation** and **ethnography** can include the use of interviews, conversational and discourse analysis, documentary analysis, film and photography and life histories and sometimes can attract criticism. Often they are seen as producing 'soft' data rather than 'hard' factual data (Hollands 2000) and certainly 'thick','rich' and ''intense' description is central to them.

Chapters 7 and 8 feature some aspects of this particular tradition, as does Chapter 11 by Jewkes. However, the chapter that perhaps best exemplifies the key features of this qualitative observational and ethnographic tradition is Chapter 9, where Faye Cosgrove and Peter Francis discuss an appreciative ethnography of police community support officers. After describing and reviewing the contribution traditional ethnographic studies of police culture have made to an understanding of police work, Cosgrove's highly original doctoral study is used to illustrative the benefit of using an appreciative ethnography to collecting deep, rich and informed qualitative data.

USING THE MEDIA AND INTERNET FOR CRIMINOLOGICAL RESEARCH

The internet and media images are both considered here as potential sources for primary and secondary data collection. Three chapters form the basis for this section. Chapter 10 by Rob C. Mawby, Chapter 11 by Yvonne Jewkes and Chapter 12 by David Wall and Matthew Williams. Each of these chapters variously address the questions of why and how to study crime *in* and *through* the media, and in the case of David Wall and Matthew Williams – the internet.

Chapter 10 by Rob C. Mawby provides a rich discussion of different types of analysis as relevant to studying crime and justice in the media, including content, narrative, semiotic, syntagmatic and paradigmatic analysis and sound and visual signifiers. In Chapter 11, Yvonne Jewkes discusses the benefits and weaknesses of using content analysis, discourse analysis, participant observation, focus groups and interviewing. Some of the most well-known and influential media/crime research studies from within the observational and ethnographic research traditions as carried out over the last 40 years are discussed. Additionally, Jewkes refers to an ethnographic study she carried out which was concerned with the ways in which men in prison use media (Jewkes 2002). This study of prison audiences adopted some of the methodological approaches of oral history or **life history**, talking to many prisoners individually for lengthy periods of time to explore the 'felt texture' of their whole lives (Deacon et al. 1999: 291). She exemplifies the value of unstructured, free-format interviewing and its usefulness in eliciting highly penetrative findings. In Chapter 12, David Wall and Matthew Williams suggests that the first two decades of the 21st century have become characterized by new social landscapes created by social networking and popular contemporary mass information systems such as *Google, Wikipedia, Twitter, Facebook, MySpace, YouTube, Flickr, Friends Reunited, SecondLife* and many others. They suggest that these new digital technologies have changed the ways that we do research in criminology. They outline how the principles of research remain much the same online as they do offline yet networked technologies have transformed research into criminological behaviour and criminal justice in three distinct ways. They look at the different ways that the internet, its digital technologies and environments can be used as a tool for researching crime and justice. The chapter explores the transformation of the criminological research environment, the ways in which networked technologies create efficiency gains for researchers and the proliferation of new information flows that can assist primary, secondary and tertiary data collection. The chapter also considers the creation of entirely new criminal environments and new forms of criminal behaviour before considering the range of new methodological and ethical challenges that arise from all of these transformations.

METHODOLOGICAL CHOICES

In terms of data collection, many key issues will connect to the ways in which you operationalize your research. Operationalization refers to the laying down of rules which stipulate when instances of a concept have occurred. **Operational rules** link abstract concepts to observations. Such observations are sometimes also known as indicators. The extent to which you, the researcher, can devise a means of observing and measuring the concepts that lie at the heart of a research problem is the extent to which there is measurement **validity**. General and abstract non-directly measurable concepts are the building blocks of theories.

The researcher needs to operationalize these concepts after careful clarification of them. While there are various checks that can be used to assess validity, including criterion validity, content validity and construct validity, we would draw attention to your ability as researcher to engage in creative decision-making. Many of you will be doing criminological research yourself while others may well be managing a research project. In both instances you will face significant moments when you must make important methodological choices. When such decision-making moments are upon you, we suggest you foreground power and give due consideration to unequal relationships between the researcher and the researched.

So, you should be continuously checking that you are studying what you want to study and that you are measuring what you should be measuring.

■ Study Questions/Activities for Students

1 Read Chapter 5 and then answer the following:

How can we best use crime data to explain and understand crime?

2 Read Chapter 6 and then answer the following:

How can large-scale surveys be designed to drill deeply into sensitive topics and with vulnerable populations?

3 Read Chapters 7, 8 and 9 and then compare the strengths and weaknesses of each of the following:

- semi-structured interviews
- biographical interviews
- participant observation
- appreciative ethnography

4 Read Chapters 10, 11 and 12 and then, drawing on the innovative ways of doing criminological research that these chapters discuss, plan a strategy to conduct research on anti-social behaviour in public areas. You should aim for methodological triangulation in your research design.

REFERENCES

Davies, P. (2006) 'Interviews', in V. Jupp (ed.), *The Sage Dictionary of Social Research*, London: Sage.

Deacon, D., Pickering, M., Golding, P. and Murdock, G. (1999) *Researching Communications*, London: Arnold.

Hollands, R.G. (2000) 'Lager Louts, Tarts, and Hooligans': the Criminalisation of Young Adults in a Study of Newcastle Night-life', in V. Jupp, P. Davies and P. Francis (eds), *Doing Criminological Research* (1st edn), London: Sage.

Jewkes, Y. (2002) *Captive Audience: Media, Masculinity and Power in Prisons*, Cullompton: Willan.

Letherby, G. (2003) *Feminist Research in Theory and Practice*, Milton Keynes: Open University Press.

Martin, C. (2000) 'Doing Research in a Prison Setting', in V. Jupp et al. (eds), *Doing Criminological Research* (1st edn), London: Sage.

Silverman, D. (2007) *Doing Qualitative Research*, London: Sage.

Stanley, L. (1993) 'On Auto/Biography in Sociology', *Sociology* 27: 41–52.

Stanley, L. and Wise, S. (1993) *Breaking Out Again: Feminist Ontology and Epistemology*, London: Routledge.

FIVE
MAPPING AND USING CRIME DATA IN CRIMINOLOGICAL RESEARCH

ALEX HIRSCHFIELD

Chapter Contents

INTRODUCTION

Crime is a complex and multifaceted phenomenon that can be studied in a number of ways and for a variety of reasons. Those of you reading this chapter will differ in terms of your interests in studying crime. For example, a student tasked with analysing burglary for a dissertation is likely to approach the subject from a different perspective from a police officer seeking to identify the latest hot spots of violence against the person. In the former situation, the student might require two years' worth of recorded crime data on domestic burglary to produce a crime profile for a deprived residential housing estate. The police officer, by contrast, might need data on incidents occurring within the last 24 hours to direct patrols dealing with alcohol-related violence in the town centre. The community safety officer, working for a Crime and Disorder Reduction Partnership (CDRP), might wish to look at how crime is changing over time in response to crime prevention measures implemented by the partnership in specific communities. The focus of attention in this case is on evaluating the impact of crime reduction strategies and projects on levels of crime within the community.

Then there are the criminologists and other academics interested not just in the timing and geographical distribution of crime, but in explaining why it occurs and understanding how and why it is changing over time (Cohen and Felson, 1979; Wikstrom and Sampson, 2006). Crucial to this exercise is the ability to drill deeper; to look at the circumstances surrounding the commission of the offence, the demographic and social characteristics of the victim, information on offender behaviour (e.g. *modus operandi*); and to relate all of this to the broader social, physical and policy environment. The latter might include housing, disadvantage, social cohesion, transport routes and accessibility. In other words, explaining and understanding crime requires more than just possessing and analysing **crime data**. It means relating crime incidents to non-crime variables in order to place offences into a broader societal context, enabling questions about risk factors and potential causal processes to be explored.

The discussion above gives a hint of the complexities involved in researching crime. The aim of this chapter is to position the mapping and use of crime data into this broader context. First, there is an examination of the different dimensions of crime, the objectives behind crime data analysis and the implication of these on the data required and the analytical methods used. Second, there is a brief examination of the importance of scale in crime analysis, that is, whether the focus is on identifying crime at the level of the individual person, the address (e.g. the residential property, business, public building) or the neighbourhood/ area. Third, special attention is then paid to the use and role of Geographical Information Systems (GIS) in mapping crime data, identifying **crime hot spots** and exploring relationships between crime, land use and the social environment. Each of the different forms of crime analysis is illustrated in a series of strategically placed information boxes, figures and tables. These draw on applied research carried out by the author and his colleagues for a range of local and central government agencies. Finally, pioneering research is introduced that relates the timing and spatial distribution of crime, not only to the social and physical environment, but also to the timing and location of crime prevention measures.

DIMENSIONS OF CRIME

The starting point in a discussion about how crime data are used to analyse and map crime is to unpack the following two questions: 'What is meant by crime?' and 'What constitutes crime analysis?'

What is crime?

Police recorded crimes are offences that are known to the authorities and classified accordingly. A domestic burglary or the theft of a vehicle would be examples of acquisitive property crimes. Other offences may be committed against individuals, such as an assault, a sexual offence or a theft from the person (e.g. the stealing of a mobile phone). Others may be damage to property (e.g. vandalism and arson) or crimes against businesses (e.g. shoplifting or fraud).

However, there are many other dimensions to the 'crime problem' not captured in police statistics. Indeed, 'data about crime', or, more specifically, data about the social, environmental and policy context within which crime occurs, are not the same as crime data. Whereas the latter usually refers to police recorded crime, it is the former (data about crime) that is often crucial when it comes to understanding and explaining crime. In fact, there are a number of different interpretations and meanings reflecting the complexity of crime as a measurable phenomenon. These are listed in Box 5.1.

BOX 5.1

DIMENSIONS OF CRIME

- Recorded crime
- Victimisation (reported plus unreported)
- Offending (detected and undetected)
- Crime opportunities (vulnerable goods, processes, people, places)
- Perceptions of crime within an area
- Perceptions of anti-social behaviour
- Perceptions of crime opportunities
- Perceptions of safety
- Fear of crime
- Anger about crime
- Shock about crime

A focus on 'victimisation' requires knowledge about offences that go unreported as well as those known to the police. The under-reporting of crime, particularly offences such as assault, sexual offences and domestic violence, means that it is not possible to get the complete picture using official statistics. A better idea of the true level of crime can be identified from surveys such as the British Crime Survey (BCS), which is a continuous survey of 40,000 households that asks respondents about their experience of crime and which of the incidents, if any, they report to the police. The difference between the number of offences identified from the BCS and those that are recorded by the police reveal the **dark figure of crime**. The BCS for 2007/08 indicated that, overall, around 42% of crimes that had taken place were reported to the police and roughly 74% of those that were reported ended up on police computers as recorded crime (Kershaw et al., 2008). Therefore, if mapping and analysing crime is about identifying the timing, location and characteristics of all or most offences that occur, then much will be missed by using police records. This is less true of theft of vehicle and domestic burglary, where, in 2007/08, 93% and 76% of incidents were reported, than it is for vandalism, assault without injury and theft from the person, where roughly two-thirds of cases go unreported (Kershaw et al., 2008).

Another way of thinking about crime is to focus not on the offence *per se*, but on the distribution and timing of opportunities that offenders have to commit crimes (Groff and La Vigne, 2001). Not all areas have equal crime risks. There will be some that contain land uses, buildings or facilities that attract and even 'generate' criminal activity, such as busy transport termini and pubs used to fence stolen goods. Others may repel crime by making it more difficult for motivated offenders to commit an offence without being challenged and act as 'crime detractors' (Brantingham and Brantingham, 1993, 1995). Crime opportunities are influenced by factors such as housing design, street layout and natural surveillance (Newman, 1972; Armitage, 2000, 2006); the accessibility of an area to the offender (Wiles and Costello, 2000); the juxtaposition of different land uses (i.e. what is next to what); the time of day; and the willingness of local residents to challenge strangers and report suspicious activity – one of the hallmarks of a socially cohesive community (Hirschfield and Bowers, 1997). Easy and concealed access to the rear of properties (poor natural surveillance) can create opportunities for burglars and drug dealers. People living in highly accessible areas (served by arterial roads, railways, bus routes) can be more susceptible to crime by travelling offenders than those living in neighbourhoods with poor communications and fewer escape routes. A secondary school next to a shopping parade may create opportunities for shoplifting, vandalism and truancy (Felson and Clarke, 1998). Situations and opportunities for crime also vary by time of day. For instance, an area that is primarily a business district during the day (with low crime) may become an entertainment area during the night (with a higher risk of theft and assault). Although there are abundant maps of crime rates and crime 'hot spots', very little systematic research, with just a few exceptions (Groff and La Vigne, 2001), has been conducted on mapping crime opportunities. This reflects a dearth of comprehensive, consistent, accessible and geographically referenced data on land use and non-residential properties (e.g. corner shops, licensed premises, bus shelters, taxi ranks, and so on).

Perceptions of safety and expressions of fear and concern about crime can be considered as different but perfectly valid dimensions of crime. Perceptions may be a particularly important barometer of how residents view their neighbourhood and may directly influence their lifestyle, behaviour and quality of life. Other emotions and responses to crime, such as anger and shock, are often overlooked but may be crucial when publicising crime prevention or formulating other policy responses (Rogerson and Christmann, 2004). None of these can be measured using recorded crime data.

What is crime analysis?

Crime analysis is primarily concerned with processing and interrogating data on criminal offences to identify patterns and trends in crime (e.g. location, timing, *modus operandi*), to identify unusual concentrations of crime in particular locations or at specific times of day (e.g. defining crime hot spots), to identify high crime communities and neighbourhoods in order to inform resource allocation, and to identify changes in levels of crime over time and benchmark these against expectations. Crime analysis also includes monitoring how crime levels change in response to the implementation of crime reduction policies and interventions as part of the **evaluation** process.

Drilling down further to identify factors that place people, property and places at a great risk of crime represents another application of crime analysis. Assessing risk can involve analysing data on victims of crime (e.g. by age, gender and experience of prior victimisation), on offenders (e.g. by age, gender, prior offending) and on the characteristics of places where crime occurs (demographics, land use, environmental design). Crime analysis can be used to support tactical responses to crime, such as the deployment of police patrols and more strategic approaches involving the targeting and implementation of crime prevention initiatives. Results from crime analysis are usually communicated by the preparation of written reports and visually through tables, graphs, charts and maps (Osbourne and Wernicke, 2003; Ratcliffe, 2004).

DATA

Although the mapping and analysis of crime requires a focus that is broader than just considering police recorded crime data, the latter, together with police calls for service (command and control data), are widely used.

A crime record will typically have a date or a date–time interval, indicating when the offence occurred or was reported, it may have a location and there may be other information about the victim (e.g. age, gender, ethnic group), how the offence was committed (the offender's *modus operandi*), goods stolen, injuries sustained and, in some cases, characteristics of the perpetrator (height, age, gender). Such data are generally comparable across different areas because they are collected using a consistent coding framework (e.g. recorded crime data broken down by Home Office crime codes). Other police data (e.g. calls for service to the police) can be subject to considerable local variations in how they are coded, although in Britain, since the introduction of a national standard for incident recording, there is greater consistency in these data (Audit Commission, 2006; Home Office et al., 2007).

Data quality, particularly the inputting of addresses and locations (geo-coding), has always been an important issue. Although the consistency of inputting addresses into police recorded crime systems has improved considerably (since the mid 1990s), the precision of the offence location is highly dependent upon the crime category. Locating residential burglaries is far easier than identifying crimes against the person, in particular, robbery, theft and assault. These are more difficult to map because of the often high degree of uncertainty about where they occur. In many information systems, their location is assigned to the nearest landmark or street intersection but in many cases it is difficult to obtain a reliable spatial reference for them.

Access to the record for each offence (**disaggregated data**) is essential for identifying **repeat victimisation**, **crime hot spots**, for producing crime profiles for non-standard user-defined areas (e.g. a housing estate, cultural zone within a city such as Chinatown) and for monitoring changes in crime patterns following the implementation of crime prevention measures such as the search for geographical displacement (Johnson et al., 2001; Bowers and Johnson, 2003). However, **disaggregated data** on crime are not in the public domain and usually can only be obtained by signing up to a confidentiality agreement and data-sharing protocol with the individual police force.

STAKEHOLDERS: WHO IS INTERESTED IN CRIME ANALYSIS AND WHY?

Just as there are variations in what constitutes crime analysis, there are different stakeholders with an interest in mapping and analysing crime. They include police officers and police crime analysts, community safety coordinators in CDRPs, regeneration practitioners, town planners, policy evaluators, academics and criminologists, businesses considering where to locate and actual/potential residents curious or concerned about crime in different neighbourhoods.

A typology of crime analyses

The various interests of these and other stakeholders imply different uses of relevant data. A typology of crime analyses is presented in Table 5.1. This shows the range of analyses that can be carried out and how these differ in terms of their rationale (e.g. describing crime patterns, crime investigations, explaining crime, evaluating prevention), the types of inquiry/research question that need to be answered and the methods that need to be applied (e.g. tables, maps, derivation of crime rates, statistical analysis).

Not all of the analyses comprising the typology are undertaken routinely or carried out with the same degree of sophistication. Much depends on the available skills and expertise of the user and access to data sets. For some users it might be sufficient to produce a table showing the number of recorded crimes by offence category within an area or across specific neighbourhoods. Others may want to establish if certain types of community (e.g. deprived areas) have higher crime rates than elsewhere. Police analysts might want to determine if offences committed in several locations are linked in some way. Community safety officers might want to explore how far changes in an area's crime rate over time can be attributed to crime prevention activity. In each of these cases, it is necessary to drill down deeper to analyse **data attributes** of the offence (e.g. timing and *modus operandi*) and to relate crime data to additional information about the context within which offences have been committed; in short, to expand the study from a concern solely with *crime data* to embrace *data about crime.*

The police, community safety partnerships and criminologists are likely to be the most prolific users of crime data. However, with an increasing number of websites offering interactive crime mapping, many other groups, including the general public, also need to be included as members of the user community. There is an abundance of systems in the USA that enable users to select areas from a map and to query a crime database using drop-down menus. Examples include systems in Chicago (gis.chicagopolice.org/), in Portland, Oregon (www.gis.ci.portland.or.us/maps/police/), in Sacramento (maps.cityofsacramento.org/website/sacpd/) and San Diego County in California (mapping.arjis.org/main.aspx). In Britain, a number of police forces now make crime data available to the public in order to communicate with and engage local communities. The West Yorkshire Police 'beat crime' system (www.beatcrime.info) is a typical example.

TABLE 5.1 A Typology of Crime Analyses

Type of Analysis	Illustrative Questions	Type of Analysis	Likely Stakeholder(s)
Descriptive	What is the main crime problem in this community? Is where I want to live (set up my business) a high crime area? Is crime increasing or decreasing?	Tabulation of offence categories by area; pie charts and bar graphs Online crime selection, querying and search facilities Street and area mapping	Community safety officers, town planners, regeneration practitioners Residents; local businesses Police forces committed to communicate and engage with local communities
Investigative	How is crime perpetrated? How do offence locations relate to those used by previous offenders and known suspects? Have these offences been committed by the same person?	Analysis of offence and offender locations Analysis of offender modus operandi Identification of patterns and associations (cluster analysis, facet analysis)	Police officers Police crime analysts, offender profilers Investigative Psychologists
Strategic & Tactical	How is crime changing at the regional level? Can we tackle the majority of crime by targeting resources into just a few areas? What are the risks in locating a business in this area? Do existing operational areas reflect workload? Where should police patrols be sent on Friday nights?	Crime rate league tables; benchmarking against other areas Spatial concentration of crime Identification of areas for store locations; pricing of insurance premiums on basis of risk Delineation and redefinition of boundaries (e.g. police beats) Real-time mapping of incidents on laptop and handheld computers	Central government departments, regional government offices, CDRPs Retail trade, insurance industry, inward investors, economic development units, town planners BCU commanders Police patrol officers
Explanatory	What drives crime? What is generating increases in crime? How can reductions in crime be explained? What are the health impacts of crime? What are the crime impacts of economic recessions?	Statistical analysis measuring the association between crime, social indicators and land use Measurement of crime change using time series analysis	Higher Education institutions, colleges, schools and research organisations Criminologists, public health specialists, social scientists
Evaluative	How appropriate are the interventions to the identified crime problems? Is this crime prevention project working? Has crime reduced beyond expectations? How far is this the result of the interventions in question ?	Changes in crime levels coterminous with the implementation of policy Initiatives Analysis of crime switch, crime displacement and diffusion of benefit Costs of crime and crime prevention Cost-effectiveness analysis	Research and consultancy organisations Central government departments Auditing bodies (Audit Commission, National Audit Office in the UK) Others with an interest in evaluation

THE IMPORTANCE OF SCALE: PEOPLE, PROPERTIES OR PLACES?

By now it will be apparent that the objectives underpinning crime data analysis can vary significantly along with the research questions and the methods. Another consideration is that of scale, which refers to the unit(s) of analysis at which the research is carried out.

TABLE 5.2 Units of Analysis in Burglary Research

Number of Properties Burgled	Number of Burglaries	Victims of Burglary	Electoral Ward with 20 or more Burglaries
260	300	575	25

Table 5.2 illustrates some of the units of analysis in a study of domestic burglary. A key unit of analysis in this case would be the 260 individual properties that had been burgled. The burglary offence, of which there are 300, would be another unit of analysis. The reason why there are more burglaries than the number of properties burgled is that some properties would have been burgled more than once (i.e. subjected to repeat victimisation). Each of the 575 victims of burglary living in those properties would constitute another 'unit of analysis'. There are far more victims of burglary than properties and this is a function of the size of the households occupying each of the properties; in this case, an average of 2.2 persons living in each property. Some properties would have been burgled and unoccupied. The victim in this case might be the landlord, who might live in an entirely different neighbourhood. Analysis at victim level would entail studying the circumstances and fortunes of 575 individuals. If the focus is on the geography of burglary across the city's electoral wards, then there are only 25 units of analysis and the only data that are available might be the total number of burglaries in each ward at one or more points in time.

Of course, an analysis of crime may employ a mix of scales, for example, studying individual properties located in the top 10% of wards with the highest overall crime rates, or interviewing female victims of burglary in properties located in wards that have seen an increase in their burglary rate in excess of 5% compared with the previous year.

It is entirely conceivable that an analysis of changes in burglary levels over a period of time conducted at the property level (e.g. in a student area) might reveal that certain properties appear again and again in the burglary data as repeatedly victimised addresses. This would not necessarily mean that the individual students living in those properties had been repeatedly burgled because a number of them may have moved home several times within a year, reflecting high levels of mobility within the student housing sector. Thus a burglary analysis at the victim level might reveal a different picture compared with that at the property level. Prior burglary, as experienced by a student victim, might have occurred at a number of different addresses, in different types of neighbourhood and under different circumstances.

MAPPING AND ANALYSIS USING GEOGRAPHICAL INFORMATION SYSTEMS

Although crime data can be tabulated, processed and analysed using spreadsheets and statistical software packages, a Geographical Information System (GIS) is needed for mapping and carrying out spatial analysis.

What is a GIS?

A GIS is essentially a system of hardware, software and procedures designed to support the capture, storage, retrieval, analysis and display of spatially-referenced information (Longley et al., 2005). Such systems enable links to be established and spatial relationships to be explored between data derived from different sources (e.g. calls to the police, crime reports, population census variables). They can be used in conjunction with grid-referenced crime data to undertake analyses which overcome the limitations inherent in the use of spatially-aggregated data for pre-determined geographical boundaries (e.g. police beats).

Figure 5.1 shows different layers of spatially-referenced information in a GIS used to analyse burglary data. These may be in the form of a grid reference referring to a specific point on a map – in this case, the locations of individual properties that have been burgled (5.1(a)). Typically, these are in the form of two readings: an 'Easting' and a Northing'. Eastings are the coordinates that stretch along the bottom x-axis of the map and Northings are the position along the side of the map (its y-axis). Spatial information may be linear features, such as a stretch of road or a network of streets, for example, a bus route running through a high crime area (5.1(b)). The boundaries of areas, such as police beats, Census Output Areas or electoral wards (referred to as a 'polygons'), represent another layer (5.1(c)). In this

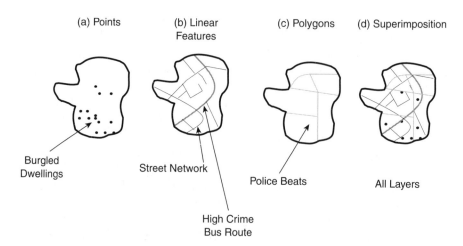

FIGURE 5.1   Spatially Referenced Data in a GIS Used for Crime Analysis

example, the polygons might be police beats or Census Output Areas with high burglary rates. Each of these features also has topography in the sense that the GIS stores data on what is next to what.

Data items referred to as 'attributes' can be linked to the geographic entities (points, lines, polygons) forming each of these data layers. For example, each burglary point may include details of the offence (e.g. date, time, *modus operandi*); each street information about speed limit, bus routes, whether it is covered by a home watch scheme; and for each polygon, its deprivation score, crime rate, demographic composition (e.g. the proportion of young males aged 18–24), and so on.

The value of GIS in crime analysis

The added value of a GIS is in the ability to manipulate the data captured for each of these layers so that relationships can be explored between them. For example, all of the layers in Figure 5.1 can be superimposed to generate a composite map of crime and land use ((d) in Figure 5.1). Alternatively, new maps can be created by selecting what to display. For example, a GIS containing data on recorded crime (offence category and date) and the location of licensed premises could be used to identify how many incidents of criminal damage or violence against the person occur in the early hours of Saturday between 1am and 2am within 100 metres of a particular pub. Clearly, the complexity of these inquiries increases with additional data. If CCTV camera positions were included, together with taxi ranks, night clubs and bus stops, then more complex queries can be answered by bringing all of these factors together. The point to reiterate here is that such information cannot be generated with ease, accuracy or speed by means other than using a GIS. Further examples of how GIS can be used in crime analysis are listed in Box 5.2.

BOX 5.2

EXAMPLES OF GIS APPLICATIONS IN CRIME ANALYSIS

- Mapping the distribution of individual and repeat incidents (offence, victim, offender locations)
- Putting contextual information on to a map of crime (deprivation, demographics, transport routes, bus stops, housing, pubs, taxi ranks, and so on)
- Calculating and mapping crime rates for administrative areas and different types of neighbourhood
- Counting how many crimes fall within a boundary, at a specific site (e.g. a car park) or within a selected radius (e.g. 200 metres surrounding a pub or a school)
- Identifying buffer zones (e.g. either side of a main road) and counting how many offences occur within them
- Identifying comparison areas for evaluation studies (e.g. similar areas with similar crime levels, one with and one without crime prevention measures)
- Tracking geographic displacement of crime

The procedures discussed above are largely problem-specific and typically require the user to specify what to look for and then to display the results on a map. A more **inductive** approach is to search for patterns in the temporal and spatial distribution of crime and display the results as series of crime hot spots. Once these have been defined, it is then possible to identify population profiles and land-use characteristics for each hot spot.

There are a number of methods for detecting patterns in crime data and delineating hot spots. The main ones include:

- **Spatial overlap analysis** – superimposing shaded maps to reveal the location of areas with the highest rates on, for example, theft from the person, vehicle crime and assault
- **Nearest neighbour analysis** – a test to distinguish random from non-random crime distributions
- **Plotting of hot spot ellipses** – these identify clusters of crime that are close in both space and time
- **Kernal density estimation** (KDE) – a process that detects hot spots by slowly moving a user-defined search window across an entire map repeatedly searching for clustering

In recent years several GIS products have been developed that incorporate crime pattern analysis software. The US National Institute of Justice (NIJ) Mapping and Analysis for Public Safety (MAPS) Initiative provides crime analysis freeware, including the CrimeStat spatial statistics programme, the Crime Analysis Spatial Extension for ESRI's ArcGIS and other products (www.ojp.usdoj.gov/nij/maps/).

EXAMPLES OF GIS APPLICATIONS

The progression from simple point mapping to hot spot delineation can be illustrated through a series of examples. Figure 5.2 shows the distribution of criminally damaged bus stops on the Wirral in Merseyside, northwest England (Newton, 2004). Each point represents a vandalised bus stop over the period of one year. Although it is possible to see where these are located individually, it is difficult to discern where the greatest spatial concentration and/or temporal clustering of incidents occur.

Mapping crime hot spots

Making judgements about the location of hot spots using experienced-based knowledge or by a cursory inspection of points on a map runs the risk of missing potentially significant crime problems. Research has shown that police officers with local knowledge are often wrong in their perceptions of where both hot spots and areas of unusually low crime are located. In fact, they get it wrong half of the time (Ratcliffe and McCullagh, 2001).

Distilling the information on a map, such as that in Figure 5.2, into a smaller number of clusters or hot spots is a useful way of synthesising the information,

FIGURE 5.2 Bus Shelters Subjected to Criminal Damage on the Wirral (Newton, 2004)

allowing the user to see the wood for the trees. The rationale behind this process is to identify the grouping together of crimes within certain time periods, in specific locations, that are unlikely to have occurred by chance; in other words the non-random bunching of incidents.

The map in Figure 5.3 draws on the criminal damage to bus stops data discussed above but covers the whole of Merseyside (Newton, 2004). The map depicts hot spots generated by the CrimeStat GIS software package available through MAPS. It uses a technique called Nearest Neighbour Hierarchical (Nnh) clustering that groups points together on the basis of their geographical proximity. The user specifies a maximum 'threshold' distance between the points and the minimum number of points that are required for each cluster. The smaller the inter-point distances, the less likely it is that the points conform to a random distribution.

First-order clusters (not shown on Figure 5.3) represent groups of points that are closer together than the threshold distance and in which there is at least the minimum number of points specified by the user. The first-order clusters are themselves grouped together to form second-order clusters and the latter are grouped together to form third-order clusters in a hierarchical manner. The value of the hierarchical approach lies in its ability to define crime clusters at different scales from a single data set.

The map identifies a single, large, third-order cluster of bus shelter damage on the Wirral and a further five in the rest of Merseyside. These are broad zones of criminal activity that can be used to guide the deployment of patrols at the county level and inform strategic planning and resource allocation. Within each large cluster are nested over 40 smaller second-order hot spots, which can be used

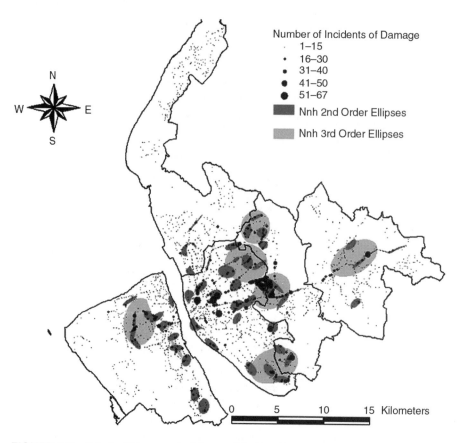

FIGURE 5.3 Criminal Damage to Merseyside Bus Stops: Hot Spots from Crime Analyst (Newton, 2004)

to investigate likely crime generators, and within these even smaller first-order hot spots can be delineated. The latter can be used to guide more site-specific surveillance and target-hardening activity. The combination of detailed information that can pinpoint criminal activity to specific locations and powerful analytical software such as Crimestat enables the user to identify specific crime hot spots, how they relate to other high-crime areas and, for the practitioner, where and when finite resources might best be targeted to reduce crime.

Crime, land use and the social environment

Additional **intelligence** about crime patterns can be gained by revealing the socio-environmental and land-use context within which they occur. The socio-demographic composition of a neighbourhood can have a strong influence on crime. High-crime neighbourhoods tend to be those where guardianship is poor and social cohesion is weak (Kelling and Coles, 1996; Sampson et al., 1997) and those with high levels of concentrated poverty and social disadvantage (Social Exclusion Unit, 1998; Hancock, 2001; Chainey, 2008). These are often communities with relatively high concentrations of both victims and offenders (Bottoms, 2006). Affluent areas tend to have lower crime and fewer offenders residing within them. Relating crime data to information about what communities are like as places enables the end user to explore such relationships, to construct hypotheses about the likely influences on crime and to identify where policy interventions, resources and crime prevention advice might be most effectively deployed.

Use of geo-demographics

Geo-demographic classifications provide a useful means for doing this by contextualising residential areas. They are derived largely from using data from the Population Census and surveys to identify similar types of residential neighbourhood in terms of their demographic, socio-economic, ethnic and housing composition. Most importantly, they can be imported into a GIS to reveal where such areas are located. The distribution of individual offences can then be superimposed upon the geo-demographic backcloth to reveal the overlap, or otherwise, between crime and specific types of community and to identify the number of crimes committed in each type of area. This moves any analysis beyond just identifying crime levels and rates for purely administrative zones (e.g. census wards). The latter typically contain several types of residential neighbourhood, making it that much more difficult to explore links between crime and any one type of neighbourhood. A geo-demographic classification enables the investigator to explore, more directly, links between crime and the social environment.

In Figure 5.4(a) one year's worth of disaggregated burglary data have been mapped directly onto a geo-demographic classification for south central Liverpool. The geo-demographics in this example come from the Super Profiles Classification (Brown et al., 2000). A number of residential neighbourhood types are represented. Three of these are labelled and include:

- a highly disadvantaged cluster referred to as the 'Have Nots'
- areas characterised by an over-representation of younger, single residents, students and transient populations ('Urban Venturers')
- areas with higher levels of owner-occupied housing and prosperity ('Affluent Achievers')

Some types of neighbourhood appear to have concentrations of burglaries, in particular the 'Urban Venturers' and 'Have Nots', while others (e.g. 'Affluent Achievers') appear to have far fewer offences.

Crime rates need to be calculated to compare the risk of victimisation across these neighbourhood types. GIS functionality facilitates this by intersecting the individual burglaries with the Super Profile area types. The outcome of this procedure, referred to as a 'point-in-polygon intersect', is the automatic appending of

(a) Burglary locations by neighbourhood type

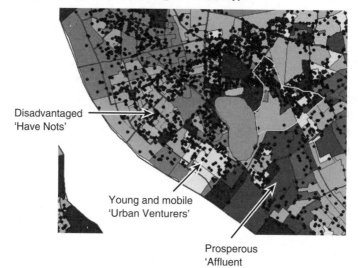

(b) Burglary rates by neighbourhood type

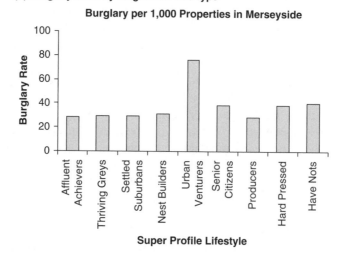

FIGURE 5.4   Relating Burglary to Neighbourhood Type

the relevant Super Profile code to each individual burglary incident. Thus each incident gains a code denoting the types of residential neighbourhood within which it occurred. The burglaries can then be aggregated by neighbourhood type and divided by the number of households in each area to construct a burglary rate.

The outcome of this analysis is shown in Figure 5.4(b), which identifies 'Urban Venturers' as the neighbourhood type with the highest domestic burglary rate. An inspection of the profile for 'Urban Venturers' suggests that this is a neighbourhood type with a high student population (an abundant supply of high value goods to steal), relatively poor levels of guardianship (many single persons, fewer people around during the day) and relatively low social cohesion (ethnically mixed population, high turnover, privately rented accommodation). This is consistent with results from the British Crime Survey, for which the Home Office has been adding geo-demographic identifiers to respondents' postcodes for many years. Using the ACORN geo-demographic classification, the BCS showed that the areas of highest risk for residential burglary included low-income areas (i.e. including social housing), and areas with a mixed social status and an over-representation of single people. Burglary rates in these areas were over twice the national average (Dodd et al., 2004).

Crime risks and the juxtaposition of different types of neighbourhood

As well as pinpointing particular neighbourhood types, geo-demographic maps also identify which types of community border them. This opens up the possibility of analysing how crime levels in a neighbourhood might be affected not only by its own internal social, demographic and land-use characteristics (e.g. housing, social cohesion, presence of offenders), but also by the characteristics of neighbouring areas. Just considering the possible impact of the geographical configuration of different types of neighbourhood on crime opens up some intriguing questions and **hypotheses**. For example:

- Do affluent areas surrounded by socially disadvantaged communities have higher levels of crime than those that border other affluent areas?
- Do disadvantaged areas that are surrounded by affluent areas have lower crime?
- Are the highest crime rates found where disadvantaged areas are at some distance from more affluent areas?
- Where within cities characterised by strong socio-economic divisions do the penalties of higher crime fall – in the disadvantaged areas or in the affluent areas that border them?

Figure 5.5(a) shows the location of cases of burglary and assault in relation to the distribution of affluent and disadvantaged neighbourhoods on the Wirral, Merseyside, in northwest England (Bowers and Hirschfield, 1999). Offences of domestic burglary are represented by a dot and those of assault by an asterisk. It is noticeable that burglaries and assaults occur in both the disadvantaged areas that appear in dark grey on the map and on the affluent side of the border shown in light grey.

Figure 5.5(b) plots the residential location of known offenders for both offences. The distribution of offenders is different from that of the offences in that the offenders are concentrated largely on the deprived side of the boundary. The hypothesis implicit from this map is that it is not just the neighbourhoods internally that make them more or less riskier places, but where they are and what is around them. This would not be apparent without adding a geo-demographic classification to the maps.

(a) Location of offences

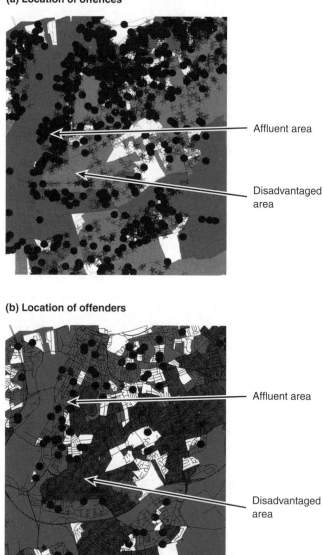

Affluent area

Disadvantaged area

(b) Location of offenders

Affluent area

Disadvantaged area

FIGURE 5.5   Assault and Burglary in Affluent/Disadvantaged Bordering Neighbourhoods

Crime and land use

While geo-demographic classifications contextualise crime maps in terms of neighbourhoods and the social environment, other backcloths can be used that do so in relation to land use, infrastructure and the physical environment (Rengert et al., 2001). For example, the distribution of offences and the location of crime hot spots often make more sense when they are mapped in relation to street lay-outs, building footprints, public open space, service delivery outlets and facilities (e.g. restaurants, pubs, schools, transport termini).

Burglaries involving access by offenders to the rear of properties make more sense when street layouts reveal that it is rows of terraced housing separated by alleyways at the rear that are being victimised. Risks of criminal damage to prop-erty and theft from vehicles can be better understood by mapping offence loca-tions directly on to a digital aerial photographic background. These can be used to visualise victimised sites and to identify if these are next to open space or shielded from view by the presence of deciduous trees.

Violence and alcohol supply points

Another example is that of establishments that sell alcohol to the public. These have specific locations and can serve as a backdrop to maps showing hot spots for violence against the person, criminal damage and disorder. Figure 5.6 gives exam-ples of different types of GIS analysis carried out in a recent evaluation of the impact on crime of the Licensing Act reforms in England and Wales. The Licensing Act gave the freedom for licensed premises to apply to be open for up to 24 hours and the aim of the evaluation was to search for evidence of any changes in the volume and timing of crime and disorder in and surrounding pubs and night clubs in five case study areas. The results from this analysis are discussed extensively elsewhere (Hough and Hunter, 2008; Newton et al., 2008a).

Figure 5.6(a) shows the location of pubs, bars and night clubs in Nottingham displayed as a series of points. The shaded ellipse in the centre of the map was generated using crime hot spotting software but is actually a 'pubs and clubs cluster' delineating the City's area of concentrated drinking. New 'pub cluster' geographies were defined in each of the case study areas and closely monitored for any changes in the volume and timing of offences occurring within them. GIS software was also used to define annular buffer zones surrounding each establishment. These are shown in Figure 5.6(b). These were used to count the number of offences in each 50-metre ring by hour of the day to search for evidence of both temporal and geographical displacement of crime and disorder. Figure 5.7(a) shows hot spots for violence against the person and Figure 5.7(b) those for criminal damage, both in relation to the distribution of pubs and clubs.

Interestingly, many of the hot spots for violence against the person (Figure 5.7(b)) coincide with the concentration of pubs, bars and night clubs. Hot spots for criminal damage (5.7(b)), on the other hand, form in a number of areas with no or very few licensed premises. Further analysis of the timing of incidents revealed that criminal damage hot spots peaked at times of the day when many bars were quiet or indeed closed, suggesting that factors other than late-night drinking were fuelling this form of criminal and anti-social behaviour (Newton et al., 2008b).

(a) Hot spot demarcating area of concentrated drinking

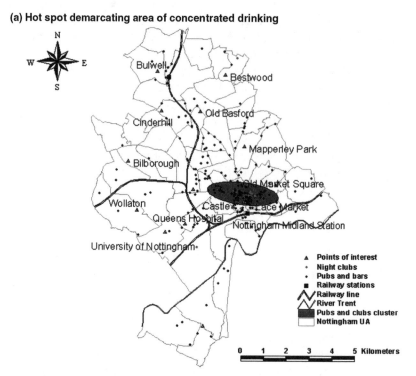

(b) Fifty-metre buffer zones surrounding licensed premises

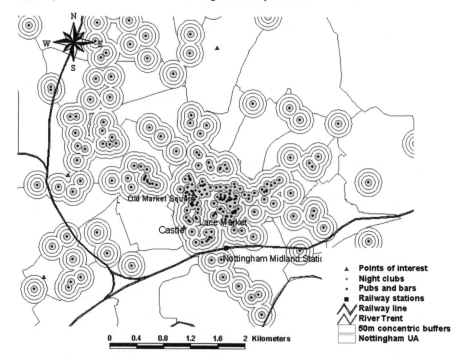

FIGURE 5.6   Licensed Premises in Nottingham

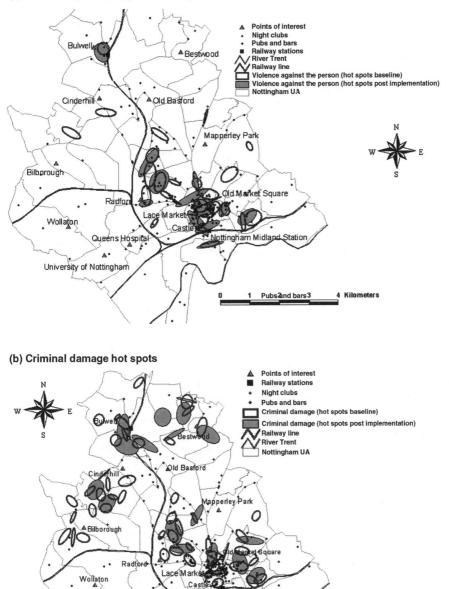

(a) Violence against the person hot spots

(b) Criminal damage hot spots

FIGURE 5.7 Licensed Premises and Crime Hot Spots in Nottingham (Newton et al., 2008b)

NEW FRONTIERS: RELATING CRIME TO CRIME PREVENTION

In addition to the social, physical and land-use environment, policies and crime prevention measures also influence crime patterns and need to be considered. Effective crime reduction measures can reduce crime, often with either no or minimal displacement (Bowers and Johnson, 2003), and offer protection to communities not immediately subjected to an intervention, a process referred to as 'diffusion of benefit' (Clarke and Weisburd, 1994). However, unlike the recording of criminal offences, which is guided by a system of crime codes (e.g. Home Office classifications), there are no commonly adopted conventions or coding schemes for recording policy interventions. Indeed, there is no statutory requirement to register policy interventions as there is with other events, such as births, marriages, infectious diseases and deaths. In many ways, this is indicative of a preoccupation with collecting data about the problems (crime, anti-social behaviour) and information about the context in which they occur (areas with poor natural surveillance, known crime generators), and a lack of attention to gathering primary data about policy interventions and the attributes of the responses to crime.

Potential uses of data on crime prevention activity

The recording of details about policy interventions remains sporadic and inconsistent. Typically, primary data about policy interventions have to be captured afresh each time there is an evaluation study, and this is time-consuming, expensive and wasteful. The absence of policy data also makes it difficult to bring crime prevention data into the mapping and analysis of crime. However, it is possible to envisage the research hypotheses that can be formulated if such data were available. Some of these are listed in Box 5.3.

BOX 5.3

QUESTIONS ABOUT THE RELATIONSHIP BETWEEN CRIME AND CRIME PREVENTION

- How geographically concentrated is crime prevention in different areas?
- How do crime prevention measures correspond to the location and timing of different types of crime?
- Is there a variation in crime prevention investment across communities with similar levels and patterns of crime?
- How far is there an 'inverse prevention law' (i.e. where areas with lower crime receive more attention)?

- How can we develop new measures, indices and tools to analyse the distribution of crime prevention measures and relate them to crime?
- How transferable are crime pattern analysis techniques (clustering and hot-spotting) to crime prevention?
- How can we measure the coalescence between crime prevention and crime risk?
- How can we better align crime prevention and crime risk?
- What effect would good quality data on crime prevention activity have on resource allocation and policy development?

The questions in Box 5.3 mirror many of the questions asked of crime data, although the extent to which it is appropriate to apply crime pattern analysis techniques to policy data needs to be researched.

A LIVERPOOL CASE STUDY

Several studies, conducted in northern England, have involved capturing data on crime prevention activity and relating this to recorded crime, not only geographically (Bowers et al., 2004), but also at the level of the individual property (Hirschfield and Newton, 2008). In a recent study, carried out in Liverpool, three years' worth of data on publicly-funded target hardening was obtained for each property offered assistance (Newton et al. 2008c). Each record contained:

- the full postal address
- information on the measures installed (locks, bolts, gates)
- the date of installation
- the amount spent on each installation.

The address for each property was matched against the National Land Property Gazetteer (NLPG) to generate a Unique Property Reference Number (UNPR) for each address. Address-referenced police recorded crime data on domestic burglary were also obtained for the same time period and UPRNs generated using the NLPG. The UPRNs were then used to join the burglary and target-hardening data for each property. This produced a very rich but complex database that enabled different subsets of properties to be defined and several scenarios to be investigated. The UPRNs also enabled incidents of repeat burglary and indeed repeat target hardening to be defined. The subgroups are listed in Box 5.4.

Figure 5.8 and Table 5.3 illustrate some of the analyses that can be undertaken. Figure 5.8 summarises the distribution of burglary across Liverpool for the period July 2005 through to December 2007. The map was produced using Kernel Density Estimation and shows hot spots of different intensities – the darker the shading the more intense the hot spot. Given the lengthy time period that these hot spots represent, they can be considered relatively stable.

The map is somewhat unusual because it also shows the location of properties that received target hardening shown as points. Much of the target hardening appears to have taken place in hot spot areas, particularly the most intense hot spots, although a sizeable number of properties outside hot spot areas were also protected.

Table 5.3 takes the analysis further by cross-referencing properties in the various subgroups (see Box 5.4) by their presence in the burglary hot spots. Each burgled property is assigned an intensity value corresponding to the intensity of the hot spot within which it is located, and five equal groups or quintiles are generated with one-fifth of burgled properties overall occupying each intensity quintile. The distribution of properties across the quintiles is then tabulated for each status group.

There was some indication that target hardening might have been less effective in the most intense burglary hot spots. This is reflected by the fact that 40% of properties 'burgled, target hardened and then burgled again' (group 5) and 33% of those 'not burgled, target hardened and subsequently burgled' (group 6) were found in these areas; markedly above the 20% even share. Significantly, 54% of the properties that had been target hardened, despite not having been burgled within the monitoring period either prior to or following target hardening (group 2), were located in the hot spot with the highest burglary risk (i.e. group 5). This possibly accounts for why they were target hardened even though they had not been victimised.

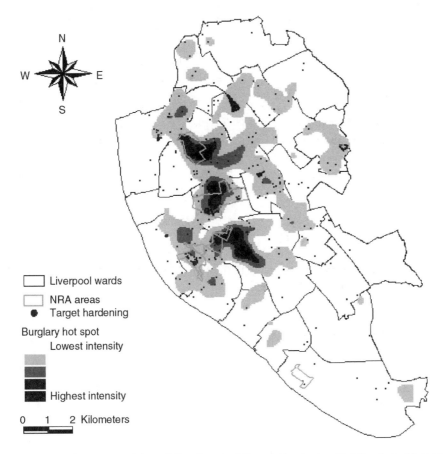

FIGURE 5.8 Superimposition of Burglary and Target Hardening Hot Spots in Liverpool

What this analysis reveals is a clear spatial dimension, not only in the allocation of target hardening to individual properties across the city, but also in levels of prior burglary risk and subsequent outcomes. None of this would be possible without adding crime prevention to the mapping and analysis of crime data. The more interesting question is whether the availability of such intelligence, updated at regular intervals, would make any material difference to future decisions on how to allocate resources for target hardening.

The incorporation of crime prevention is undoubtedly a new frontier in crime analysis. However, undertaking this is far from straightforward. The analysis shown in Table 5.3 was the culmination of considerable data processing and cross-referencing, involving the joining of target-hardening and burglary data, and their integration with sophisticated spatial analysis software using a GIS. There are many unresolved issues around the practicalities of mainstreaming such analyses. These include the need to develop a national classification of policy interventions, the identification of an agency or body responsible for implementing data capture

TABLE 5.3 The Concentration of Property Status Groups in Liverpool's Burglary Hot Spots

		Hot spots					
		Lowest risk<--------->Highest risk					
Group	Description	1	2	3	4	5	Total
1	All properties burgled	20.0	20.0	20.0	20.0	20.0	100 (N=15088)
2	Burgled and never target hardened	21.5	21.0	20.2	19.4	18.0	100 (N=11540)
3	Never burgled, target hardened, no subsequent burglary	2.2	3.5	8.1	32.1	54.1	100 (N=1466)
4	Prior burglary, then target hardened, no subsequent burglary	6.3	7.5	14.5	32.1	39.6	100 (N=159)
5	Prior burglary, then target hardened, subsequently burgled	10.0	15.0	20.0	15.0	40.0	100 (N=20)
6	No prior burglary, target hardened, then subsequently burgled	7.4	16.0	20.2	23.4	33.0	100 (N=94)
	All properties burgled and target hardened	*7.0*	*11.0*	*16.8*	*27.8*	*37.4*	*100 (N=273)*

and, crucially, sufficient funding to pay not only for the creation of databases, but also for maintaining, updating and archiving such information.

SUMMARY

This chapter has taken a broad look at the mapping and analysis of crime. It has introduced dimensions of crime that are not measurable solely through the use of police recorded crime data but are, nevertheless, important in contextualising crime. The relevance of crime analysis to stakeholders beyond the police and community safety partnerships has been explored and a typology of crime analyses has been presented. The varied nature of the latter reinforces the fact that there are multiple objectives in undertaking crime analysis that reflect the roles, interests and concerns of the various stakeholders.

The utility and limitations of recorded crime data have been touched upon briefly and the practical implications of choosing different scales and the units of analysis have been discussed.

The valuable role that Geographical Information Systems can play in crime analysis was illustrated through a series of case studies. These demonstrated the extra insights that can be gained by overlaying crime data with information on land use and different types of residential neighbourhood, as revealed through geo-demographic classifications.

Finally, the inclusion, in crime analysis, of data on crime prevention was discussed. This is a highly under-researched area but one that displays considerable potential for the formulation and testing of hypotheses about the alignment between the nature and deployment of crime prevention measures and the timing and location of crime. The extent to which crime pattern analysis techniques can be adapted to detect patterns in the distribution of crime prevention activities was highlighted as an area for future research.

■ Study Questions/Activities for Students

1 Study the crime analyses typology in Table 5.1 and ask where you would place yourself.

2 Look up the meaning of the term 'ecological fallacy' and discuss why this might have implications for the use of geo-demographics in crime analysis.

3 Think of where you live and where you go for a night out. Can you identify any crime opportunities in the areas? If so, what would they be?

RESOURCES

Sources relevant to some of the issues raised in this chapter fall into two broad categories, namely: crime analysis and GIS and crime mapping.

Crime analysis

For a clearly written overview of the field of crime analysis, see Clarke, R. and Eck, J. (2003) *Becoming a Problem-Solving Crime Analyst in 55 Steps*. Jill Dando Institute of Crime Science, University College London (downloadable from www.jdi.ucl.ac.uk).

A series of useful guides on crime analysis in a policing context has been produced by the US Department of Justice. The guides produced by the DOJ's Office of Community Oriented Policing Services (COPS) are available from www.cops.usdoj.gov.

GIS and crime mapping

Excellent overviews of the field include Chainey, S. and Ratcliffe, J.H. (2005) *GIS and Crime Mapping*, Sydney: Federation Press; Boba, R. (2005) *Crime Analysis and Crime Mapping*, London: Sage.

An excellent discussion on the identification of different types of hot spot can be found in Ratcliffe, J. (2004) The Hot Spot Matrix: A Framework for the Spatio-temporal Targeting of Crime Reduction. *Police, Practice and Research*, 5(1): 5–23.

Innovations in hot spot analysis can be found in Johnson, S. and Bowers, K. (2004) The Burglary as Clue to the Future: The Beginnings of Prospective Hot Spotting. *European Journal of Criminology*, 1(2): 237–255; Johnson, S.D., Bowers, K. and Pease, K. (2005) Predicting the Future or Summarising the Past? Crime Mapping as Anticipation. In M. Smith and N. Tilley (eds), *Launching Crime Science*. Cullompton: Willan.

Mapping and Analysis for Public Safety (MAPS), National Institute of Justice, USA, provides a plethora of material on crime mapping and analysis plus a listserver: www.ojp.usdoj.gov/nij/maps/. The International Association of Crime Analysts website, www.iaca.net, houses information on conferences, publications and training materials. A listserver for analysts is provided. In the UK, the Home Office Toolkits are worth consulting, especially the page on Focus Areas: http://webarchive.nationalarchives.gov.uk/20100413151441/http://crimereduction.homeoffice.gov.uk/toolkits/fa00.htm.

A wide range of UK social and demographic data for small areas, useful for Crime Environment Analyses, can be downloaded from the Office for National Statistics (ONS) Neighbourhood Statistics website: www.neighbourhood.statistics.gov.uk.

The Association of Geographic Information (AGI) host a Crime and Disorder Special Interest Group, which can be found at: www.agi.org.uk.

REFERENCES

Armitage, R. (2000) An Evaluation of Secured by Design Housing in West Yorkshire. Home Office Policing and Reducing Crime Unit Briefing Note 7/00. September.

Armitage, R. (2006) Predicting and Preventing: Developing a Risk Assessment Mechanism for Residential Housing. *Crime Prevention and Community Safety: An International Journal*, 8(3): 137–149.

Audit Commission (2006) *Crime Recording 2005: Improving the Quality of Crime Records in Police Authorities and Forces in England and Wales*. London: Audit Commission.

Bottoms, A.E. (2006) Incivilities, Offence, and Social Order in Residential Communities. In A. Von Hirsch and A.P. Simester (eds), *Incivilities: Regulating Offensive Behaviour*. Oxford: Hart Publishing.

Bowers, K.J. and Hirschfield, A. (1999) Exploring Links Between Crime and Disadvantage in North West England: an Analysis Using Geographical Information Systems. *International Journal of Geographical Information Science*, 13(2): 159–184.

Bowers, K.J. and Johnson, S.D. (2003) Measuring the Geographical Displacement of Crime. *Journal of Quantitative Criminology*, 19(3): 275–301.

Bowers, K.J., Johnson, S.D. and Hirschfield, A. (2004) The Measurement of Crime Prevention Intensity and its Impact on Levels of Crime. *British Journal of Criminology*, 44(3): 419–440.

Brantingham, P. and Brantingham, P. (1993) Environmental Routine and Situation: Towards a Pattern Theory of Crime. *Advances in Criminological Theory*, (5): 259–294.

Brantingham, P.L. and Brantingham, P.J. (1995) Criminality of Place: Crime Generators and Crime Attractors. *European Journal on Criminal Policy and Research*, 3: 5–26.

Brown, P.J.B., Hirschfield, A. and Batey, P.W.J (2000) Adding Value to Census Data: Public Sector Applications of the Super Profiles Geodemographic Typology. *Cities and Regions*, X: 19–32.

Chainey, S. (2008) Identifying Priority Neighbourhoods Using the Vulnerable Localities Index. *Policing*, 2(2): 196–209.

Chainey, S. and Ratcliffe, J. (2005) *GIS and Crime Mapping*. Chichester: Wiley.

Clarke, R.V. and Weisburd, D. (1994) Diffusion of Crime Control Benefits: Observations on the Reverse of Displacement. In R.V. Clarke (ed.), *Crime Prevention Studies* (Vol. 2). Monsey, NY: Willow Tree Press.

Cohen, L. and Felson, M. (1979) Social Change and Crime Rate Trends: A Routine Activity Approach. *American Sociological Review*, 44: 588–608.

Dodd, T., Nicholas, S., Povey, D. and Walker, A. (2004) *Crime in England and Wales 2003/2004*. Home Office Statistical Bulletin 10/04. London: Home Office.

Felson, M. and Clarke, R.V. (1998) *Opportunity Makes the Thief: Practical Theory for Crime Prevention*. Home Office Policing and Reducing Crime Unit Police Research Series Paper 98. London: Home Office.

Groff, E. and La Vigne, N. (2001) Mapping an Opportunity Surface of Residential Burglary. *Journal of Research in Crime and Delinquency*, 38(3): 257–278.

Hancock, L. (2001) *Community, Crime and Disorder: Safety and Regeneration in Urban Neighbourhoods*. Basingstoke: Palgrave.

Hirschfield, A. and Bowers, K.J. (1997) The Effect of Social Cohesion on Levels of Recorded Crime in Disadvantaged Areas. *Urban Studies*, 34(8): 1275–1295.

Hirschfield, A. and Newton, A. (2008) The Crime–Crime Prevention Relationship: A Manchester Case Study. *Built Environment*, 34(1): 104–120.

Home Office, Association of Chief Police Officers (ACPO), Association of Police Authorities (APA) (2007) *The National Standard for Incident Recording (NSIR): Counting Rules, Instructions for Police Forces in England and Wales*. London: Home Office, ACPO and APA.

Hough, M. and Hunter, G. (2008) The 2003 Licensing Act's Impact on Crime and Disorder: An Evaluation. *Criminology and Criminal Justice*, 8(3): 239–260.

Hough, M. and Maxfield, M. (2007) *Surveying Crime in the Twenty-first Century*. Collompton: Willan Publishing.

Johnson, S.D., Bowers, K.J., Young, C.A. and Hirschfield, A. (2001) Uncovering the True Picture: Evaluating Crime Reduction Initiatives using Disaggregate Crime Data. *Crime Prevention and Community Safety: An International Journal*, 3(4): 7–24.

Kelling, G.L. and Coles, C.M. (1996) *Fixing Broken Windows: Restoring Order and Fixing Crime in Our Communities*. New York: Free Press.

Kershaw, C., Nicholas, S. and Walker, A. (2008) *Crime in England and Wales 2007/08: Findings from the British Crime Survey and Police Recorded Crime*. London: Home Office.

Longley, P.A., Goodchild, M.F., Maguire, D.J. and Rhind, D.W. (2005) *Geographic Information Systems and Science* (second edition). Chichester: John Wiley & Sons.

Newman, O. (1972) *Defensible Space: Crime Prevention Through Urban Design*. New York: Macmillan.

Newton, A.D. (2004) Crime and Disorder on Buses: Towards an Evidence Base for Effective Crime Prevention. Unpublished PhD thesis, Department of Civic Design, University of Liverpool.

Newton, A.D., Hirschfield, A., Armitage, R., Rogerson, M., Monchuk, L. and Wilcox, A. (2008a) *Evaluation of the Licensing Act: Measuring Crime and Disorder in and around Licensed Premises. Research Study SRG/05/07. Final Report Prepared for the Home Office*. Huddersfield: University of Huddersfield.

Newton, A.D., Hirschfield, A., Armitage, R., Rogerson, M., Monchuk, L. and Wilcox, A. (2008b) *Evaluation of the Licensing Act: Measuring Crime and Disorder in and around Licensed*

Premises. Research Study SRG/05/07. Final Report Prepared for the Home Office. Annex 5, Nottingham. Huddersfield: University of Huddersfield.

Newton, A.D., Rogerson, M. and Hirschfield, A. (2008c) Relating Target Hardening to Burglary Risk: Experiences from Liverpool. *Papers from the British Criminology Conference: An Online Journal Published by the British Society of Criminology*, 8: 153–174.

Nicholas, S., Kershaw, C. and Walker, A. (2007) *Crime in England and Wales 2005/2007.* London: Home Office.

Osbourne, D. and Wernicke, S. (2003) *Introduction to Crime Analysis: Basic Resources for Criminal Justice Practice.* New York: Haworth Press.

Pease, K. (1998) *Repeat Victimisation: Taking Stock.* Crime Prevention and Detection Series 90. London: Home Office.

Ratcliffe, J. (ed.) (2004) *Strategic Thinking in Criminal Intelligence.* Cullompton: Willan Publishing.

Ratcliffe, J.H. and McCullagh, M.J. (2001) Chasing Ghosts? Police perception of high crime areas. *British Journal of Criminology*, 41(2): 330–341.

Rengert, G., Mattson, M. and Henderson, K. (2001) *Campus Security: Situational Crime Prevention in High-density Environments.* Monsey, NY: Criminal Justice Press.

Rogerson, M. and Christmann, K. (2004) *Crime, Fear of Crime and Quality of Life, Identifying and Responding to Problems.* NDC National Evaluation Research Report 35. Sheffield: CRESR.

Sampson, R.J., Raudenbush, S.W. and Earls, F. (1997) Neighborhoods and Violent Crime: A Multilevel Study of Collective Efficacy. *Science*, 227: 918–924.

Social Exclusion Unit (1998) *Bringing Britain Together: A National Strategy for Neighbourhood Renewal.* CMD Paper 4045. London: HMSO.

Walker, A., Flatley, J., Kershaw, K. and Moon, D. (2009) Crime in England and Wales 2008/09: Findings from the British Crime Survey and Police Recorded Crime. *Home Office Statistical Bulletin 11/09*, Volume 1. London: Home Office.

Wikstrom, P.O. and Sampson, R.J. (2006) *The Explanation of Crime: Context, Mechanisms and Development.* Cambridge: Cambridge University Press.

Wiles, P. and Costello, A. (2000) *The 'Road to Nowhere': The Evidence for Travelling Criminals.* Home Office Research Study 207. London: Research, Development and Statistics Directorate, Home Office.

SIX
SENSITIVE SURVEY RESEARCH: AN OXYMORON?

JO DEAKIN AND JON SPENCER

Chapter Contents

This chapter:

- Assesses the suitability of surveys when dealing with sensitive topics
- Examines how the British Crime Survey approaches sensitive topics
- Introduces the design of research tools for sensitive topics
- Details conducting ethical research with children and other vulnerable groups
- Offers examples of survey research on sensitive topics and with hard-to-reach groups

INTRODUCTION

A few days after the 'MPs' expenses scandal' hits the headlines in 2009, a team of researchers sit around a table. Their task is to devise a suitable method to investigate expenses claimed by academics visiting conferences. After agreeing on the key areas of investigation (what respondents would and would not claim for, what they consider to be dishonest, their own experiences of 'fiddling' claims, and views on appropriate penalties or punishments), the researchers begin to look at suitable methodological approaches. They know the data could be embarrassing for the respondents, have legal, procedural or disciplinary ramifications, or have wider implications for the reputation of academics. After weighing up the different approaches, the researchers decide on a large, national sample of academics at various stages of their careers and agree that the **survey** method will generate the required data. However, a key point of concern is whether a questionnaire will allow the researchers to treat this difficult subject sensitively.

So, is it possible to gather sensitive research data through a large-scale survey? Quantitative survey research has been maligned for failing to deal sensitively with research topics and respondents, and, in particular, for employing predefined terms and a static agenda (Reinharz, 1979; Fox Keller, 1980; Oakley, 1981). These criticisms are especially problematic where sensitive issues and vulnerable populations are concerned.

It would appear, on first impression, that the survey is not a suitable choice of method for a sensitive research topic, or where the respondents are vulnerable. However, in this chapter we explore how surveys *can* be an acceptable method to gather data on sensitive issues. We review the literature on survey methodology and conducting sensitive research with vulnerable populations, and provide a brief guide to devising and administering a survey on a sensitive issue.

WHAT IS A SENSITIVE TOPIC?

The term 'sensitive research' is used to describe taboo, or difficult, topics, for example victimisation or deviant behaviour. The term may be used where research elicits the views of vulnerable or 'powerless' groups such as children (see Box 6.1). In criminology and victimology, many of the central **research questions** are of a 'sensitive' nature because the topics may be difficult for respondents to discuss, can cause distress and may elicit information that can be damaging to the respondent with serious implications for the respondent, their communities and, on occasions, the researcher.

BOX 6.1

A FOCUS ON RESEARCH WITH CHILDREN

Research with children presents specific ethical and methodological issues (Hood et al., 1996; Mahon et al., 1996; Morrow and Richards, 1996). The British Society of Criminology's guidelines, *Code of Ethics for Researchers in the Field of Criminology* (2006), reinforces the need for caution to be exercised with research concerning children:

> Researchers should consider carefully the possibility that the research experience may be a disturbing one, particularly for those who are vulnerable by virtue of factors such as age, social status, or powerlessness and should seek to minimise such disturbances. (BSC, 2006: 4.1)

Morrow and Richards (1996) argue that the difference between research with children and adults can be reduced to two perceptions that adults hold of children. First, that children are vulnerable and adults should take responsibility for them and, second, that children are not as competent as adults (Morrow and Richards, 1996). Further, they argue that these perceptions are reinforced by legal notions of the child as powerless and irresponsible. These perceptions have implications for gaining consent for research, the choice of methods and the interpretation of data.

Children are potentially vulnerable in two respects: first, because of their comparative physical weakness and lack of experience and knowledge; and second, 'because of their total lack of political and economic power and their lack of civil rights' (Lansdown, 1994: 35). According to Lansdown, it is children's lack of civil status that has not been adequately addressed as a factor that produces vulnerability.

Some researchers have assumed that children lack the competence to provide valid sociological data (see Morrow and Richards, 1996). American researchers, Fine and Sandstrom (1988), for example, have likened the knowledge gained from children during participant observation to that gained from kittens, and fear that an adult interpretation of the data may be inaccurate. A further question of competence is raised around children's informed consent to the research (Kinaird, 1985). This requires a respondent to 'voluntarily agree to participate in a research project, based on a full disclosure of pertinent information' (Tymchuk, 1992: 128). However, in the case of research with children, who are usually not seen as competent enough to give consent, consent must come from a parent, teacher or guardian.

> In the UK, consent is usually taken to mean consent from parents or those 'in loco parentis', and in this respect children are to a large extent seen as their parents' property, devoid of the right to say no to the research. (Morrow and Richards, 1996: 94)

Research with children must address the fundamental problem associated with gaining informed consent: can children be informed enough of the implications of the research to give informed consent?

Lee (1993: 4) argues that sensitive research should be understood as that 'which potentially poses a substantial threat to those who are or have been involved in it'. Lee defines the threat in three ways:

> The first is where the research poses as an 'intrusive threat', dealing with areas which are private, stressful or sacred. The second relates to the study of deviance and social control and involves the possibility that information may be revealed which is stigmatising or discriminating in some way. Finally, research is often problematic when it impinges on political alignments, if 'political' is taken in its widest sense to refer to the vested interests of powerful persons or institutions, or the exercise of coercion or domination. In these situations researchers often trespass into areas which are controversial or involve social conflict. (Lee, 1993: 4)

Within criminological research **hard-to-reach groups** are not readily available or able or willing to be 'the researched' and so have been under-represented. Engaging positively with hard-to-reach groups in order to give them 'a voice' in research requires a particular set of methodological skills that we consider below. See Box 6.2 for the Home Office definition and examples of hard-to-reach groups.

BOX 6.2

DEFINITION OF HARD-TO-REACH GROUPS

Taken from the Home Office crime reduction website, a hard-to-reach group can be any group which is difficult to access for any reason, such as:

- physical inaccessibility (e.g. older frail people)
- language (e.g. first-generation immigrants to the UK)
- cultural perceptions and traditions (e.g. disadvantaged young people)
- social expectations (e.g. children and young people who are often not considered an appropriate consultee and who often also do not consider themselves as likely to be taken seriously)

Hard-to-reach groups could include:

- homeless people
- children and young people
- drug users
- gay men, lesbian women, transsexual and transgendered people
- minority ethnic communities (particular sections of)
- victims of domestic abuse
- older people (especially older frail people and isolated older people)
- travellers
- asylum seekers

- people with learning difficulties
- people with disabilities
- people with mental health problems
- faith communities
- people who travel or commute into the area
- small businesses
- rural communities
- tourists

Source: www.crimereduction.homeoffice.gov.uk/toolkits/p03110701.htm

SURVEY RESEARCH

Survey research involves the systematic collection of large quantities of data, by means of questionnaires and/or interviews, from a broad **sample** of a target population. A range of complex issues are involved, including sampling methods, developing meaningful research instruments (questionnaires, interviews), administering the survey, maximising response rates, and a variety of ethical considerations (protection of respondents, confidentiality, etc.) (see, for example, Seale, 2004; Bachman and Schutt, 2008; Fowler, 2009). Here we provide an overview of survey research, signpost key areas for further reading, and focus more closely on the use of surveys in the area of sensitive topics and with hard-to-reach groups.

Surveys are an important tool of the social scientist in collecting, categorising and quantifying data. They allow the researcher to frame a research problem using a structured set of questions. Surveys are most commonly used to answer questions about the extent of beliefs or experience and can be used with a whole population or a sample of a population to provide data that can be generalised across a larger group. For this purpose, the sample or cross-section must accurately reflect the complexity and heterogeneity of the population to be studied. A cross-section of the prison population, for example, may be surveyed to gain information that can be applied to the whole of the prison population. A prison-based sample must reflect the characteristics of the whole prison population as closely as possible, including gender, Black and Minority Ethnic populations, those serving different sentence lengths for different types of crime, and so on. A prison-based survey must also take account of differing levels of literacy (a self-completion questionnaire would not be suitable for those who cannot read and write) and should be translated where necessary. An example of such a survey is the Measuring the Quality of Prison Life Survey (MQPL) which surveys a sample of prisoners in each prison in relation to a number of key elements of prison life, including, trust, respect, fairness, order and safety (see Ross et al., 2008).

The aim of survey research may be to generate statistics to describe the characteristics of a population, known as descriptive statistics (e.g. the extent of physical violence suffered by children), or to explore the correlation between two variables, known as analytic statistics (e.g. the relationship between the extent of physical violence suffered and the level of fear of violence experienced by children). The statistics generated are often used to inform policy- and decision-making.

CRITICISMS OF SURVEYS

The disadvantages of a quantitative survey methodology largely centre around five claims:

1 That the complexities of social data cannot reasonably be measured or recorded using an intrinsically positivistic method (Cicourel, 1964).

2 That the survey method assumes respondents all understand and interpret the world around them in the same way, as if one were measuring a natural, unthinking phenomena (Schutz, 1962).

3 That the meanings and definitions people assign to their experiences are ignored through the use of a structured method (Oakley, 1981; Cicourel, 1982), creating a 'static' image of social experience (Blumer, 1956).

4 That they present an obstacle to open discussion and prevent flexibility and spontaneity (Reinharz, 1979; Fox Keller, 1980; Oakley, 1981).

5 That where surveys involve interviews, the influence of the interviewer and the location of the interview significantly distort responses (Phillips, 1971).

Marsh (1982) counters these claims by arguing that when surveys are well designed and properly administered they make a key contribution to our under-standing of the social world. She suggests that it is a particular style of survey research, known as *smash 'n' grab*, which has resulted in the bad press associated with this method. For Marsh, *smash 'n' grab* refers to the process whereby researchers design research instruments, undertake fieldwork and analyse data within a very short time frame, literally 'smashing' into the field, 'grabbing' data and exiting quickly. The result is a hastily developed, carelessly designed and poorly implemented survey.

The questionnaire is the most heavily criticised element of survey research. Questionnaires conducted in interview form are accused of failing to acknowledge the respondents' or the researchers' experiences. It is argued that such an approach objectifies the respondent as data while their subjective experiences and personal meanings become lost in the process (Oakley, 1981). Self-completion question-naires that do not require direct contact between the researcher and the respond-ents are viewed as generating detached, stilted data and preventing 'an interactive process' (Kennedy Bergen, 1993: 203).

However, problems with questionnaires, and the survey method more generally, are not insurmountable, as Kelly (1990) demonstrates with the use of questionnaires in her research on child sexual assault. With a background in **qualitative research**, Kelly's transition towards **quantitative methods** came as a result of experimenting with different approaches suitable for answering particularly sensitive research questions. She recognised the significance of collecting quantitative data from large groups of respondents to answer questions about the *extent* of personal experience, and began to explore the survey method. However, for a survey to deal with sensitive issues ethically, it must allow for subjective definitions and experience, and create space for views to be expressed (Kelly, 1990). Since most surveys work on predefined categories and tick-box style answers, Kelly needed to rethink the traditional survey style to fit her sensitive topic. Kelly's questionnaire, in addressing these problems, allowed respondents to define their own experiences and provided support for participants as required, thereby minimising distress.

Perhaps most importantly, the research team spent several days prior to administering the questionnaire working in the participating institutions to facilitate links and develop relationships. This type of participatory approach to research allows researchers to begin to understand the research environment and become known to potential respondents. Through participation, researchers can gain the respondents' trust, provide appropriate support and have an active role in facilitating change. Even when self-completion questionnaires are the chosen method, the process doesn't have to be detached and stilted. Engaging with the participants in the research environment before and after collecting the data can encourage an interactive process that values the meanings people assign to their experiences and provides support.

The value of the survey method lies in its ability to gather large amounts of data to reveal the extent of a phenomenon. In so doing, it does *not* have to adhere to the stilted, bullish image it has so often been associated with. For the most part, the charges levelled at the survey are failings of the smash 'n' grab method; they are not failings of *all* surveys. Perhaps questionnaires will always have elements of inflexibility in their stable agenda and predefined categories, but in sensitive research, these elements have probably been derived from a qualitative **pilot study** conducted to explore the area.

LARGE-SCALE SURVEYS: THE BRITISH CRIME SURVEY AND ITS APPROACH TO SENSITIVE TOPICS

The British Crime Survey (BCS) provides annual data about the nature and extent of crime and victimisation. The survey collects data about individual experiences of victimisation and the information gathered informs government policy. In terms of sensitive research, the BCS has it all: taboo topics (such as sexual assault and domestic violence); vulnerable populations (children); responsibility to include hard-to-reach groups; and the potential to reveal incriminating information. The survey consists of a set of core 'modules' that are asked of all respondents in face-to-face interviews, a set of secondary modules asked of sub-samples of respondents in the interview, and a final set of self-completion modules for all respondents. The self-completion modules deal with the most sensitive issues addressed in the survey. So how does the BCS approach questions on topics that may be considered particularly sensitive, such as domestic violence and sexual assault?

In the 2007/08 BCS, the questions dealing with domestic violence and sexual assault were located in the self-completion module entitled 'Domestic violence and sexual assault'. All respondents over the age of 16 are asked to complete this section. The module comprised 24 pages of questions covering aspects of the respondents' experiences of and attitudes to domestic violence and sexual assault. The questions on the 'Domestic violence and sexual assault' module are considered to be too sensitive to be read out in a face-to-face interview and are completed on a laptop. This approach is intended to minimise embarrassment to the respondent and improve the reporting rate. The questions are carefully phrased, free from jargon and easily understood by respondents of all ages (see Box 6.3), and reiterate that the respondent does not have to answer the questions:

> The next few questions are about serious sexual assaults, such as rape and indecent assault that can affect both men and women. Although the language used is very explicit and direct, this is because the Home Office needs to understand how common different types of serious sexual assault are and how best to deal with them.

> Remember, if the questions upset you in any way you can just pass by them by pressing 'Don't wish to answer'. However, we hope you will continue to the end.

BOX 6.3

DOMESTIC VIOLENCE AND SEXUAL ASSUALT MODULE

Thinking about ANY relationships you have had since you were aged 16, has any partner ever done any of the following things to you? By partner, we mean any boyfriend or girlfriend as well as a husband or wife.

1   Prevented you from having your fair share of the household money
2   Stopped you from seeing friends and relatives
3   Repeatedly belittled you to the extent that you felt worthless
4   Frightened you, by threatening to hurt you or someone close to you
5   Pushed you, held you down or slapped you
6   Kicked, bit or hit you with a fist or something else, or thrown something at you
7   Choked or tried to strangle you
8   Threatened you with a weapon, for example a stick or a knife
9   Threatened to kill you
10 Used a weapon against you, for example a stick or a knife
11 Used some other kind of force against you
12 None of these
13 Have never had a partner/been in a relationship
14 Don't know/can't remember
15 Don't wish to answer

In addition, a number of procedural safeguards were put in place to ensure an ethical approach. For example, new researchers are required to attend full briefing sessions and further refresher courses are compulsorily attended by the more experienced researchers. Confidentiality of data is ensured, and advice on how to obtain further help is offered to respondents as necessary.

GENERATING SURVEY DATA ON SENSITIVE TOPICS AND WITH VULNERABLE GROUPS

We now consider how to use surveys and questionnaires to produce ethically sound data on sensitive topics and with hard-to-reach groups. There is a significant literature dedicated solely to the theory and practice of survey research and this includes consideration of designing questions, developing sampling frames, dealing with non-responses and processing data. Here, we outline key points for consideration before undertaking sensitive survey research and show how these work in action by providing two examples of surveys that we have worked on. One of our examples, 'The Children and Young People's Safety Survey' (Gallagher et al., 1998), involves a vulnerable population and a sensitive topic, and the other, 'Public Attitudes to Sex Offenders' (Brown et al., 2007), concerns a particularly emotive and taboo topic. The design and implementation of the survey methods affect the quality, **validity** and **reliability** of the data. When the topic or the population to be researched are defined as sensitive, a further level of complexity is added as sensitivity affects almost every stage of the research process (Renzetti and Lee, 1990; Lee, 1993) and should be considered in the conceptualisation, **piloting**, implementation and dissemination processes.

To provide a valid method of gathering attitudes and experiences, surveys should be constructed to be ethically sound, discreet and anonymous. Key questions that all researchers should ask when undertaking any project are:

- Who will benefit from this research?
- What is the cost (emotional and financial) to respondents?
- What are the barriers to this research and how can we address them? For example, legal barriers, ethical barriers, political barriers and practical barriers such as access.
- Ultimately, the researcher needs to ask 'can the research be justified?' If the answer is no, the researcher should withdraw from the research. If the answer is yes, then even though there will be problems along the way, it is appropriate to proceed.

Identifying and designing suitable research questions

Surveys are frequently associated with studies of prevalence and incidence and research on sensitive topics is often concerned with estimating the extent of a phenomenon that is hidden. Uncovering the extent or frequency of a particular type of deviant behaviour, the size of a hidden deviant population, or the extent of experiences of taboo victimisations are all appropriate topics for survey research. Survey methods can be used to research attitudes and opinions, and to explore perceptions and definitions given to sensitive topics. Box 6.4 gives examples of different types of question used in survey research.

BOX 6.4

SOME TYPICAL SURVEY QUESTIONS

Closed-question types

Dichotomous

Are you male/female?

Ordinal scale

How old are you?
0–20, 21–40, 41–60, 61–80, over 81

Rating scale

How satisfied are you with the response of the police following the crime you reported?

- ☐ Very satisfied
- ☐ Moderately satisfied
- ☐ Neutral
- ☐ Moderately dissatisfied
- ☐ Very dissatisfied
- ☐ Don't know/don't want to say

Likert scale

Please indicate by circling your preference the extent to which you agree or disagree with the following statement:

   A person found guilty of a serious sexual offence should always be imprisoned

Strongly agree, agree, neither agree nor disagree, disagree, strongly disagree, don't know

Open-question types

Unstructured

How do you see your role as a prison officer in a prison today?

Focused semi-structured response

What do you think is an appropriate sentence (if any) for a first-time offence of stealing a car?

Specific, factual response

Who would you initially seek help from if you'd been burgled?

Response to stimulus or hypothetical situation

The government have recently proposed to prosecute men who are caught kerb-crawling. What do you think of this proposal?

(See also section on vignettes below.)

Designing a survey so that it is accessible to the respondent group seems obvious but can be surprisingly difficult. For example, how are respondents going to understand and answer this question? How can I make the question more interesting? Researchers needs to put themselves in the respondents' shoes and stay there throughout the design and piloting phases. This ensures that the presentation and phrasing of questions is appropriate, engaging, interesting and as unthreatening as possible. The role of the survey researcher is to minimise the feeling of threat so as to gain detailed, accurate and reliable data in an ethical manner. There are a number of threat-reducing techniques that can be used, such as leading gently up to sensitive questions and using computers for self-completion questions. But by far the most significant factor in desensitising a topic is the choice of suitable questions. Here we provide an overview of different types of question and discuss the potential advantages and pitfalls in question design.

Open and closed questions

Closed questions containing pre-coded or 'fixed-choice' responses are useful for gathering factual data such as personal background information, or data about events or behaviours. These data are often complete and easy to analyse. However, where sensitive topics are involved, closed questions can inhibit accurate reporting as respondents may avoid ticking the outermost response categories (Lee, 1993). Such problems can be circumvented by ensuring that response categories cover all possible behaviours and incorporate the extremes. To achieve the most appropriate closed questions, it can be helpful to take data from a small sample of respondents answering open questions and use this knowledge to design closed-response questions for a larger sample (Gomm, 2004). This technique is called a pilot study and typically involves conducting a number of qualitative interviews from which quantitative, fixed-choice questions can be generated.

Open questions can be more difficult to answer as respondents are required to write down a few words rather than tick one of a number of pre-given answers. However, open questions have the advantage of allowing the respondent to answer freely without being confined by a set of answers. This is particularly valuable in research focused on people's experiences and perceptions. For example, it is more useful to ask someone to describe what it felt like to be sentenced to prison rather than to provide them with a list of emotions to tick. Both open and closed questions have a central place in survey research and are used effectively to draw out different types of information.

Once the questionnaire has been devised it should be 'piloted' to check that it operates effectively. Piloting involves testing the questionnaire with a small set of respondents who are comparable to the target respondents. As Bryman (2001: 155) notes, piloting 'may be particularly crucial in relation to research based on the self-completion questionnaire, since there will not be an interviewer present to clear up any confusion'. Problems with questionnaires and survey interview schedules can be identified through this process and alterations to the research instruments can be made.

Long questions

Sensitive research provides the exception to the rule about question length. It is commonly believed that lengthy questions are detrimental on surveys, confusing the respondent and leading to hasty responses (Bryman, 2001). Longer questions allow the researcher to talk around the issue before asking the question so, with sensitive research, this may help to desensitise the topic (Lee, 1993) and a longer question may aid recall (Sudman and Bradburn, 1982). A word of warning: use them sparingly and only where necessary as respondents can become tired of reading or listening to lengthy questions.

Loaded questions

The tone of a question can have an effect on the types of replies it elicits. Loaded questions are accused of leading the respondent towards a particular response (Bryman, 2001). However, loaded questions can help a respondent feel more comfortable when talking about an uncomfortable subject and provide a forum in which taboo behaviour can be revealed. Sudman and Bradburn (1982) describe four ways to load a sensitive question to achieve more accurate reporting of behaviour. The examples they provide are intended to encourage parents to discuss taboo feelings of anger towards their children (see Box 6.5).

BOX 6.5

SUDMAN AND BRADBURN'S LOADED QUESTIONS

Type of approach	Loaded question
Everybody does it	Even the calmest parents get mad at their children sometimes. Did your children do anything in the past week to make you angry?
Assume the behaviour	How many times during the last week did your child do something that made you angry?
Use expert opinion	Many psychologists believe it is important for parents to express their pent-up frustrations. Did your children do anything in the past week to make you angry?
Explain the behaviour	Parents become angry when they're tired or distracted or when their children are unusually naughty. Did your children do anything in the past week to make you angry?

Adapted from Sudman and Bradburn (1982)

Vignettes

Vignettes are an alternative to traditional questions and are used in surveys to reveal attitudes and behaviour. The main element of a vignette is a description of a scenario involving a number of key factors. However, there are different ways of using them in a survey. For example, Alexander and Becker (1978) describe the use of vignettes in a study concerned with rape victimisation attitudes among police and nurses. The vignette described the attack but varied factors relating to the victim, for example marital status, relationship to the attacker, injuries sustained, and so on. In total, the variations produced 64 possible combinations that were distributed randomly across the sample of 680 respondents. Differences in attitudes between the two groups could then be measured by looking at the average response to each version of the vignette (Alexander and Becker, 1978).

Finch (1987) used vignettes in a qualitative study to establish family obligations. The vignettes follow a story that is presented in several stages adding further information, and with questions asking what the protagonists should do after each stage. The questions were designed to allow the respondent to define a situation and to reveal norms of behaviour. While she notes some problems with this method, particularly around the recall of details as the story develops, Finch argues that using stages within a vignette allows the respondent to imagine how a story evolves (Finch, 1987).

Another approach to vignettes involves devising a set of different scenarios linked under a common theme that are distributed to each respondent. This thematic approach can be useful as part of a pilot study or an exploratory investigation into a topic, particularly where definitions or perceptions of a particular term or activity are required. In our nationwide study of public attitudes towards sex offenders (detailed as Survey Example 2, below), we developed thematic vignettes to reveal opinions about the classification and severity of a range of offences (Brown et al., 2007). The vignettes provided respondents with an opportunity to explore their thoughts on this sensitive topic while retaining an 'outsider' perspective (see Box 6.6).

BOX 6.6

VIGNETTES USED IN PUBLIC ATTITUDES TO SEX OFFENDER RESEARCH (BROWN ET AL., 2007)

ACCOUNT 1: Ted rents his house to a group of young professionals. Unknown to any of the tenants, Ted routinely records their bedrooms and bathroom via a digital camera system. He collects hours of footage per day and has videos dating back a number of years.

1 Do you think that Ted is a sex offender? Why?

2 How serious do you consider his actions?

(Continued)

(Continued)

Very serious	☐	1
Serious	☐	2
Not that serious	☐	3
Trivial	☐	4

ACCOUNT 2: Jim lends his computer to Sarah for a couple of weeks while he is on holiday. Sarah finds a folder containing general pornographic material downloaded from the internet. One of the pictures is of someone in their early teens.

1 Do you think that Jim is a sex offender? Why?
2 How serious do you consider his actions?

Very serious	☐	1
Serious	☐	2
Not that serious	☐	3
Trivial	☐	4

ACCOUNT 3: Karen and Robert attended a party together. Robert encourages Karen to drink spirits. Karen says that after a few hours of flirting with Robert she went into a bedroom to sleep off some alcohol. The next morning she claims to have been sexually assaulted by Robert. Karen says that no consent was given. Robert states that Karen had implied consent throughout the night.

1 Do you think that Robert is a sex offender? Why?
2 How serious do you consider his actions?

Very serious	☐	1
Serious	☐	2
Not that serious	☐	3
Trivial	☐	4

ACCOUNT 4: From a window inside his own home, Brian intentionally exposes himself to a passer-by. The passer-by laughs at first, but becomes concerned for others who might be offended and reports the incident to the police. The police question Brian. Brian states that the person whom he flashed laughed at him and did not seem to find his behaviour upsetting.

1 Do you think that Brian is a sex offender? Why?
2 How serious do you consider his actions?

Very serious	☐	1
Serious	☐	2
Not that serious	☐	3
Trivial	☐	4

These different approaches to the use of vignettes allow for the simulation of a situation. This has the advantage of 'desensitising' the topic and allowing the respondent to remain detached. However, one problem is that the use of a simulated scenario may produce simulated responses that do not match up with what a respondent would do or think in a real situation. For this reason, Lee (1993) concludes that vignettes are best used to reveal 'normative patterns' (or how respondents think things ought to be), rather than actual behaviours. Despite the drawbacks, the vignette method is a popular tool of the survey researcher. It allows for creativity in the design process, can be shaped to fit sensitive issues very effectively and encourages respondent engagement in the survey.

Confidentiality

While ensuring confidentiality with participants is imperative in any research, reassurance of water-tight confidentiality is arguably the make or break of sensitive research. For respondents, the thought of disclosing personally sensitive information in an interview or on a questionnaire can be daunting and assurances of confidentiality may be essential for their participation. It is imperative that respondents enter into the research process with the knowledge that the data gathered will be collected, handled and stored without fear of leakage or loss. One way to reassure respondents of confidentiality is, where possible, to spend time in the research environment before and after the data collection.

A range of methods can be used to ensure data collected remains confidential. Collecting anonymised data is the most secure method, but is obviously a problem if a follow-up interview is required in a longitudinal study. Alternatively, data could be anonymised at a variety of stages during the fieldwork or analysis phases, using separately stored codes to identify respondents for follow-up.

EXAMPLES OF SURVEY RESEARCH

We now discuss our own experiences of survey research. The following section presents two examples of surveys in which we have been involved. Both focus on sensitive topics and involve vulnerable or hard-to-reach groups, and each presents specific methodological problems.

SURVEY EXAMPLE 1: CHILDREN AND VICTIMISATION

The Children and Young People's Safety Survey (CYPSS) (Gallagher et al., 1998) is an ESRC-sponsored survey that was conducted between 1996 and 1998. The survey was carried out in 26 primary and secondary schools in the north-west of England by a sizeable multidisciplinary group and the data produced has provided various analyses of children's fears and experiences of victimisation (Gallagher et al., 1998, 2008; Deakin, 2006). We were able to explore these sensitive issues through questionnaires and follow-up interviews, generating quantitative data about the prevalence of victimisation and providing a forum for discussion on how victimisation and fear are recognised, defined and dealt with by children. We administered questionnaires to 2,420 children and young people between the ages of 9 and 16 from four types of area: the inner city, peripheral council estates, suburban and rural locations.

Questionnaires were completed during class-time, and follow-up interviews were conducted with a sub-sample of 52 victims and 52 non-victims in their homes. Our method highlights the importance of the children's subjective experiences by allowing them to define victimisation and fear, and it provided support and advice to children and their parents about the issue of abuse (Deakin, 2006).

Questions around the confidentiality of data or disclosure of children's experiences either to parents or to child protection agencies were perhaps our greatest concern during the fieldwork. The National Children's Bureau argues that complete confidentiality can never be guaranteed to children because the researcher has a duty to pass on relevant information to professional agencies as appropriate (Mahon et al., 1996). The children involved in the study were informed that their answers would, for the most part, be confidential, but that, in certain circumstances, they might be encouraged to disclose information to an appropriate professional (Gallagher et al., 2008).

Design

The questionnaire was designed to provide children with a forum to describe their feelings and experiences. It included straightforward language, graphics and colour to appeal to children and feel informal. The number of questions was kept to a minimum, while as much information as possible was gathered about victimisation, safety and fears. The more sensitive questions exploring victimisation were carefully worded to allow children to define their own experiences, to avoid causing distress, and to be acceptable to schools and parents. Sensitive parts of the questionnaire were introduced after less sensitive questions and followed by a discussion about safety measures intended to leave the child in a positive frame of mind (Gallagher et al., 2002).

Access and piloting

Schools were selected as the most representative of each area and letters were sent to each school explaining the nature of the study, the proposed uses of the research and requesting participation. Most of the schools contacted agreed to take part in the study after a period of consultation with parents. For the follow-up interviews, consent was sought from both children and parents. Piloting of the questionnaire and the interview schedule were extensive due to the sensitive nature of the study, and as a result a number of changes were made, including order and wording of questions.

Implementation

Before handing out the questionnaires, the children were briefed on its content and purposes in an age-appropriate manner. We gave the children examples of the types of question and explained the structure of the questionnaire. We also explained to the children that everything they wrote down was confidential and would be anonymised, and told them they could ask for help, or stop answering the questions at any time. After the questionnaire had been completed the children were offered the opportunity to talk to the researcher privately and were given information about further sources of help and advice (Gallagher et al., 2002).

From our questionnaires we were able to gather detailed, robust and subtle data in relation to children's fears and experiences of victimisation. This study demonstrated that questionnaires can tackle sensitive topics with a vulnerable population. They can use questions that leave definitions open to the respondent and they can be administered ethically providing advice and support where needed.

SURVEY EXAMPLE 2: PUBLIC ATTITUDES TO SEX OFFENDERS IN THE COMMUNITY

Our second example of sensitive survey research details a project we conducted in 2004/05 aimed at revealing public perceptions of sexual offences and attitudes towards the sentencing and potential reintegration of those convicted (Brown et al., 2007). Two distinct problems were raised by this research:

1   How to approach the emotive topic of sex offender reintegration sensitively
2   Ensuring that the sample of the general public is representative and includes some respondents from **hard-to-reach groups**

Just under 1,000 responses were gathered using a range of techniques, including a targeted postal questionnaire, a web-based questionnaire promoted via various USENET groups, and a community-based questionnaire delivered to community groups, local meetings, health services and local businesses (Brown et al., 2007).

Previous research has shown that gauging public attitudes to offenders and sentencing, in general, is fraught with problems (Stalans, 2002). Results have been varied (often contradicting the common perception that people are generally punitive). Stalans argues that this variance is caused by methodological issues: '… researchers have measured attitudes in a variety of ways and the public's response often depends on the manner in which the question is asked and the context in which it is located' (Stalans, 2002: 16).

Stalans (2002) goes on to argue that research considering public attitudes to sentencing tends to be relatively superficial without fully exploring the depth of public opinion. Clearly, attempting to unravel the layers of attitudes to offenders, sentencing and their management in the community is no easy task.

In our study of public attitudes towards sex offenders, the task was further complicated by the 'taboo' nature of offences that have been termed 'sex crime' and the emotive response they provoke. Our decision to conduct a survey of the general public about this controversial topic resulted in a range of challenges to be met and problems to be overcome.

Sample selection and data gathering

Our first challenge was to ensure that we constructed a representative sample. The sample needed to include people from different social, demographic, ethnic and geographic groupings, and include those that could be considered 'hard to reach' (see Box 6.2). In order to take account of these differences within the sample we used several different sampling methods.

First, using social and demographic research data accessed via the Office for National Statistics, we identified a range of socio-economic locations. We were then able to select postal areas from within our larger, targeted, geographic area. We included two areas that had high levels of deprivation, two areas with 'average' levels of economic activity and one area that was 'affluent'. We also included one area that was defined as multicultural. Two of the areas identified were rural areas and the remaining geographic locations were close to city centres. Once we had decided upon the geographic locations we began to negotiate access with local community-based groups and health centres (these were across a spectrum of pursuits and concerns so that we could ensure variations of age and interests). We were available to explain the purpose of the questionnaire, be on hand while respondents completed the questionnaire and administer the questionnaire verbally or translate it if necessary. Through this method, we were able to include some respondents within the hard-to-reach category, and we were able to offer advice and support to this group. However, this is a very time-consuming method of data gathering. Spending time at each of the community groups was a highly labour-intensive means of data gathering and at times the questionnaire return was small due to the number of people attending the meetings. We collected 98 questionnaires from community groups and health centres.

At the same time, we mailed out a total of 5,000 questionnaires. The questionnaires were split across our geographic areas to named respondents. This was an attempt to embed an element of control in the structure of the sample. We also mailed the questionnaire into large workplaces. In total, we received a 15% response rate to our postal questionnaire.

Additionally, we placed a web-based questionnaire on a news-group site which consisted of mainly open questions. This was intended to supplement the data gathered through the other, more targeted, sampling methods. The problem with the web-based method is that while you can gain rich data, you have no control over the structure of the sample. The very nature of the respondents using news groups meant that the data could have been skewed towards those with a greater interest in, and knowledge of, current or topical issues. Additionally, people likely to respond to web-linked questionnaires are often those with the most extreme views. There were 72 web-questionnaires returned, which we used separately from the postal and community responses as additional, illustrative data to support (and sometimes confound) the rest of our results (Brown et al., 2007).

Making sense of the data

In total we had 979 responses to our questionnaire. We had attempted to elicit a range and depth of information from respondents and so had used a number of survey data gathering methods. For example, we included a range of open questions and vignettes to create space for attitudes to be expressed and definitions to be explored. We asked a number of questions in relation to definitions of sex crime, attitudes towards sex offender sentencing and rehabilitation, views on the effectiveness of current resettlement strategies and the sex offenders register. All respondents were provided with an information sheet about the project that included the contact details of relevant help and support organisations (for a more detailed report of this research, see Brown et al., 2007).

The data generated from the various survey methods was rich and allowed us to analyse attitudes to sex offenders against the variables of gender, age, socio-economic status and type of area of residence, for example urban or rural. The responses were varied and in sufficient volume to enable us to complete a range of statistical tests on the data. In general, our results were consistent with those of previous research studies and highlighted that attitudes towards sex offenders were much more nuanced and complex than the claims made by the tabloid press. Our survey method had effectively uncovered these complexities through a combination of vignettes and open and closed questions directed at revealing attitudes.

The research highlighted the problem that policy-makers face in continually having to reproduce high levels of trust in the criminal justice system in order to ensure that the public retain confidence not only in the delivery of justice, but also in the management of offenders in the community (Brown et al., 2007). Our research suggests that the level of public trust in the criminal justice system and in criminal justice professionals is essentially very fragile. We were able to discover the fragility of public trust through the use of a survey in what is a very sensitive area.

SUMMARY

Sensitive survey research is not an oxymoron, providing care is taken throughout each stage of the process. Clearly, sensitive research poses unique ethical and methodological challenges whatever the chosen method. We have demonstrated in this chapter that it is possible to undertake ethically sound and appropriate survey research in relation to sensitive topics. Through the careful and thoughtful construction and administration of a questionnaire, extensive piloting, participation in the research environment, and by structuring the sample to take account of difference, it is possible to give respondents, some of whom have little voice in research, a forum to share their experiences and thoughts with safety and without threat or coercion. This highlights one of the core principles of any research: that the respondent is never a means to an end but rather an end in themselves. Above all else, criminological research should value the experiences and thoughts of those who agree to participate in our projects.

So, when you are thinking about undertaking research, you should consider the following questions carefully:

- **Is my proposed research sensitive?** Think about the types of question you are going to be asking respondents and remember to put yourself in their shoes. If the question feels sensitive to you, then by and large it probably is and it therefore needs to be treated with respect and care.

- **What are the key criticisms of my survey research?** In other words, can you justify what you are doing? If you can't, then you probably should not proceed with the research.

- **What are the advantages and disadvantages of using different methodological techniques in my survey?** Think about the various ways you could gather data and judge which would be the most appropriate research instruments to develop.

- **How can I engage with the respondents?** Can you spend time in the research environment before the survey is administered? What support can you provide after the fieldwork has finished? How will you disseminate the findings?

- **What ethical issues does this research pose?** Be alert to the variety of ethical issues posed by sensitive research and the specific ethical issues when research respondents are under 18. You need to be able to satisfy rigorous ethical scrutiny in order to justify your project.

■ Study Questions/Activities for Students

1   What are the main criticisms of survey research?

2   What issues are included under the umbrella term 'sensitive'?

3   What is a 'hard-to-reach' group?

4   Are surveys ever an appropriate method to use when considering sensitive issues?

5   What ethical issues would you need to consider when conducting survey research with children?

6   Using one of the vignette types described in Box 6.6, design a series of vignettes to explore one of the following topics:

    (a) Employees' understanding of workplace bullying.
    (b) Attitudes of the general public to methods used by the police in the prevention of terrorism.

7   You are directing a research project to reveal employers' attitudes towards employing ex-problem drug users (PDUs). Devise a briefing note to the research team with what you think may be the problems with gathering data from employers and how these may be avoided in the questionnaire design.

8   You are designing a survey to find out the experiences of foreign national (FN) women in prisons in the UK. In particular, you want to know how they experience their relationships with prison staff. Design some questions to be part of a survey using each of the following question types: ordinal, open, interval, yes/no.

9   You are thinking about conducting a survey with children between the ages of 11 and 16 to investigate the relationship between truancy and offending.

    (a) Make a list of the key factors you would want to ask your respondents about.
    (b) Make a list of the key ethical considerations and how you would approach them.

10 Using Sudman and Bradburn's examples of loaded questions (Box 6.5), what questions could you use to research the following topics? Try loading your questions using the four different approaches.

    (a) The extent of promiscuity among college students.
    (b) The nature of anti-social behaviour engaged in by 16–18-year-olds.
    (c) The extent of feelings of insecurity experienced by residents of a high-crime estate.

RESOURCES

On researching sensitive issues, see:

Lee, R. M. (1993) *Doing Research on Sensitive Topics*, London: Sage. Chapter 5 discusses sensitive survey research.

On survey research, see:

Bachman, R. and Schutt, R. (2008) *Fundamentals of Research in Criminology and Criminal Justice*, Thousand Oaks, CA: Sage. Chapter 6.

Bryman, A. (2001) *Social Research Methods*, Oxford: Oxford University Press. Chapters 4, 5, 6, 7.

Fowler, F. J. (2009) *Survey Research Methods* (4th Edition), Los Angeles: Sage.

Gomm, R. (2004) *Social Research Methodology: A Critical Introduction*, Basingstoke: Palgrave Macmillan. Especially Chapters 4 and 8.

Groves, R.M., Fowler, F.J., Couper, M.P., Lepkowski, J.M., Singer, E. and Tourangeau, R. (2004) *Survey Methodology*, New York: Wiley.

Marsh, C. (1982) *The Survey Method: The Contribution of Surveys to Sociological Explanation*, London: Allen and Unwin.

Seale, C. (ed.) (2004) *Social Research Methods: A Reader*, London: Routledge.

REFERENCES

Alexander, C.S. and Becker, H.J. (1978) 'The Use of Vignettes in Survey Research', *Public Opinion Quarterly*, 42: 93–104.

Bachman, R. and Schutt, R. (2008) *Fundamentals of Research in Criminology and Criminal Justice*, Thousand Oaks, CA: Sage.

Blumer, H. (1956) 'Sociological Analysis and the Variable', *American Sociological Review*, 21: 683–90.

Brown, S., Deakin, J. and Spencer, J. (2007) 'Public Attitudes towards Sex Offenders', *Howard Journal of Criminal Justice*, 47, 3: 259–74.

Bryman, A. (2001) *Social Research Methods*, Oxford: Oxford University Press.

BSC (British Society of Criminology) (2006) *Code of Ethics for Researchers in the Field of Criminology*. London: BSC.

Cicourel, A.V. (1964) *Method and Measurement in Sociology*, New York: Free Press.

Cicourel, A.V. (1982) 'Interviews, Surveys and the Problem of Ecological Validity', *American Sociologist*, 17: 11–20.

Deakin, J. (2006) 'Dangerous People, Dangerous Places: The Nature and Location of Young People's Victmisation and Fear', *Children and Society*, 20: 376–90.

Finch, J. (1987) 'The Vignette Technique in Survey Research', *Sociology*, 21: 105–14.

Fine, G.A. and Sandstrom, K.L. (1988) *Knowing Children: Participant Observation with Minors*, Qualitative Research Methods Series, 15, Newbury Park, CA: Sage.

Fowler, F.J. (2009) *Survey Research Methods* (4th Edition), Los Angeles: Sage.

Fox Keller, E. (1980) 'Feminist Critique of Science: A Forward or Backward Move?', *Fundamenta Scientiae*, 1: 341–9.

Gallagher, B., Bradford, M. and Pease, K. (1998) *The Nature, Prevalence and Distribution of Sexual and Physical Abuse of Children by Strangers*. Final Report to the ESRC. Manchester: University of Manchester. R000 23 5996.

Gallagher, B., Bradford, M. and Pease, K. (2002) 'The Sexual Abuse of Children by Strangers: Its Extent, Nature and Victims' Characteristics', *Children and Society*, 16: 356–9.

Gallagher, B., Bradford, M. and Pease, K. (2008) 'Attempted and Completed Incidents of Stranger Perpetrated Child Sexual Abuse and Abduction', *Child Abuse and Neglect*, 32: 517–28.

Gomm, R. (2004) *Social Research Methodology: A Critical Introduction*, Basingstoke: Palgrave Macmillan.

Hood, S., Kelley, P. and Mayall, B. (1996) 'Children as Research Subjects: A Risky Enterprise', *Children and Society*, 10: 117–28.

Kelly, L. (1990) 'Journeying in Reverse: Possibilities and Problems in Feminist Research on Sexual Violence', in L. Gelsthorpe and A. Morris (eds), *Feminist Perspectives in Criminology*, Milton Keynes: Open University, pp. 107–14.

Kennedy Bergen, R. (1993) 'Interviewing Survivors of Marital Rape', in C.M. Renzetti and R.M. Lee (eds), *Researching Sensitive Topics*, Newbury Park, CA: Sage.

Kinaird, E.M. (1985) 'Ethical Issues in Research with Abused Children', *Child Abuse and Neglect*, 9: 301–11.

Lansdown, G. (1994) 'Children's Rights', in B. Mayall (ed.), *Children's Childhoods: Observed and Experienced*, London: Falmer Press.

Lee, R.M. (1993) *Doing Research on Sensitive Topics*, London: Sage.

Mahon, A., Glendinning, C., Clarke, K. and Craig, G. (1996) 'Researching Children: Methods and Ethics', *Children and Society*, 10: 145–54.

Marsh, C. (1982) *The Survey Method: The Contribution of Surveys to Sociological Explanation*, London: Allen and Unwin.

Morrow, V. and Richards, M. (1996) 'The Ethics of Social Research with Children: An Overview', *Children and Society*, 10: 90–105.

Oakley, A. (1981) 'Interviewing Women: A Contradiction in Terms', in H. Roberts (ed.), *Doing Feminist Research*, London: Routlegde & Kegan Paul.

Phillips, D.L. (1971) *Knowledge from What? Theories and Methods in Social Research*, Chicago: Rand McNally.

Reinharz, S. (1979) *On Becoming a Social Scientist*, San Francisco: Jossey-Bass.

Renzetti, C.M. and Lee, R.M. (eds) (1990) *Researching Sensitive Topics*, Newbury Park, CA: Sage.

Ross, M.W., Diamond, P.M., Liebling, A. and Saylor, W.G. (2008) 'Measurement of Prison Social Climate: A Comparison of an Inmate Measure in England and the USA', *Punishment Society*, 10: 447.

Schutz, A. (1962) *Collected Papers I: The Problem of Social Reality*, The Hague: Martinus Nijhof.

Seale, C. (ed.) (2004) *Social Research Methods: A Reader*, London: Routledge.

Stalans, L. (2002) 'Measuring Attitudes to Sentencing', in J. Roberts and M. Hough (eds), *Changing Attitudes to Punishment: Public Opinion, Crime and Justice*, Cullompton: Willan Publishing.

Sudman, S. and Bradburn, N.M. (1982) *Asking Questions: A Practical Guide to Questionnaire Design*, San Francisco: Jossey-Bass.

Tymchuk, A.J. (1992) 'Assent Processes', in B. Stanley and J.E. Sieber (eds), *Social Research on Children and Adolescents: Ethical Issues*, London: Sage.

SEVEN
DOING INTERVIEWS IN PRISON

PAMELA DAVIES

Chapter Contents

KEY POINTS

This chapter:

- Explores the methodological choice of using interviews for doing prison-based research
- Draws on my experience of conducting qualitative, in-depth interviews with female offenders in a prison setting
- Illustrates that the 'planning' and 'doing' of research go hand in hand and that practicalities and politics often present key decision-making junctures
- Exemplifies some dilemmas associated with doing valid and ethical criminological research

INTRODUCTION

This chapter is about doing research through interviewing. It flows on from earlier chapters that were devoted to the topic of preparing to conduct criminological research and it connects with many of the issues discussed within the planning stages of research. It reinforces some of the detail in relation to **research design**. The chapter acknowledges that the 'planning' and 'doing' of research go hand in hand and that practicalities and politics often interrupt/disrupt both. Through an emphasis on the doing of research through interviewing, some of these 'interruptions' become key illustrations and examples, and form the basis for discussion of research practice and **decision-making** junctures. In particular, this chapter draws on my experience of conducting interviews with female offenders in a prison setting in the north-east of England.

The chapter commences with an overview of issues related to choosing interviews as a research tool and prison as a location for conducting them. The chapter then moves into an account which focuses upon the contextual factors surrounding the whole experience of doing qualitative interviews. In 'official publications' such as those often emanating from the Home Office and police sources, we are presented with an uncluttered, clean and sanitised version of the research findings clearly set out for us to 'read off'. Rarely do these and most policy-related research publications draw our attention to, or ask us to think about what goes on behind the scenes and about the often painful and slow process of the research experience – how it is 'arrived at' and what the research dilemmas are along the way. Examples of researchers and practitioners 'telling it like it is' include exposing subjective reflections where the researcher as observer makes personal statements about feelings that might have been evoked during the fieldwork or interviews (Berg, 2007). Research is often not a neat and tidy process and the day-to-day business of conducting it can be frustrating if it is not accepted that there are fuzzy edges to such work.

Such accounts of experience give us added value in the form of observational and 'reflective' data in addition to the 'literal dialogue' (Mason, 1996). 'Methods' and 'good research practice' instruction has traditionally come in textbook formats which are littered with warnings about how not to do research. After reading such texts, students and prospective researchers may be easily discouraged from embarking upon any form of original research or fieldwork. Awareness of the guiding principles of doing good research is essential, but some readers ought, and may prefer, to be enticed into doing criminological research by reading about these principles in real contexts.

RESEARCH IN PRISON

Interviews

So why did I make the methodological choice to conduct interviews and why conduct them in prison? First, why interviews rather than alternatives such as mail or internet-based surveys and why face-to-face interviews rather than alternatives such as telephone interviews? Interviewing, as defined earlier, is a method of data collection, information or opinion gathering that specifically and typically involves asking a series of questions in the form of a dialogue where rich data can be unearthed with the help of deep probing. My methodological choices were influenced by the attempt to follow good reflective research practice. They were also influenced by my research problems, which focused on women and economic crimes and motivations for such female offending.

Feminist research

Decisions about doing qualitative interviews with female offenders – the example drawn upon in this chapter – suggest a feminist orientation. These issues include conscious choices made at the outset by a female researcher; the fact that the sample included only offending women; and that the subject matter explores a research question that has a specific gender bias to it. The use of the semi-structured, in-depth interview method is generally seen as consistent with feminist research because such interviews seek not to be exploitative but to be appreciative of the position of women. Face-to-face interviews steer towards an 'appreciative stance' or 'standpoint position', which are consistent with a feminist approach.

Feminist research practice has been explored by various writers (Gelsthorpe 1994; Gelsthorpe and Morris, 1994; Maynard and Purvis, 1994; Naffine, 1997; Stanley and Wise, 1993) and many others have brought their own feminist perspective to bear on their fieldwork and analysis of different areas of sociology and criminology (Carlen, 1988; Carlen et al., 1985; Daly, 1994; Heidensohn, 1985; Hudson, 1994; Maher, 1997; Walklate, 2003), while contributing to challenging debates surrounding feminist perspectives in criminology (Gelsthorpe and Morris, 1994; Naffine, 1997) and with philosophy and epistemologies (Cain, 1994). Such debates continue to reveal more about the various 'truths' of doing research. This loose-knit body of work also clearly demonstrates that there is no single feminist viewpoint or perspective. Nevertheless, as Naffine has argued:

> Many feminists are of the view that the angle from which the dominant class views the world is one which provides a poor field of vision. Subjugation, and reflection upon that status, makes for a better appreciation of the world. (Naffine, 1997: 51)

This particular view is similar to the approach to research that is grounded. Grounded research might involve several of the following principles: first, collecting data at first hand from informants. Second, collecting it in their own terms and in the light of what they think is significant (not what pre-existing theory thinks is significant). Third, developing theory grounded in the actor's words and/or actions (Glaser and Strauss, 1967). In this way, my research would hopefully elicit common data but also differences and variations while remaining faithful to the sources from which the information came. These latter points also raise issues pertinent to doing feminist and ethically imbued research, to which I return below.

As intimated in the Introduction to Part II of this volume, particular research issues are raised when planning to conduct interviews in a prison setting as detainees are hard to reach by virtue of their incarceration and they might be deemed 'vulnerable', being a 'captive sample'. Several research issues will be explored throughout the remainder of this chapter that directly relate to the respondent's 'status' as prisoner. First, however, at the preparation and planning stage of all research and perhaps especially research proposed in prison, there are issues concerning security and access to address.

First, security. Prisons are categorised by their main role and there are broadly two main types: local and remand institutions and training prisons. The former deal with prisoners awaiting trial or sentence (on remand), those serving short sentences and those being assessed before being sent elsewhere. Training prisons can be 'open' or 'closed' and for men these are categorised according to a security level score from Category A, which are most secure and house prisoners whose escape would be highly dangerous to the public or national security, through to 'D Cat' which means 'open' conditions. For women, the four categories range from 'Cat A' to closed, semi-open and open. Thus when planning to conduct research with inmates, the type and security level of the proposed prison are important and this impinges upon issues concerning access too.

There are various routes into doing prison-based research but research contracts are rarely awarded to a novice and it is a difficult world to enter before one even arrives at the prison gates, whereupon the unpleasant world of the prison begins (Martin, 2000). The women's prison estate is much smaller and less populated than the men's, and while the female prison population has been steadily rising over the last 10–15 years, women still represent only a small fraction of the total prison population (around 6%) (Medlicott, 2007). This may make the researcher's prospects of gaining access both easier and more difficult, depending upon local, regional and national politics and idiosyncrasies. Broadly speaking, it is really quite a task to get into prisons to do any kind of research. At the very least you, as an individual researcher within a university or other appropriate body, will need the permission of the Governor and most likely also that of the Head of Psychology and the permission also of the Regional Psychologist if your research is to take place in one region (see Box 7.1). Unless you already have a strong 'foot in the door' via a personal contact, you will probably need to complete a standard application form and have supporting documentation, including your questionnaires, ethics approval, consent forms, CVs, etc. If your research involves offender health issues, access can be quite cumbersome and lengthy, and the application procedure and ethics procedures are very strict and rigorous. The Offender Health Research Network has a website with useful links (see www.ohrn.nhs.uk/toolkit/).

THE CONTEXT: WOMEN AND CRIME FOR ECONOMIC GAIN

The main vehicle used for illustration in this chapter relates to a part of my research that has investigated women who commit crime for economic gain (see Davies, 1999). While the fieldwork encompassed various different strategies and stages of gathering data, a major part of it involved one-to-one interviews with women who had committed 'economic crimes'. Where specific terms are used in the formulation of research problems, it is important to define these in the context of the project. In this case, the definition of 'economic crimes' proved highly complex but in general terms it incorporates most varieties of property crimes such as thefts (including shoplifting and pilfering, frauds and forgery, as well as many crimes that come under the general heading white-collar crimes), burglary and car crimes as well as prostitution and drug-related offences.

Interviews were conducted with 21 women in prison. All the women interviewed were white and can be loosely described as working class. The majority were in their twenties although their ages ranged from 17 years to 46 years. Ten of the women had a total of 21 children between them with two of these same women pregnant again in prison. Eleven had a partner and the remainder described themselves as single. Ten of the women were on remand while the remainder were serving sentences of either three, four, six, eight, nine or 15 months and one of two years. All had been convicted of at least one, and in the majority of cases several, criminal offences. The crimes the women were most frequently engaged in, and discussed in interviews, were thefts, in particular shoplifting, fraud and deception, but also employee and car theft. Burglary, drugs and prostitution-related offences also figured significantly in their offending profiles, while a variety of other offences were also included in the range of crimes they had committed. As economically marginal women committing petty offences (Steffensmeier and Allen, 1996), these women might generally be characterised as 'hustlers' (Campbell, 1991; Maher, 1997). Crime appeared to constitute a major source of income for these women.

BEFORE INTERVIEWING

Before interviewing takes place, much research, organisation and planning are needed. Indeed, by this stage many important decisions about the research have already been made. For example, decisions have been made about whether to conduct personal interviews or perhaps administer a postal survey. Decisions then need to be made about how to introduce the research and how best to describe what it is all about to the various gatekeepers as well as the interviewees. Decisions need to be made about how to organise the interviews and thought should be given to where interviews might take place. It is important to consider how the interview will be conducted. Time and length restrictions as well as other non-scheduled interruptions may affect the way in which the interview is conducted and strategies need to be thought through in order to achieve a good interview. Factors likely to affect a good interview might include whether or not tape recording will be an option or whether copious note-taking will be required. All decisions regarding research, organisation and planning before interviewing need to be considered carefully. Certainly, flexibility needs to be built into the early preparations for interviewing.

In respect of the period before my own interviewing took place, several methodological choices were made regarding interviewing and the type of interview. My decision to employ the use of personal and semi-structured in-depth interviews was largely based upon the nature of the research questions being explored. These questions included exploring the types of crime the interviewees engaged in and details on the ways in which they conducted them. Preliminary research and pilot discussions had shown similarities between the women in respect of types of crime committed and there were also commonalties between the ways in which their crimes were executed. This could have suggested a structured format but I preferred to keep the research grounded and maintain respect for the women's narratives as far as possible. The semi-structured interview format I adopted moved beyond 'conversation' but remained naturalistic and in-depth, with discussions steered by my questions and prompts, but the substantive content largely determined by the respondent.

Ethically imbued research

Because ethical dilemmas are endemic to social research (Sumner, 2006), learned societies of academic researchers and professional associations produce published guidelines to promote good practice and high ethical standards by which behaviour should be regulated. For example, the British Society of Criminology has devised and regularly updates its code of ethics, which offers guidance to criminological researchers. The British Sociological Association has a similar code of ethics. The Social Research Association (SRA), the Economic and Social Research Council (ESRC), Market Research Society and Higher Education Academy (HEA) all offer their own sets of principles or guidelines that are useful benchmarks for practising researchers and useful starting points for conducting ethically imbued research.

Informed consent is an ethical principle implying a responsibility on the part of the social researcher to strive to ensure that those involved as participants in research not only agree or consent to participating in the research of their own free choice, without being pressurised or influenced, but that they are fully informed about what it is they are consenting to (Davies, 2006). Research must not harm or put the researched at risk in any way, and the researcher has a responsibility to conduct themselves with honesty and integrity and with consideration and respect for the research subjects, whose rights should be respected. This particular responsibility that researchers have towards research participants implies that researchers should base research, so far as possible, on the freely given informed consent of those studied. Research participants should be made aware of their right to say no, decline or refuse permission and to participate. They should be able to exercise this right whenever and for whatever reason they wish. Moreover, while the researched may agree to participate generally, they should nevertheless also feel free and be free to exercise their powers of veto during the research process and reject the use of specific data-gathering devices such as tape recorders and video cameras.

Therefore, for consent to be fully informed it is incumbent upon the researcher to explain as fully as possible, and in terms meaningful to participants, the questions of what, who, why and how. That is, what the research is about, who is undertaking and financing it, why it is being undertaken, how it is to be promoted and how any research findings are to be disseminated. None of these aspects of the research design is clear-cut or straightforward. *Who*, for example, are the participants in the research? It is one of the responsibilities of the researcher to determine from whom informed consent must be obtained. If access to research is gained through a 'gatekeeper', for instance, informed consent should be sought directly from the research participants to whom access is required. This may mean adhering to the principle of informed consent at several different levels of access. Special care in this respect must also be taken where research participants are vulnerable by virtue of factors such as age, social status or powerlessness, or are ill or infirm, or where proxies may need to be used in order to gather data. Doing interviews in the prison setting brings forth several ethical considerations about informed consent and decision-making, and doing research in prisons involves following strict criteria for ethical approval, as noted earlier in this chapter. Once approval has been gained, however, as Martin has observed, 'one distinct advantage of carrying out research among such a literally captive audience is that the refusal rate is usually low' (Martin, 2000: 228). Ethically though, this could remain a worrisome issue.

There is also a strong onus on the researcher to decide what is meant by anonymity and confidentiality, and the researcher and the researched should be clear and in agreement about what each of these mean. Research participants should be informed about and understand how far they will be afforded anonymity and/or confidentiality. My own respondents provided me with a name which may or may not have been their given name. I changed all names and gave respondents pseudonyms, which goes some way towards providing anonymity but is no guarantee.

The researchers' responsibility extends to a careful consideration about making promises or unrealistic guarantees that might later be difficult, impossible or tempting not to keep.

While informed consent ought to be integral to any robust and effective research design, this can prove difficult to adhere to in practice during the conduct of social and criminological research, and research done in prison in particular. Informed consent might be seen as an ideal-typical principle to which all social research should aspire. In reality it may be impossible to achieve consent that is fully informed, and in practice informed consent is never likely to be fully attained.

As the research progresses it often creates a range of ethical choices and dilemmas. In some research contexts informed consent may need revisiting as the research develops and evolves. The aims and objectives of a research question may be clearly stated at the outset and empirical or experimental fieldwork will be conducted according to an original research design. For example, informed consent might be sought at an early stage but research is often dynamic and developmental. Consequently, the nature and use of the material obtained from the research is likely to alter. It may be necessary for the obtaining of informed consent to be regarded not as a one-off event at the outset, but as a process subject to renegotiation or reminder, especially during the course of research over prolonged periods of time. Informed consent is an ethical principle that may demand continuous dialogue and communication if participants are to fully understand what the research is about, who is doing and financing it, why it is being done and how it will be used.

Access, case selection and inducements

Prior to entering the field, more issues present or re-present themselves, such as gaining access to interviewees and control over case selection. Politics may complicate the research process as well as practical difficulties.

For me, initial access to prison-based interviewees was made surprisingly easy via the cooperation of the Governor and staff members at a regional remand centre. Prisons have traditionally been 'closed' institutions and gaining access for research purposes, as noted earlier, can be troublesome and a considerable undertaking for most. Research efforts can often be thwarted once carefully planned research becomes fieldwork, and access at various levels of the prison staff hierarchy may need negotiating and re-negotiating, allowing each layer of personnel to be put in the picture, kept abreast of the research and given the opportunity to give approval and grant access. Access is often therefore a recurring issue rather than a one-off hurdle.

Although fieldwork is often a part of the research process to look forward to, doing interviews with known criminals who have apparently done something serious enough to warrant their loss of liberty can be a daunting prospect. In respect of case selection (who to interview), in theory you can exercise some measure of control over the selection of inmates for interview. The offence categories which were of interest to me were made explicit. It was emphasised that economic crimes, that is fraud and forgery, thefts and shoplifting-type offences (excluding violent offences), were to be investigated. Such parameters can be built into the research design (see Chapter 2 in the volume) for genuine reasons related to the research question, but they also help to lessen anxiety about your close proximity to dangerous and violent offenders.

Another decision concerns the offering of inducements to interviewees. Should payment be offered to the women for the interviews? Others conducting research with vulnerable and impoverished women had done so and there are valid arguments both for and against this practice. For many, this option is fairly swiftly dismissed, as funding is often not available even if it was preferred, but other 'inducements' might be considered. In carrying out my own research, small quantities of cigarettes were taken to all interview venues together with a lighter (with permission from wing staff in the prison). This practice could be seen as part of the 'research bargain' and proved particularly useful in the prison setting and in (re-)gaining control of my sample.

DURING INTERVIEWS

During the interview process many issues represent themselves and others arise. Here I dwell on snowball sampling, managing interviews, validity and reflexivity.

Snowball sampling

Snowball sampling has been defined as a form of non-probability sampling. The researcher begins by identifying an individual perceived to be an appropriate respondent willing to provide data. This respondent is then asked to identify another potential respondent and the process is repeated until sufficient data has been accumulated (Oliver, 2006). Thus, snowball sampling is a way of selecting a sample (which is akin to a 'chain letter') where the sample becomes self-selecting. It is an acceptable and ethical method of sampling, although there are problems associated with this method in respect of typicality, representativeness and bias.

Having described to the officers on the wing the types of offence (and therefore I hoped the types of offender) I was keen to interview, the selection of inmates to approach was initially at their discretion. In the event, the vast majority of the women had at some time committed offences relevant to the research. This was mostly established early on in the interview as the purpose of the discussion was described. On the first afternoon of interviewing in prison, however, I was introduced to a diminutive woman who was on remand for alleged murder. We continued our discussion, talking about her circumstances and her life in general, before our conversation came to a close, whereupon she politely thanked me for spending time talking with her. The member of staff, curious after each interview, was keen to know once again how it had progressed. *He* was clearly amused and was testing out my reactions and how I would cope. It was all done in good humour and although the interview had proved an interesting experience, it was not useful for the purposes of gathering hard data. After this occasion greater control was exercised over the selection of interviewees in prison. This was achieved by asking women who were particularly helpful and forthcoming about their committing of 'economic crimes' to suggest other inmates' names to me for interviewing purposes.

This snowball sampling method signified a more grounded form of research practice, but also a degree of collusion and connection with the inmates was achieved that allowed them to become self-selecting. Several inducements were also clearly contributing to this pattern of recruitment. It became apparent on the wing that 'Miss' (later I became Pam) wanted to talk to them. This held out the prospect of getting them out of cleaning the floor, or their cell, or simply doing nothing, and they heard she had cigarettes with her. This spread of rumour, interest and curiosity all combined to my advantage. Self-selecting interviewees were presenting themselves while checks and balances within the interview schedule were ensuring that the stories were their own and individual accounts were emerging. This last point raises the question of validity which is further discussed after the next section.

Managing interviews

Once in the one-to-one interview situation, interviewing skills are important. The interviewer has to do, say and think about several things all at once. Most important is to listen, then prompt and encourage when appropriate, but without 'leading', and to steer the discussion back on track if it appears to be heading off down a less promising avenue. Encouraging a respondent to elaborate further on something mentioned in passing during a lengthy narrative is an important technique, which also supports a naturalistic style of interviewing. Thus some of my brief notes from an interview with Angela looked similar to those shown in Box 7.2 and were scribbled beneath my typewritten prompt sheet, as used for each and every respondent. The simple note M&S easily catches the eye when there is a pause in the dialogue and can be picked up on later and probed further to elicit another account of a shoplifting experience.

This prompting of shoplifting stories from the past and how it was done in different shops lead to a lengthy 'thick' or 'deep' description of the details on how, what and where to shoplift. When these illustrations came to a close I sought more clarification on how to avoid security obstacles – an issue raised in the narrative extract in Box 7.2 by the interviewee but glossed over. Further prompting of that issue is achieved by repeating the words of the respondent, as noted on the prompt sheet. The words 'foil bag' are remembered and catch the eye from my notes:

BOX 7.2

EXTRACT FROM PROMPT SHEET

Offending – nature and extent/means and methods/reasons

4.   SHOPLIFTERS
Explore: Which shops, preferences? What taken, how, why?
M&S

PD: You said before that you preferred certain shops and you mentioned M&S.
A: Yeah – good for underwear and that and it would go easy, people would want it
PD: So how did you actually do it in M&S?
A: Two of us would go in separately. I'd fill a foil bag up with underwear and leave it in such a place and she'd walk out with it. If someone clocks me putting them in they've got nothing on me. At Asda we'd work…

PD: You've mentioned when stealing clothes that you used a foil bag? How does that work?
A: To put the gear in, how it works right…

An experienced interviewer is able to encourage a natural narrative along restricted topics using the semi-structured interview schedule in order to introduce the topics. Equally important is the ability to encourage women to provide a fuller picture of how their offending is achieved. This can be done by asking them to focus on particular techniques or their use of specialist equipment, as the notes above show in relation to shoplifting and as the notes from an interview with Patricia, a drug dealer, show here:

PD: You mentioned before that you opened up two other shops?
P: I was a big drugs dealer; I opened up two other shops in our area…

Following a detailed explanation, I prompted further:

PD: And did you use any special equipment?
P: I had scales and I weighed up. I had equipment for drug dealing. Electric scales, lottery papers – the long ones – and a bag for grams…

In all of the interviews done in prison, contemporaneous notes were taken. Note-taking in the interview situation is neither easy nor unobtrusive. Both parties' use of language as well as the nature of the accounts being offered also complicates this. Interviewees' language and the subject matter might be humorous or violent, distressing and shocking. The interviewer's language can be adapted to suit that of the interviewee by repeating some of the words and phrases used by the women. Sometimes direct questions or comments may need to be further explained or clarified. Having asked Rebecca to describe a typical (shoplifting) day, the extract in Box 7.3 illustrates how respondents use their own vernacular but also shoplifting slang:

Sometimes prison or street slang has to be quickly absorbed and used. Sometimes specific phrases and words used by the women are the only ones to properly encapsulate the meaning and description of events and these are worth recording verbatim. Other times it is the gist of the account that is sufficient to record and a balance has to be struck between stemming the flow of the narrative, maintaining it and getting it all down on paper. It is useful to adopt a method of knowing which bits of the interview are précised and which are direct quotes as these are often very difficult to decipher after the interview. 'Cryptic jottings' are useful techniques to

---

BOX 7.3

REBECCA – WRITTEN-UP FIELD NOTES

R: I'd get up in the morning early, I'd have to be, about 9, I was at me friends. I'd go out on my own up the town, walking. I'd get a graft – (shoplift) either at a food store for meat or clothes shops and go back and sell that door to door and then I'd got me money about £50 and then I'd go and score – anywhere – depends. I'd hand over £40 for the drugs – heroin. I'd have that, smoke it on my own – Billy no mates – (laughing). It would be about 9.45. I'd go back to town, come back and score about 2–3 times and then go back to me friends and lie on the bed cabbaged. It's weird with the gear you get a buzz at first and then you don't get a buzz. It makes you normal so you don't turkey and then ... sometimes you get a good gouch (mongin) ((off your head)). I'd be cabbaged by 7pm but still awake and then I'd go to sleep at 11. I'd watch TV at night or if it was the weekend I'd go out with friends – get up to the same stuff...

---

use in the field and during interviewing. These may include brief statements, sketches, short-hand notes and odd or unusual terms or phrases that serve as a memory trigger when writing the full field notes (Berg, 2007). Relevant details must be recorded without missing anything that could be further explored as more qualitative data. It is important to strike a balance between reacting naturally to disclosures and not appearing too shocked. Discussions inevitably involve some distressing stories about childhood relationships, victimisations and circumstances, some of which might be expected but nevertheless might be distressing to both disclose and to hear about. On occasions, such experiences of interviewing may have affects on the interviewer as researcher in the longer term. Secrets and confidences divulged by the interviewee can have a traumatic effect on researchers who are unprepared for them or who have built up a rapport with a female interviewee.

Validity and reflexivity

Good research is valid research. Validity is 'the design of research to provide credible conclusions' (Sapsford and Jupp, 1996: 1). Valid research incorporates valid

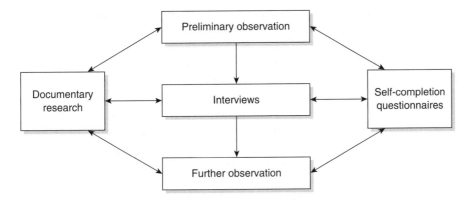

FIGURE 7.1 Triangulation of Methods in Prison Research

measurements and validity of generalisation. The process of monitoring and reflecting upon all aspects of a research project from the formulation of research ideas through to the publication of findings and their utilisation (Jupp, 2006) is important in the process of qualitative research (Hammersley and Atkinson, 1983).

Validity checks on some of the data obtained from interviewing women in prison could have been achieved using a combination of different sources, such as interview data combined with offender records. Combining these forms of data for validity checks is a form of **triangulation,** that is, the use of different methods to study the same phenomenon, or the observation of the research issue from (at least) two different points (Jupp, 2006). This, together with supporting literature and a reflective practice, generally would enable very robust checks on the reliability and validity of the research. For example, observational techniques combined with interviewing and documentary research allow the researcher to start with some preliminary observation, move into the interview phase while conducting the documentary research alongside, and conclude with more observation. This is illustrated in Figure 7.1.[1]

As a specific example, Harvey (2007) used what he described as an embedded, multi-method approach which included semi-structured interviews, quantitative measures, social network analyses and observations of key areas in a Young Offenders Institution in order to explore the psychosocial experience of imprisonment for young men. In my own prison-based research, although there was some measure of triangulation, elaborate lengths were not deemed necessary in this fieldwork as the data of interest concerned the *modus operandi* and offender networks information, which is not reliably and consistently collated and stored by official sources on female offenders. Internal checks and balances on offenders' explanations for their part in crime were employed.

Beyond the mechanics of valid methodologies are issues related to reflexivity and subjective reflexivity. Highly reflexive research can significantly enrich the

---

[1]This table appeared in Chapter 12 of the first edition of *Doing Criminological Research* (2000) by Carol Martin.

validity of any research. Some of these considerations are explored by Piacentini, who argues 'for a process of acquiring penal knowledge based on criminology of emotional attentiveness' (Piacentini, 2007: 153). In my own research, the vast majority of those interviewed within the prison suffered from an addiction to drugs – in the main, speed, amphetamines, heroin and cocaine – but also to alcohol. At the time of conducting the prison-based interviews, I was both surprised and shocked to discover the high proportion of female inmates who had a drug problem. Since these interviews were conducted, increased numbers of women received into prison have been sentenced for drugs-related offences (Devlin, 1998; Malloch, 2000) and in 2004 the Home Office reported that 66% of the sentenced women in prison were either dependent on drugs or drinking heavily before they came to prison (Medlicott, 2007). Although drugs offences were not generally the reason for their most recent sentence, many of the women I interviewed were close to, or involved with, drug use. This complicated their patterns of offending, exacerbating the extent of it (particularly their crimes for economic gain), and it also affected the way in which some of the interviews were conducted. The provision of cigarettes to smoke during the interview helped calm and compose the women who often found concentration and conversation difficult to maintain.

It is not unknown for some commentators to denigrate research conclusions based on interviews with known criminals (see, for example, Jupp, 1989) and drug users. The research described here also relies on self-report data provided by offenders. In self-reports there is always a risk of under-reporting or of over-exaggeration. The fact that some of the women discussing their experiences of committing crime were drug users invites criticism of the research. Some women interviewed in prison did exhibit signs of restlessness and an inability to concentrate, but the majority were keen to talk and be listened to. The discussions primarily focused upon the manner in which they carried out their activities, the locations in which they took place and details on the methods and networks of which they were a part. Little of the information could be exaggerated or specific crimes referred to made up. Most respondents were highly comfortable narrating their criminal activities and expertise. The greatest problem experienced was in finding the detail. Stealing and 'grafting' had become such a way of life and routine activity for many of the women that they took it for granted that the methods and techniques employed to carry out their crimes were commonly known and understood. Although the women interviewed had in the main been labelled dishonest by the police and courts, there is no reason to suggest that their stories and narrative accounts in interviews were fabricated.

AFTER INTERVIEWING

Remaining faithful

It is good practice to transcribe and/or write up interviews within a day or so after they have taken place. In this way the nuances of the conversation that might not be captured on paper are remembered more accurately and can be noted as reflective, added data. I noted earlier that in all of the interviews I conducted in the prison setting, contemporaneous notes were taken as permission was not obtained to use a tape recorder. Some of the extracts above illustrate how these became written up. Writing up naturalistic style interviews is a time-consuming and consequently costly activity and a well-planned and realistically timetabled research project will need to take account of this. It is always likely to be useful to record extra details surrounding the interviews, such as where and when they took place, what else was going on in the background (alarm bells, the clip clop of female officers heels in corridors and shouting in prison), who else was around and other contextual but factual details. Other thoughts about the interviews are also likely to prey on the researcher's mind. Transcribing discussions, words and facts is part of the interviewing process but so too is the writing up of these other thoughts. These are part of what was referred to earlier as good reflective practice and subjective reflexivity. Reflecting on the experiences of interviewing is natural and ongoing (I am still reflecting upon my faithfulness and ethical positioning with regard to doing prison-based interviews over 10 years later) and it is useful to adapt the use of a research diary to record these 'extra' ideas and thoughts, concerns and feelings.

Doing interviews in prison is an emotionally and physically draining form of interaction and, upon returning home from doing prison-based interviews, the researcher may feel not only exhausted but have a feeling of anti-climax. To immediately commence the time-consuming task of writing up is not realistic. After a period of being alone subsequent to interviewing, the need to get the interviews down on paper is important. Talking about the interviews without disclosing confidences or compromising anonymity is a useful practice and serves several functions, including diffusing feelings of stress and euphoria after the intensity of the interview situation, as well as preparing for their analysis and discussing fieldwork with other colleagues and supervisors in an ethical manner.

Remaining ethical

While the principle of informed consent might be generally adhered to, at any stage of the research it is questionable how far consent can ever be fully informed, especially where research cuts across cultural and linguistic divides. Similarly, it is questionable how far participants can ever fully understand what it is they are committing themselves to and what use will be made of the research of which they are a part.

There are a host of ethical issues in qualitative interviewing which are similar to those faced by ethnographic researchers and those engaged in **participant observation** work, as noted in Chapters 8 and 9 of this volume. While I was able to follow a fairly standard ethical checklist about what I asked, how I asked it, what I let my interviewees tell me, about confidentiality and anonymity, consent and power relations (Mason, 1996), some of the knowledges derived from interviews remain ethically ponderous well after the final research report or dissertation or thesis has been written up.

For instance, though I was able to check some of the transcripts with women interviewed in the community, this was not viable with those interviewed in prison. Women in prison are transient and vulnerable populations and the opportunity to revisit and check some of the finer details was not practical. The onus on us to perform ethically principled research applies to a range of stages and personnel, and my own reflective checklist of questions still rings true and asks:

Did I remain ethically principled in my research in all my thinking, acting and in all phases? To:

- the women I interviewed?
- the prison?
- my contacts?
- the gatekeepers?

SUMMARY

This chapter has focused on the preparation, planning and experience of conducting qualitative, in-depth interviews with female offenders in a prison setting. In terms of doing criminological research, a number of summary points emerge. Most notably, research of this nature can be understood as a series of methodological choices, a continuous process of decision-making and negotiation. Being reflexive in your approach to and conducting of criminological research has been shown as important. There are always decisions and trade-offs to be made in fieldwork-based research, which in turn affect the research experience and outcome. In sum, this chapter has explored the methodological choice of using interviews for doing prison-based research. It has given specific attention to issues concerning access and gatekeeping, case selection, sampling and inducements, interviewing skills, politics, ethics, reflexivity and validity. It has illustrated that the 'planning' and 'doing' of research go hand in hand and that practicalities and politics often present key decision-making junctures where dilemmas associated with doing valid and ethical criminological research need to be faced.

■ Study Questions/Activities for Students

1 *Activity*: Visit the website of the ESRC and examine its *Research Ethics Framework*.

   Questions:

   (a) In the context of your own research, how useful are the principles laid out in this framework?

   (b) In the context of doing interviews in prison, how useful are the principles laid out in this framework?

2 *Activity*: Visit the websites of the British Society of Criminology and the British Sociological Association. Examine these codes of ethics offering guidance to criminological and social researchers and revisit the questions posed in question 1.

Question: To what extent do you agree that giving voice to the researcher and presenting subjective disclosures provides you, through sharing the research experience, insights into the world of research?

RESOURCES

Cowburn, M. (2007) 'Men Researching Men in Prison: The Challenges for Pro-Feminist Research', *The Howard Journal of Criminal Justice*, 46 (3): 276–288.

King, R.D. and Wincup, E. (2007) *Doing Research on Crime and Justice.* Oxford: Oxford University Press.

Liebling, A. and Maruna, S. (eds) (2005) *The Effects of Imprisonment.* Cullompton: Willan.

REFERENCES

Berg, B.L. (2007) *Qualitative Research Methods for the Social Sciences* (sixth edition). London: Pearson.

Burgess, R.G. (1984) *In the Field: An Introduction to Field Research.* London: Unwin Hyman.

Cain, M. (1994) 'Realist Philosophy and Standpoint Epistemologies or Feminist Criminology as a Successor Science', in L. Gelsthorpe and A. Morris (eds), *Feminist Perspectives in Criminology.* Milton Keynes: Open University Press.

Campbell, A. (1991) *The Girls in the Gang* (second edition). New York: Basil Blackwell.

Carlen, P. (1988) *Women, Crime and Poverty.* Milton Keynes: Open University Press.

Carlen, P., Christina, D., Hicks, J., O'Dwyer, J. and Tchaikovsky, C. (1985) *Criminal Women.* Cambridge: Polity Press.

Daly, K. (1994) *Gender, Crime, and Punishment.* New Haven, CT and London: Yale University Press.

Davies, P. (1999) 'Women, Crime and an Informal Economy: Female Offending and Crime for Gain', in *British Criminology Conferences: Selected Proceedings* (Volume 2) (www.lboro.ac.uk\departments\ss\bsc\bccsp\vol02\\01davie.htm).

Davies, P. (2006) 'Informed Consent', in V. Jupp (ed.), *The Sage Dictionary of Social Research Methods.* London: Sage.

Devlin, A. (1998) *Invisible Women.* Winchester: Waterside Press.

Gelsthorpe, L. (1994) 'Feminist Methodologies in Criminology: A New Approach or Old Wine in New Bottles?', in L. Gelsthorpe and A. Morris (eds), *Feminist Perspectives in Criminology.* Milton Keynes: Open University Press.

Gelsthorpe, L. and Morris, A. (eds) (1994) *Feminist Perspectives in Criminology.* Milton Keynes: Open University Press.

Gilbert, N. (ed.) (2008) *Researching Social Life* (third edition). London: Sage.

Glaser, B. and Strauss, A. (1967) *The Discovery of Grounded Theory.* Chicago: Aldine.

Hammersley, M. and Atkinson, P. (1983) *Ethnography: Principles in Practice.* London: Tavistock.

Harvey, J. (2007) *Young Men in Prison: Surviving and Adapting to Life Inside.* Cullompton: Willan.

Heidensohn, F. (1985) *Women and Crime.* London: Macmillan.

Hudson, A. (1994) '"Elusive Subjects": Researching Young Women in Trouble', in L. Gelsthorpe and A. Morris (eds), *Feminist Perspectives in Criminology*. Milton Keynes: Open University Press.

Jupp, V. (1989) *Methods of Criminological Research*. London: Allen and Unwin.

Jupp, V. (ed.) (2006) *The Sage Dictionary of Social Research Methods*. London: Sage.

Kvale, S. and Brinkmann, S. (2008) *InterViews: Learning the Craft of Qualitative Research Interviewing* (second edition). London: Sage.

Maher, L. (1997) *Sexed Work: Gender, Race and Resistance in a Brooklyn Drug Market*. Oxford: Clarendon Press.

Malloch, M.S. (2000) *Women, Drugs and Custody*. Winchester: Waterside Press.

Martin, C. (2000) 'Doing Research in a Prison Setting', in V. Jupp et al. (eds), *Doing Criminological Research*. London: Sage.

Mason, J. (1996) *Qualitative Researching*. London: Sage.

Maynard, M. and Purvis, J. (eds) (1994) *Researching Women's Lives from a Feminist Perspective*. London: Taylor and Francis.

Medlicott, D. (2007) 'Women in Prison', in Y. Jewkes (ed.), *Handbook on Prisons*. Cullompton: Willan.

Naffine, N. (1997) *Feminism and Criminology*. Cambridge: Polity Press.

Oliver, P. (2006) 'Snowball Sampling', in V. Jupp (ed.), *The Sage Dictionary of Social Research Methods*. London: Sage.

Piacentini, L. (2007) 'Researching Russian Prisons: A Consideration of New and Established Methodologies in Prison Research', in Y. Jewkes (ed.), *Handbook on Prisons*. Cullompton: Willan.

Sapsford, R. and Jupp, V. (1996) *Data Collection and Analysis*. London: Sage in Association with the Open University.

Stanley, L. and Wise, S. (1993) *Breaking Out Again: Feminist Ontology and Epistemology*. London: Routledge.

Steffensmeier, D. and Allen, E. (1996) 'Gender and Crime: Toward a General Theory of Female Offending', *Annual Review of Sociology*, 22: 459–487.

Sumner, M. (2006) 'Ethics', in V. Jupp (ed.), *The Sage Dictionary of Social Research Methods*. London: Sage.

Silverman, D. (2005) *Doing Qualitative Research* (second edition). London: Sage.

Walklate, S. (2003) 'Can there be a Feminist Victimology?', in P. Davies, P. Francis and V. Jupp (eds), *Victimisation: Theory, Research and Policy*. Basingstoke: Palgrave/Macmillan.

EIGHT
'ESSENTIALLY BARBARIANS'? RESEARCHING THE 'YOUTH UNDERCLASS'

ROBERT MACDONALD

Chapter Contents

KEY POINTS

This chapter:

- Describes a theoretical approach that sees youth crime in the UK as an outcome of the emergence of a new, welfare-dependent underclass
- Outlines how methodological problems have affected the underclass debate
- Describes a set of qualitative youth studies that tested the claims of underclass theory
- Reports the findings of these studies in respect of young men's criminal careers
- Draws on these findings to argue against underclass theory

INTRODUCTION

What is criminological research? Answers to this question will have been given, directly and indirectly, in other chapters of this edition – so why ask it here? Because the research studies discussed at the heart of this chapter were not strictly or narrowly criminological ones and nor do the theoretical, methodological and empirical issues raised sit solely within the confines of criminology. Criminological research might be best understood as that which seeks answers to criminological questions. Ours did but they also had a broader basis in the sociology of youth transitions and social exclusion. This wider perspective and the methodological approach used are valuable in throwing light on some important criminological questions about the relationships between an alleged youth **underclass**, youth transitions and criminal careers in contexts of social exclusion.

The main aim of the chapter is to demonstrate how *methodological* choices and approaches are crucial in shaping the findings and theories that come from research about young people and crime.

A 'YOUTH UNDERCLASS'?

John Muncie (2004) has described the special place of young people, historically and still, as the subjects of much criminology. Since the emergence of youth as a recognised age category in the early industrial era, social commentators have constructed young people as a vulnerable group in a hostile adult world and, simultaneously, as an uncivilised, threatening presence requiring discipline (Gillis, 1974). The governance of this social category through successive waves of state intervention has been driven by these ideological representations of youth 'as/in trouble', of 'control' versus 'care' (Hebdige, 1988; Griffin, 1993).

Debates about the emergence of a 'youth underclass' provide a classic example of these paradoxical, ideological ways of thinking about young people. Whereas Gans (1990) describes the 'underclass' as a racial code word in US debates, in Britain much of the underclass debate has been implicitly, sometimes explicitly, about the condition and situation of poor, 'socially excluded' *young* people (MacDonald, 1997). There are different types of underclass theory (see Box 8.1). This chapter concerns itself primarily with the most widely known variant: 'conservative' or 'cultural' underclass theory. This has been championed by the American academic Charles Murray (1990, 1994). The archetypal protagonists in the development of this 'new rabble', welfare-dependent underclass are feckless, work-shy, criminally inclined young men ('essentially barbarians', to cite Murray 1990) and parentally irresponsible, promiscuous, welfare-draining young single mothers who, together, do no less than threaten 'the survival of free institutions and a civil society' (Murray, 1994: 127).

BOX 8.1

WHAT IS 'THE UNDERCLASS'?

The 'underclass' has been defined in numerous ways and has different meanings to different authors. This is a key problem in debates about it. The most well-known version, from Charles Murray, stresses the *cultural* causation of the underclass. Some sociologists, on the other hand, emphasise its *social structural* origins. Still others argue strongly that there is 'no such thing' as the underclass and that we should abandon the concept. MacDonald (1997: 4) offers this working definition that conflates structural and cultural theories. *If* such a thing has empirical validity, the underclass can be understood as:

> a social group or class of people located at the bottom of the class structure who, over time, have become structurally separate and culturally distinct from the regularly employed working class and society in general though processes of social and economic change (particularly de-industrialisation) and/or through patterns of cultural behaviour, who are now persistently reliant on state benefits and almost permanently confined to living in poorer conditions and neighbourhoods.

Since the late 1990s, underclass terminology has largely been replaced in the UK by the lexicon of 'social exclusion'. There are important differences in language and conceptualisation between theories of social exclusion and of the underclass (see Byrne, 1999; MacDonald and Marsh, 2005). For instance, on the face of it, social exclusion discourses are less controversial in their depictions of the poor and give more room to social structural explanations of poverty (as opposed to cultural or individualised ones). As Levitas (1998) points out, however, moralising tendencies about 'the undeserving poor' remain in many approaches to defining and tackling social exclusion, including New Labour's. One example can be found in the British government's emphasis upon making welfare benefits increasingly conditional upon participation in various training and job-search activities, reflecting a view that without such compulsion the unemployed would prefer idleness to actively seeking work. So, while explicit talk of 'the underclass' has declined, this does not mean that ideas about the underclass have disappeared or been disproven.

For Murray, three social developments, when concentrated together in poor neighbourhoods – rising 'illegitimacy', crime and unemployment – are signals of the emergence of this underclass. In a key, often quoted paragraph, he says:

> If illegitimate births are the leading indicator of an underclass and violent crime a proxy measure of its development, the definitive proof that an underclass has arrived is that large numbers of young, healthy, low-income males choose not to take jobs. (1990: 17)

METHODOLOGICAL QUESTIONS IN THE UNDERCLASS DEBATE

What methodological strengths underpin Murray's controversial theory? Space only allows attention to one problem here (see MacDonald and Marsh, 2005). Taking the final clause in the quotation, above, obviously the key word is 'choose'. No one really doubts that at the time of writing in the early 1990s (and now) there was significant unemployment among the young, male working-class. That is not a point of dispute. That this can be interpreted as *voluntary* unemployment is. Murray provides no evidence for this claim, bar scraps of unconvincing anecdote, and ignores the hundreds of items of British research evidence from the preceding decade that demonstrated that youth unemployment was primarily a result of labour market restructuring and retrenchment. *No* serious empirical study has concluded that voluntary idleness has any quantitative significance.

The methodological weaknesses of Murray's work beg the question, why is it given any credence? Interestingly, many people find Murray's arguments attractive and agreeable. His writing is short in length and adopts a folksy, accessible style – appealing to the common-sense, 'what we all know' truths of the 'man in the street' (set rhetorically against the out-of-touch, woolly-headedness of university 'intellectuals'). Critically, his theories meshed with the (conservative) temper of the political times. Indeed, public and political consumption of academic research is chiefly *not* related to the quality of that research, even when a government professes a keenness for 'evidence-based' policy.

Most British social scientists had little truck with the sort of conservative, cultural underclass thesis developed by Murray (variants that stressed the social structural causation of a dispossessed underclass *were* more popular; see Westergaard, 1992). Critics such as Bagguley and Mann (1992) reject the underclass thesis outright, regarding it as a 'social scientific myth' (p.122) and a 'demonstrably false set of beliefs' (p. 125). They eschew academic discussion and investigation, seeing this as unnecessary and politically dangerous. They paraphrase Murray's depiction of the underclass as 'idle, thieving, bastards' (1992: 113).

Why, then, did *we* engage theoretically and empirically with Murray's ideas? ('We', rather than 'I', is used throughout in recognition of the collective work of the Youth Research Group at Teesside University in undertaking the studies discussed in the chapter; www.tees.ac.uk/sections/research/social_futures/youth_ research.cfm.) Despite its critics, underclass theory is not *necessarily* mistaken. Murray is correct that underclass theory tends to be more popular 'out there' than within academia. Some reputable sociologists describe the theoretical potential of the social developments he describes (Roberts, 1997, 2001). And, as John Mcnicol, an avid critic of underclass theory, put it: 'no thoughtful visitor to the now-blighted inner city areas of Britain or America, whether Meadowell [in northeast England] or Chicago's South Side, could deny that *something* new and frightening has happened' (1994: 30).

Importantly, many of the sorts of studies said to disprove the underclass thesis are not methodologically fit for that purpose (MacDonald, 1997; Roberts, 1997, 2001). Putting it baldly, critics of underclass theory have often looked in the 'wrong' places, at the 'wrong' times, at the 'wrong' people with the 'wrong' methods. Payne and Payne use findings from a large-scale **survey** of the young unemployed of the 1980s to reject the underclass thesis but, in a telling caveat, they say:

> This is not to deny that in some parts of the country there may already exist minority underclass cultures. ... Indeed, if such minority cultures do exist, they are not likely to be identified by large surveys ... which rely on conventional methods of sampling and data collection. (Payne and Payne, 1994: 18)

It is quite feasible that those individuals *most likely* to be part of 'an underclass' are the *least likely* to be listed on the official records that provide research **sampling** frames or to respond to questionnaire surveys. Even then it is unlikely that individuals would be keen to tick off answers that depicted them as immoral, indolent and criminal. Resultant findings are therefore likely to be biased against uncovering the alleged underclass. Murray notes this methodological problem himself:

> There is an ecology to poverty. Cross-sectional surveys of poor people or of the unemployed are useless in either confirming or disconfirming this hypothesis ... those who say that there is no underclass tend to rely on studies in which scholars go into poor neighbourhoods for a few hours at a time with clipboards and multiple choice questionnaires. Those who say there is an underclass tend to rely on studies in which scholars live in poor communities, and get their information from long conversations conducted over weeks and months with the people who live there. (Murray, 1990: 69–70)

If we are to engage properly with underclass theory, what is needed are studies which are able to explore in depth the values, activities and outlooks of the most likely members, in the most likely places and during the most likely periods in which underclass phenomena might show themselves. In broad terms, this is what we did. (Box 8.2 sketches the different positions in the underclass debate.)

BOX 8.2

A SKETCH OF POSITIONS AND METHODOLOGICAL APPROACHES IN THE UNDERCLASS DEBATE (SEE MACDONALD, 1997)

Murray's cultural underclass theory

- Strong support for the idea of a culturally generated, welfare-dependent 'new rabble' underclass in the UK
- Based on:
  - ➤ research and theory developed in relation to the USA
  - ➤ correlation of UK local social statistics about crime, unemployment and 'illegitimate' births
  - ➤ anecdotal conversations with key respondents in a few British cities

(Continued)

Mainstream British social science perspectives on the underclass questions

- Rejection or non-engagement with cultural, conservative underclass theory because of:
  - ➢ political distaste for the theory
  - ➢ existing research evidence that apparently disproved underclass theory in relation to the UK
- Preference for more social–structural versions of underclass theory

Teesside studies of youth transition and social exclusion

- Social scientific engagement with cultural, conservative underclass theory because of:
  - ➢ its theoretical possibility, influence and popularity
  - ➢ the weakness of existing research claimed to disprove it (e.g. cross-sectional, quantitative surveying or out-of-date research)
- Focused, qualitative, extensive and critical case study investigation of the key claims of cultural underclass theory in a prime 'underclass' locale using methods most likely to uncover evidence in support of its claims
- As a consequence, empirical rejection of conservative underclass theory

THE TEESSIDE STUDIES OF YOUTH TRANSITIONS AND SOCIAL EXCLUSION

We refer here to three, related studies (see Box 8.3). The first two of these, *Snakes and Ladders* (Johnston et al., 2000) and *Disconnected Youth?* (MacDonald and Marsh, 2005), both explored how working-class young people (aged 15–25 years) made transitions to adulthood in contexts of multiple deprivation, with critical investigation of theories of the underclass and concepts of social exclusion as prime foci. When pushed to state where British researchers might be most likely to locate the alleged underclass, Murray (1994) cited Middlesbrough because of its high rates of crime, unemployment and 'illegitimacy'. Fortuitously for us, this is also where we work. We selected the poorest neighbourhoods of this town for our critical case study. We use pseudonyms for research participants and particular neighbourhoods.

At the time of fieldwork in the late 1990s and early 2000s, the seven wards that comprised our research sites all featured in the top 5% most deprived nationally (DETR, 2000) and two of them ('Orchard Bank' and 'Primrose Vale') were in the worst five – of 8,414 – in England. Both studies used **participant observation** (e.g. regular, repeated visits to particular sites to be in the company of groups of young people) and, in total, interviews with approximately 50 professionals who worked with young people (such as drugs advisers, youth workers, employment advisers). These studies relied on lengthy, tape-recorded, **biographical interviews** (Chamberlayne et al., 2002) with 186 young people (82 females and 104 males) from the predominantly white, (ex)manual working-class population resident in 'one of the most de-industrialised locales in the UK' (Byrne, 1999: 93).

For the first two studies, sample recruitment was a mixture of **purposive**, **theoretical** and **convenience sampling**. The starting point was to recruit individuals of the right age (15–25 years) from these places. It was imperative to focus on aspects of young people's experiences that would help test the claims of underclass theory at the same time as being as open as possible in recruitment. Thus, we sought out individuals who were single parents, who had plentiful experience of unemployment and who had significant histories of offending, but we also sought out people who were not parents, who were employed (or training/studying) and who were not known to us as offenders. Agencies and organisations were helpful in introducing us to potential interviewees (e.g. training schemes, further education colleges, New Deal for Young People programmes, drugs advice services, the Probation Service, local Young Offenders Institutes, community groups). From early interviewees we would seek suggestions for others (in a **snowballing method**). These two strategies generated the bulk of interviewees. A few responded to posters and flyers advertising the research. One of the projects offered a small financial compensation for participation (of £10), the other did not. This made little difference to recruitment (apart from, in the first case, we came across some people who appeared to be mainly participating for financial reasons, which is perhaps one example of the financial hardship that participants faced).

Because of our recruitment methods we cannot claim that this combined sample of 186 people is statistically representative of young adults in these neighbourhoods. We therefore cannot and do not seek to *quantify* aspects of youth experience (e.g. *how many* local young people are unemployed or use drugs). Because of our efforts to sample different experiences of youth transition, our varied points of contact and the relatively large size of the sample, we do believe, however, that we achieved a sample that was representative of the range of experiences typical of young adults in these neighbourhoods.

The third study *Poor Transitions* (Webster et al., 2004), was designed as a follow-up to the two earlier ones. The key research question was where earlier youth transitions *led* individuals in their mid to late twenties. Fieldwork was undertaken in 2003, between two and four years after our first interviews. We re-interviewed 34 people (18 females and 16 males), now aged 23 to 29 years, from the two original samples. We sampled theoretically so as to understand key experiences in longer-term transitions (see Box 8.3).

Again, no claim can be made that these 34 individuals are strictly representative of the larger samples of the first studies. Our knowledge of the research site and of *potential* re-interviewees makes us think that those we did speak to were broadly representative of the initial, larger samples (see Webster et al., 2004).

BOX 8.3

THE TEESSIDE STUDIES OF YOUTH TRANSITIONS AND SOCIAL EXCLUSION: RESEARCH DESIGN

Study 1 (*Snakes and Ladders*, Johnston et al., 2000)

- Funded by Joseph Rowntree Foundation
- Fieldwork in 1998–99, in one very deprived ward in Teesside
- 20 interviews with professional 'stakeholders'
- Some limited observational work in the research site
- 98 one-off, qualitative interviews with young adults, aged 15–25 years

Study 2 (*Disconnected Youth?* MacDonald and Marsh, 2005)

- Funded by Economic and Social Research Council
- Fieldwork in 1999–2001, in five neighbouring, very deprived wards in Teesside
- 30 interviews with professional 'stakeholders'
- Participant observation with young people in three sites over a year
- 88 qualitative interviews (some repeated) with young adults, aged 15–25

Study 3 (*Poor Transitions*, Webster et al., 2004)

- Funded by Joseph Rowntree Foundation
- Fieldwork in 2003
- 34 qualitative interviews with young adults, aged 23–29, drawn from the samples of studies 1 and 2, exploring three sub-themes:
  - Young parenthood (n. 11)
  - Persistent 'poor work' (n. 11)
  - Long-term criminal and drug-using careers (n. 12)

Longitudinal, qualitative youth research like this is relatively rare in British social science (see Henderson et al., 2007, for a very good example). The sort of (working-class) 'socially excluded' young adults we talked to are often described as 'hard to reach' in (middle-class) research and policy circles (Merton, 1998). In fact, there was nothing *particularly* difficult about finding suitable participants and undertaking interviews with them. Our experience is that powerless, working-class people, especially underemployed ones, are usually happy to participate in research if asked – certainly more so than the powerful and middle-class. *They* are more '**hard to reach**'.

Being honest about the aims of the research and the likely minimal or zero benefits to participants helped. Methodology textbooks describe the necessity of researchers building relationships with 'hard to reach' young adults over time, so as to establish the trust and **rapport** vital for successful interviewing (Spradley, 1979; May, 1993), particularly where '**sensitive topics**' such as involvement in crime are envisaged. This is why 'insider research' is often seen to be advantageous; the researcher is already part of the scene or group under study and his or her cultural identity eases access and trust (see Hodkinson, 2002). Our experience was not quite like this. In the first studies, certainly, we were strangers to the interviewees and typically carried out lengthy, detailed interviews at first contact. Nevertheless, in most cases 'rapport' appeared to develop very quickly, leading to frank, revelatory and sometimes emotional interviews about people's lives, experiences and viewpoints.

We had little difficulty in finding out about supposedly 'sensitive topics' (e.g. their involvement in 'dole fiddling', crime or drug use). Indeed, our status as strangers possibly helped the achievement of these interviews. *Because* we did not know these people it was safe to open up. We were struck by this most directly in interviews with young men in Young Offenders Institutes. They were used to showing a hard face to the world and displaying resilience and bravado. Yet these private, confidential, *safe* interviews were often marked by what we judge to be great candour, reflection and depth on their part. They told sometimes tearful stories of 'things gone wrong', failure, loss, regret and personal shame.

Admittedly, some of these interviewees with criminal justice system records had previously been asked to account for themselves and their situations (and, occasionally, more polished and apparently partial story telling sometimes needed to be interrupted and our status and purpose re-explained). Most interviewees, however, had never talked about themselves (and expressed bemusement about why anybody might be interested). Finally, we would note that it is rare for anyone, no matter what their social status, to receive attentive, non-judgemental questioning about their lives from someone who is genuinely interested in only that. Our interviewees responded very generously, providing the core of the empirical material of the studies. Here we focus only on what informants told us about their 'criminal careers'.

UNDERSTANDING 'CRIMINAL CAREERS': YOUTH TRANSITIONS AND SOCIAL EXCLUSION

While it is important to re-iterate that these were not statistically representative samples, analysis of the biographical accounts of interviewees can help us sketch out the *nature* and *shape* of criminal careers. Of the 186 interviewees across the *Snakes and Ladders* and *Disconnected Youth?* studies, 168 gave accounts of crime that were deemed detailed enough to use. Of these, 100 reported no offending whatsoever and 21 described 'one-off' or very short-lived offending. Forty-seven reported recurrent offending, all of whom had convictions and 33 of whom had been imprisoned. Of these 47, 26 were or had been opiate users.

Although each case differed, there were enough of them and enough shared between them to allow valid, theoretical descriptions of criminal careers among young people like this in this place at this time. Here we merely provide an overall sketch. We also refer to one cameo – of Richard – presented as a 'life-grid' (Table 8.1), that helps exemplify in one biography the general pattern among young men.

TABLE 8.1 One Criminal and Drug-using Career – Richard, 20 (at first interview)/23 (at second interview)

Age	School to work	Family/housing	Leisure/networks	Crime	Drugs
11–14	**'Loads of truancy'**	Living with mother and step-father in East Kelby (father left when Richard was age 4)	**Street-based socialising** with friends, while truanting	Occasional shop-lifting (**'leisure crime'**) 'I think I went off the rails with my Dad being away'	Cannabis use
14–16	**Re-engagement** with school: 5 (low grade) GCSEs	(Ditto)	Some dis-engagement from peer group	Reduced offending	(Ditto) [Heroin arrives in East Kelby] 1st heroin use: 'Me and my friends thought we'd have a daft go at it [heroin] and before we knew it a few of us were [cold] turkeying and then we all were. Hooked'
16–19	'Typical' post-16 career: Youth Training schemes, unemployment, short-term unskilled jobs, New Deal, unemployment	(Ditto)	(Ditto)		Attempts to desist, with methadone

TABLE 8.1 (Continued)

Age	School to work	Family/housing	Leisure/networks	Crime	Drugs
19–20	Unemployed	**Ejected from family home** (accused of theft), sleeps rough, assaulted/hospitalised, moves to homeless hostel	Immersed in new, heroin-using peer group at hostel	Accelerated rate of shop lifting to fund drug use, increasingly **chaotic, acquisitive crime,** burglary, period on remand, release, further burglary and shoplifting, on remand then probation.	Relapses to heroin – **addicted, daily use**
				'You don't think about anything else at all. All you think is heroin – where do you want to go for a mooch [to thieve], where to score a bag [purchase heroin], where to do it [to administer the drug]'	
	Aspires to return to college	Hopes to be reunited with family	Wants to dissociate from drug-using/criminal associates	Attempts to desist from offending	Persisting with new, methadone programme
			'It's 'cos I don't occupy myself. No job to keep me busy. It does me head in just wandering around. Nothing to do. So I end up knocking around with me old mates. I just get back into it'		
21–23	No jobs, no training, unemployed	**New partner** Lives with her and her two children	Processes of dissociation from previous peer group, socialising with partner	Further offending, further imprisonment 'Fragile desistance'	Failed methadone programme New methadone programme

As noted, 21 interviewees had a very short-lived 'criminal career', with typically one or two offences of shoplifting or criminal damage in their early to mid teenage years. For many, their transgressions ceased there.

Two key movements can be identified in the consolidation of the most serious, longer-term criminal careers (of 47 participants). The first of these was the hardening up of school disaffection (again, a common experience of the samples overall) into full-blown educational disengagement. This was usually displayed in frequent, persistent truancy (see Table 8.1, Richard aged 11–14 years). A process of simultaneous disengagement from school and engagement with 'street corner society' (MacDonald and Shildrick, 2007) further established oppositional identities and was the cornerstone for the evolution of most careers of crime that extended beyond early to mid-teenage. Thus, Richard spent much of the first years of secondary schooling involved in 'loads of truancy' with friends, sometimes shoplifting to relieve the boredom (receiving two police cautions for these offences). He said of this period: 'I think I went off the rails a bit with my Dad being away' (i.e. his natural father had left the family home in Richard's childhood). His mother tried to deter his truancy: 'she used to give me a good hiding'. In general, dull truant time was enlivened by the camaraderie of shoplifting jaunts, other petty thieving and speeding around the estates in stolen vehicles: crime as leisure for bored, out-of-school teenagers (see Stephen and Squires, 2003).

For some, this marked the early phases of criminal apprenticeships. They began to learn the routines of more acquisitively-oriented offending (e.g. how and what to thieve from cars) and were drawn into local criminal markets (e.g. the best shops and pubs for fencing stolen property, the market rate for 'knock-off gear', etc.). For many, though, these sorts of infringements – coupled with underage drinking and recreational use of drugs such as cannabis, speed and ecstasy – marked the extent, and end-point, of criminal careers.

Thus, the relatively large numbers involved in (petty) offending in early teenage lessened as the years passed.

The second, most significant moment – that helped to drag out a smaller number of individuals' criminal career into later years and to transmute them into something more destructive – is when heroin enters the scene. Parker and colleagues (1998) map the 'second wave of heroin outbreaks' in Britain during the mid-1990s. Middlesbrough provides a classic case. Local police and drugs workers reported how very cheap, smoke-able heroin flooded into the working-class housing estates of Teesside in the mid-1990s. MacDonald and Marsh (2002) describe how some of Teesside's young people seem unprepared to resist the temptations of this 'poverty drug' and made speedy transitions from occasional, recreational use of drugs such as cannabis and speed to often daily, dependent use of heroin (and later in the 1990s, crack cocaine) (see Table 8.1, Richard aged 14–16 years). Richard described how he and his friends made the shift from cannabis to heroin use:

> We'd all been smoking tack [cannabis] for ages. Ever since we were 14 or 15. We'd smoke it all day and it'd get to the point where it had no effect. It wasn't getting us stoned

> ... [so] ... me and my friends thought we'd have a daft go at it [heroin] and before we knew it a few of us were [cold] turkeying and then we all were. Hooked. It's dead hard to come off ... they say 'once a smackhead, always a smackhead'. Maybe they're right.

For this minority (n. 26), dependent use of heroin was the driving force behind exclusionary transitions which distanced them from their families, from their previous lifestyles, from the labour market and which entangled them in chaotic, damaging careers of drug-driven crime (see Simpson, 2003). Heroin use became central to an understanding of their unfolding biographies.

For individuals like Richard (see Table 8.1, Richard aged 19–20 years), increasingly desperate acquisitive criminality was fuelled by the need for daily drug money. He estimated that he committed around 150 separate thefts from shops in different towns around the north-east during this period (having been 'barred out' of his local town centre by private security guards who were aware of his criminal record). At one point he was making around £300 per day from the selling on of stolen goods and 'most of it was going on heroin'. By the age of 20, this close combination of drug and crime careers had progressively closed down options for a more 'mainstream' lifestyle. He had failed to complete several government training programmes, had been employed only once (and briefly), had been unemployed recurrently, had become estranged from his family, had been homeless and slept rough, had a lengthy and worsening record of offending, had been imprisoned twice and, at the age of 20, was living in a bail hostel, struggling to maintain his commitment to a methadone programme and scratching around trying to find ways, beyond heroin, to fill tedious, direction-less days. Cases like that of Richard represent perhaps the most intractable forms of social exclusion that were uncovered in the research.

Yet our follow-up study, *Poor Transitions* (Webster et al., 2004), uncovered a happier story. To recap, one of the 'types' of transition that we were particularly interested in tracking into the interviewees' mid and late twenties was that where careers of persistent offending and dependent drug use were combined. Richard was one of those re-interviewed for this project, some three years later. The intervening period had been typified by a familiar pattern of heroin use, offending, prison, attempts to 'go straight' and relapse to heroin use. He said:

> It's [heroin-crime] like a vicious circle. It's like one, big, magnetic circle ... when you get out of jail it starts again, you're slowly getting drawn back in all the time ... slowly you end up back on the circle again, moving round and round and back in the same direction all the time.

Despite the depths of his troubles at age 20, at 23 Richard – like the majority of the 12 interviews in this group in the follow-up study – was in a state of 'fragile desistance' from crime and dependent drug use. By this we mean that *we* agreed that he was making a sustained, new and – at that point – apparently successful attempt to take the long, precarious journey back to 'a normal life', as he described it. We stress the fragility of desistance as a *process* (rather than a single, simple

BOX 8.4

FACTORS THAT AID DESISTANCE FROM CRIMINAL AND DRUG-USING CAREERS, TEESSIDE FINDINGS

- **New, lawful, purposeful activity** (which could revolve around activities such as youth work projects or college attendance)
- **Employment**
- **Parenthood**
- **Partnerships**
- **Drug treatment** (that was quickly accessible, non-punitive)
- **Housing moves** (away from the immediate home neighbourhood)
- **Separation from earlier peer groups** (and 'street corner society')

event) because, of course, the biographies of this sub-sample were replete with failed attempts and because success was contingent on several factors beyond individual motivation (see Box 8.4).

Just as the perceived purposelessness of school had set the context for the drift into offending – and later unemployment sometimes helped informants down 'the wrong path' into more serious crime – the availability of 'purposeful activity' (MacDonald and Marsh, 2005) in which individuals could invest their time, energy and identity helped in the shift away from drug and criminal careers. This purposefulness could be found in normal aspects of youth transition and, confirming other criminological research, the getting of jobs, the forming of new partnerships and becoming a parent motivated and facilitated the process of 'growing out of crime' (Rutherford, 1992). The problem, though, is that a corollary of cumulative, sustained, heroin-driven crime is often largely 'empty' school-to-work careers punctuated by repeated spells of imprisonment. This makes the achievement of these sorts of resolution much harder. People like Richard are unlikely to appear attractive as potential employees, partners and fathers. With 'purposeful activity to engage energies and through which to redefine personal identity, liberating oneself from addiction was hard enough. Without it, relapse was common. Heroin helped "fill the void" [and] make life bearable' (Foster, 2000: 322).

Easy access to therapeutic, non-punitive drug treatment services was reported as a significant aid to the process of desistance, as was separation from previous peer groups. Physical and emotional detachment from earlier subcultural lives and alliances was crucial. Peer networks had eased the transition to offending and now blocked the path to desistance. Even when people had come to a point where they felt a desire to 'go straight', they perceived no easy way forward. Dependent heroin users were unanimous on this point; their lives since mid-teenage had been lived within social networks that reinforced drug behaviour. For many of them, imprisonment often provided a welcome opportunity to do their 'rattle', albeit under a harsh, non-therapeutic regime ('rattle' refers to the physical effects of heroin detoxification). A few had even purposefully sought a prison sentence (rather than probation supervision) as a way of escaping the recurrent drug temptations of 'the street'. Release from prison was normally viewed with trepidation because it signalled a return to the environment that had generated their initial drug dependency.

WHAT IS WRONG WITH UNDERCLASS THEORIES OF YOUTH CRIME?

Returning to Murray's theory of a cultural underclass, on the face of it, there is *some* 'fit' between what he says in respect of young men and crime and what we found in the 'underclass' locales we researched. Many young men had not been brought up by two, married birth parents. Crime rates were significantly above average and drug markets (for heroin and more lately crack cocaine) and drug use have had a terrible effect upon the place. Unemployment, and associated welfare payments, have become a common and recurrent feature of life. Young men and women often do not have clear, successful labour market 'careers'. Poverty is widespread. Clearly, some do make choices that, on the face of it, lead them toward crime, drug use and welfare.

So what *is* so wrong with underclass theory? We can understand how simplistic sketches of social statistics pertaining to this place and brief conversations with some residents (i.e. the sort of methods adopted by Murray) might lead one to positive conclusions of its existence. Yet we come to a different conclusion. We raise four points of objection here. Each, we think, demonstrates the importance of our *methodological* choices and approach (i.e. had we done things differently we may not have been able to make these arguments).

1   Underclass theory misinterprets apparent evidence of support for its ideas among poor people. An easy explanation of crime in terms of cultural degeneration and moral failure will always find popular support. It benefits from simplicity and chimes with the human desire to apportion blame; to label the wrong-doers and the 'bad'. Murray heard exactly this sort of moral castigation of 'the underclass' Other, in his few and brief visits to poor, working-class areas. We heard the same in our interviews. When put in lay terms, underclass theory was well received by the sort of people deemed by Murray to *be* the underclass. This is odd.

   Yet the difference between our method and his is that we were able to talk to many such people over time and in depth. Our qualitative **interview** method allowed us to question, challenge, probe, argue, follow-up and explore. This led us to a different understanding from Murray's. Unsurprisingly, negative diatribes about 'idle, thieving bastards' (Bagguley and Mann, 1992) were never self-applied; they were always about a usually un-named 'them'. *Personal*, biographical accounts of why and how 'I am' a young, lone mother, or unemployed and claiming benefits, or involved in crime, *never* fitted the claims of underclass theory (and were far more detailed, complex, human and convincing), yet this theory was used widely and roughly to explain the alleged failings of others in the same situations as them. Occasionally, members of the supposed underclass were named. When we pursued these leads again we found the same popular disdain for 'the undeserving poor' rhetorically displaced on to vague others. In short, we interpret this popular discourse about 'the underclass' among the alleged underclass not, as Murray does, as evidence of its empirical existence, but as the desperate, untutored rhetoric of the socially insecure and materially poor. It shored up personal and family respectability by distancing themselves from commonly heard diatribes about people like them and places like this.

2   The *length* and quasi-longitudinal focus of our research – using the concept of youth transition, employing biographically focused interviews (that recounted the past, described the present and scanned the future) and returning to the same interviewees over time – also makes us cast doubt on underclass theory. It is hard to reconcile the life stories told to us with a theory that sees criminal engagement as driven by delinquent values and cultures inherited from underclass parents. People change. Lives change. The twists, turns, choices and decisions of complicated 'criminal' biographies were influenced more by chance, contingency and 'critical moments' than by inbred, hard-set deviancy.

'Critical moments' (see also Thomson et al., 2002) were 'out of the blue' episodes or experiences that buffeted lives that always lacked material comfort and sometimes lacked emotional/social support. Many but not all critical moments came from the ill-health and bereavement that shadowed these life stories. The sheer preponderance of death in interview transcripts (of friends, parents, siblings, children) was surprising at first glance, but predictable with the knowledge of the socio-spatial concentration of health inequalities. What was less predictable was the personal consequence of these sorts of critical moment. For instance, judging by our evidence, traumatic bereavements could help turn individual transitions 'off the rails', towards desperate offending behaviour and heroin use (see Allen, 2007), but they could equally serve to influence people away from the same. The contingency of when, in a biography, such critical moments impacted upon individuals, the other pressures they faced previously and currently, the level of support they had and, no doubt, factors beyond our sociological gaze came together in ways that were too complicated and complex to allow for the prediction of who (of the sample) would develop criminal careers and who would not. Certainly, the orthodox 'risk factor' approach to understanding criminal development did not seem to work for the samples in this context. So many had so many of the risk factors said to predict criminality but proportionately so few fulfilled this theoretical prediction (see MacDonald, 2006; Webster et al., 2006). In short, individual life stories (including those with criminal careers) were not set in stone. They were determined neither by positivistic checklists of risks, nor by inherited value systems of the alleged underclass.

3   It is hard to square our findings with a theory that posits that a new, criminally-inclined and deviant underclass is 'contaminating the life of entire neighbourhoods' (Murray, 1990: 195). The sort of youth transition and criminal career followed by people like Richard was one among many. The 'delinquent solution' remains very much a minority one, even in a prime 'underclass' locale among prime candidates. Indeed, a more interesting question – that might also be asked of more serious, contemporary criminological investigations in de-industrialised neighbourhoods (e.g. Hall et al., 2008) – is why proportionately so *few* young adults adopt a criminal response to the restricted opportunities and impoverishment facing them.

Elsewhere (MacDonald and Marsh, 2005) we describe the sheer, stubborn normality of the values, outlooks and ambitions of young people here, particularly in respect of family life and their working futures, defining these by their 'hyper-conventionality'. (Even most of those with committed criminal/drug-using careers, like Richard, held to these values and goals.) We explain this in terms of the durability of entrenched *working-class* – not underclass – culture. Importantly, though, we would not have been able to claim this without the very simple methodological decision to recruit a broad sample and to ask them about a broad range of topics. Our reflections on these criminological questions were not restricted by a sample consisting of only those known to be involved in crime, or by questions only about crime. Criminal careers cannot be fully understood by *only* talking to those with criminal careers about crime. We have described how criminal careers emerged in relation to other aspects of transition, particularly 'leisure careers' and 'school-to-work careers'. The previous point was about the length of our research. This one is about its *breadth*.

4 Underclass theory of the sort offered by Murray overplays individual choice and underplays the ways that life choices are socially structured and constrained (by the inequalities of social class and place). History is important here. Key among the social processes that we argue create the forms of economic marginality and social exclusion experienced by our samples is the de-industrialisation of Teesside. In 1974, 54% of Middlesbrough 16-year-olds left school for jobs or apprenticeships. By 1998, when our first fieldwork began, 6% did. In between came the global economic crises of the mid-1970s with the local impact of an extremely steep and speedy decline of Teesside's economic base, which saw half of all manufacturing and construction jobs (and a quarter of all jobs) lost (see Beynon et al., 1994). The economic basis of youth transitions to respectable, secure, working-class adulthood was shattered. Ineffective, government-sponsored training and employability schemes (that tend not to lead to jobs), education courses that are questionable in their quality and labour market 'dividend' and insecure, low-paid 'poor work' now provide the framework through which transitions are made. In other words, the 'structure of opportunities' facing young people here has radically altered.

One cannot understand choices without understanding the structure of choices available (and the way that class and gender, in particular, texture perceptions of these choices). Thus, to take just one example, Murray's 'definitive proof' (1990: 17) of an underclass – young men *choosing* not to take jobs – seems wildly ignorant of the social–structural and historical conditions that create or deny choices for employment. And, in fact, young men and women persistently *did* 'choose' the low-quality jobs that were available (MacDonald and Marsh, 2005). The significance of place and history in framing the possibilities of youth transitions is also evident in the impact of a significant heroin market (and associated criminal economy) in Teesside during the mid-1990s. Our interviewees (i.e. professionals who worked in these neighbourhoods, young people who had and who had not used these drugs) unanimously reported the rapid deterioration of community life caused by criminality fuelled by dependency on illegal drugs. Putting it baldly, young people like Richard would not have been able to make the 'choices' he did, and have the heroin-dependent youth phase he has had, if he had been born 10 years earlier. The 'choices' and dramas of individual biographies cannot fully be understood unless situated within the wider landscape of place, economy and history in which lives are lived.

SUMMARY

The chapter has noted the long-running representation of 'youth as trouble' and how young people are commonly the subject of criminological research and theory. Conservative underclass theory is both controversial and influential, and seeks to explain youth crime in relation to the emergence of a new, welfare-dependent underclass at the bottom of the social heap. British social science tended not to engage empirically with Charles Murray's underclass theory, often pointing instead to studies said to disprove it. These, however, typically had methodological shortcomings. Our Teesside-based studies of youth and social exclusion were designed to provide a critical case study of underclass theory. These have been described in some detail, with reflection particularly on their methodology and our experience of research. The chapter sets out findings in respect of young men's criminal and drug-using careers, which are drawn upon in outlining four key problems with underclass theory.

Overall, the chapter demonstrates the value of qualitative research that aims to get close up to young people's lives and which seeks extensive understandings of them. By 'extensive' we mean studies that explore the range of interdependent 'careers' that comprise transitions **and** how these transitions unfold over the years. This broad, sociological approach to youth transitions – when set in the panoramas of history, place and economy that shape 'structures of opportunity' – can, among other things, help us better understand the causes and meanings of offending among young people.

■ Study Questions/Activities for Students ■

1 What are the methodological strengths and weaknesses of:

   (a) Murray's underclass theory?
   (b) the Teesside studies of youth transitions and social exclusion?

2 Which set of ideas do you find most convincing in understanding youth crime and why?

3 The chapter outlines four main objections to underclass theories of youth crime. Can you rephrase them in your own words and think of others?

4. If *you* wanted to research the relationship between 'the underclass', social exclusion, youth transitions and criminal careers, how would you go about it?

5 Describe what you understand by the following terms:

   (a) 'youth transition'
   (b) 'the underclass'
   (c) 'social exclusion'
   (d) 'criminal career'
   (e) 'leisure career'
   (f) 'school to work career'
   (g) 'the structure of opportunities'

6 Identify three things that the chapter says about research methodology that you think are interesting, controversial or wrong.

RESOURCES

Bagguley, P. and Mann, K. (1992) 'Idle, thieving bastards: scholarly representations of the "underclass"', *Work, Employment and Society*, 6(1): 113–26.

Jones Finer, C. and Nellis, M. (eds) (1998) *Crime and Social Exclusion*, Oxford: Blackwell.

MacDonald, R. and Marsh, J. (2005) *Disconnected Youth? Growing up in Britain's Poor Neighbourhoods*, Basingstoke: Palgrave.

Morris, L. (1994) *Dangerous Classes*, London: Routledge.

Murray, C. (1990) *The Emerging British Underclass*, London: Institute of Economic Affairs.

Murray, C. (1994) *Underclass: The Crisis Deepens*, London: Institute of Economic Affairs.

REFERENCES

Allen, C. (2007) *Crime, Drugs and Social Theory*, Aldershot: Ashgate.

Bagguley, P. and Mann, K. (1992) 'Idle, thieving bastards: scholarly representations of the "underclass"', *Work, Employment and Society*, 6(1): 113–26.

Beynon, H., Hudson, R. and Sadler, D. (1994) *A Place Called Teesside*, Edinburgh: Edinburgh University Press.

Byrne, D. (1999) *Social Exclusion*, Milton Keynes: Open University Press.

Chamberlayne, P., Rustin, M. and Wengraf, T. (eds) (2002) *Biography and Social Exclusion in Europe*, Bristol: Policy Press.

Foster, J. (2000) 'Social exclusion, crime and drugs', *Drugs: Education, Prevention and Policy*, 4(7): 317–30.

Gans, H. (1990) 'Deconstructing the underclass', *American Planning Association Journal*, 52: 271–7.

Gillis, J. (1974) *Youth and History*, New York: Academic Press.

Griffin, C. (1993) *Representations of Youth*, Cambridge: Polity Press.

Hall, S., Winlow, S. and Ancrum, C. (2008) *Criminal Identities and Consumer Culture*, Cullompton: Willan.

Hebdige, D. (1988) *Hiding in the Light*, London: Comedia/Routlege.

Henderson, S. et al. (2007) *Inventing Adulthoods*, Milton Keynes: Open University Press.

Hodkinson, P. (2002) *Goth: Identity, Style and Subculture*, Oxford: Berg.

Johnston, L., MacDonald, R., Mason, P., Ridley, L. and Webster, C. (2000) *Snakes and Ladders: Young People, Transitions and Social Exclusion*, Bristol: Policy Press.

Levitas, R. (1998) *The Inclusive Society? Social Exclusion and New Labour*, Basingstoke: Macmillan.

MacDonald, R. (1997) 'Dangerous youth and the dangerous class', in MacDonald, R. (ed.), *Youth, the 'Underclass' and Social Exclusion*, London: Routledge.

MacDonald, R. (2006) 'Social exclusion, youth transitions and criminal careers: five critical reflections on risk', *Australian and New Zealand Journal of Criminology*, 39(3): 371–83.

MacDonald, R. and Marsh, J. (2002) 'Crossing the Rubicon: youth transitions, poverty, drugs and social exclusion', *International Journal of Drug Policy*, 13: 27–38.

MacDonald, R. and Marsh, J. (2005) *Disconnected Youth? Growing up in Britain's Poor Neighbourhoods*, Basingstoke: Palgrave.

MacDonald, R. and Shildrick, T. (2007) 'Street corner society', *Leisure Studies*, 26(3): 339–55.

Macnicol, J. (1994) 'Is there an underclass? The lessons from America', in White, M. (ed.), *Unemployment and Public Policy in a Changing Labour Market,* London: Policy Studies Institute.

May, T. (1993) *Social Research*, Buckingham: Open University Press.

Merton, B. (1998) *Finding the Missing*, Leicester: Youth Work Press.

Muncie, J. (2004) *Youth and Crime*, London: Sage.

Murray, C. (1990) *The Emerging British Underclass*, London: Institute of Economic Affairs.

Murray, C. (1994) *Underclass: The Crisis Deepens*, London: Institute of Economic Affairs.

Parker, H., Bury, C. and Eggington, R. (1998) *New Heroin Outbreaks amongst Young People in England and Wales*, Police Research Group, Paper 92, London: Home Office.

Payne, J. and Payne, C. (1994) 'Recession, restructuring and the fate of the unemployed: evidence in the underclass debate', *Sociology*, 28(1): 1–21.

Roberts, K. (1997) 'Is there a youth underclass? The evidence from youth research', in MacDonald, R. (ed.), *Youth, the 'Underclass' and Social Exclusion*, London: Routledge.

Roberts, K. (2001) *Class in Modern Britain*, London: Palgrave.

Rutherford, A. (1992) *Growing Out of Crime: The New Era*, London: Waterside Press.

Simpson, M. (2003) 'The relationship between drug use and crime', *International Journal of Drug Policy*, 14: 307–19.

Spradley, J. (1979) *The Ethnographic Interview*, New York: Holt, Rinehart and Winston.

Stephen D. and Squires, P. (2003) '"Adults don't realize how sheltered they are": a contribution to the debate on youth transitions from some voices on the margin', *Journal of Youth Studies*, 6(2): 145–64.

Thomson, R., Bell, R., Holland, J., Henderson, S., McGrellis, S. and Sharpe, S. (2002) 'Critical moments: choice, chance and opportunity in young people's narratives of transition', *Sociology*, 36(2): 335–54.

Webster, C., Simpson, D., MacDonald, R., Abbas, A., Cieslik, M., Shildrick, T. and Simpson, M. (2004) *Poor Transitions: Social Exclusion and Young Adults*, Bristol: Policy Press.

Webster, C., MacDonald, R. and Simpson, M. (2006) 'Predicting criminality?', *Youth Justice*, 6(1): 7–22.

Westergaard, J. (1992) 'About and beyond the underclass: some notes on influences of social climate on British sociology', *Sociology*, 26: 575–87.

NINE
ETHNOGRAPHIC RESEARCH IN THE CONTEXT OF POLICING

FAYE COSGROVE AND PETER FRANCIS

Chapter Contents

KEY POINTS

This chapter:

- Describes the core characteristics of ethnographic research, including its relationship to forms of participant observation

- Reviews the tradition of using ethnography to research the police occupational culture

- Examines the development of appreciative ethnographies in some police and criminal justice research

- Reports on the findings of one doctoral study that utilised an appreciative ethnography to research Police Community Support Officers

- Draws the discussion together to reflect upon the suitability of an appreciative ethnography in understanding contemporary police occupational cultures

INTRODUCTION

In much criminological literature, police officers are described as sharing a set of collectively understood and often taken-for-granted norms, cultural attitudes, values and beliefs, frequently referred to in the literature as 'cop culture'. For Reiner, cop culture is a 'patterned set of understandings which help officers to cope with and adjust to the pressures and tensions which confront the police' (2000: 87), and is 'crucial to an analysis of what they do, and their broad political function' (2000: 85).

Much of our knowledge and understanding of the existence of a police occupational culture has arisen from ethnographic studies carried out by researchers operating overtly or covertly within the police organisation. Often mixing methods including **participant observation** and ethnographic interviews, ethnographers have not only identified the core characteristics of the police culture as involving mission, solidarity, suspicion, isolationism, cynicism and pragmatism (Reiner, 2000), but have also testified to its strength – some researchers finding that the pressure to 'go native' jeopardised the research they were doing (Punch, 1979).

Yet while such studies have brought a welcome insight to debates on police culture, for some they misrepresent what the police do (and why they do it), provide insufficient comparisons for the claims they make and reflect the perspectives of the researcher more than they do the police officers being researched (Hunt and Manning, 1991; Waddington, 1999). For these writers what is required is an ethnographic methodology that appreciates rather than condemns and one that explains rather than describes.

The aim of this chapter is to review ethnographic studies of police culture. In so doing, the chapter outlines the core characteristics of ethnographic research, reviews its use in traditional sociological studies of police culture, examines the development of a more appreciative ethnography to understanding organisational culture in contemporary society and describes our own approach to doing appreciative ethnography with police community support officers. Throughout the chapter a series of boxed illustrations add depth to the discussion and the chapter is supported by glossary terms, exercises and activities.

ETHNOGRAPHIC RESEARCH

Ethnography is a methodology widely used by researchers across social science disciplines, and has a long-established research tradition in criminology (Noaks and Wincup, 2004). It is a form of qualitative research that involves the utilisation of a range of methods with the aim of gaining an insight into a culture or cultures 'that a group of people share' (Van Maanen, 1995). It is typically described as committed to observing 'intact cultural groups in their natural settings over long periods of time' (Lee, 1999: 26). Support for its applicability to the study of culture is provided by Denscombe (1998: 79), who argues, 'ethnographic research is well suited to dealing with the way members of a culture see events – as seen through their eyes'. This commitment to the subjective interpretations of social reality of the observed (Hammersley and Atkinson, 1983) and Robinson and Reed's (1998) observation that ethnography is typically adopted when little is known about a subgroup and as a means of developing an understanding of the views, values and beliefs of that group clearly suggests the suitability of it for researching the police organisation, as we demonstrate later on in the chapter.

The origins of ethnography are located in the work of the Chicago sociologists of the 1920s and 1930s. It draws upon symbolic interactionism, phenomenological and hermeneutic perspectives and views social phenomena as characteristically different from physical phenomena. Given that actions are based on meanings and are constructed and reconstructed as people interpret and reinterpret the situations in which they find themselves, ethnography has developed as a means through which access to and an understanding of meanings, actions, decisions and situations is achieved. To do this the researcher will learn the codes, language and practices of the group he or she is observing. Ethnography therefore combines cultural interpretation – that is eliciting an understanding of the shared meanings of a group so as to develop understanding of their actions – with prolonged participant engagement in the natural settings within which the group operate.

Despite their time-consuming nature and the lack of generalisability of findings generated through the intensive study of relatively small populations (Miles and Huberman, 1994), ethnographic methodologies are useful in providing detailed description and insights into specific populations (Silverman, 1993) that cannot be achieved by **quantitative** methodologies. Ethnography involves the researcher:

- actively immersing him/herself overtly or covertly in the daily lives of those being researched before a period of distance in order to develop an informed assessment
- utilising one or more of the following: participant observation, the collection of documents, **ethnographic conversations** and semi-structured interviews
- disturbing the process of social interaction as little as possible so as to secure detailed descriptions of actions and behaviours grounded in social meanings, and cultural norms to be understood
- operating with a fairly 'open-ended' direction and focus, with research questions remaining broad and a research design that develops with what looks interesting and available
- identifying a small sample often through a case study approach allowing for the development of strong, deep, complex and long-term research relationships with those involved.

Ethnography is often misrepresented in terms of either what it involves or what it hopes to achieve. Noaks and Wincup (2004: 91–92) offer a useful debunking of four myths that have arisen around ethnography (see Box 9.1).

BOX 9.1

FOUR MYTHS OF ETHNOGRAPHY

- **Ethnography is synonymous with participant observation**. While it can involve forms of observation, ethnography is associated with a range of different research methods, delivered alone, mixed or triangulated.
- **Ethnography is 'telling it like it is'**. While ethnographers seek to understand the natural setting, they are involved both as participant and social scientist, and thus bring their own perspectives and decision-making to the research, including what to collect, record, analyse and present.
- **Ethnography is simple to do**. Ethnographic research involves planning, preparation and rigour in order that the researcher is able to gain access, build rapport, know what data to collect and how to analyse and present it.
- **Ethnographic research lacks rigour**. For some, its lack of replicability and generalisability, coupled with the lack of 'controls' associated with more traditional forms of research design, means that it lacks rigour. However, its rigour is derived from the experience, design and approach of the researcher involved.

Participant observation is one method of ethnographic research and aims to give the researcher an insider's view to enable as complete an understanding as possible of the cultural meanings and social structures of the group and how these are interrelated (Aull-Davies, 1999). Definitions of participant observation frequently distinguish between participation and non-participation. However, participant observation involves varying levels of participation, from non to full, and variation in roles adopted by the observer, from full to marginal involvement (Atkinson and Hammersley, 1994). The widely used fourfold typology of researcher roles developed by Gold (1958) and later Junker (1960) – complete observer, observer as participant, participant as observer and complete participant – provides a subtle analysis of degrees of participation (see Box 9.2).

BOX 9.2

DEGREES OF PARTICIPANT OBSERVATION

- **Complete participant**. The researcher is actively involved in the group, operates covertly, and conceals his/her research intentions.
- **Participant as observer**. The researcher is actively involved in the group, operates overtly, and does not conceal his/her research intentions.
- **Observer as participant**. The researcher participates with the group as if he or she is a member of the group and the research intentions are not concealed.
- **Complete observer**. The researcher does not participate in the group, remaining in the background as an observer.

Source: Gold (1958), *Roles in Sociological Field Observations.*

The level of active involvement depends on the response of the group being researched and whether the researcher is treated as an insider or outsider, although it should be noted that the level of participation can change (see Punch, 1979; Van Maanen, 1988) and is in itself not an accurate assessment of the quality or success of the research. Thus, the key challenge for the researcher is to become accepted within the group being studied since their participation in the field becomes the main means of verifying their account (Ellen, 1984). The success of a study is therefore largely determined by the capacity of the researcher to manage impressions in a way that facilitates observation and insight and erodes barriers to social access (Walsh, 1998).

While opportunities to participate can increase as fieldwork progresses, observation remains the most important consideration. As Rabinow (1977, in Aull-Davies, 1999: 79–80) explains,

> Observation ... is the governing term in the pair. ... However much one moves in the direction of participation, it is always the case that one is still both an outsider and an observer. ... In the dialectic between the policy of observation and participation, participation changes the anthropologies and leads him [sic] to new observation, whereupon new observation changes how he participates.

Since the observer is the primary research instrument within participant observation, the method of observing itself is necessarily reflexive (Atkinson, 1990). The observer is required to be sensitive to assumptions, to consider observations within their wider context and to be reflexive in relation to their own participation, observing interactions and action introspectively in an attempt to overcome the effects of misinformation and to be accepted by the group. However, while emphasis has been placed upon the importance of reflexivity, authenticity and creativity in ethnographic practice, there is little methodological rigour associated with it, preferring instead to focus wholly on 'the personalised, seeing, hearing, experiencing in specific social settings'. It is this close interaction and engagement between the observer and observed that enables mutually understood expectations and meanings to be observed and interpreted (Wolcott, 1998, in Ely et al., 1994: 44).

It is equally important to acknowledge the potential bias resulting from being a part of the observed behaviour itself that can effect **reliability** and **validity** (Tedlock, 1991; Spano, 2005). However, in his research into observer bias in police observational research, Spano (2005) suggests that such negative effects are not determined. For example, he argued that rapport between officers and the observer improves over time, and that police officers do not shield observers from the more brutal aspects of police work. He also found little evidence of observer bias in the form of going native or observer burnout, effects typically associated with ethnographic studies.

STUDIES OF POLICE CULTURE

Ethnography is particularly suited to the study of **police culture** because it allows the researcher to actively involve themselves in the police culture on the street, in the station, in the canteen, as well as alongside officers in their interactions with others. However, the nature and type of active involvement can differ between studies. For example, Holdaway (1979) used his position as a serving police officer to undertake ethnographic research covertly; Van Maanen (1988) undertook a 13-week police training course and did not conceal his intentions; while Punch (1979) started out as a researcher but soon became actively involved, searching houses and cars with the officers he was studying. Conducting his research covertly while serving as a police officer, Young (1991: 15) argues that the ethnographic method is suited to a study of police culture 'for it requires an extended field of study to reveal much about the unspoken agenda which determines many aspects of police practice'. That is, ethnographic approaches are able to offer important insights beyond so-called 'official' accounts of the police and their role in society.

Ethnographic studies of police culture have reported that police officers form specific cultural attitudes, values and beliefs due to their common experience of the strains and challenges associated with police work (Skolnick, 1966; Van Maanen, 1974; Manning, 1988). While it is the case that officers do not create their own symbolic environments in isolation of other occupational and organisational factors, the discretion associated with policing equips police officers at all ranks with a good deal of personal and structural power. The law itself obviously constrains the police in some ways and aspects, but it itself is often discretionary, ambiguous and requiring interpretation. It is not surprising therefore that police officers deal with this discretion and the confusion it sometimes generates through the construction of collectively understood and often taken-for-granted norms and values, frequently referred to in the literature as cop culture (see Box 9.3).

BOX 9.3

WHAT IS POLICE CULTURE?

For Chan (1997: 43), police culture is a concept that refers to 'a layer of informal occupational norms and values operating under the rigid hierarchical structure of police organisations'.

Manning (1989: 360) defines police cultures as the 'core skills, cognitions, and affect which define "good police work"...which includes accepted practices, rules and principles of conduct that are situationally applied and generalised rationales and beliefs'.

It is acknowledged (Foster, 2003; McLaughlin, 2007; Rowe, 2009) that Michael Banton's 1964 study *The Policeman and the Community* was instrumental in paving the way for ethnographic studies of the police occupational culture. Writing at the height of public support for policing (Reiner, 1992), and in a period of limited academic research of the police (Westley's study of violence in the police undertaken in the 1940s in Illinois and Indiana using participant observation and interviews was an exception that Banton drew upon but considered too extreme and pessimistic for a British context), Banton wanted to understand the role and the pressures that came to bear on the police officer, particularly in relation to the tensions between law enforcement and peacekeeping, and the relationship between the police and the public. His study utilised participant observation of police officers working within the Lothian and Borders police in Scotland, UK, and officers working within three cities in the USA.

In the decades following the publication of *The Policeman in the Community*, a number of ethnographic studies of the police have been carried out. These studies have been intent on developing an understanding of the nature and impact of police culture, its relations to social processes, its effect on how policing is performed, and

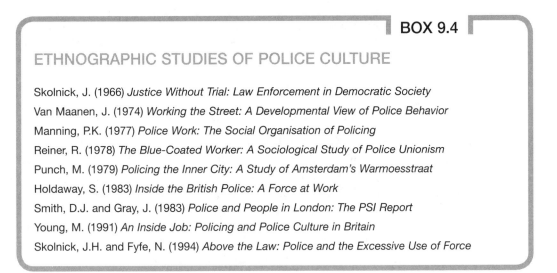

BOX 9.4

ETHNOGRAPHIC STUDIES OF POLICE CULTURE

Skolnick, J. (1966) *Justice Without Trial: Law Enforcement in Democratic Society*

Van Maanen, J. (1974) *Working the Street: A Developmental View of Police Behavior*

Manning, P.K. (1977) *Police Work: The Social Organisation of Policing*

Reiner, R. (1978) *The Blue-Coated Worker: A Sociological Study of Police Unionism*

Punch, M. (1979) *Policing the Inner City: A Study of Amsterdam's Warmoesstraat*

Holdaway, S. (1983) *Inside the British Police: A Force at Work*

Smith, D.J. and Gray, J. (1983) *Police and People in London: The PSI Report*

Young, M. (1991) *An Inside Job: Policing and Police Culture in Britain*

Skolnick, J.H. and Fyfe, N. (1994) *Above the Law: Police and the Excessive Use of Force*

how the central tasks of police work are interpreted. Box 9.4 details a number of the more celebrated ethnographic studies of the police occupational culture that have been undertaken during this period.

Despite the specificity of focus, ethnographic design, location and time frame of each of these studies, a number of shared themes arise from a reading of them:

- *Police occupational norms and a shared police culture.* Police officers develop specific attitudes, values and norms in relation to their work as a means of coping with the strains and demands of police work.

- *Variations in occupational and organisational police cultures.* While many studies appear to confirm the stability and universality of police culture across countries and police forces (Skolnick and Fyfe, 1994; Crank, 2004), some suggest the need 'to acknowledge differences, internal tensions, contradictions and paradoxes' (Manning, 1994: 4, cited in Paoline, 2003: 204). Studies have identified different officer typologies (Broderick, 1977; Muir, 1977; Reiner, 1978; Cochran and Bromley, 2003), gendered orientations (Martin, 1980) and organisational variations (Wilson, 1968; Reuss-Ianni, 1983; Foster, 1989; Loftus, 2008).

- *The dominance of crime fighting within the police culture.* Despite the broad parameters of an officer's role, studies constantly report the ways in which crime fighting is emphasised and transmitted into the culture at the expense of other roles, most notably the social service and community policing roles. Moreover, some of the more negative connotations associated with malpractice and corruption, including rule breaking (Punch 1979), rule deviation (Chatterton, 1979) and status protection (Holdaway, 1983), appear in many studies.

- *Differentiation and categorisation of the public within the police culture.* There is a marked tendency to suggest that the police categorise individual members of the public and treat them differently according to the level of perceived threat they present (Van Maanen, 1978, in Newburn, 2005), either to the society or to the legitimacy and authority of the police, or both.

- *Racism, sexism and homophobia within the police culture.* There is a tendency to identify prejudice particularly among the lower ranks (Smith and Gray, 1983), although questions remain as to whether such prejudice is a product of the individual police officer, of the nature of the work the police undertake or reflective of the society from which recruits are drawn. Furthermore, the gendered nature of policing is well documented, whereby masculine values are both a by-product of and an influence on the internal police culture (Heidensohn, 1992; Walklate, 2001; Westmarland, 2001).

CRITICAL APPROACHES AND APPRECIATIVE INQUIRY

Many ethnographic studies of police culture, largely undertaken following the demise of the golden era of consensus policing, and during periods of social upheaval, increasing politicisation of policing, and publicised accounts of corruption and abuse of police power, have been influenced by critical perspectives of police work (Holdaway, 1989). While the majority did not set out to be critical, many of the studies described above concentrate on the negative characteristics and attitudes of police officers towards the public and their work (Foster, 2003). Often 'The police culture has been used', as Paoline (2004: 230) notes, 'in explanations for legitimizing the misuse of police authority, including the use of force, and has also been noted as a major barrier to police reform'. Despite efforts from some researchers to acknowledge the challenges and pressures faced by the police in delivering crime control (Reiner, 1992, 2000), to understand aspects of police culture as coping mechanisms to the danger and uncertainty inherent within police work (Skolnick, 1966; Paoline et al., 2002), and to note that police officers are not passive and do not just imbibe culture, that culture actually has the potential for change and not just resistance to it (Chan, 1996), such critical approaches to policing continue to be promoted (Sanders and Young, 2003; Sharp, 2005).

In a wide-ranging critique of mostly ethnographic studies of police culture, Waddington (1999) argues that the use of observation, conversation and interview has lead to an over-emphasis on the connections between talk and action. It is his view that many studies, based as they are on the researcher spending extended periods of time watching and listening to serving officers in the canteen, on the street and in the station, tend to adopt the talk as an explanation for police action. For Waddington, however, 'this conceptual bridge looks rather rickety as it spans the obvious and frequently acknowledged chasm between what officers say and what they do' (1999: 288). Rather than supporting what he sees as a condemnatory position on police culture found in much ethnographic police research, he articulates an 'appreciative' conception of the talk itself. He goes on to argue that 'Observational studies of police behaviour on the streets have overwhelmingly concluded that the principal explanatory variables are contextual' (1999: 288). Thus, he asks, 'if the rhetoric of the canteen is divorced from actions on the streets, how is the latter explained? Does this approach consign officers to being the playthings of situational constraints lacking agency? Not at all: it does mean that what officers in one area (the canteen) do is not necessarily, or substantially carried out into quite a different area…'. As Waddington (1999: 302) urges, 'if we wish to explain (and not just condemn) police behaviour on the streets, then we should look not in the remote recesses of what they say in the canteen or privately to researchers, but in the circumstances in which they act'. That is:

> In other words, if talk does not inform police practice why do police officers invest so much effort in talking about their work? If policing is mundane and boring, why do police officers spend so much time trying to convince each other and themselves that it is action-packed? If women officers perform their role indistinguishably from their male colleagues why do those male colleagues insist that they do not? (Waddington, 1999: 294)

Box 9.5 provides an overview of Waddington's appreciation of police culture as a response to the structural contingencies that police officers face.

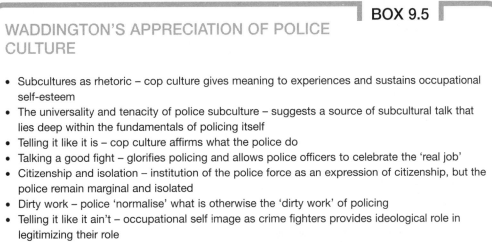

BOX 9.5

WADDINGTON'S APPRECIATION OF POLICE CULTURE

- Subcultures as rhetoric – cop culture gives meaning to experiences and sustains occupational self-esteem
- The universality and tenacity of police subculture – suggests a source of subcultural talk that lies deep within the fundamentals of policing itself
- Telling it like it is – cop culture affirms what the police do
- Talking a good fight – glorifies policing and allows police officers to celebrate the 'real job'
- Citizenship and isolation – institution of the police force as an expression of citizenship, but the police remain marginal and isolated
- Dirty work – police 'normalise' what is otherwise the 'dirty work' of policing
- Telling it like it ain't – occupational self image as crime fighters provides ideological role in legitimizing their role
- The rhetoric of exclusion – cop culture allows distinctions to be drawn between populations they encounter
- Defensive solidarity – cop culture allows the police to group together

Source Waddington (1999)

Similarly, Paoline (2003: 199) argues that while ethnographic studies have allowed for the collection of rich descriptive data on police culture, few studies actually 'explain its causes, prescriptions and outcomes'. For Paoline (2004), not all officers carry the undesirable attributes often associated with the police culture. Moreover, he argues that we need to acknowledge that there have been changes in the composition of police personnel (sex, race, education) and in the philosophical and organisational approach of it (Paoline, 2003, 2004). Survey-based research, Paoline suggests (Paoline et al., 2000), identifies that old cop culture views of the thrill of policing has changed, with officers much more able to acknowledge the importance of responsibility, citizenship and cooperation within the broadening approach to community policing. Paoline and colleagues also suggest that 'we do not find these differences are patterned by officers' characteristics' (Paoline et al., 2003: 601).

The work of Waddington and Paoline, alongside that of Chan (1997), Fielding (1989), Foster (1989, 2003) and Marks (2004), are all representative of what can be called an appreciative sociological approach to police culture that illuminates the existence of multiple police subcultures within the police organisation influenced by hierarchy, occupational status and duties, and group norms and values. These authors suggest that studies that present police culture as a unifying, one-dimensional entity are misleading and provide an uncritical account of the existence and expression of police culture (Foster, 2003) rather than a valid account of police actions and decision-making. In more appreciative studies, emphasis is placed on positioning individual police officers at the centre of analysis to explore more fully their active role in adopting or rejecting aspects of the culture that they find personally acceptable (Fielding, 1988; Waddington, 1999), since ultimately police make sense of their work better than most researchers (Chan, 2006).

In respecting diversity and the role of the individual, these studies collectively identify the significance of adopting a more appreciative methodological approach to understanding police culture and how things work within the context of

---

BOX 9.6

APPRECIATIVE INQUIRY WITH PRISON OFFICERS

Liebling and Price's (2001) exploratory study *The Prison Officer* provides a detailed understanding of staff–prisoner relationships, the nature of the work of prison officers and their use of discretion in a maximum security prison. Liebling and Price (2001) argue that while traditional social science research focuses on problems and difficulties, appreciative inquiry tries to allow good practice, best experiences and accomplishments to emerge through supporting and developing rather than criticising and condemning staff. Appreciative inquiry might accentuate the positive, but in doing so it has the potential to confront the negative by developing a richer understanding of the circumstances in which negative experiences occur (Braithwaite, 1999; Liebling et al., 1999). Furthermore, Liebling (2000) suggests that appreciative inquiry offers some significant pathways towards criminological *verstehen* or understanding.

Appreciative inquiry was deemed most relevant to the study due to:

- its potential for new and valuable ways of looking at the work of prison officers
- its capacity for identifying what is working within an organisation – in this case, illuminating how positive staff–prisoner relationships and collaboration between officers could best be achieved and identifying elements of a positive working environment

(Continued)

- its potential for exploring the processes and skills of conflict avoidance and peacekeeping between officers and prisoners
- its ability to generate trust and rapport with research participants and facilitate their active involvement in the research process

The study involved:

- a nine-month period of extended observation of prison officers
- 'reserved participation' by the research team
- secondary analysis of institutional data

organisational change and policing reform. One such effort to provide a more appreciative approach, albeit within the criminal justice system is Liebling and Price's (2001) study of prison officers (Elliot, 1999) (see Box 9.6).

The benefits of utilising an appreciative ethnographic approach extended to the research process itself. Liebling and Price (2001: 10) identified that prison officers responded unconditionally and were more likely to be generous in communicating and providing information and perceptions to uncritical observers of their work. Although drawing upon experiences of using appreciative inquiry within business, Busche (1995) similarly suggests that people 'love to be interviewed appreciatively', and using an appreciative lens to understand organisational change provides rich stories and insight about the meanings people attach to their work.

DOING AN APPRECIATIVE ETHNOGRAPHY OF POLICE COMMUNITY SUPPORT OFFICERS

In 2006, one of us (Peter) secured funding for the other (Faye) to undertake full-time doctoral research on the occupational culture of Police Community Support Officers (PCSOs). Introduced in the Police Reform Act (2002), and part of what many have described as a growing pluralisation and diversification (Johnston, 2006; Jones and Newburn, 2006) of policing involving commercial, municipal and

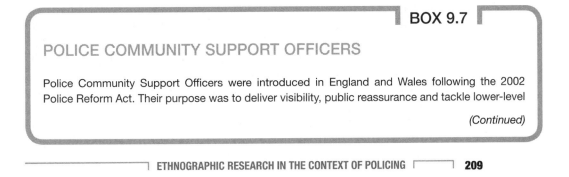

BOX 9.7

POLICE COMMUNITY SUPPORT OFFICERS

Police Community Support Officers were introduced in England and Wales following the 2002 Police Reform Act. Their purpose was to deliver visibility, public reassurance and tackle lower-level

(Continued)

disorder through the provision of dedicated foot patrols. While the nature and scope of activities in which PCSOs are involved varies between forces, PCSOs are involved in increasing public safety and supporting victims of crime, intelligence gathering, tackling anti-social behaviour, confiscating alcohol consumed in a public place and working alongside neighbourhood police officers.

As civilian officers, PCSOs do not hold full powers of enforcement and have a non-confrontational role. PCSO powers of enforcement were standardised in December 2007. Standard powers include the power to issue fixed penalty notices for environmental nuisance, the power to request the name and address of someone acting in an anti-social manner, and the power to confiscate alcohol from persons under 18 years of age. Despite the introduction of standardised powers, Chief Officers in each police force may also designate PCSOs with a number of discretionary powers, including the power to issue penalty notices for disorder, the power to detain, the power to enforce licensing offences and the power to use reasonable force in relation to detained persons.

public forms, PCSOs are employed by the public police but provide a civilian role dedicated to the provision of visible patrol and reassurance that does not involve the acquisition of powers of a sworn police officer. Box 9.7 describes the introduction and core aspects of the PCSO role.

Our initial interest in PCSOs developed out of an **evaluation** we had carried out into their implementation in a north-east police force between 2003 and 2005. During the evaluation, we became aware of the different composition, skill set, motivations and practices of PCSOs compared to regular sworn officers and started to question whether our group of PCSOs would be enveloped by the wider police culture, or would develop their own. The potential of a study on PCSO culture was confirmed when we went back to review the literature on PCSOs, which was either impact oriented (Crawford et al., 2004; Chatterton and Rowland, 2005; Cooper et al., 2006) or concerned with the capacity of PCSOs to improve equality and diversity within police forces (Johnston, 2006). Little research shed light on their motivations, working practices, skills or their capacity to deliver reassurance, and we were convinced that the proposed doctoral research provided a valuable opportunity to develop an analysis of a subculture within the police organisation that had not previously been studied. And as PCSOs represented a major shift in the civilianisation of police work, an ethnography appeared particularly pertinent if the nature of PCSO practices, decision-making and experiences within the context of police modernisation and reform was to be understood.

From the outset we agreed that a critical ethnographic approach would not provide the depth of data required to discover the complexities and defining characteristics of a PCSO (sub)culture, their unique experiences of police work or the organisational and political context in which they worked. Rather, we shared the view that adopting a more appreciative approach might well assist in providing the time and support necessary to access and build trust among those involved in the study. Emphasis was subsequently placed on appreciating the separate

assumptions held by individual PCSOs and their subjective meanings and interpretations of police work and their occupational environment (see Box 9.8).

BOX 9.8

APPRECIATIVE ETHNOGRAPHY AND PCSOs

Throughout the study, emphasis was placed upon the individual PCSO and their subjective meanings and interpretations of police work and their occupational environment. The research sought to identify PCSO achievements and 'what is working', rather than highlighting negative aspects of PCSO practice, since an empathetic, non-judgemental and supportive approach to interaction in the field is more likely to develop a deeper understanding of 'what it is like to be a PCSO'. By placing the PCSO at the centre of analysis and adopting a supportive 'participant as observer' role, the research aimed to achieve an in-depth ethnographic account written from the perspective of the researched rather than the researcher and situated within the context of wider civilianisation and police reform.

The research was concerned with developing:

- an understanding of PCSO decision-making and behaviour within the context of their limited authority and training and structured position within the police organisation
- an understanding of the challenges faced by each individual PCSO in developing the key skills of policing and in dealing with their occupational environment
- an understanding of PCSO orientations to police work and the impact of organisational factors on effective practice and PCSO integration

---

Research design, access and location

A **mixed methods** approach to research design was adopted. Data **triangulation** through mixed methods was deemed essential to understand how PCSO attitudes, experiences, working practices and identities combine to form a PCSO culture within the context of the wider police organisational structure. The research employed participant observation, qualitative interviews and focus groups within the context of a case study approach (Yin, 2003). Despite initial concerns about the researcher accompanying PCSOs on patrol, access was granted by the host police force without difficulty, most likely due to the two of us having already established a positive reputation with senior officers and as a consequence of our use of presentational techniques. Brewer (2000), Punch (1983) and Noaks (1999) suggest that it is often necessary to adopt a range of presentational strategies as part of a 'research bargain' (Brewer, 2000) to secure the support of senior officers and to ensure minimal interference in the research design. First, we emphasised the appreciative methodological position and the benefits that would emerge from the research. We were keen to dispel a 'politics of distrust' (Hughes, 2000) by presenting the researcher as a critical friend rather than a critical commentator.

Second, we confirmed that the research would adhere to strict ethical guidelines, and finally, we ensured that the phrase 'police occupational culture' was avoided during initial discussions in order to avoid the negative connotations and controversy associated with police cultural studies.

At the beginning of the study, the force employed 133 PCSOs. By March 2010 it employed 438 PCSOs, over one-third of whom were female and 1% were minority ethnic (Mulchandani and Sigurdsson, 2009). However, the distribution of PCSOs across the force's six area commands was unequal. The area command selected for the research was chosen because of the volume of PCSOs allocated to it, the higher than average crime and disorder rates reported within it and the ethnic mix of the communities residing throughout it. The location also had a reputation for a proactive approach to neighbourhood policing, and there was enthusiasm from management to encourage effective PCSO practice. With a population of over a quarter of a million (259,500), two out of eight sectors were selected as case study areas. The two sectors identified were similar in nature in terms of composition, housing tenure and levels of deprivation, but differed in the ways in which area commanders had chosen to deploy PCSOs.

Observation, conversations and interviews

The study involved 150 hours of observation within each case study area. PCSOs were observed while on patrol, in the station, when dealing with incidents, and during encounters with members of the public. PCSOs were observed when working in pairs for the most part, but were also observed when working individually and when working alongside neighbourhood police officers (NPOs). As recognised by Junker (1960) and Van Maanen (1978), the roles adopted by the researcher shifted as relations, and therefore trust, developed. When observing PCSOs, the researcher embodied the observer as participant role and did not reach full member status. However, research roles and identities overlapped and varied throughout the period of observation depending upon the specific context. There were times when PCSOs would welcome an input regarding incidents and/or individuals encountered on patrol and they would ask for assistance. This implies a role of the full participant, and it was not uncommon for members of the public to mistake the researcher as a police officer, albeit one in plain clothes.

PCSOs were fully informed that written notes would be taken but that every effort would be made to avoid doing so in view of members of the public. Field notes tended therefore to be cursory, relying upon memory triggers while in the field, and acting as an *aide-mémoire* to interpretation and analysis following each period of observation. Recordings were made in relation to the physical setting, interactions and relationships, police decision-making, conflict between PCSOs and the public, crucially distinguishing between views and observations. As suggested by Ely et al. (1994) and Walsh (1998), the focus of observations inevitably shifted as the research progressed, from a general overview, recording as much as possible to a focus on the detailed, concrete and contextual aspects of the situation and an interpretation of events. Notes were shared with PCSOs to check for clarity and to increase their validity.

Simply by accompanying PCSOs on patrol and sharing common experiences meant that conversation would spontaneously occur. During the early stages of the research, **ethnographic conversations** focused upon building rapport. However, as trust developed, PCSOs became increasingly willing to reflect upon their experiences and express their views, and the challenge for the researcher, as Flick (2009) notes, is to shape the conversation into interviews drawing upon common experiences and towards issues of interest in a systematic way. Additionally, semi-structured individual **interviews** were conducted at the end of the fieldwork with each PCSO. Interviews were recorded in order to enable attention to be entirely focused on the participant rather than writing field notes. Interviews were a way of obtaining the depth of knowledge required about PCSO values, attitudes and orientations to the job that could not be obtained through observation and conversation. In addition, they enabled PCSOs to express themselves without the presence of colleagues, which might hinder their participation and responses. Finally, as identified by Waddington (1999), interviews were a means of comparing PCSO accounts of what they 'say' they do, during interview, with what they 'do' in practice, as measured during observations.

Two focus groups were conducted with neighbourhood police officers working in each case study area. Both **focus groups**, involving four participants, took place within the station and were not recorded. Focus groups were conducted to examine the reactions of neighbourhood officers to the introduction of PCSOs, to explore officer perceptions of the value of PCSOs to frontline police work and in so doing highlight PCSO accomplishments and good practice.

Data handling and analysis

Before data analysis could begin, each period of observation needed to be prepared, written up from jottings and notes, and numbered by the date on which it occurred. While every effort was made to minimise inference and ensure personal reflections remained distinct from the raw data, field notes are subject to memory work and selectivity even at the early stages of data collection. As argued by Wolcott (1990: 35, in Stake, 1995), 'the critical task ... is not to accumulate all the data you can, but to [get rid of] most of the data you accumulate. This requires constant winnowing'. Observation field notes are necessarily and inevitably subjective constructs as the observer continually makes judgements about the importance and relevance of the events, actions and behaviour they observe (Van Maanen, 1988; Sanger, 1996). Interview data also goes through a similar process of preparation. Conventions for transcription differ according to the purpose and methodological approach of the study and judgement of the individual researcher about significant categories or themes.

As identified by Becker (1970: 26–27, in Boulton and Hammersley, 2006), within participant observation research, 'analysis is carried on sequentially, important parts of the analysis being made while the researcher is still gathering his data'. In our study, analysis of observational data commenced after the first period of observation and continued throughout the process of data collection. Observational data from each case study area was then analysed using manual content analysis, also referred to as thematic qualitative analysis (Flick, 2009). All logs and transcripts were closely read to support familiarisation with the material and to identify significant relationships between events, behaviour and comments. Informed by **research objectives** and themes identified within the existing literature, a wide range of categories or themes were identified and marked on each observation log. This stage is particularly important when handling large amounts of data since it enables the researcher to understand the character of the data and to control for original assumptions, for example, of a traditional police culture (Boulton and Hammersely, 2006).

Following this initial identification of categories or subcategories, similarities and differences within and patterns and relationships between all data assigned to the same category were identified and explored. Field notes were subject to another close reading, with the intention of identifying the unique features of each case study area and confirming the accuracy and recurrence of subcategories or codes. This process, identified as 'constant comparative method' by Glaser and Strauss (1967), inevitably leads to some categories becoming more prominent than others as data is transformed from loosely defined categories into more analytical, definitive concepts. Significant categories identified from the original data were revisited for accuracy and recurrence for the purpose of mapping typicality and meaning as opposed to quantification (May, 2001).

Subcategories were then refined and grouped into wider themes – for example, skill development, authority, legitimacy, role conflict, performance culture – and each observation was illustrated and colour-coded according to these themes. Interview data were similarly handled, becoming subject to the same iterative process. The relevance of themes was explored on an interview-by-interview basis (Rapley, 2007) and while additional data and differences between case study areas emerged, themes identified through content analysis of field notes were also identified within both the interview transcripts and the notes from focus groups, thereby adding to the validity of findings. These overarching themes were then used to frame the presentation of findings.

UNDERSTANDING PCSO CULTURE

Achieving an appreciative understanding of PCSO experiences, practices and decision-making was wholly dependent upon the development of trust and rapport. The only way in which this could be secured was through gaining informed consent. The aims and objectives of the study were made clear from the outset, assurances of confidentiality and anonymity were made and PCSOs provided their consent to engage. Accompanying PCSOs on patrol during bad weather, during unsociable hours, and sharing their frustrations and challenges in conducting the role over a sustained period of time led to shared and common experiences and served to demonstrate commitment on the part of the researcher to an accurate understanding of the reality of their occupational environment. Shared experience and ethnographic interviewing while on patrol facilitated an ongoing relationship of trust and encouraged PCSOs to reflect upon their work in the context in which decisions were made. Furthermore, encouraging PCSOs to reflect upon their experiences frequently led to them gaining new insight into their role and/or their professional development, particularly for less experienced PCSOs, promoting confidence that claims to appreciation were genuine. Positive questioning and the adoption of an empathetic, interested and relaxed persona over time led to greater familiarity with subjects; as rapport developed, PCSOs revealed incidents of misconduct of other officers, discussed personal problems and became increasingly candid in their accounts of the 'working rules' of the organisation.

An appreciative approach therefore enabled the researcher to occupy a 'liminal' status (Van Maanen, 1979) and to occupy a participant role that was 'betwixt and between' the status of outsider and insider. It produced a perspective that was 'shared by and produced in the actual encounter between the participant observer and the subjects' (Hunt, 1984: 283). In so doing, the research was able to achieve insight into the hidden dimensions of the occupational world of the PCSO and the nuances of police culture not typically achieved within traditional critical studies.

This research contributes to the study of police subculture in three key ways. First, by demonstrating the resilience of the traditional characteristics of the police culture and the ways in which PCSOs endorse these characteristics to support their integration within the organisation. Second, by detailing the approaches and tactics utilised by PCSOs in delivering reassurance and maintaining order. Third, by illustrating the emergence of specific PCSO cultural characteristics and orientations to police work as a result of their unsworn status and limited authority, thereby offering support for multiple subcultures within the police organisation.

The resilience of the traditional police culture

The majority of PCSOs were principally motivated by a desire to become a sworn police officer. In their efforts to support their integration into the organisation and achieve a sense of value, PCSOs emulated the police officers whom they aspired to become and aligned themselves with the traditional characteristics of the police culture, including suspicion (Skolnick, 1966), solidarity, isolation (Van Maanen, 1974), cynicism (Young, 1991) and a sense of mission (Reiner, 2000). The traditional crime fighting ethos presented within the police performance culture of the organisation exerted a powerful influence upon PCSO occupational identities and orientations to the role.

PCSO approaches to engagement and maintaining order

In order to become effective and feed into organisational objectives, PCSOs must learn the necessary 'craft skills' of policing (Fielding, 1989). However, unlike sworn officers, PCSOs do not have recourse to the law to secure compliance. Operating within a context of limited consensus and authority, and drawing upon craft skills of communication, persuasion and negotiation, PCSOs adopted one of two approaches in their dealings with those they sought to control. The first approach – the befriending approach – was characterised by high levels of discretion, efforts to engage and the use of persuasion and negotiation to encourage compliance. The second approach – the authoritative approach – was adopted by PCSOs as a reaction to challenges to their legitimacy and/or frustration with the role. However, unable to exert the necessary authority, PCSOs were ultimately dependent upon fully sworn officers to restore order. As a result, the majority of PCSOs relied upon the 'befriending approach' to engage and encourage compliance. Despite their dependence upon fully sworn officers to provide enforcement, PCSOs were, for the most part, able to reassure law-abiding sections of the community and to support organisational objectives of crime control through engagement, intelligence gathering and coordinating their activities with those of neighbourhood police officers.

The emergence of a PCSO subculture

PCSOs also developed cultural characteristics that were distinct from police officers as a result of their unique experience, limited authority and position in the organisation, providing evidence of a distinct police subculture. The tensions inherent within the PCSO role therefore lead to the construction of cultural attitudes and competing orientations to the role that both aligned and set them apart from sworn police officers. The study identified a threefold PCSO typology:

- Professional PCSOs, who remain committed to the delivery of reassurance but perceive the role as a means of securing the necessary craft skills of policing to support entry into the police force.

- Frustrated PCSOs, who define the role entirely in terms of its capacity to contribute to crime fighting and the crime control objectives of the organisation and in so doing are most likely to embrace the traditional characteristics of the police culture.

- Disillusioned PCSOs, who become cynical due to their lack of authority and incapacity to provide enforcement, causing a loss of commitment to the role and its remit of reassurance.

SUMMARY

The chapter has noted that traditional representations of the police found in much ethnographic research suggests that officers share a common set of understandings, values, beliefs and attitudes, frequently referred to in the literature as cop culture. This overview must, however, be understood as ideal-typical (Chan, 2003). It is important that the breadth of police culture is understood. Research has identified that variations abound, not only across rank (chief constables have a broader view of the police role than do constables) but also within specialisms (such as CID and Community Policing) and sectors (public/private) and within forces. Differences also can be found within officers' personal styles, policing styles across forces and areas, and between old and young. Nevertheless, as Reiner (2000) argues, these are variations around a theme as opposed to yawning chasms.

Yet, for a number of academic researchers and commentators (Chan, 1996; Waddington, 1999; Paoline, 2000), the limitations of many ethnographic studies lie in their condemnatory approach to the police and policing, and particularly in their failure to go beyond describing the 'walk' and 'talk' of police decision-making. Our appreciative ethnography of community support officers provides a critical case study of ethnographic studies of police culture in a changing context of contemporary policing. The civilianisation of aspects of community policing in the form of PCSOs, alongside the broader modernisation and professionalisation of the service, provides a contemporary context to explore the continuing strength or otherwise of the police occupational culture. Additionally, the use of an appreciative methodology provides an alternative approach to developing understanding of the thoughts and values of civilian officers, and assists in securing the time and support necessary to build access, rapport and understanding.

Overall, the chapter demonstrates the value of an appreciative ethnography that aims to place the researched at the centre of analysis in order to understand the contextual, structural and political reality in which such accounts are gained. This broad, sociological approach to police culture – when set alongside changes in the nature, composition and structure of the police and policing – can, among other things, help us better understand the causes, meanings and impact of police occupational cultures (see Cosgrove, 2010).

■ Study Questions/Activities for Students ■

1   What are the methodological strengths associated with ethnography and why are they suited to the study of police occupational culture?

2   What are the characteristic features traditionally associated with police culture and how might these features impact upon police working practices?

3   The chapter identifies a number of limitations of many ethnographic studies of police culture. What are they and can you identify any others?

4   To what extent do you agree with Waddington's view that the talk that contributes much of what passes for police subculture provides little explanation of police behaviour?

5   What are the core characteristics of appreciative inquiry/ethnography and what are the methodological strengths associated with it?

6 If you wanted to develop an ethnographic study of the police occupational culture, what would be the major issues you would have to overcome when developing and carrying out your research?

RESOURCES

Chan, J. (1996) 'Changing Police Culture', *British Journal of Criminology*, 36(1): 109–134.

Fielding, N. (2008) 'Ethnography', in Gilbert, N. (ed.), *Researching Social Life.* London: Sage.

Liebling, A. and Price, D. (2001) *The Prison Officer*. London: Waterside Press.

Newburn, T. (2003) *Key Readings in Policing*. Cullompton: Willan. Chapters 17–22.

Noaks, L. and Wincup, E. (2004) *Criminological Research: Understanding Qualitative Methods.* London: Sage.

O'Neil, M., Marks, M. and Singh, A.M. (2007) *Police Occupational Culture: New Debates and Directions 8.* New York: Elsevier.

Reiner, R. (2000) *The Politics of the Police* (3rd edition). Oxford: Oxford University Press. Chapter 3.

Rowe, M. (2009) *Introduction to Police.* London: Sage.

Waddington, P.A.J. (1999) 'Police (Canteen) Sub-Culture: An Appreciation', *British Journal of Criminology*, 39(2): 286–308.

REFERENCES

Atkinson, P. (1990) *The Ethnographic Imagination: Textual Constructions of Reality*. London: Routledge.

Atkinson, P. and Hammersley, M. (1994) 'Ethnography and Participant Observation', in Denzin, N.K and Lincoln, Y.S. (eds), *Handbook of Qualitative Research.* London: Sage.

Aull-Davies, C. (1999) *Reflexive Ethnography: A Guide to Researching Selves and Others*. London: Routledge.

Banton, M. (1964) *The Policeman in the Community*. London: Tavistock.

Boulton, D. and Hammersley, M. (2006) 'Analysis of Unstructured Data', in Sapsford, R. and Jupp, V. (eds), *Data Collection and Analysis* (2nd edition). London: Sage.

Brewer, J. (2000) *Ethnography*. Milton Keynes: Open University Press.

Broderick, J.J. (1977) *Police in a Time of Change.* Morristown, NJ: General Learning Press.

Busche, G.R. (1995) 'Advances in Appreciative Inquiry as an Organisation Development Intervention', *Organisation Development Journal*, 13(3): 14–22.

Chan, J. (1996) 'Changing Police Culture', *British Journal of Criminology*, 36(1): 109–134.

Chan, J. (1997) *Changing Police Culture: Policing in a Multicultural Society.* Cambridge: Cambridge University Press.

Chatterton, M. (1979) 'The Supervision of Patrol Work under the Fixed Points System', in Holdaway, S. (ed.), *The British Police.* London: Edwin Arnold.

Chatterton, M. and Rowland, D. (2005) *Community Support Officers: Report on Focus Group Discussions and Statistical Data*. London: Police Federation of England and Wales.

Cochran, J.K. and Bromley, M.L. (2003) 'The Myth of the Police Sub-Culture', *Policing: An International Journal of Police Strategies and Management*, 26(1): 88–117.

Cooper, C., Anscombe, J., Avenell, J., McLean, F. and Morris, J. (2006) *A National Evaluation of Community Support Officers.* Home Office Research Study 297. London: Home Office.

Cosgrove, F. (2010) An Ethnographic Study of the Socialisation and Occupational Culture of PCSOs in a Northern Force. Unpublished thesis, Northumbria University.

Crawford, A., Blackburn, S., Lister, S. and Shepherd, P. (2004) *Patrolling with a Purpose: An Evaluation of Police Community Support Officers in Leeds and Bradford City Centres.* Leeds: Centre for Criminal Justice Studies, University of Leeds.

Denscombe, M. (1998) *The Good Research Guide: For Small-scale Social Research Projects.* Buckingham: Open University Press.

Denzin, N.K. and Lincoln, Y.S. (eds) (2003) *Strategies of Qualitative Inquiry.* London: Sage.

Ellen, R.F. (1984) *Ethnographic Research: A Guide to General Conduct.* London: Academic Press.

Elliot, C.M. (1999) *Locating the Energy for Change: A Practitioner's Guide to Appreciative Inquiry.* Winnipeg, MB: IISD.

Ely, M., Anzul, M., Friedman, T., Garner, D., McCormack, S. and Steinmetz, A. (1994) *Doing Qualitative Research: Circles within Circles.* London: The Falmer Press.

Fielding, N. (1988) *Joining Forces: Police Training, Socialisation and Occupational Competence.* London: Routledge.

Fielding, N. (1990) 'Mediating the Message: Affinitiy and Hostility in Research on Sensitive Topics', *American Behavioural Scientist*, 33: 608–620.

Fielding, N. (2008) 'Ethnography', in Gilbert, N. (ed.), *Researching Social Life.* London: Sage.

Flick, U. (2009) *An Introduction to Qualitative Research.* Los Angeles: Sage.

Foster, J.A. (1989) 'Two Stations: An Ethnographic Study of Policing in the Inner City', in Downes, D. (ed.), *Crime and the City.* Basingstoke: Macmillan.

Foster, J.A. (2003) 'Police Cultures', in Newburn, T. (ed.), *Handbook of Policing.* Cullompton: Willan.

Glaser, B. and Strauss, A. (1967) *The Discovery of Grounded Theory.* Chicago: Aldine.

Hammersley, M. and Atkinson, P. (1983) *Ethnography: Principles in Practice.* London: Tavistock.

Heidensohn, F. (1992) *Women in Control? The Role of Women in Law Enforcement.* Oxford: Clarendon Press.

Holdaway, S. (ed.) (1979) *The British Police.* London: Edwin Arnold.

Holdaway, S. (1983) *Inside the British Police: A Force at Work.* Oxford: Blackwell.

Holdaway, S. (1989) 'Discovering Structure: Studies of the British Police Occupational Culture', in Weatheritt, M. (ed.), *Police Research: Some Future Prospects.* Aldershot: Avebury.

Hughes, G. (2000) 'Understanding the Politics of Criminological Research', in Jupp, V., Davies, P. and Francis, P. (eds), *Doing Criminological Research.* London: Sage.

Hunt, J. (1984) 'The Development of Rapport through the Negotiation of Gender in Fieldwork among the Police', *Human Organisation*, 43: 283–289.

Hunt, J. and Manning, P.K. (1991) 'The Social Context of Police Lying', in Pogrebin, M. (ed.) (2003), *Qualitative Approaches to Criminal Justice: Perspectives from the Field.* Thousand Oaks, CA: Sage.

Johnston, L. (2006) 'Diversifying Police Recruitment? The Deployment of Police Community Support Officers in London', *The Howard Journal of Criminal Justice*, 45(4): 388–402.

Jones, T. and Newburn, T. (2006) *Plural Policing: A Comparative Perspective*. London: Routledge.

Junker, B.H. (1960) *Field Research: An Introduction to the Social Sciences*. Chicago: Chicago University Press.

Lee, R.M. (1995) *Dangerous Fieldwork*. London: Sage.

Liebling, A. and Price, D. (2001) *The Prison Officer*. London: Waterside Press.

Loftus, B. (2008) 'Dominant Culture Interrupted: Recognition, Resentment and the Politics of Change in an English Police Force', *British Journal of Criminology*, 48(6): 765–777.

McLaughlin, E. (2007) *The New Policing*. London: Sage.

Manning, P.K. (1977) *Police Work: The Social Organisation of Policing*. Cambridge, MA: MIT Press.

Manning, P.K. (1988) 'Community Policing as a Drama of Control', in Green, J.R and Mastrofski, S.D. (eds), *Community Policing: Rhetoric or Reality*? New York: Praeger.

Manning, P.K. (1989) 'Occupational Culture', in Bayley, W.G. (ed.), *The Encyclopaedia of Police Science*. New York: Garfield.

Marks, M. (2004) 'Researching Police Transformation: The Ethnographic Imperative', *The British Journal of Criminology*, 44(6): 866–888.

Martin, S.E. (1980) *Breaking and Entering: Policewomen on Patrol*. Berkeley, CA: University of California Press.

May, T. (2001) *Social Research: Issues, Methods and Process* (3rd edition). Buckingham: Open University Press.

Miles, M.B. and Huberman, A.M. (1994) *Qualitative Data Analysis*. Thousand Oaks, CA: Sage.

Muir, W.K. (1977) *Police: Streetcorner Politicians.* Chicago: University of Chicago Press.

Mulchandani, R. and Sigurdsson, J. (2009) *Police Service Strength: England and Wales.* Home Office Statistical Bulletin. London: Home Office.

Newburn, T. (ed.) (2005) *Key Readings in Policing.* Cullompton: Willan.

Noaks, L. (1999) 'Cops for Hire: Methodological Issues in Researching Private Policing', in Brookman, F., Noaks, L. and Wincup, E. (eds), *Qualitative Research in Criminology*. Aldershot: Ashgate.

Noaks, L. and Wincup, E. (2004) *Criminological Research: Understanding Qualitative Methods.* London: Sage.

Paoline, E.A. III (2001) *Rethinking Police Culture: Officer's Occupational Attitudes.* New York: LFB Publishing.

Paoline, E.A. III (2003) 'Taking Stock: Towards a Richer Understanding of Police Culture', *Journal of Criminal Justice*, 31: 199–214.

Paoline, E.A. III (2004) 'Shedding Light on Police Culture: An Examination of Officers' Occupational Attitudes', *Police Quarterly*, 7(2): 205–236.

Paoline, E.A., Myers, S.M. and Worden, R.E. (2000) 'Police Culture, Individualism and Community Policing: Evidence from Two Police Departments', *Justice Quarterly*, 17: 575–605.

Punch, M. (1979) *Policing the Inner City: A Study of Amsterdam's Warmoesstraat*. London: Palgrave Macmillan.

Punch, M. (1983) 'Officers and Men: Occupational Culture, Inter-Rank Antagonism, and the Investigation of Corruption', in Punch, M. (ed.), *Control in the Police Organisation*. Cambridge, MA: MIT Press.

Rapley, T. (2007) *Doing Conversation, Discourse and Document Analysis*. London: Sage.

Reiner, R. (1978) *The Blue-Coated Worker: A Sociological Study of Police Unionism*. London: Cambridge University Press.

Reiner, R. (1992) 'Police Research in the United Kingdom: A Critical Review', in Tonry, M. and Morris, N. (eds), *Modern Policing: Crime and Justice: A Review of Research* (Volume 15, pp. 435–508). Chicago. University of Chicago Press.

Reiner, R. (2000) *The Politics of the Police* (3rd edition). Oxford: Oxford University Press.

Reuss-Ianni, E. (1983) *Two Cultures of Policing.* London: Transaction Books.

Robinson, D. and Reed, V. (eds) (1998) *The A–Z of Social Research Jargon*. Aldershot: Ashgate.

Rowe, M. (2009) *Introduction to Police.* London: Sage.

Sanders, A. and Young, R. (2003) 'Police Powers', in Newburn, T. (ed.), *Handbook of Policing*. Cullompton: Willan.

Sharp, D. (2005) 'Who Needs Theories in Policing?', *The Howard Journal*, 44(5): 449–459.

Silverman, D. (1993) *Interpreting Qualitative Data*. London: Sage.

Skolnick, J.H. (1966) *Justice Without Trial: Law Enforcement in Democratic Society*. New York: Macmillan College Division.

Skolnick, J.H. and Fyfe, J.J. (1994) *Above the Law: Police and the Excessive Use of Force*. New York: The Free Press.

Smith, D.J. and Gray, J. (1983) *Police and People in London: The PSI Report*. Aldershot: Gower.

Spano, R. (2005) 'Potential Sources of Observer Bias in Police Observational Data', *Social Science Research*, 34: 591–617.

Tedlock, B. (1991) 'From Participant Observation to the Observation of Participation: The Emergence of Narrative Ethnography', *Journal of Anthropological Research*, 47: 69–94.

Van Maanen, J. (1974) 'Working the Street: A Developmental View of Police Behavior', in Jacob, H. (ed.), *The Potential for Reform of Criminal Justice*. Sage Criminal Justice System Annual Review, Volume 3. Thousand Oaks, CA: Sage.

Van Maanen, J. (1978) 'The Asshole', in Newburn, T. (ed.) (2005), *Policing: Key Readings.* Cullompton: Willan.

Van Maanen, J. (1979) *Qualitative Methodology*. Beverly Hills, CA: Sage.

Van Maanen, J. (1988) *Tales of the Field: On Writing Ethnography*. Chicago: University of Chicago Press.

Van Maanen, J. (1995) *Representation in Ethnography*. Beverly Hills, CA: Sage.

Waddington, P.A.J. (1999) 'Police (Canteen) Sub-Culture: An Appreciation', *British Journal of Criminology*, 39(2): 286–308.

Walklate, S. (2001) *Gender, Crime and Criminal Justice*. Cullompton: Willan.

Walsh, D. (1998) 'Doing Ethnography', in Seale, C. (ed.), *Researching Society and Culture*. London: Sage.

Westmarland, L. (2001) *Gender and Policing: Sex, Power and Police Culture*. Cullompton: Willan.

Wilson, J.Q. (1968) *Varieties of Police Behaviour: The Management of Law and Order in Eight Communities.* Cambridge, MA: Harvard University Press.

Yin, R.K. (2003) *Applications of Case Study Research* (2nd edition). Applied Social Research Methods Series, Volume 34. London and Thousand Oaks, CA: Sage.

Young, M. (1991) *An Inside Job: Policing and Police Culture in Britain*. Oxford: Clarendon Press.

TEN
USING THE MEDIA TO UNDERSTAND CRIME AND CRIMINAL JUSTICE

ROB C. MAWBY

Chapter Contents

KEY POINTS

This chapter:

- Argues that media representations of crime and criminal justice are a worthwhile subject for criminological study
- Suggests the analysis of media representations of criminal justice is a significant research activity

(Continued)

INTRODUCTION

There currently exists strong research interest in the relationship between crime and the media (see Jewkes, this volume) and you may undertake a research project on crime and the media or pursue a dissertation in this subject area. The term 'media' can refer to communications organisations or professionals, or to communications channels (e.g., print, radio, television and internet), or to outputs or 'texts' (e.g., newspapers, films, computer games, blogs, and factual and fictional television and radio programmes). Accordingly, student projects take different forms, depending on the media under investigation. However, for many projects the emphasis falls on how crime and criminal justice is represented, which requires the analysis of *media texts* – the focus of this chapter. It encourages you to think as criminologists rather than as passive consumers; it prompts you to think about why some crime stories make the front pages of newspapers and others don't. It provides information about how to decode or 'read' crime-related media texts and how to carry out crime-focused media projects. There are a number of media analysis methods that can be drawn on and the chapter considers several that fall within the categories of **content analysis, narrative analysis** and **semiotic analysis.** These are explained, with examples, which are of practical value.

The chapter first considers why it is important to study media representations of crime and justice; second, an overview is provided of key questions that academics have asked concerning the relationship between crime and the media; third, approaches to studying media representations are explained and examples are provided; and finally, the chapter concludes by suggesting a number of media analysis activities.

WHY STUDY CRIME *IN* AND *THROUGH* THE MEDIA?

There are substantive reasons to support the argument that the study of media representations of crime is a worthwhile criminological activity. First, consider Box 10.1, which presents some results from an Ipsos MORI survey. To explore the gap between recorded crime trends and public perceptions, researchers asked a sample of 2001 people who they trusted to tell the truth about crime (for further details see Duffy et al., 2007). The results show a high level of trust in television news and documentaries and in local and broadsheet newspapers. This suggests that one reason the media should be taken seriously is because people use media outputs as an influential source of crime information. The results also illustrate that the media are not a monolith. In this respect there are interesting differences between the 'trust status' of television and newspapers, and between broadsheet, tabloid and local newspapers. Tabloid newspapers are trusted less, but achieve higher circulations, while broadsheet newspapers have relatively lower circulations but are trusted more.

BOX 10.1

WHO DO YOU TRUST TO TELL THE TRUTH ABOUT HOW CRIME IS BEING DEALT WITH?

1	Relatives'/friends' experience	89%
2	TV news/documentaries	87%
3	Local newspapers	77%
4	Police	68%
5	Broadsheet newspapers	60%
6	What you learned in class	57%
7	Newsletter from police	49%
8	Telephone helpline	36%
9	Internet/websites	30%
10	Tabloid newspapers	22%

From Duffy et al. (2007)

There are other reasons why media representations of crime are worthy of study, including:

- **Criminal justice operates in a media-saturated society.** Much of our knowledge of the world is mediated. There are national and local newspapers, numerous television channels, hundreds of radio stations and the internet is constantly available as a source of information and entertainment. Established information sources are supplemented by citizen journalists and global events of significance such as the attack on New York on '9/11' and the Mumbai terrorist attack of November 2008 are reported almost as they unfold (Allan, 2006; Thussu, 2009). In this media-saturated context, crime is a frequent and popular subject and it is important that representations are not taken for granted, but are interrogated and interpreted.

- **Media representations of criminal justice contribute to accountability.** The police, prison and probation services are accountable public institutions and the media are channels through which the services can express transparency and be held accountable.

Criminal justice agencies and interest groups are active in managing their visibility and through the media they can articulate their world view and lobby for their interests. Police forces, for example, have substantial media and public relations departments (Mawby, 2002). Criminal justice agencies are, on occasions, also held accountable in the media, as evidenced through Mark Daley's BBC investigative documentary *The Secret Policeman* (BBC, 2003), which uncovered unacceptable racism within the police service. The study of media representations helps us to understand these struggles to establish dominant meanings and images of criminal justice (Mawby, 2003).

- **Media representations can reflect criminal justice debates.** The media provide a forum for reflecting crime issues. For example, Reiner (1994; see also Leishman and Mason, 2003) has tracked the debate over whether the police are primarily a force or service through dominant television representations of policing. More recently *Life on Mars* (BBC, 2006–) contrasted the prevailing ethics of policing in the 1970s and 2000s. In the prison domain, dramas (e.g., *Bad Girls* (ITV, 1999–2002)) and documentaries (e.g., *Holloway* (ITV, 2009)) have reflected arguments about women and imprisonment (Wilson and O'Sullivan, 2004; Jewkes, 2006). Analysis of media representations therefore contributes to debates about important criminal justice issues.

CRIME AND THE MEDIA

Numerous research studies have focused on the relationship between crime and the media (see Reiner, 2007, for an excellent summary), but as Kidd-Hewitt (1995) and Newburn (2007: 85) have noted, much research has grouped around attempts to answer three core questions, namely:

Do the media cause crime?

In addition to being of interest to academics, this theme is a staple ingredient of public discourses and media commentaries that debate whether violent films, DVDs and computer games encourage violent or criminal behaviour in some people who watch and play them. This question has been debated throughout the history of media development (Reiner, 2007), and is commonly debated following crimes in which it is argued the perpetrators have been influenced by the media. For example, it was suggested that the video *Child's Play 3* had influenced the murderers of 16-year-old Suzanne Capper in December 1992 and two-year-old James Bulger in February 1993. Home Office funded research subsequently failed to establish the link between violent videos and aggressive behaviour in young people (Livingstone, 1996).

Researchers have also explored whether the presentation of crimes in the media has influenced people to copy the depicted methods to commit new crimes. For example, criminologists who have written about *Crimewatch UK* (BBC, 1984–), a programme that reconstructs unsolved crimes, have argued that the programme does lead to copycat crimes (Jewkes, 2004). This, unsurprisingly, is rebuffed by the programme makers, who naturally shun such associations (Miller, 2001: 14), but is supported by **surveys** of armed robbers (Matthews, 2002: 31–2).

Do the media distort the reality of crime and stereotype certain groups?

In this area studies have examined whether the media overrepresent certain crime types and exaggerate crime levels, possibly leading to moral panics (Cohen, 2002) and deviancy amplification (Wilkins, 1964). Hall et al. (1978) explored the role of the media in creating an image of black youths as 'muggers' and young people have frequently been the focus of mediated panics, recent examples being concerns over 'hoodies' and anti-social behaviour generally (Marsh and Melville, 2009).

Do media representations of crime cause people to be fearful?

This question has been asked in respect of the impact on viewers of programmes like *Crimewatch UK* that reconstruct violent interpersonal crimes and it has also been asked in terms of the reporting of crime news across print and visual formats. In recent years, the government and researchers have become interested in the so-called 'perception gap', namely the difference between people's fears of becoming a victim and their statistical chances of being that victim (Duffy et al., 2007; Casey, 2008). Duffy et al. found some evidence that the media contributed to this perception gap. In particular, as Box 10.2 illustrates, they found that watching television and reading newspapers influenced people's beliefs that crime had increased.

BOX 10.2

WHAT MAKES YOU THINK THERE IS MORE CRIME THAN TWO YEARS AGO?

Watching TV	57%
Reading newspapers	48%
Experience of people I know	24%
Personal experience	20%
Radio	15%
Feel generally less safe	12%
Teenagers hanging around	7%
Internet	3%
More police on the streets	1%
Other/don't know	6%

From Duffy et al. (2007)

Implicit in these three questions is an ongoing theoretical debate concerning whether representations of crime and law and order in the media are 'hegemonic' or 'subversive' in relation to the dominant social order and the agencies of criminal justice (Reiner et al., 2003: 13–14; Reiner, 2007). Proponents of the former perspective argue that the media are an ideological apparatus that support existing power relations in society, that the media exaggerate crime which fuels public anxieties and builds support for authoritarian criminal justice policies and methods (e.g., zero tolerance policing and tougher sentences). In contrast, proponents of the latter perspective perceive the media as a threat to morality and authority, and fear that media representations undermine respect for law and order and criminal justice agencies.

STUDYING CRIME AND CRIMINAL JUSTICE IN THE MEDIA

If you are embarking upon a project or dissertation that involves researching some aspect of crime or criminal justice in a media setting, you will need to consider at least three questions:

1 What am I interested in studying?
2 What object(s) do I need to study?
3 What methods are available and appropriate?

First, you will need to determine the *focus* of the project. Your choice will determine the *object* of your research, and then you will need to decide which methods are appropriate to generate the kind of data that will answer your questions or throw light on the topic under investigation. Box 10.3 shows how the object of study flows from the project focus. It sets out three distinct areas that can be studied either separately or in combination:

1 **Texts.** This involves the study of television programmes, films, magazine articles, newspapers and 'new' media outputs (e.g., blogs or podcasts).
2 **Organisations**. This involves examination of the circumstances behind the media representations (e.g., the work of crime reporters, programme makers and producers), and the ways in which criminal justice agencies seek to manage their reputations.
3 **Audiences.** This involves undertaking research with media consumers to analyse how they respond to media representations.

You might, for example, decide that you wish to explore gender representation in a criminal justice-focused television programme – this would be your 'project focus'. You would then need to select your 'object of study', which in this example would be an appropriate television programme. You might choose one particular programme, such as the investigative documentary *Undercover Copper* (ITV, 2006), which exposed sexism in Leicestershire Police force, or you might choose a drama, such as *The Bill* (ITV, 1984–), which would enable the study of gender

BOX 10.3

PLANNING A MEDIA STUDY

Project focus (What are you interested in studying?)	Object of study (What do you need to study?)	Methods of analysis (What are the appropriate methods?)
Examples	**Text(s)**	
1 The representation of gender in contemporary television criminal justice programmes	TV programme – drama or fact-based programmes	Content analysis Narrative analysis Semiotic analysis
2 The representation of black youth and gun crime in national newspapers	Newspapers (hard copies or online archives)	
	Organisation(s)	
1 The work of crime reporters	Television/radio stations or newspapers	Interviews Observation Questionnaire survey
2 The use of social networking websites by police forces	One or more police force(s)	Documentary analysis
	Audience(s)	
1 Do people think there is a connection between watching Crimewatch UK and 'fear of crime'?	Sample – either specific groups (e.g., old people) or a representative sample	Interviews Focus groups Questionnaires
2 Do people think Bad Girls provides an accurate portrayal of women's imprisonment?	Sample – either specific groups (e.g., ex-prisoners) or a representative sample	

(e.g., of offenders, victims and main police characters) in a fictional setting over a number of episodes.

Having determined your project focus and the object of study, the next steps are to determine the method of analysis and then to design the research activities. This involves matching the most appropriate methods to the object of study. You will need to choose one or more method of data collection that will generate data that are relevant to answering your research question. To continue the example of examining gender in a documentary or drama series, suitable methods include content analysis, narrative analysis and semiotic analysis, which are explained in the sections that follow.

Using a combination of methods can strengthen a project. For example, if you were interested in researching how newspapers' presentation of crime news relates to people's perception of crime levels (the 'project focus'), you could combine a content analysis of a sample of newspapers with a questionnaire survey of students that explored which newspapers they read and their perceptions of crime levels. Alternatively, or in addition, you could arrange one or more focus groups to discuss newspaper reading habits and perceptions of crime. The methods chosen will reflect the project focus, the time available and the resources that can be accessed.

For projects involving audience research, the methods will typically involve interviews, questionnaires and/or **focus groups**. For projects involving organisational research, the methods will include **interviews**, observation, questionnaire surveys and documentary analysis. Guidance on designing, planning and undertaking survey and interview-based research and focus group research is addressed in other chapters in this volume.

Content, narrative and semiotic analysis can be porous terms. What the methods share is a concern with examining texts in detail and in a systematic way, though the emphasis may change from counting the numbers of something to eliciting the manifest and latent meanings of that something.

Content analysis

Content analysis, as the name suggests, is a term given to the systematic counting and analysis of phenomena in one or more texts. It is used widely for the study of news in the press and on television (Philo, 1995), for the study of television programmes and films, and has been used to study the content of comics and internet websites (McMillan, 2000).

Content analysis has both **quantitative** and **qualitative** traditions. The method is generally described as being quantitative because it involves counting and categorising (e.g., the frequency of different crime types in a newspaper). Some researchers (e.g., Krippendorff and Bock, 2009) deploy extremely quantitative research designs that are rooted in the **positivist** social scientific approach. However, other researchers (e.g., Mason, 2006a) use a more qualitative content analysis approach that combines content analysis with other types of analysis (e.g., narrative or semiotic analysis as described below) to examine not only the quantity of the phenomena being examined, but also the manifest and latent meanings of the phenomena. For example, counting the number of different types of crime in a national newspaper will generate raw data on the types and numbers of each crime, but analysis of the crime types, whether they are solved, who committed the crimes and who the victims are will elicit meanings about how newspapers portray crime. If the newspaper coverage is then compared to official crime statistics, it allows the analysis to say something about whether newspaper representations reflect official statistics (see Jewkes, this volume).

Remaining with newspapers, a content analysis of crime types, victims and offenders can be deepened through an analysis of the '**news values**' evident in the newspaper coverage. The concept of news values was brought to academic attention in 1965 through a study of Norwegian newspapers (Galtung and Ruge, 1965). Galtung and Ruge were not writing about crime issues, but they identified common themes that enabled them to identify a system by which news items were selected and prioritised for publication. Since this original paper, the concept of news values has been used by researchers with an interest in determining what factors will elevate a story into the news. In a classic study of crime reporting, Chibnall (1977) identified a number of news imperatives, which he argued structured crime news, and this has since been revisited by Leishman and Mason (2003) and by Jewkes (2004). Jewkes explains that news values are the combined outcome of the production processes of news organisations and the assumptions of media professionals about audience needs. News values that shape crime news are summarised in Box 10.4.

BOX 10.4

NEWS VALUES

News value	Description
Threshold	Events have to meet a certain level of perceived importance or drama to be considered newsworthy. The threshold differs at local, regional, national and global level.
Predictability	Predictable news stories (e.g., the release of crime figures) allow news organisations to plan ahead.
Simplification	Reducing the news to a minimum number of themes or parts, e.g. 'drugs and crime'. Whenever possible social situations must be reduced to binary oppositions.
Individualism	Individual definitions of crime and responses to crime are preferred to complex explanations. Issues are reduced to conflict between individuals (e.g., the Prime Minister's views on law and order compared with those of the Leader of the Opposition).
Risk	Misrepresentation of the risk of crime. Media present serious crime as random, meaningless and unpredictable.
Sex	Over-reporting of crimes of a sexual nature. Misrepresentation of women victims.
Celebrity or high status persons	The level of deviance required to attract media attention is significantly lower for celebrities than for 'ordinary' citizens.

(Continued)

(Continued)

News value	Description
Proximity	Proximity is both spatial – the geographical nearness of an event – and cultural – the relevance of an event to an audience. Proximity varies between local and national news. Cultural proximity can pertain to perpetrators and victims; more coverage will be afforded to missing 'respectable' girls than 'tearaway' council estate lads.
Violence	Violence fulfils the media's desire to present dramatic events in the most graphic possible fashion.
Spectacle and graphic imagery	Quality pictures help to demonstrate the 'truth' of a story. Violent acts with a strong visual impact will receive media attention. Increased use of CCTV footage and video footage shot by amateur witnesses.
Children	Any crime involving children can be lifted into news visibility, both children as victims and children as offenders.
Conservative ideology	A version of 'populist punitiveness' dominates. This agenda emphasises deterrence and repression and voices support for more police, more prisons and a tougher criminal justice system.

Summarised from Jewkes (2004: 40–60)

Using Box 10.4, it is possible to examine the coverage of crime stories in newspapers and to make judgements about which news values are important and how they might differ in prominence across newspapers. For example, in July 2009, newspapers featured the story of Greater Manchester Police's decision to halt the investigation to find the body of Keith Bennett, one of the five young victims of the Moors Murderers, Ian Brady and Myra Hindley (e.g., 'Moors hunt ends', *Sunday Times*, 5 July 2009, and 'Agony as cops stop Moors hunt', *The Sun*, 1 July 2009). This story possesses many news values: the original crime met the *threshold* of being of national importance; the murderers achieved a degree of criminal *celebrity*; the victims were all *children*; their deaths involved *violence* and the cultural *proximity* was, and remains, cogent, evidenced through interviews with the victim's mother. However, the extent to which different newspapers foregrounded each news value in their coverage depended upon their tabloid or broadsheet style and target readership.

Content analysis is highly adaptable and has the advantages of being cheap and accessible. For example, newspapers can be collected over a determined period and physically examined or individual newspaper websites can be interrogated online or search engines can be used to search for key terms across selected newspapers (though see Jewkes, this volume, for a 'health warning' on using search engines). For example, in a study that I undertook with a colleague, we examined newspaper coverage of the crime risks associated with the accession of Bulgaria and Romania to European Union membership on 1 January 2007 (Mawby and Gisby, 2009).

Using *LexisNexis*, we were able to swiftly interrogate the archives of all UK national newspapers (using 'crime', 'European Union', 'Romania', 'Bulgaria' and 'police' as our key search words) for a two-year period that captured the pre- and post-accession periods. Following our examination of an initial sample of 1,905 articles, we refined our search criteria to focus on two contrasting daily and Sunday broadsheet and tabloid newspapers. This produced a sample of 216 articles. We read each of these, assessing their content by categorising the types of crime featured and identifying recurring themes. We noted the tone and use of language and the deployment of signifying metaphors, such as 'waves' and 'floods' of 'undesirable' migrants into the UK. We then used the data to assess the extent to which the perceived crime concerns could be understood as a moral panic (Cohen, 2002). In a similar way, if the object of study is a single television programme or a film or a television series, these can be recorded or purchased on DVD and stored in preparation for analysis.

When contemplating a content analysis, students often ask how many episodes of a television series or how many newspaper articles constitute an adequate sample. The answer to this is that the sample needs to be representative of the subject being investigated and the sample must be capable of being justified. Therefore an analysis of the television drama *The Wire* that focused on one episode would be insufficient, but an analysis that focused on series one (13 episodes) would be adequate. Similarly, a newspaper analysis of a particular crime story would require a sample of representative newspapers (e.g., tabloid and broadsheet, daily and Sunday) over a reasonable time period, as illustrated in the example above.

Textbooks and published examples generally suggest that there are common steps in conducting a content analysis and these are laid out in Box 10.5.

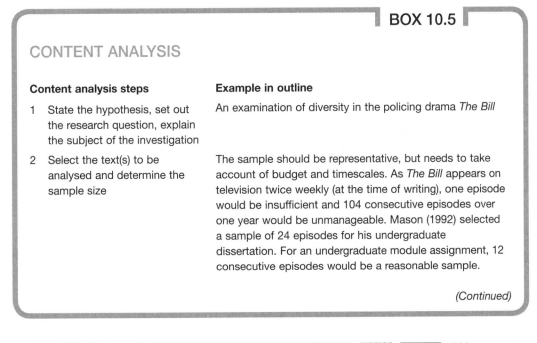

BOX 10.5

CONTENT ANALYSIS

Content analysis steps	Example in outline
1 State the hypothesis, set out the research question, explain the subject of the investigation	An examination of diversity in the policing drama *The Bill*
2 Select the text(s) to be analysed and determine the sample size	The sample should be representative, but needs to take account of budget and timescales. As *The Bill* appears on television twice weekly (at the time of writing), one episode would be insufficient and 104 consecutive episodes over one year would be unmanageable. Mason (1992) selected a sample of 24 episodes for his undergraduate dissertation. For an undergraduate module assignment, 12 consecutive episodes would be a reasonable sample.

(Continued)

(Continued)

Content analysis steps	Example in outline
3 Design the data collection: determine what is to be counted; set out the categories to be recorded and their definition	Set out a coding sheet that enables you to record the diversity profile (age, ethnicity, gender, sexuality, physical/mental disabilities) of police officers, offenders, victims, witnesses. This does not need to be sophisticated; it requires drawing up a matrix that allows easy recording of the diversity profile of each character. Also code the crime types perpetrated by and against each character.
4 Examine the text and code the data, summarise the results	Watch the sample of episodes, filling in the coding sheets. Record the diverse characteristics of each police officer, victim, witness and offender. Also record the frequency and types of crime involving offenders and victims. Summarise the data on a separate form.
5 Analyse and interpret the results, taking into account the hypothesis/research question	Compare the diversity profiles of police, victims and offenders. Compare the profiles of police officers in *The Bill* with official statistics. Compare the profiles of offenders with who commits crime according to official statistics.
6 Write up the study and its findings	The written assignment should include: introduction, literature review, background and context, methods, results and analysis, conclusion, references, appendix detailing the titles of watched episodes and time and date of broadcasting.

Content analysis with narrative analysis

Narrative analysis includes a variety of methods concerned with examining the overall structure of a text and with identifying patterns within the structure (e.g., watching episodes of a crime drama series and identifying recurring themes). Sometimes the text is broken into units for analysis. These can then be analysed in a variety of ways to reveal deeper meanings within the text. Narrative analysis is perhaps best explained through examples, and two studies by Paul Mason illustrate how it can be combined to good effect with content analysis.

Mason undertook a content and narrative analysis of *The Bill* for his undergraduate dissertation, which he subsequently published (Mason, 1992). The aim was to analyse the television representation of the police. His study involved watching and coding 24 episodes. These were analysed under the headings of: *criminals*, *police*, *victims* and *offenders* (with age, gender and ethnicity recorded for each). Crimes were classified in terms of location, type and motive. Significantly,

Mason's content analysis revealed that the crime detection rate was 78.7% in his sample compared with 34% in official statistics. Therefore Mason's analysis demonstrated how the series exaggerated the success of the police in solving crime, arguably helping to construct a more positive image of policing than was the case in reality. The study was enriched by a narrative analysis, in which Mason analysed and compared the development of the characters of police officers and criminals. He explored 'police ideology' by recording officers' comments on their job, on crime and on criminals. Looking beyond *The Bill* to other popular police series, such as *Dixon of Dock Green* (BBC, 1955–76) and *The Sweeney* (ITV, 1974–78), he also identified patterns of continuity across police series, for example the recurring central roles of a solid uniformed sergeant and a maverick detective. He also examined how production techniques contributed to the narrative structure, namely by recording details of the use of cameras, commercial breaks and scene-setting.

A more recent study by Mason, from 2006, of media representations of prisoners provides another good example. He combined content analysis with a narrative analysis that included 'several elements of discourse analysis' to 'explore how the media produce and contribute to a discourse of imprisonment through their power to represent prison and the prisoner in a particular way' (Mason, 2006a: 253). Over a period of one calendar month, October 2005, Mason collected and analysed media representations of the British penal estate in 19 national newspapers, in television news bulletins and in television dramas, documentaries and films. He found that the dominant narratives constructed prisoners as constantly dangerous (e.g., by labelling prisoners as 'killers' and 'thugs' and by highlighting violent offenders and offences, particularly rape and murder) and projected prison as a soft option (e.g., the news focused on such stories as: comparing the reception at Holloway Prison to a hotel; highlighting the availability of drink and drugs; and criticising a lax regime, e.g., 'killers' in open prisons enjoying 'luxury' conditions). In contrast with these dominant narratives, Mason's analysis of 65 stories in the newspapers revealed a failure to explore substantive reasons for prison overcrowding or to offer any critique of penal policy. Mason concluded that the media represent prison uncritically as a solution to crime.

Narrative analysis of prison films

As mentioned previously, narrative analysis can take a number of forms. Wilson and O'Sullivan put forward the argument that prison films can have a number of functions in relation to prison reform. These functions are: *revelatory, benchmarking, defence, news/memory* and *humanising/empathy* (they are explained in Box 10.6). Having posited the five functions, they then examine closely the narrative storylines of a number of prison films. They apply the five functions to the narrative structure, asking the types of question set out in Box 10.6. For example, in respect of the *defence* of gains function, the narrative of a film is examined to determine whether it is making a statement that will 'combat backsliding by penal authorities' (Wilson and O'Sullivan, 2004: 98) on such matters as the humane treatment of prisoners. They conclude that some films (e.g., *Brubaker* in Box 10.6) may perform all five functions, while others will carry out none. This framework provides an analytical structure that can be applied to any prison film. Box 10.6 outlines each function and the extent to which two prison films perform them. *Brubaker*, set in 1960s Arkansas, follows a reforming warden in his attempts to change a corrupt and brutal prison regime. *The Shawshank Redemption* follows the path through prison of a wrongly convicted man.

BOX 10.6

THE APPLICATION OF WILSON AND O'SULLIVAN'S NARRATIVE ANALYSIS APPROACH

Function	Description	Film 1: Brubaker (1980)	Film 2: The Shawshank Redemption (1994)
Revelatory	*Bringing to light practices which are or should be disapproved of.* What does the film reveal that we didn't know about?	The film reveals minor and major unacceptable conditions and practices. *Inhumane conditions:* leaking buildings; insufficient beds, overcrowding; worm-infested food. *Corrupt practices:* selling blood; internal markets for food and favours. *Corrupt regime:* warden providing prisoners as free labour to local businesses; beating of prisoners by trustees; murder.	The film is set in the period 1946 to 1975 and reveals: innocent people in prison; a regime of fear and brutality; inmate rape; exploitation of prisoners' skills for warden's profit; obstruction of justice; the murder of a prisoner.
Benchmarking	*Helping to set standards of decency for what is and what is not acceptable practice in prisons.* Does the film indicate/establish common acceptable standards?	The film benchmarks what prisons should not be like through the device of sending in the new warden disguised as an incoming prisoner. The new warden subsequently proceeds to reform the prison, benchmarking acceptable standards relating to food, living conditions and prisoners' rights.	The film indicates what a prison should not be like. It documents the failure of the prison regime from the brutality of the guards to the corruption of the warden.

Function	Description	Film 1: Brubaker (1980)	Film 2: The Shawshank Redemption (1994)
Defence	**Attempting to combat backsliding by penal authorities on gains established.** Is the film defending a position – e.g., the reasonable treatment of prisoners, rights of prisoners, anti corporal punishment?	The film is loosely based on Thomas Murton's (1969) book. As a former warden, he had tried to reform the Arkansas penal system in the late 1960s. It provides a reminder that corporal punishment is inhumane and its reintroduction would be a retrograde step.	The film has little to say about prison reform with its feel-good ending of prisoner escape and the suicide of the warden. It does not appear to be defending a position.
News/memory	***Spreading the news that certain events happened and keeping alive a memory of them.*** Is the film a reminder of certain practices – good or bad?	The film reminds us of US prison conditions in the 1960s.	The film depicts a flawed prison regime during the period 1946 to 1975.
Humanising/ empathy	***Representing prisoners as people in an attempt to counter processes of dehumanisation.*** Does the film help to humanise prisoners? Does it encourage empathy?	The film has characters who have been dehumanised by the brutal regime and who lack warmth. However, under the new enlightened regime, some prisoners regain their self-worth and earn our compassion.	The film has sympathetic characters, including the innocent protagonist Dufresne and also older, guilty prisoners Red and Brooks.

Semiotic analysis

Semiotics, the 'science of signs', derives from the work of the linguist Ferdinand de Saussure (1915/1983). Saussure argued that signs comprised two components: the 'signifier' and the 'signified', and that the relationship between the two was arbitrary. Semiotics is therefore concerned with interpretation and media texts are seen as 'sign systems' that can be decoded. The semiotic analyst is interested in the generation and conveying of meaning and semiotic analysis involves the decoding and 'reading' of texts to elicit their latent meanings. This section outlines and provides three examples of semiotic analysis. These are (1) 'syntagmatic' and (2) 'paradigmatic' analysis, which can be applied to narratives, and (3) the decoding of how media texts are visually and audibly presented.

Syntagmatic analysis

A syntagmatic analysis focuses on the chain of events that comprise a narrative structure, such as the storyline that is played out in a television drama, novel or film. This type of analysis identifies the relationships that exist between elements within the text. It dissects the text, identifies the component parts, their relationship to each other and to the overall text. This process enables analysis of the functions of textual elements and of characters within the text.

This form of analysis is associated with the work of Vladimir Propp and his 1928 book *Morphology of a Folk Tale* (1928/1968). The book recorded Propp's study of nineteenth-century Russian folk tales. He made a comprehensive collection of these and then examined each one, noting down the actions (or 'functions' as he described them) of each character in each story. Propp argued from his analysis that the same narrative units reappeared across the folk tales, as did the characters who performed the functions. What's more, the functions tended to appear in the same order across folk tales. In total, Propp identified 31 narrative units, including: *villainy* – the villain harms the family; *mediation* – the misfortune is made known and the hero is dispatched; and *victory* – the villain is defeated. He also identified a limited number of characters and concluded that all folk stories form repeatable patterns. Propp's formula provides a template for investigating texts for patterns of repeated characters and plots.

Propp's framework can be considered in relation to prisons films which have been the subject of renewed academic interest (O'Sullivan, 2001; Mason, 2003, 2006a, 2006b; Wilson and O'Sullivan, 2004, 2005; Rafter, 2006). In academic discussions over whether a prison film genre exists and, if so, what it comprises, it has been argued consistently that prison films comprise stock plots, characters, scenes and themes. For example, Rafter (2006) has suggested there are just two main prison film plots – the *riot* and the *escape*, while others (O'Sullivan, 2001; Mason, 2003; Nellis, 2006) have identified the plots of *escape, riot, corruption, violence* and *wrongful conviction*. These plots are supported by stock themes: triumph over adversity, the lone hero against the system, the spectacle of punishment and the prison as a machine that dehumanises prisoners (Mason, 2003). In terms of characters, Rafter (2006: 163–4) suggests that the pattern of stock characters that appear in the 1930 film *The Big House* has endured, namely:

1   The hardened criminal

2   The 'yellow-bellied snitch'

3   The handsome (middle-class) hero, convicted of a minor crime

4   The wise, tough, fair warden

5   The 'Rat' who gathers information for the authorities

6   The ensemble of convict buddies

Box 10.7 applies Propp's ideal characters to a typical prison film and also shows how they might appear in a typical television police drama.

BOX 10.7

PROPP'S CHARACTERS AND THEIR APPLICATION

Propp's characters	Applied to a prison film	Applied to a police drama
The Villain	The brutal guard	The offender
The Hero	The innocent in prison	The cop
The Helper (aids hero in solving problem)	The old lag that befriends the hero	The cop's side-kick
The False Hero (unmasked)	The corrupt warden	The 'bent copper'
The Donor (provides hero with magical agent)	The prisoner who reveals vital information	The informer/key witness
The Princess (sought for person) and Father (assigner of tasks)	The victim of the original crime	The victim
The Dispatcher (sends hero on mission)	The campaigning lawyer on the outside	The cop's boss

In summary, syntagmatic analyses are concerned with applying formulas to reveal the manifest meanings within a text; they examine the chain of events and the roles and activities of characters. In contrast, other forms of analysis move beyond what is happening in the text to what the text *means*. These forms of analysis are concerned with the latent, rather than the manifest, meanings in a text. They are interested in what texts connote, rather than what they denote. One such method is paradigmatic analysis.

Paradigmatic analysis

Paradigmatic analysis of a text involves 'a search for a hidden pattern of oppositions that are buried in it and that generate meaning' (Berger, 2005: 24). This can be achieved by analysing narrative structures for binary oppositions within the text, for example, identifying in crime dramas the tension between upholding the rule of law (exemplified by the criminal justice system and its agents) and the breaking of the law (exemplified by offenders and their criminal plots). Although oppositions are not always so immediately obvious in texts, Berger (2005: 25) argues that 'some kind of systematic and interrelated sets of oppositions can be elicited in all texts … without differences, there is no meaning'. To undertake a paradigmatic analysis of a text, it is necessary to identify and explain the central oppositions at play. For example, to return to prison films, examination of a film involving the wrongful conviction of a citizen who experiences a corrupt and brutal regime that dehumanises and degrades prisoners might reveal one or more of the following oppositions:

- guilt v. innocence
- individual v. the system
- rehabilitation v. punishment
- prisoners v. guards
- power v. morality
- law v. justice
- humanity v. the prison machine
- brutality v. kindness
- freedom v. oppression

Having identified these oppositions, it is then possible to examine how the narrative provides examples of these underlying themes. For example, to take the film *The Shawshank Redemption*, under the 'guilt v. innocence' opposition, you might note that the film's hero is a prisoner who is innocent of the crime he has been convicted of, yet the warden managing the prison is not convicted of any crime but is guilty of gross malpractice. From this inverse representation of the guilt/innocence opposition, you might infer that the prison system is corrupt. Similarly, when the prisoner breaks the law and escapes at the same time as making public the corruption of the warden and appropriating some of his ill-gotten gains, this raises the moral question of whether the means can justify the ends; justice has been achieved but at the cost of breaking the law.

An example of this form of analysis is provided by Geoffrey Hurd (1979), who examined two television series, *Z Cars* (BBC, 1962–78) and *The Sweeney* (ITV, 1974–78). Hurd set out to examine the points of tension within policing dramas by identifying oppositions in two series that provided benchmarks of police media representation. His purpose was to go beyond 'what a programme intends to be or say … to the more important meanings that are embedded in its structures' (1979: 134). The analysis results in the following binary oppositions:

- police v. crime
- law v. rule
- professional v. organisation
- authority v. bureaucracy
- intuition v. technology
- masses v. intellectuals
- comradeship v. rank

Hurd's analysis remains a helpful example for the way that it identifies the underlying oppositions within the text. It also offers the challenge of updating the analysis in a student project, for example, using *The Sweeney*'s natural successor, *Life on Mars*.

Decoding sound and visual signifiers

In addition to examining the narratives of films and television programmes for manifest and latent meanings, you can also examine how media texts look and sound, and infer meanings from these. For example, in television and films, camera shots and techniques of filming and editing are selected and deployed to indicate and infer certain meanings. For example, Box 10.8 summarises the ways in which camera techniques are routinely used to generate meaning. As Berger (2005: 34) points out, these techniques provide us with 'a kind of grammar of television', which help us to understand what is happening. For example, jerky camera work of the sort used in many crime dramas, from *NYPD Blue* to *The Shield*, suggests reality and closeness to the main drama, such that viewers might feel that they are following the detectives around, from crime scene to back stage at the police station.

BOX 10.8

CONNOTING MEANING THROUGH FILMING TECHNIQUES

Camera work (signifier)	Implied meaning (signified)
Screen fades in	Beginning
Camera looks down (pan down)	Power
Camera looks up (pan up)	Weakness
Rapid cutting from image to image	Panic, speed
Grainy film tone	Documentary realism
Close-up shot	Intimacy
Soft focus	Romance, nostalgia
Long, panning shot	Context-setter
Screen fades out	Ending

Following Selby and Cowdery (1995: 57–8) and Berger (2005: 34)

Lighting can also be used to generate particular atmospheres. For example, in the television adaptation of David Peace's *Red Riding* trilogy (Channel 4, 2009), the dull days, unremitting rain and smoke-laden bars evoked a gloominess that captured the feel of a 'grim up-North' 1970s Yorkshire. Similarly, sound and music are used to connote and infer. Music can build tension and convey danger. In the film *Jaws*, the same sound sequences are used each time the shark is about to attack, which builds anticipation. It can connote fear (e.g., a victim being pursued by the homicidal killer in numerous crime thrillers); or, it can connote nostalgia (e.g., the use of classic 1960s pop music in the policing golden age drama, *Heartbeat*).

These techniques apply just as much to reality programmes as dramas. Their influence, for example, is recognised in crime reconstructions. The BBC has editorial guidelines which outline the standards for crime reconstructions with the intention of avoiding gratuitous scenes that may contribute to anxiety about crime. These stipulate that the appropriate use of camera angles should be carefully considered and unnecessary close-ups of weapons should be avoided, as should incidental music and irrelevant sound effects (www.bbc.co.uk/guidelines).

SUMMARY

This chapter has argued that media representations of crime and criminal justice are a significant subject, worthy of academic attention. The relationship between crime and the media has been the focus of much research and three key areas are: the media as a possible cause of crime; the media's role in stereotyping particular groups as deviant; and the media's relationship to people's anxieties over crime.

Studying crime and criminal justice in the media is a suitable enterprise for an undergraduate project and the focus may be on media texts, their context of construction and/or on audiences. This chapter has focused on media texts, which can be studied in a number of ways. Content analysis is commonly used to study crime in newspapers and on television. Narrative analysis takes a number of forms, and narrative and content analysis can be combined. Semiotic approaches to understanding media representations include syntagmatic and paradigmatic analysis. The former focuses on the chain of events within a narrative structure to draw out manifest meanings within the text, while the latter seeks to identify underlying oppositional themes in the text which elicit latent meanings.

■ Study Questions/Activities for Students

1 Keep a media diary for a week, noting the quantity and character of crime and criminal justice coverage in the media you routinely interact with. What does the coverage tell you about the media representation of crime and wider criminal justice issues?

2 Watch an episode of a television crime drama series. How many of Propp's ideal characters can you identify and what functions do they perform in the narrative?

3 Conduct a content analysis of a criminal justice story or issue (e.g., a trial, a crime, a series of crimes, a type of crime, a crisis within the criminal justice system, or an aspect of criminal justice policy) in two contrasting newspapers. Critically examine the coverage. How is crime and criminal justice represented?

4 Compare the coverage of a criminal case in one broadsheet and one tabloid newspaper. Which news values are evident? Do they differ for each paper?

5 Watch a DVD of a film set in a prison. Analyse the extent to which the film fulfils Wilson and O'Sullivan's five prison film functions.

RESOURCES

Two good overviews of 'crime and the media' are Reiner (2007) and Chapter 4 of Newburn (2007), which are strongly recommended, as is Jewkes (2004). Students approaching media analysis for the first time should find Stokes (2003) helpful. For further advice and instruction on applying media analysis methods, I would suggest that students consult one or more of Berger (2005), Marsen (2006), Chandler (2007) and Devereux (2007).

REFERENCES

Allan, S. (2006) *Online News*. Maidenhead: Open University Press.

Berger, A.A. (2005) *Media Analysis Techniques* (3rd edn). London: Sage.

Casey, L. (2008) *Engaging Communities in Fighting Crime*. London: Cabinet Office.

Chandler, D. (2007) *Semiotics: The Basics* (2nd edn). London: Routledge.

Chibnall, S. (1977) *Law-and-Order News: An Analysis of Crime Reporting in the British Press*. London: Tavistock.

Cohen, S. (2002) *Folk Devils and Moral Panics: The Creation of the Mods and Rockers* (3rd edn). London: Routledge.

Devereux, E. (2007) *Understanding the Media.* London: Sage.

Duffy, B., Wake, R., Burrows, T. and Bremner, P. (2007) *Closing the Gaps: Crime and Public Perceptions*. London: Ipsos MORI Social Research Institute.

Galtung, J. and Ruge, M. (1965) 'Structuring and selecting news', in Cohen, S. and Young, J. (eds) (1981), *The Manufacture of News: Social Problems, Deviance and the Mass Media* (4th edn). London: Constable, pp. 52–63.

Hall, S., Critcher, C., Jefferson, T., Clarke, J. and Roberts, B. (1978) *Policing the Crisis: Mugging, the State, and Law and Order*. London: Macmillan.

Hurd, G. (1979) 'The TV presentation of the Police', in Holdaway, S. (ed.), *The British Police*. London: Edward Arnold, pp. 118–34.

Jewkes, Y. (2004) *Media and Crime.* London: Sage.

Jewkes, Y. (2006) 'Creating a stir? Prisons, popular media and the power to reform', in Mason, P. (ed.), *Captured by the Media: Prison Discourse in Popular Culture.* Cullompton: Willlan Publishing, pp. 137–53.

Kidd-Hewitt, D. (1995) 'Crime and the media: a criminological perspective', in Kidd-Hewitt, D. and Osborne, R. (eds), *Crime and the Media: The Post-modern Spectacle.* London: Pluto Press, pp. 1–24.

Krippendorff, K. and Bock, M.A. (eds) (2009) *The Content Analysis Reader.* London: Sage.

Leishman, F. and Mason, P. (2003) *Policing and the Media.* Cullompton: Willan Publishing.

Livingstone, S. (1996) 'On the continuing problem of media effects', in Curran, J. and Gurevitch, M. (eds), *Mass Media and Society* (2nd edn). London: Arnold, pp. 305–24.

Marsen, S. (2006) *Communication Studies.* Basingstoke: Palgrave Macmillan.

Marsh, I. and Melville, G. (2009) *Crime, Justice and the Media*. London: Routledge.

Mason, P. (1992) *Reading The Bill: An Analysis of the Thames Television Police Drama*. Bristol: Bristol and Bath Centre for Criminal Justice.

Mason, P. (2003) 'The screen machine: cinematic representations of prison', in Mason, P. (ed.), *Criminal Visions: Media Representations of Crime and Justice.* Cullompton: Willan Publishing, pp. 278–97.

Mason, P. (2006a) 'Lies, distortion and what doesn't work: monitoring prison stories in the British media', *Crime Media Culture: An International Journal*, 2(3): 251–67.

Mason, P. (ed.) (2006b) *Captured by the Media: Prison Discourse in Popular Culture.* Cullompton: Willan Publishing.

Matthews, R. (2002) *Armed Robbery.* Cullompton: Willan Publishing.

Mawby, R.C. (2002) *Policing Images: Policing, Communication and Legitimacy*. Cullompton: Willan Publishing.

Mawby, R.C. (2003) 'Completing the "half-formed picture"? Media images of policing', in Mason, P. (ed.), *Criminal Visions: Media Representations of Crime and Justice.* Cullompton: Willan Publishing, pp. 214–37.

Mawby, R.C. and Gisby, W. (2009) 'Crime fears in an expanding European Union: just another moral panic?', *The Howard Journal*, 48(1): 37–51.

McMillan, S.J. (2000) 'The microscope and the moving target: the challenge of applying content analysis to the World Wide Web', *Journalism and Mass Communication Quarterly*, 77: 80–98.

Miller, H. (2001) *Crimewatch Solved.* London: Pan Macmillan.

Nellis, M. (2006) 'Future punishment in American science fiction films', in Mason, P. (ed.), *Captured by the Media: Prison Discourse in Popular Culture*. Cullompton: Willan Publishing, pp. 210–28.

Newburn, T. (2007) *Criminology*. Cullompton: Willan Publishing.

O'Sullivan, S. (2001) 'Representations of prison in nineties Hollywood cinema: from *Con Air* to *The Shawshank Redemption*', *The Howard Journal*, 40(4): 317–34.

Philo, G. (ed.) (1995) *The Glasgow University Media Group Reader* (vols I and II). London: Routledge.

Propp, V. (1928/1968) *Morphology of the Folk Tale*. Austin, TX: University of Texas Press.

Rafter, N. (2006) *Shots in the Mirror: Crime Films and Society* (2nd edn). Oxford: Oxford University Press.

Reiner, R. (1994) 'The dialectics of Dixon: the changing image of the TV cop', in Stephens, M. and Becker, S. (eds), *Police Force Police Service*. London: Macmillan, pp. 11–32.

Reiner, R. (2007) 'Media made criminality: the representation of crime in the mass media', in Maguire, M., Morgan, R. and Reiner, R. (eds), *The Oxford Handbook of Criminology* (4th edn). Oxford: Clarendon Press, pp. 302–37.

Reiner, R., Livingstone, S. and Allen, J. (2003) 'From law and order to lynch mobs: crime news since the second world war', in Mason, P. (ed.), *Criminal Visions: Media Representations of Crime and Justice*. Cullompton: Willan Publishing, pp. 13–32.

Saussure, F. de (1915/1983) *Course in General Linguistics.* London: Gerald Duckworth.

Selby, K. and Cowdery, R. (1995) *How to Study Television.* London: Macmillan.

Stokes, J. (2003) *How to Do Media and Cultural Studies*. London: Sage.

Thussu, D. (2009) 'Turning terrorism into a soap opera', *British Journalism Review*, 20(13): 13–18.

Wilkins, L.T. (1964) 'The deviance-amplifying system', in Carson, W.G. and Wiles, P. (eds) (1971), *Crime and Delinquency in Britain: Sociological Readings.* London: Martin Robinson, pp. 219–26.

Wilson, D. and O'Sullivan, S. (2004) *Images of Incarceration: Representations of Prison in Film and Television Drama*. Winchester: Waterside Press.

Wilson, D. and O'Sullivan, S. (2005) 'Re-theorizing the penal reform functions of the prison film', *Theoretical Criminology*, 9(4): 471–91.

ELEVEN
THE MEDIA AND CRIMINOLOGICAL RESEARCH

YVONNE JEWKES

> ### Chapter Contents

> ### KEY POINTS

This chapter:

- Discusses four different aspects of media/crime research: texts, audiences, media organisations and criminal justice institutions

(Continued)

(Continued)

- Highlights the benefits and weaknesses of various quantitative and qualitative methodologies, including content analysis, discourse analysis, participant observation, focus groups and interviewing
- Discusses some of the most well-known and influential media/crime research studies carried out over the last 40 years

INTRODUCTION

While research by media scholars into topics of criminological importance has a long and distinguished history and has shaped our understanding of topics as diverse as wartime propaganda and the effects of cartoon violence on impressionable young minds, it is arguable that criminologists have been slow to recognise the significance of media to their work and, at best, tentative in their engagement with interdisciplinary research in the field. Yet, interest in the relationship between media and crime among students has never been so keen. In every annual cohort of undergraduate and Masters-level Criminology students, there will be a significant number who wish to write their dissertation on some aspect of the role of media in shaping our ideas about crime and criminal justice. Among the dissertations I have supervised have been studies of media representations of domestic violence, internet sites that promote suicide, paedophilic images in Japanese *manga* and *anime*, Victorian attitudes to surveillance, and the gendered differences in news reporting of infanticide. These topics represent a fraction of potential research projects linking crime and media, but illustrate the scope of criminological research into media texts and technologies that might be pursued by students.

With this broad spectrum of researchable topics in mind, the chapter is divided into four parts, each of which will explore research into a different aspect of the relationship between media and crime. First, the chapter discusses the study of *media texts* – that is, newspapers, TV news bulletins or any other 'readable' text – using content analysis and discourse analysis. These approaches can be particularly useful for examining the biases, prejudices and omissions in media reporting. The second part of the chapter examines researching *media audiences*. Typically this type of research uses ethnography to try to get 'inside' people's worlds and explain them in all their richness, complexity and specificity. The third section examines ethnographic research into *media organisations*, notably the newsrooms occupied by crime correspondents. Finally, the chapter considers the role of *media within criminal justice* and the part that research can play in illuminating aspects of a system that is usually not only hidden from public gaze but can also be shrouded in myth and mystique.

RESEARCHING MEDIA TEXTS

Content analysis

When researchers refer to media 'texts', they mean both written texts (such as newspaper articles) and visual texts (TV programmes, films, etc.) which can be read semiotically (see Mawby, this volume). Media texts may be analysed using methods that are both predominantly quantitative (e.g. content analysis) and qualitative (e.g. discourse analysis). **Content analysis** – the largely quantitative approach – involves the systematic assignment of media content to categories, and the analysis of relationships involving those categories using statistical methods (Riffe et al., 2005). Usually, a sample of news items from a particular medium is selected and content is numerically coded for predetermined characteristics (e.g. 'sex' or 'violence'). The frequency of each item is then compared with some other representation of reality (such as the British Crime Survey) to evaluate the media's construction of the issue being investigated.

To give an example, Ditton and Duffy (1983) obtained a sample of 116 Scottish newspapers (both tabloid and broadsheet, and Sunday as well as daily titles) from March 1981, together with official statistical data on crimes and court trials for that month. Newspaper coverage was assessed in two ways: first, by the area in millimetres of news space given to crime news; and second, by the number of relevant reports. Each report was classified as a member of one of seven groups, ranging from 'non-sexual crimes of violence or implied violence against the person, including murder, serious assault and robbery' and 'crimes involving indecency, including rape and prostitution' to 'fire-raising, malicious and reckless conduct, including vandalism' and 'offences relating to motor vehicles'. The crime incidence data were similarly classified and the totals within the two samples were then compared. Content analysis allowed the researchers to ascertain which types of crime were under-reported by the press and which were over-reported, compared to official statistics. Among their findings was that in Strathclyde in March 1981, crimes involving sex and violence accounted for only 2.4% of recorded incidents, yet occupied 45.8% of newspaper coverage. While Ditton and Duffy focused on press reporting, other studies have examined the role of television in perpetuating selective and distorted understandings of crime. To take one example, a content analysis of reality-based US police TV shows found that 87% of criminal suspects portrayed were associated with violent crime compared with official FBI statistics of 13% (Oliver, 1994).

BOX 11.1

A LONGITUDINAL CONTENT ANALYSIS

Content analysis provides a 'snapshot' of mediated crime in a given period – usually one month to a year. A study which took a more ambitious approach to media content was the longitudinal analysis of crime in newspapers, television and cinema between 1945 and 1991 conducted by Reiner and Livingstone (1997). Their aims were to examine how media representations of crime and criminal justice have changed since the Second World War and to understand how audiences of different generations interpreted these changes over their lifetimes. Their methods involved randomly selecting sizeable samples from each medium. For *film*, the analysis combined a sample

(Continued)

(Continued)

of all films released in Britain since 1945 (which included an increasing proportion of US films over the period), with a subsequent focus on box office hits, as the films most viewed by audiences. For *television,* they focused on fictional crime series as these provide the most sustained portrayals of police and the criminal justice system. For the *press,* they sampled from the newspaper of record throughout most of the period, *The Times*, and a paper which contrasts with it in terms of both market (tabloid versus quality) and politics (left-of-centre versus right), *The Mirror*. While these selections are limited, this was nonetheless a larger sampling across crime, media and time than any found in the research literature. The historical dimension allowed Reiner and Livingstone to interrogate familiar discourses such as the assumption that the media increasingly sensationalise deviance, glamorise offending and undermine moral authority. They found that the proportion of newspaper stories about crime has increased considerably (from 7% in *The Times* during the period 1945–1951 to 21% in 1985–1991). The numbers of crime programmes on TV also increased, while films showed no significant change: crime has always been a staple of cinema and remained stable across the period at 20%, with a further 45–50% of films 'containing central crime contents' (Reiner and Livingstone, 1997: 6). One of the most surprising findings was that there have been significant changes in the representation of offenders and victims. In the period following the Second World War, news stories encouraged compassion for offenders by providing details designed to elicit sympathy for their circumstances, thus endorsing the rehabilitative ideal that dominated penal policy at that time. Victims, on the other hand, had a 'shadowy and functional role' in crime narratives (ibid.). It is only relatively recently that victims have moved to an increasingly pivotal position in crime narratives (again, reflecting changing directions in policy and practice), 'their suffering increasingly constituting the subject position or the *raison d'être* of the story' (ibid.).

Discourse analysis

Related to content analysis is **discourse analysis** (also called **narrative** or **semiotic** analysis). Here it is not frequency of stories about a particular issue that is of interest, but rather frequency and type of words used to *describe* a story. Discourse analysis aims to reveal the hidden motivations behind a text, 'deconstructing' ideas, belief-systems, or generally held social values and assumptions. Teun van Dijk explains the differences between content and discourse analysis:

> Traditional approaches to the role of the media … were largely content analytical: quantitative studies of stereotypical words or images representing minorities. … Discourse analytical approaches, systematically describe the various structures and strategies of text or talk, and *relate these to the social or political context*. For instance, they may focus on overall topics, or more local meanings (such as coherence or implications) in a 'semantic' analysis. But also the 'syntactic' form of sentences, or the overall 'organisation' of a news report may be examined in detail. (Van Dijk, 2000: 35, my emphasis)

Discourse analysis is, then, very effective for looking at the ways in which discourse is linked to power and social interests. A contemporary example is that carried out by the Prison Media Monitoring Unit (PMMU) established by Paul Mason at the

University of Cardiff's School of Journalism, Media and Cultural Studies (see also Mawby's discussion of Mason's work, this volume). PMMU examined British media coverage of prison and prisoners, highlighting errors, misinformation and distortion about prison issues which, the Unit believed, may have a significant effect on government policy and public attitudes towards prison, punishment and social control (www.jc2m.co.uk/pmmu.htm). The work of PMMU is especially interesting because it used the online database LexisNexis (web.lexis-nexis.com/xchange-international/).

LexisNexis

LexisNexis is a valuable research tool, widely used by undergraduate students with limited time and money. In brief, LexisNexis is a searchable online archive of content from newspapers and other printed sources and is a relatively quick and easy way to build up a picture of media reporting of any given topic. In the case of the PMMU, data was collected from all 19 UK national newspapers using the search terms: 'prison', 'prisoner', 'jail', 'punishment', 'inmate' and 'detention'. These terms were applied to three LexisNexis criteria: words appearing in a headline; a 'major mention'; or appearing three or more times in the article. Stories were also classified according to the sources of information relied on: Her Majesty's Chief Inspector of Prisons, Home Secretary, serving prisoners, academic experts, and so on. Finally, the results were processed through SPSS software to produce statistical analyses.

The approach adopted by PMMU allowed researchers to highlight an identifiable range of textual strategies in press accounts of prison and the prisoner. For example, discrete themes in the reporting of prisons were found to be linked together to form an overall picture conveying prisons as cushy environments full of dangerous individuals. The dominant discourse in their sample from 2006–07 was 'prison as a "soft option"', accounting for 22% of all prison reports. A related theme was the privileges and luxuries afforded rapists and other serious offenders, which was combined with the themes of a prison system unable to cope and an incompetent Home Office to create an impression of prisons being risky and volatile places. Even the issue of prison overcrowding – a prevalent theme in prison reporting, accounting for 14% of all stories – was reported in terms of 'mayhem', 'chaos' and 'meltdown', contributing to the overall picture of dangerousness, rather than in the context of, say, prisoners' human rights (www.jc2m.co.uk/pmmu.htm). The work of PMMU provides qualitative and quantitative evidence of negative and judgemental news reporting of prisons and prisoners which, it can reasonably be surmised, contribute to the 'othering' of prisoners from mainstream society, and generate support for more draconian criminal justice measures and, in particular, the increased use of prison.

However, searchable online databases such as LexisNexis have several shortcomings, one of which is that they strip stories of much of their textual and visual meaning:

> Reduced to words on a computer monitor, printed 'news' becomes decontextualized, shorn of structure and style, disconnected from defining images and surrounding stories – and so, ultimately, left with little similarity to the increasingly spectacular, brilliantly colourful products that media audiences consume on a daily basis. (Greer et al., 2007: 6)

For this reason, documentary sources such as *The Times* digital archive have the advantage that, once a relevant story has been identified, it can be viewed online as a facsimile of the original news page, along with accompanying photographs and other images, and the stories composed around it.

The ways in which we engage with the physicality of newspapers are radically different from the ways in which we use online news sources, not least because when we browse 'real' newspapers, we have a healthy lack of control. By exercising control through our choice of **keywords** to search for, we limit our opportunities to chance upon stories that are of interest and relevance to our research topic, but which did not contain the words we inputted. For example, one could use the database to research UK press coverage of asylum seekers and refugees and, by using certain keywords, one might construct an argument that many newspapers report immigration issues in a negative and sensationalist manner, and may even conflate asylum seekers and terrorists in order to create 'extremes of otherness' and perpetuate the discourses of fear that characterise a risk-attuned society (Greer and Jewkes, 2005). But in doing so, one might miss balancing stories, compassionate stories, reports of suicide/self-harm in immigration detention centres, and any number of other issues that make the reporting of politically sensitive subjects more complex than they might first appear. See Box 11.2 for a summary of the limitations and strengths of LexisNexis.

BOX 11.2

LEXISNEXIS: LIMITATIONS AND STRENGTHS

Strengths

- Inexpensive
- Easily accessible
- Useful for building up a picture of news reporting of any topic

Limitations

- Photographs and other images cannot be included in the analysis
- Researchers tend to focus on narrow categories of analysis based on 'keywords' and exclude reports that might be peripherally important or balance the stories selected
- Questions are raised about validity in so far as LexisNexis is reliant on the skills of the researcher to interpret the data and present meaningful findings without simply 'cherry-picking' examples that make the points they were hoping to find
- It is estimated that more people get their news online than from newspapers. For example, a US survey found that 37% of Americans go online for news compared to 27% who only read a print newspaper (people-press.org/report/444/news-media). People who consume news in this way may interact with the journalist, editor and other readers via comment pages, networking sites (e.g. Twitter) and blogs, and they may also access video clips as well as still images, all of which will be absent from a LexisNexis search

Triangulation

Discourse analysis is, then, *always* a matter of interpretation, with the **reliability** and the **validity** of the research findings depending entirely on the cogency of the researcher's arguments. For this reason, many researchers combine discourse analysis with other methodologies to '**triangulate**' their findings. For example, the Glasgow University Media Group (GUMG) employ a wide range of research techniques that enable them to analyse both production and consumption factors. They will, for example, supplement discourse analysis with interviewing journalists and audience members. Further, in a development of traditional discourse analysis, the GUMG have pioneered an approach that enables them to show how news accounts of major events not only shape the audience's immediate understanding of those events, but also have a measurable influence on people's long-term understanding and memory of them. They do this by inviting audience members to imagine they are journalists and to write their own news items. They are given photographs from TV news footage of an event (e.g. the Israel–Palestine conflict) and told to use these as a stimulus. Not only does this show what audiences have retained from news programmes, but it has demonstrated that audience members accurately reproduce the language, structure and sequence of accounts as they had most frequently occurred on TV news (www.gla.ac.uk/centres/mediagroup/PDFs/PhiloMethods.pdf).

Finally, relatively little research has been devoted to crime fiction, either in terms of its production or consumption (but see literary theorist Todorov's 1966 typology of detective genres, reproduced in Greer, 2009: 293–301). An exception is Clarke's (2001) discussion of the detective novel, which looks at how different types of detective story have treated the relationship between crime, criminality, detection and social order and stresses that, just as defining 'crime' as a problem is a central issue, so too is the question of how 'crime' also becomes a source of pleasure. Clarke conducted a narrative discourse analysis (see Mawby, this volume) of the detective novel genre, which led him to divide detective stories into four main categories: the classic English murder mystery; the private eye; the police procedural; and the deviant detective (Clarke, 2001: 72–106). By paying close attention to the text, Clarke is able to 'unpack' the generic pleasures of each of these kinds of detective story and make wider observations about shifting social perspectives on the societies portrayed in detective novels.

More common are studies of cinematic and televisual representations of crime, policing and imprisonment (e.g. Leishman and Mason, 2003; Mason, 2005; Reiner, 2007; see also *Crime, Media, Culture: an International Journal*: cmc.sagepub.com for numerous examples). During my time as co-editor of *CMC*, the journal received dozens of articles containing textual analyses of the American forensic crime drama *CSI*. By the time this volume is in print, I anticipate that *Crime, Media, Culture* will be inundated with articles about the HBO series *The Wire*, described by renowned American sociologist William Julius Wilson as having done more to enhance our understandings of the challenges of urban life and inequality than 'any other media event or scholarly publication including studies by social scientists' (tinyurl.com/6jxnvh).

RESEARCHING MEDIA AUDIENCES

While most of the 'classic' audience studies have much to tell us about gendered power relations, social class, typical roles adopted within families, and fan communities (see Dickinson et al., 1998, for an overview), there are relatively few audience studies which set out specifically to interrogate the relationship between audiences and media content that is concerned with crime, despite the enduring popularity of the genre. This is in contrast to the vast body of research known as 'media effects', which is psychology-based and typically employs very different research methods. Generally not found to be credible by UK researchers (see Jewkes, 2010, for an overview), much effects research emanates from the USA, is conducted under laboratory conditions, and seeks to find a direct, causal relationship between violent or sexual media content and imitative behaviour. Bandura and his colleagues' experiments with children and Bobo dolls in the 1950s are still widely cited despite their obvious flaws (see Jewkes, 2010, for a critique).

Surveys

The most straightforward type of audience research is the survey, which usually seeks to provide empirical data collected from a population of respondents on their media habits. The basic tool for surveying is the questionnaire, which has been used in many of the studies discussed in this chapter. However, because this quantitative approach can only elicit fairly short answers to a finite set of questions (usually questions starting with *what* or *how many*), it is commonly used in conjunction with qualitative methods such as observing audience members *in situ*, conducting **focus groups**, or interviewing individuals about their viewing, reading and listening preferences, all of which provide more in-depth findings about the *hows* and *whys* of people's attitudes, opinions and behaviour (see Dickinson et al., 1998: Chapter 9).

Focus groups

Focus groups are relatively quick, cheap and straightforward to organise. They are good for obtaining rich data in participants' own words and developing deeper insights than would be elicited from a questionnaire. Gillespie and McLaughlin (2003) conducted focus groups to try to discover the relationship between media and overtly punitive public attitudes to offenders. Ninety-three viewers were interviewed in nine focus groups between January and March 2002 in Swansea, South Wales. Approximately three-quarters of the sample were from working-class backgrounds, 75% were female and 25% male, with a balance across age groups. The focus groups were self-selecting and drawn from pre-existing social and communication groups. For example, the working-class male group was drawn from a local Working Men's Club; the middle-class women's group was drawn from a professional social network. This ensured that the groups were already familiar with each other and were used to exchanging opinions on topical issues. Participants are also able to build on each other's responses and come up with ideas they might not have thought of in a one-to-one interview. Sometimes group members act as checks and balances on one another, for example, identifying factual errors or extreme views. Because they are essentially conversational, focus groups are also useful for obtaining data from children and from people with low levels of literacy.

Gillespie and McLaughlin's choice of focus groups as a research methodology enabled them to conclude that the viewing and reading public understand far less about sentencing and punishment than they do about crime and policing. Moreover, as much information is learned from television dramas and soaps as from factual TV programmes such as news, although tabloid newspapers are still *most* influential in shaping strongly punitive attitudes. Focus group discussions also facilitated one of their most interesting findings, which was that when people 'knew' the offender (for example, a character in a TV soap) and had insight into their background, motives etc., they held far less punitive opinions about that individual than if they knew little or nothing about them. Like the GUMG, Gillespie and McLaughlin found that punitive attitudes are often articulated through the language and phrases of tabloid and mid-market newspapers. But while initial conversations replicated the kind of punitive rhetoric of news headlines and sound bites, as the discussions continued, more subtle moral positions were adopted as the complexities of particular individual cases emerged. Where a questionnaire or structured **interview** usually yields either a long-held opinion or a 'don't know', the focus group encourages discursive reflection, debate and deliberation, which – in this research – led to participants' expressing empathy and understanding towards offenders, thus contradicting what is often assumed about the supposedly punitive public.

However, focus groups are not always appropriate or useful for all research participants. For example, an ethnographic study I carried out was concerned with the ways in which men in prison use media (Jewkes, 2002). In addition to individual interviews, I decided to try focus groups, anticipating that respondents might make sense of their experiences differently and in greater depth by talking them through in conversation with others. For most of us, media consumption is primarily a social activity, and interaction between people in a group situation is a normal feature of most people's viewing, reading, listening and browsing. In the prison context, however, media use is generally a solitary activity and I found that focus groups simply encouraged consensus. In addition, prisoners – especially male prisoners – are frequently rather more inhibited in volunteering their thoughts and experiences in front of each other than when they are simply talking to a researcher.

The gendered differences in focus group constitution are highlighted in a study authorised by the Broadcasting Standards Commission (BSC) called *Men Viewing Violence* (1998), a follow-up to a study of *Women Viewing Violence* (Dobash et al., 1992), in which groups split by gender were asked questions about the violence contained within a spectrum of broadcast television material, ranging from drama to sport. In brief, the men were not as forthcoming as the women in focus group discussions, and were less engaged with both the characters and storylines in the material they saw (BSC, 1998).

Life history

Part of the difficulty for the researcher in eliciting information about how any audiences understand and interpret media content is that most people do not consciously think about, let alone articulate, how they *use* media content in their daily lives (Hansen et al., 1998). In my study of prison audiences, I ended up adopting some of the methodological approaches of oral history or **life history**, talking to many prisoners (especially lifers and long-termers who had very long histories in the prison system) individually for two hours or more about their early memories, pre-prison experiences and time(s) inside, in order to explore the 'felt texture' of their whole lives (Deacon et al., 1999: 291). As a result, my research was able to go beyond straightforward findings about prisoners' media preferences and elicit more penetrative findings about the relationship between their uses of media and their sense of self, identity, masculinity, power, powerlessness, and so on (Jewkes, 2002).

Life history as a methodological tool was made famous by the Chicago School of Sociology in the 1920s (which combined it with other methods, including participant observation) and it has been successfully used in several studies of offenders, including Carlen's (1985) study of 'criminal women'. Another example is King and Maruna's psychosocial research into punitive public opinion. Following an initial research phase during which postal surveys were sent to 3,600 households seeking views on a range of criminal justice issues, the researchers followed up by inviting 40 of the respondents to participate in 'life story interviews'. Half the **sample** had, in the postal survey, expressed 'punitive' attitudes, and half low or 'non-punitive' attitudes. Individuals were, among other things, asked about crime-related stories in film and literature that they had found particularly meaningful or significant. The researchers found that highly punitive individuals sought out media content which sustained their world view and clearly delineated between 'right' and 'wrong', while the less punitive individuals enjoyed more morally ambiguous media messages (King and Maruna, 2006). Interestingly, phone-in radio programmes appear to be driven by a strong conservative rather than liberal agenda, and shows such as those presented by Jeremy Vine on Radio 2 and Nicky Campbell on 5Live generally attract callers who would be classified as holding 'high punitive' attitudes on King and Maruna's scale. Frequently described as the 'Cinderella' of media studies because of its relative neglect by researchers, 'talk radio' would provide a fruitful area for future criminological research.

RESEARCHING MEDIA ORGANISATIONS

Participation observation

There have been a number of 'classic' **participant observation** studies which have sought to go beyond trying to find the 'meanings' embedded or encoded in media texts or, alternatively, the 'meanings' decoded (i.e. understood) by media audiences, and instead have borrowed from social anthropology methods that enable them to explore the organisational, bureaucratic, political and ideological processes involved in making news. In the main, these studies have relied on the researcher(s) immersing themselves in the field of news production: typically spending a great deal of time in newsrooms and with journalists, both on and off duty, in order to explore the full range of institutional and socio-cultural factors which shape and determine news output. As Ericson et al. drily observe in one of their influential studies of the news media in Toronto, 'some aspects of newsmakers' orientations can be gleaned from content but the inferences will be weak without knowledge of the actual methods of newsmakers' (Ericson et al., 1987: 79; cf. Greer, 2009: 98). Collectively, these studies of newsrooms have demonstrated the ways in which the problem of crime is distorted by the media: they have illustrated that the level of crime reporting remains much greater than its actual incidence and that the police feed journalists stories which give false impressions about 'crime waves' and their own success in clear-up rates (Roshier, 1973; Fishman, 1978). Studies have also shown that the police are engaged in competitive, self-promoting struggles to shape their own images and the policy agenda (Schlesinger and Tumber, 1994; Mawby, 2002).

Other than the classic trilogy of news-making processes in Canada written by Ericson, Baranek and Chan (1987, 1989a, 1989b), the most well known of the research studies of crime reporting (in the UK) are arguably those by Cohen (1972/2002), who popularised the phrase 'moral panic' in his analysis of clashes between mods and rockers in the 1960s; Hall et al. (1978), who examined the 'mugging' phenomenon in the 1970s and coined the term 'primary definers' to describe the powerful sources to which media reporters habitually turn in order to produce 'news'; and Chibnall (1977), who analysed the symbiotic relationship between the police and the media in post-war Britain.

Given the current tendency within popular culture to look back at police procedures from the 1960s and 1970s with nostalgia and even a degree of affection (thanks in large part to the BBC series *Life on Mars* and *Ashes to Ashes*, with the corrupt but charismatic DCI Gene Hunt), it is instructive to revisit some of the academic research studies conducted during that period. In *Law and Order News* (1977), Chibnall explores the institutional and cultural pressures faced by journalists who had a vested interest in 'keeping their [police] contacts sweet' (1977: 144). In spending a lot of time with reporters and editors, he was able to establish trust and rapport between himself and those he was observing. He notes that journalists' perceptions of public expectations inform editorial decisions because, quite simply, people want to be able to feel they can trust their police to protect them. Stories about police corruption and police brutality (bearing in mind that Chibnall's research was conducted at a time when both were relatively common) were handled carefully by news teams, who attempted to tread a precarious line between being pro-police and anti-police corruption. The result, however, was that the police remained a powerful institutional source of news who maintained a sufficiently cosy relationship with specialist reporters to ensure that it was many years before the extent of police malpractice, corruption, brutality and institutional racism were revealed in the UK's police forces. In more recent times, it is arguably more likely that these kinds of problems would be uncovered by an investigative journalist than by an academic researcher (see, for example, stories uncovered by freelance journalist Nick Davies, www.nickdavies.net/).

Interestingly, none of the three 'classic' studies by Cohen, Hall et al. and Chibnall has much to say about the methodologies employed; the emphasis is firmly on theory and evidence. This is not to question their methodological rigour, merely to observe that, for these scholars, their methodological approaches were considered secondary to their findings. For example, Cohen's 1972 study, *Folk Devils and Moral Panics: The Creation of Mods and Rockers*, has undeniably become one of the all-time 'classics' of media criminology and has inspired and influenced countless researchers in the decades since it was published. Yet he relegates his indisputably impressive sources of data to an Appendix (see Box 11.3). It is perhaps precisely this methodological exactitude that helps to explain why this kind of empirical research is now so rare. As one specialist in the field observes, we have witnessed the 'death of ethnography' in media criminology (Greer, 2009).

BOX 11.3

THE MULTI-METHOD APPROACH

Cohen's documentary sources included:

- national and local press cuttings from the entire two-and-a-half-year research period;
- tape recordings of most radio and television news bulletins over the Bank Holiday weekends during which the incidents took place;
- local publications with restricted circulation (parish newsletters, council minutes and the like);
- *Hansard* reports;
- letters received by the National Council for Civil Liberties alleging police malpractice.

In addition to these secondary sources, Cohen took several primary, empirical methodological approaches:

- administered questionnaires to trainee probation officers;
- interviewed news editors;
- held informal discussions with local hotel owners, shop assistants, taxi drivers etc.;
- interviewed 65 members of the public who had witnessed the clashes between the mods and rockers;
- wrote letters to MPs and other public officials, some of which were followed up with interviews;
- talked to local action groups;
- participated as a volunteer worker for a youth project in one of the seaside towns in which conflict had occurred (Cohen, 1972/2002: 173–177).

RESEARCHING MEDIA IN THE CRIMINAL JUSTICE SYSTEM

Interviewing

Of all the approaches to researching the relationship between media and crime discussed so far, studies of the role of media within the criminal justice system are arguably the least commonly undertaken. The reasons for this are largely pragmatic; negotiating access, getting past 'gatekeepers', persuading busy criminal justice professionals and wary 'clients' to grant interviews, and treading fine ethical lines are all potential obstacles to carrying out research in the relatively 'closed' settings of police stations, legal practices, courtrooms and prisons. There are exceptions, however, one of which is my own ethnographic study of the *Captive Audience* in prisons discussed previously (Jewkes, 2002). Another is Helen Jones' (2007) study of the experiences of suicide and self-harm among boys in a Young Offender Institution which found, via in-depth interviewing, that being denied video games, play stations and personal computers contributed to feelings of boredom, loneliness and despair. A very different piece of research was that conducted by Newburn and Hayman (2002) into the introduction and impact of CCTV cameras in the custody suites (that is, the police cells, interview rooms, medical rooms, and so on) at Kilburn police station in London. Their aim was to discover what the arrival of surveillance media did for ways in which privacy and protection were experienced within the custody suites. In addition to analysing documentary sources which permitted them to trace the history behind the decision to introduce CCTV (including the controversial case of the death in custody of Marlon Downes in 1997), data was gathered from in-depth interviews with police and individuals held in custody. Further supplementary interviews were conducted with solicitors, lay visitors, forensic medical examiners and other 'appropriate adults' who had reason to visit the custody suite.

In studies such as the Kilburn CCTV project, interviewing provides a rich seam of data allowing the researchers not only to evaluate the success of the new media experiment and offer sensible suggestions for future policy direction, but also to make profoundly important points about wider social issues – in this case around themes of power, governance and human rights. Similarly, in Lynn Chancer's (2005) study of high-profile, newsworthy legal cases, her groundbreaking access to key personnel, interviewed over a period of seven years, allowed her to trace the cultural dynamics that turn certain criminal events (e.g. the trial of O.J. Simpson) into catalysts for wider racial, gender or class hostilities. She conducted over 200 personal interviews with judges, lawyers and jurors, as well as editors and reporters on the *New York Times*, journalists working in local news, and people who had strong opinions about the cases, including those who had physically protested, written to the newspapers, attended community meetings, or worked in or near the courthouses where the trials took place.

Chancer's central argument, which she was able to formulate as a direct result of her close contact with judges and jurors, is that, whether intentionally or unwittingly, individuals involved in judicial proceedings are subtly yet profoundly intertwined with the media. This interdependence, she argues, can affect understandings of subsequent cases, which are tried in the knowledge, and under the influence, of what has occurred previously. The actions, decisions and 'performances' of judges, lawyers and jurors, conveyed to the public at large by the mass media, become part of the cultural fabric of society, subtly manipulating public understandings of a wide range of social issues. For these reasons, decisions about whether to allow television cameras into courtrooms have never been so apposite. While this remains a relatively under-researched area, Stepniak has spent 15 years researching audio and visual coverage of court trials around the world. His research, which combines interviewing with documentary analysis, observation and participant observation, aims to invigorate the debate in the UK about the potential benefits of televising court trials (Stepniak, 2008). Critics of the proposal maintain that media technologies fundamentally alter the stages on which criminal justice is played out, and may thus change the nature of justice itself.

SUMMARY

At the start of this chapter, it was noted that many criminologists have been slow to recognise the significance of media to their work and frequently ignore the vast, interdisciplinary body of literature and research in the field. Even when the role of media is noted in studies of, say, public opinion about offenders, or anxieties about crime, the reference is frequently perfunctory, and anything but the most cursory glance at the kinds of authoritative, interdisciplinary research that has been reviewed in this chapter is not evident. In many cases, criminologists make brief and bold statements about the crime–media nexus, while clearly having no engagement with research in the field whatsoever. In fact, while the brief for this chapter was to discuss criminological research into media, the outcome is that the majority of studies mentioned were conducted and written by scholars in departments of journalism, media or cultural studies.

The chapter has discussed media–crime research in four different areas: texts; audiences; organisations; and within criminal justice. For practical reasons, the chapter has concentrated mainly on: traditional media (i.e. the media of greatest penetration historically); the methods most likely to be adopted by university students in their own research; and some, if by no means all, of the most influential criminological studies of media over the last 30 years or so. But as demonstrated by the healthy growth of research into crime in cyberspace and the role of new and emerging media in offending, victimisation and policing, there are many exciting – if ethically challenging – avenues for the researcher to explore (see, for example, DiMarco and DiMarco (2003) on researching in online chat rooms and Bell (2001) on researching cybercultures; and Chapter 12, this volume). Yet, while criminological research into media technologies is relatively buoyant in the fields of surveillance studies and cybercrime, there is very little credible, rigorous criminological research on, for example, gaming on computers and consoles and its relationship to crime and deviance. New media technologies are creating new types of consumer – perhaps more accurately called 'users' rather than 'audiences'. Texts are becoming txts; consumers surf, blog, network, tweet and game in addition (or as an alternative) to reading, watching and listening; traditional media industries have, of necessity, embraced the virtual realm, and the criminal justice system is adopting media technologies at a brisk pace. These areas all provide unlimited scope for future research that is fascinating, topical, imaginative and relevant to our everyday lives.

◗ ■ Study Questions/Activities for Students ▬▬▬▬▬▬▬

1 What are the relative merits and limitations of using actual newspapers and other documentary sources for discourse analysis, as opposed to online sources?

2 It was noted in this chapter that discussions of crime on 'talk radio' would provide a fruitful area for future research. How might you go about conducting such research? What methods would you employ?

3 A question that is frequently asked by academic scholars is 'Where is today's Chibnall?' (or versions thereof). Why do you think that sociologically informed ethnographic studies of crime news production appear to have all but disappeared?

4 As this chapter underlines, most criminological research into media understandably focuses on 'traditional' media texts, technologies, audiences and institutions. How might future criminological research develop our ideas about, and understandings of, the relationship between new and emerging media and crime-related issues? What kinds of innovative research methods might be employed?

5 When high-profile crimes occur, newspapers frequently carry in-depth analysis and editorials in addition to straightforwardly reporting the events. What would you say are the key differences between investigative journalism and academic research?

RESOURCES

For real insight and understanding of the joys and pitfalls of doing research into crime and media, you can do no better than to refer to some of the classic studies mentioned in this chapter. While extracts from the likes of Cohen's *Folk Devils and Moral Panics* (1972/2002) and Chibnall's *Law and Order News* (1977) usefully appear in many criminology readers – see, for example, Greer, C. (ed.) (2009) *Crime and Media: A Reader*, London: Routledge, and Jewkes Y. (ed.) (2009) *Crime and Media* (3 vols), London: Sage – there is no substitute for getting hold of the original texts. That said, the editors' commentaries in both of these editions are worth reading for their insight into crime–media research and Greer's reader includes an immensely useful section devoted to 'researching media', including a critique of internet-assisted content and discourse analysis. To keep up to date with current research in the field, *Crime, Media, Culture: an International Journal* (http://cmc.sagepub.com) is a valuable resource which includes 'research notes' that focus on data collection methods as well as full-length articles. There are too many books on media research methods to mention more than a couple. A useful collection on audiences is Dickinson, R. et al. (eds) (1998) *Approaches to Audiences: A Reader*, London: Hodder. A good all-round introduction is Hansen, A. et al. (1998) *Mass Communication Research Methods*, Basingstoke: Macmillan; an updated and more extensive edition of which has been published in four volumes by Sage (2009).

REFERENCES

Bell, D. (2001) *An Introduction to Cybercultures*, London: Routledge.

Broadcasting Standards Commission (1998) *Men Viewing Violence*, London: BSC. Available at: www.ofcom.org.uk/static/archive/bsc/pdfs/research/m_view.pdf.

Carlen, P. (1985) *Criminal Women*, Cambridge: Polity Press.

Chancer, L.S. (2005) *High-Profile Crimes: When Legal Cases Become Social Causes*, Chicago: University of Chicago Press.

Chibnall, S. (1977) *Law and Order News*, London: Tavistock.

Clarke, J. (2001) 'The pleasures of crime: interrogating the detective story', in J. Muncie and E. McLaughlin (eds), *The Problem of Crime* (2nd edition), London: Sage.

Cohen, S. (1972/2002) *Folk Devils and Moral Panics: The Creation of Mods and Rockers*, London: MacGibbon and Kee; 3rd edition with revised introduction, London: Routledge.

Deacon, D., Pickering, M., Golding, P. and Murdock, G. (1999) *Researching Communications*, London: Arnold.

Dickinson, R., Harindranath, R. and Linne, O. (1998) *Approaches to Audiences: A Reader*, London: Hodder.

DiMarco, A. and DiMarco, H. (2003) 'Investigating cybersociety: a consideration of the ethical and practical issues surrounding online research in chat rooms', in Y. Jewkes (ed.), *Dot. cons: Crime, Deviance and Identity on the Internet*, Cullompton: Willan.

Ditton, J. and Duffy, J. (1983) 'Bias in the newspaper reporting of crime news', *British Journal of Criminology*, 23(2): 159–165.

Dobash, R.P., Weaver, C. and Scheslinger, P. (1992) *Women Viewing Violence*, London: British Film Institute.

Ericson, R., Baranek, P. and Chan, J. (1987) *Visualizing Deviance: A Study of News Organization*, Toronto: University of Toronto Press.

Ericson, R., Baranek, P. and Chan, J. (1989a) *Negotiating Control: A Study of News Sources*, Toronto: University of Toronto Press.

Ericson, R., Baranek, P. and Chan, J. (1989b) *Representing Order: Crime, Law, and Justice in the News Media*, Toronto: University of Toronto Press.

Fishman, M. (1981) *Manufacturing the News*, Austin, TX: University of Texas Press.

Gillespie, M. and McLaughlin, E. (2003) 'Media and the shaping of public knowledge and attitudes towards crime and punishment', in *Rethinking Crime & Punishment*. Available at: www.rethinking.org.uk.

Greer, C. (ed.) (2009) *Crime and Media: A Reader*, London: Routledge.

Greer, C. and Jewkes, Y. (2005) 'Images and processes of social exclusion', *Social Justice*, special edition, 32(1): 20–31.

Greer, C., Ferrell, J. and Jewkes, Y. (2007) 'It's the image that matters: style, substance and critical scholarship', *Crime, Media, Culture: an International Journal*, 3(1): 5–10.

Hall, S., Critcher, C., Jefferson, T., Clarke, J. and Roberts, B. (eds) (1978) *Policing the Crisis: Mugging, the State and Law and Order*, London: Macmillan.

Hansen, A., Cottle, S., Negrine, R. and Newbold, C. (1998) *Mass Communication Research Methods*, Basingstoke: Macmillan.

Jewkes, Y. (2002) *Captive Audience: Media, Masculinity and Power in Prisons*, Cullompton: Willan.

Jewkes, Y. (2010) *Media and Crime*, second edition, London: Sage.

Jones, H. (2007) 'The pains of custody: how young men cope through the criminal justice system', Unpublished PhD Thesis, University of Hull.

King, A. and Maruna, S. (2006) 'The function of fiction for a punitive public', in P. Mason (ed.), *Captured by the Media: Prison Discourse in Popular Culture*, Cullompton: Willan, pp. 16–30.

Leishman, F. and Mason, P. (2003) *Policing and the Media: Facts, Fictions and Factions*, Cullompton: Willan.

Mason, P. (ed.) (2005) *Captured by the Media: Prison Discourse in Popular Culture*, Cullompton: Willan.

Mawby, R. (2002) *Policing Images: Policing, Communication and Legitimacy*, Cullompton: Willan.

Newburn, T. and Hayman, S. (2002) *Policing, Surveillance and Social Control: CCTV and Police Monitoring of Suspects*, Cullompton: Willan.

Oliver, M. (1994) 'Portrayals of crime, race and aggression in "reality based" police shows: a content analysis', *Journal of Broadcasting and Electronic Media*, 38(2): 179–192.

Reiner, R. (2007) *'Media made criminality'*, in M. Maguire, R. Morgan and R. Reiner (eds), *The Oxford Handbook of Criminology*, Oxford: Oxford University Press.

Reiner, R. and Livingstone, S. (1997) *Discipline or Desubordination? Changing Media Images of Crime: Final Report.* Available at: www.lse.ac.uk/collections/media@lse/pdf/discipline.pdf.

Riffe, D., Lacy, S. and Fico, F.G. (2005) *Analyzing Media Messages: Using Quantitative Content Analysis in Research* (2nd edition), Mahwah, NJ: Lawrence Erlbaum Associates.

Roshier, B. (1973) 'The selection of crime news by the press', in S. Cohen and J. Young (eds), *The Manufacture of News*, London: Constable.

Schlesinger, P. and Tumber, H. (1994) *Reporting Crime: The Media Politics of Criminal Justice*, Oxford: Clarendon Press.

Stepniak, D. (2008) *Audio-visual Coverage of Courts: A Comparative Analysis*, Cambridge: Cambridge University Press.

Van Dijk, T. (2000) 'New(s) racism: a discourse analytical approach', in S. Cottle (ed.), *Ethnic Minorities and the Media: Changing Cultural Boundaries*, Buckingham: Open University Press.

TWELVE
USING THE INTERNET TO RESEARCH CRIME AND JUSTICE

DAVID S. WALL AND MATTHEW WILLIAMS

Chapter Contents

KEY POINTS

This chapter:

- Argues that the philosophical principles of empirical research remain much the same online as they do offline

- Discusses how networked technologies have transformed criminological research into criminal behaviour and criminal justice systems in three distinct ways. They:

(Continued)

- provide researchers with new sources of information that can assist with the collection of primary, secondary and tertiary data
- provide researchers with new opportunities to study new (criminological) research environments
- create new forms of criminal (and criminal justice system) behaviour that generate new research questions

INTRODUCTION

If the leitmotif of the 1990s was information technology, then the 'noughties' (2000s) were characterised by new social landscapes created by social networking and popular contemporary mass information systems such as *Google, Wikipedia, Twitter, Facebook, MySpace, YouTube, Flickr, Friends Reunited, SecondLife* and many others. The expansion of the domestic internet since the mid-1990s has seen the internet grow from an information sharing and retrieval tool to a fully interactive, immersive and transformative social arena. The **Web 1.0** technologies common to the early internet included email, newsgroups, instant message chat (such as MSN Messenger) and websites that had no capacity for collaborative content generation. These latter websites were static and were meant solely for information retrieval. The leap to **Web 2.0** technologies was accompanied by a sea-change in web content generation and interpersonal interaction and also the potential democratisation of web content production. Web 2.0 technologies also therefore allow 'readers' of websites to easily contribute to their content and include Wikis, blogs and social networking sites such as *Facebook, Myspace, eBay* and *Bebo*, and also 2D and 3D graphical spaces such as *SecondLife, Habbo Hotel* and *Active Worlds*. Technology commentators have now begun to talk of **Web 3.0**, a label that is yet to be fully defined, but is said to include technologies that provide internet users with a more 'realistic' interactive online experience (Williams 2006a).

The mass population of these new 'social' spaces has, in one way or another, shaped social, unsocial and criminal behaviour to the point that they are now part of our everyday lives and lexicon. Even if we ourselves do not connect to the internet, others, who either make decisions about us or support our lives, do so. This transformation is significant because we have almost reached the technological point where every single informational transaction that we make or involves us is recorded in databases that are searchable by those with access. Yet, despite this startling informational shift, there is little systematic discussion in the criminological literature about how new digital technologies have changed the ways that we conduct research in criminology and criminal justice.

This chapter will map out the relationship between criminological research and network technologies. In so doing it will explore three fundamental ways that network technologies and the environments they create can facilitate research into crime, criminal justice and the information society. The first part will explore the ways in which technologies can assist criminological researchers to conduct criminological research in 'conventional' offline (kinetic) environments, especially the collection of primary and secondary data. The second part will look at some challenging research issues that result from the creation of entirely new (non-kinetic) criminal environments. The third part will focus upon researching cybercrimes. The final part will discuss how these developments give rise to a range of new methodological and ethical challenges.

RESEARCHING TRADITIONAL CRIME AND CRIMINAL JUSTICE PROCESSES USING THE INTERNET

Networked technologies provide criminologists with powerful new communications and computing tools that enable them to research 'conventional' criminological and criminal justice topics much more effectively and also at a distance (Lash 2001). Such efficiency gains can be a considerable advantage on the pre-internet experience. Advances in information collection, retrieval and information technology-based working practices mean that individual researchers now have far more personal control over the whole research process than they once had.

When collecting and analysing primary data, researchers are no longer confined to their office or institution's computing resources because these facilities are now portable. Statistical analysis that once required access to a large static mainframe computer can now be run off a laptop or notebook computer. Furthermore, respondents can also be located and accessed by researchers through the utilisation of individuals' social networks. Once respondents have been located, then one-to-one **interviews** can be conducted with respondents at a distance by using **digital communication technologies.** These advances are augmented by a new arsenal of online research methods that can be utilised to research offline settings, such as online **focus groups** (see next section), online interactive interviews (via IRC (Internet Relay Chat) and *Facebook*-type environments) and online survey technology (such as the *Bristol Online Survey Tool, Survey Monkey, Zoomerang, SurveyGizmo, LimeSurvey, Magic Survey Tool, QIPM Web Survey Tool* and others). Such tools collect data from respondents on offline or online topics (see the next section). Not only do these online data collection methods allow criminologists to conduct online surveys at a distance and in the respondent's, and not researcher's, time, but they can also download the collected data directly into a statistical data analysis software package such as SPSS. Even voice recordings can now be transcribed electronically into a word processor or directly into **qualitative** analysis packages such as NVivo or Atlas.ti. In addition to advances in the collection of research data, developments in networking, such as Cloud Computing and the (GRID) e-infrastructure, are also changing the way that research collaborations can take place. **The GRID** can facilitate data collection and analysis by distributed research teams across the UK (Fielding and Macintyre 2006), where researchers in

Edinburgh, Cardiff, London and Belfast can, for example, simultaneously collect and analyse data in real-time by utilising high-capacity video link and networked online methods 'tools'.

As more and more of our offline activities become mediated by **networked technologies**, this increases the number of information flows that can become a potential resource for the researcher. Even resolute offliners – those individuals who adamantly reject the internet and networked technologies – will find personal data about themselves, or their movements or participation in activities, being digitally recorded somewhere. More and more data about our everyday activities are being deposited into searchable networked databases. Specific to criminal justice research, network technologies are helping the police, courts, prisons and related criminal justice agencies organise themselves more effectively, efficiently and economically. They are opening up entirely new (often interactive) lines of communication between criminal justice agencies and their constituent components: related key agencies, government and the general public. Importantly, for research, each of these digital methods of communication generate new types of information stream that potentially provide new sources of data. With authorisation for access, these have the potential to be utilised for research into both criminal and institutional activity. Legal access to the data notwithstanding, new **data-mining** techniques can efficiently explore this massive amount of data to identify links between variables and reveal important new information about 'social' relationships and change over time.

These new online sources of information place vast amounts of data and information at the researcher's fingertips that can be accessed by search engines or 'browsers'. This development has led to the **keyword search** becoming a basic organising concept behind contemporary research methods. Carefully chosen combinations of keywords can provide researchers with the means to interrogate internet search engines such as *Google*, *Bing* and *Yahoo*. In more advanced forms, variants of keyword research can be used to interrogate large databases of, say, transactional data. In short, new technologies allow researchers to expand their research sample and conduct traditional-type research in ways not tempered by traditional physical constraints so that research can take place within a shorter time frame and at a distance.

RESEARCHING NEW ONLINE CRIMINAL ENVIRONMENTS

An important effect of networked technologies has been the emergence of new online environments that have become a new focus for researchers. Early debates about these online environments as 'communities' (see Rheingold 1993) saw a notable shift in the ways that social scientists perceive human activity on the internet. Sociologists and criminologists began viewing online behaviour as an extension of everyday life (see discussion in Wall and Williams 2007). As a result, traditional 'terrestrial' research methods began to be adapted to operate in these new digital areas. However, faster 'broadband' connections in the twenty-first century have intensified activity in these new environments and have caused researchers to now consider whether existing research methods still apply. We suggest that in most cases they do, but the applicability of particular methods and similarities between environments should not be assumed without consideration of their dynamics and the research question being asked. The 'virtual' **ethnography** of 'communities' of networked individuals, for example, may not necessarily be the same as the ethnography of more geographical social communities. Whereas the former can arguably withdraw easily from the virtual environment, the latter may not have as much choice of mobility because of their socio-economic situation and geographical location.

While new virtual, globalised and networked social settings can differ from the forms of social interaction that preceded the internet, the applicability of offline social science methods remains. However, these methods often need to be adapted in light of what the internet affords its users: anonymity, multiple identities, the ability to visit and belong to a multitude of online social networks, to rapidly alter and shape personal online spaces, etc. 'Traditional' field methods of participant and non-participant observation, interviewing, focus groups and **survey research** have been used to collect data from online social groups with varying degrees of success (see Baym 1995a, 1995b; Correll 1995; Markham 1998; Witmer et al. 1999; Gatson and Zweerink 2004; Williams 2006a). The survivability of 'traditional' methods within a networked and digital environment is dependent upon their capacity to be utilised and adapted to the technology that mediates human interaction online. Each manifestation presents new opportunities for the evolution of the 'traditional' methods of social investigation. Two practical examples of how 'terrestrial' methodological techniques have been adapted to the online setting are shown in Box 12.1 and Box 12.2.

BOX 12.1

ONLINE DISCUSSION/FOCUS GROUPS

One of the earliest documented uses of online focus groups in academic social research was Murray's (1997) study of a geographically dispersed group of healthcare professionals who all had an existing expertise in computer-mediated communication. The characteristics of Murray's population made the use of an online focus group appropriate to the study. Murray replicated the format of face-to-face focus groups by ensuring that the online groups composed 6–8 members. Online, this group size prevented simultaneous conversational threads developing. Threads occur where multiple topics of conversation overlap simultaneously, which can become disorienting to an outsider. In naturally occurring online discussions, such 'threading' is commonplace, and although initially apparently chaotic to a novice, participants are soon adept at maintaining distinctions between the threads. Also notable from Murray's groups was that too high a level of questioning from the researcher led to serial direct answering by participants to the researcher, rather than it stimulating discussion. Around the same time, Robson's (1999) use of online focus groups involved a patient population group, again allowing for the inclusion of geographically dispersed members in the sample.

(Continued)

Robson's group was larger than Murray's, with 57 participants in one email-based discussion. Here, threading did occur, allowing multiple topics to be discussed simultaneously with the group remaining open, responsive and familiar with each other, requiring minimal questioning from the facilitator.

Unlike Murray's and Robson's email-based groups, Stewart et al. (1998) conducted a real-time online focus group with young women to investigate the usefulness of the internet as a qualitative public health research tool. Again, the method allowed a geographically dispersed sample to be used, with participants simultaneously contributing from four separate sites. The facilitator made minimal contributions, interjecting to make sure all topics were covered. Facilitating the discussions was more problematic than in asynchronous online focus groups, such as those of Murray and Robson, due to the speed and frequency with which the topics changed, making it harder to ensure all planned topics were covered.

BOX 12.2

ACCESSING ONLINE POPULATIONS FOR QUALITATIVE RESEARCH

The respective research projects of Murray (1997), Robson (1999) and Stewart et al. (1998) into health issues were aided by a definable and captive online population. Identifying and gaining access to populations for research purposes is very often the first obstacle for researchers to overcome. Researching internet populations is no exception. Indeed, there are some similarities, such as ascertaining what kind of population is required for the research, and the criteria to which the population must adhere. While focus groups have been employed both in market research and the social sciences, in neither case has there been the goal to generalise the findings to a wider population. The aim of the focus group is to elicit data from small groups of people on the meanings, processes and normative understandings that lie behind group assessments that are unlikely to be statistically applied to a general population (Bloor et al. 2001). Instead of generalising findings, the emphasis is placed upon achieving a depth of understanding. Typical methods of recruitment in offline settings have therefore relied on tapping into pre-existing social groups or samples, individual canvassing and snowball sampling. However, these recruiting conventions, as applied to online settings, have been met with varying degrees of success. Taking advantage of existing social groups online is by far the most common and successful method of recruiting participants (see Robson 1999). Notably medical sociology and health research has capitalised upon 'captive populations' online. Health and illness support networks have been used to conduct online focus groups (Murray 1997; Stewart et al. 1998; Robson 1999; Stewart and Williams, 2007).

Many criminologically relevant captive online populations, with whom researchers can engage, exist on the internet. Wall, for example, observed the practices of on-hacking communities in his 2000 research (Wall 2007: 66), and Williams (2006a) observed vandalism in online communities. Beyond observation, there are, in the UK, several forums supporting victims of crime, such as the Centre for Action on Rape and Abuse forum (www.crcl.org.uk/forum.html). Such forums provide a population of victims as potential research participants. Assuming that appropriate ethical practices are employed in gaining access to respondents, these forums facilitate access to potential research participants as well as providing an appropriate medium for discussion on the research topic.

The challenge of sampling online populations

Before the novice researcher sets about spending time searching for relevant online captive populations, due attention should be given to the limits of online sampling. Depending upon the researcher's epistemological perspective (theory of knowledge – e.g. **positivism** vs. **interpretivism**), representative populations may or may not be of importance. However, regardless of whether the researcher subscribes to realism or interpretivism, the **digital divide** cannot be ignored. Not all of the UK population are online, and usage of online technologies varies greatly by user demographics. For example, only a small number of victims of rape or sexual abuse will seek advice online, and even fewer will be prepared to engage in an online discussion of their experiences. Recruiting solely from an online source has its limitations and researchers risk a 'skewed' sample if due care is not taken during respondent recruitment. Findings will be specific to only the sample studied if relevant offline **sampling** conventions are not applied online.

The challenge of conducting virtual ethnography in online environments

Central to the discussion about researching popular new online environments are debates about the interesting opportunities that they open up for conducting virtual ethnography and the research challenges that they raise. One thorny question is whether or not a virtual ethnographic account is a true reflection of the virtual culture, place or people it claims to have studied. Here, as with debates over offline ethnography, issues of naturalism and realism collide with constructivist notions that reconceptualise ethnographic authenticity. While reflexivity allows researchers to produce 'open' accounts in the 'real' or offline (kinetic) world, recent concerns have been cast on the reproduction of grounded accounts in the virtual arena. Epistemological and methodological questions complicate the application of research methods to the online setting. Questions have been raised about:

- the extent to which the researcher is able to write in a convincing way about the people studied when anonymity inherent in internet interactions casts doubts upon the identities of research participants

- how the participant observer manages his/her identity in settings mediated by text and graphics, and what impact this has on data collection

- how researchers conceptualise the boundaries of online settings and the experiences of those observed.

The works of Markham (1998), Hine (2000), Leander and Mckim (2003) and others have addressed the application and adaptation of ethnography to online *textual* environments. This work primarily relates to the observation of textual exchanges, both synchronous and asynchronous, within MUDs (Multi User Dimension), MOOs (MUD Object Oriented), newsgroups, discussion lists and IRC (Internet Relay Chat). The experience gained by these authors from conducting

participant observation in disparate online spaces enabled them to raise important methodological and epistemological questions. Questions ranging from the difficulties associated with analysing discourse in textual spaces where lurkers (non-participating observers) are abundant (Hine 2000) to epistemological concerns over the role of the observer in online settings (Leander and Mckim 2003).

In comparison to textual online environments such as Internet Relay Chat, more advanced graphical spaces such as *SecondLife*, *Active Worlds* and *Habbo Hotel* pose unique methodological challenges. Williams' (2006a, 2006b) study of an online graphical world reflects that the simulation of presence and the importance of the visual in interactions within graphical settings requires that the participant observer pay more attention to his/her *avatar's* appearance (the graphical representation of a user's online persona), the frequency with which it changes physical form and the use of gesture (virtual non-verbal cues). Considerations of the pseudo-physical extend beyond avatars to the field-site. The visual design of graphical spaces impacts significantly upon avatar and observer behaviour. As visual stimuli become abundant, research observation shifts from textual discourse to interactions between avatars and artefacts. In addition to the mapping of the physical boundaries of the field-site, the online ethnographer must therefore attempt to map out the multi-sited experiences of those observed. Asynchronously travelling to other worlds, associated newsgroups and web-pages allows the participant observer to build up an experiential picture of users' online lives.

Online qualitative data

Although data collected from online environments are in many respects similar to data collected in any other environment, online environments lack the non-verbal information found in tactile and physical environments, such as setting, expression, movement, phatic noise and the like (see Mann and Stewart 2000; Denscombe 2003). Whereas these separate elements are easily distinguishable in conventional face-to-face interactions, which allow them to become primary subjects for analysis and contribute to a whole meaning, researchers have to remember that text-only online data is 'all-inclusive text', making its different elements harder to identify. Researchers therefore have to impose such separation on online data and tease out any non-verbal elements in order to capture the meaning of textual online communication. Three features have comparable characteristics with accepted offline data categories; they are form, style and content.

- *Form* – is comparable to 'context' in offline research. Email, web-board messages, chat rooms and the like all have particular background expectancies and shared understandings that contribute to our understanding of the data. Email communications provide more formed, considered, 'literate' rather than 'oral' responses, and also assume an air of privacy and intimacy. Being asynchronous, web-based discussion boards share some of these 'literate' characteristics but carry with them a greater sense of public or group discussion compared to group circulated emails. Finally, synchronous forms of discussion, such as chat rooms, are characterised by more fast-paced, punchy, spontaneous discussion.

Overly stylistic content, disrupted adjacency, overlapping exchanges and topic delay all have to be contended with during mediation and analysis. In summary, setting up a focus group within a chat room creates quite distinct challenges and generates data quite different from that generated through a distribution list.

- *Style* – is comparable to non-verbal cues in offline research and idiomatic forms of expression such as emoticons, line width, use of capitals, colour and font convey meaning. Phrasing emphasis is given in a variety of ways, such as mewing words within asterisks, using text characters to convey recognisable facial expressions, and capitalising words to denote shouting, anger or impatience. While these conventions may appear stilted or confusing to the novice, users swiftly develop the ability to decipher the nuances of conversation from these tactics. Thus, for the researcher there is richer meaning to written words if they are able to interpret them.

- *Content* – is comparable to the verbal elements of offline data. Content comprises the words participants use to express themselves.

All three elements have considerable bearing on where criminological online research might take place, how that research is conducted and what kind of analysis is used to explain the data. Situations, conventions, emotions and senses are conveyed through readable channels and 'reconstituted' by the recipient reader.

RESEARCHING NEW ONLINE CRIMINAL BEHAVIOURS: CYBERCRIME

Traditional environments for research have changed radically and new online research has emerged as the result of the networked technologies. New forms of criminal and harmful behaviours have also arisen and these too are the subject of contemporary research inquiry. Identity theft (phishing), cyberterrorism, information warfare, spamming, denial of service attacks, hacker and cracker programs, hacktivism, e-frauds, auction fraud, click fraud, scams, scareware, hate crime, cyberbullying, illegal online gambling, extreme pornography, viruses, worms and Trojans are just some of the terms that now encompass 'cybercrime' (Wall 2007: 52–129).

As these activities become a new research focus, it is very important to distinguish methodologically between the different levels of technological mediation to which criminal behaviour has been subjected. Traditional forms of offending that simply use computers to assist their organisation are very different in character from behaviours that are purely the spawn of the internet. In the former group, offending such as drug trafficking, simple bank frauds, the gathering of precursor information to help commit or organise a crime are low-end cybercrimes because the behaviours will persist by other means if the networked technologies were to be removed. Cybercrimes born of the internet fall into two subcategories. The first are 'hybrid' cybercrimes, which are those 'traditional' or legislated crimes for which network technology has created entirely new global opportunities, such as e-auction frauds. The second category are the 'high-end', true cybercrimes that are solely the product of the internet and not possible without it. They include spamming, phishing (identity theft) and pharming (hijacking browsers), scareware (fake anti-virus software) and variations of online intellectual property piracy (Wall 2007: 44–48).

The main methodological distinction to be made between these different categories of cybercrime is that both traditional crimes using computers and hybrid cybercrimes already tend to be the subject of existing laws. Therefore, any new legal problems relate more to understandings of legal procedures than to substantive law, which means that the researcher therefore needs to focus more effort upon the policing process rather than the courts. The 'true' cybercrimes, however, are new behaviours that are *sui generis* (of themselves), often requiring new legislation, as has been the case with (among other examples) spamming in the European Union, USA and elsewhere (see Wall 2007, 2008). Researching these latter forms of offending may require a very different research approach. For example, a research project might examine threat analysis data from cyber-security reports in order to identify potential levels of victimisation. These might then be compared with the findings of online surveys that identify actual experiences of victimisation.

Three further distinctions can be made between different types of cybercrime. First, *crimes against the machine* assault the integrity of computer network access mechanisms, such as hacking/cracking, cyber-vandalism, spying, DDOS (distributed denial of service) attacks and viruses. Second, *crimes using machines*, such as phishing or advance-fee frauds, use networked computer systems (often legitimately) to engage victims with the intention of dishonestly acquiring cash, goods or services. Third, *crimes within the machine* relate to the illegal content of networked computer systems, such as the trade and distribution of pornographic, hate crime materials or materials that intend to deceive (Wall 2007: 52–129). This threefold typology links the different behaviours to distinct bodies of law and associated professional experience, but it also identifies where the research focus might lie in order to obtain data. Research into *crimes against the machine* will, for example, focus more upon the computer system and the mindset that wishes to gain access to it, whereas research into *crimes using the machine* focuses upon the harmful or criminal act that the computer was used for. Both types contrast with research into *crimes in the machine*, which explores the impact of harmful content upon shaping social behaviour.

Tensions in the production of criminological knowledge about cybercrimes

Because cybercrimes are a relatively new phenomenon, little is known about them. Often they have a very short time frame and within this, new types of cybercrime behaviour can quickly escalate. Cybercrime rapidly evolves alongside new technological developments. Online ID theft has evolved from 'phishing', using fake bank emails to deceive individuals into giving away their private financial details, into 'smishing', where mobile phone SMS text messages replace the emails. It has recently morphed into 'vishing', which uses phone messages sent by VOIP (Voice Over Internet Protocol technology). Such rapid escalation and evolution exacerbate a range of other tensions that already exist in the ways that knowledge about cybercrimes are produced and impede understanding of them (identified in Wall 2007: 17–28). These tensions (outlined below) have to be recognised by researchers so that they do not skew their data collection and subsequent analysis.

The existence of multiple discourses about cybercrime. Cybercrime means different things to different groups of people and so it is viewed differently by each in terms of their respective functions. A typical confusion in contemporary debates about cybercrime is between those with specific interests in the respective impacts of cybercrime on the individual, organisation and nation state. This confusion is compounded by a range of legal–political, technological, social and economic discourses that have led to some very different epistemological constructions of cybercrime in the literature.

The disintermediation of news sources. The networking of information and the proliferation of different and alternative news sources has disintermediated the reporting of news. News sources today are arguably not subjected to the same level of editorial control as would have been the case prior to the internet. Not only has the editorial role arguably lost the control it once exercised over the news process, but there has also been 'a major restructuring of the relationship between public and media' (Sambrook 2006) with the effect that public discourse itself has become disintermediated because the public can now directly access politicians and the political process, and vice versa.

The disintermediation of statistical information. Just as news sources have become disintermediated, then so have the ways that statistics about cybercrime are collected. Without commonly applied standards, there are arguably fewer checks on information quality, thus raising the possibility for misinformation to be circulated. Not only are there disagreements about what constitutes cybercrime and therefore what is included in statistical compilations, but there are also no recognised centralised data collection points.

The primary source of statistical information about cybercrimes tends to be the many annual threat reports produced by the cybercrime security industry. It has often been argued that the cybercrime security industry has an economic interest in perpetuating the illusion of high levels of cybercrime and some scaremongering clearly did occur in the industry's early days. But today, it is arguable that the industry now has more to gain by producing reliable data and considered findings rather than sensationalising the threats. More important is the fact that these statistics are regularly produced with transparent methodologies and they are available to all, and in the absence of other data they are all we have to use. Therefore, if we understand how the data is collected, what it represents and what its limitations are, then we can use the threat reports within that specific context. Threat reports are just that, reports of threats, and do not represent personal or corporate reports of victimisations. They thus represent infringements of scientific rules (not the law) that have been reported automatically by the firms' proprietary brand of security software and recorded on a database. Sometimes threat reports are supplemented by other forms of data-mining research. This data has great limitations in that it will never indicate the true level to which individuals regard themselves as victims of cybercrime. What it does do effectively, however, is provide a valuable indication of the range of different types of potential ways that individuals and organisations can fall victim. Furthermore, this data can also very usefully indicate changes in trends over time, space and place.

Over-reporting the threat of cybercrime. A recurring problem with threat reports is that in seeking the story, journalists often confuse 'threats' with impacts, and in so doing significantly change the meaning of the reports (Wall 2008: 53). Consequently, the reporting of industry-generated statistics to indicate actual levels of victimisation is greatly misleading and has in the past led to an over-reporting of the problem and an exaggeration of the levels of actual risk. Once the methodologies of threat statistics are understood then, they may be of some use when describing, for example, levels of potential online risk, or data trends over time.

Under-reporting victimisation. In contrast to the tendency for media to over-report levels of cybercrime is the simultaneous tendency of victims to under-report cases. Some of the automatically reported threats will, of course, eventually result in actual victimisations, for example, if personal information stolen by Trojans is subsequently used to defraud the owner of the data. Yet there also exist a number of distinct reasons why these crimes are under-reported. A fraud, for example, may be reported straight to the bank rather than the police and may not ever appear as an internet-related statistic (assuming such a collection category existed). Even when there is a clear internet link, individuals may be embarrassed to report their victimisation, or their loss may be small. Otherwise, the dangers posed may not be immediately evident, or not regarded as serious by the victim, or the loss may genuinely not be serious. Alternatively, it may be the case, as with credit card frauds, that police refer reportees back to their banks, which are viewed as the real victims. Where the victims are corporate entities, such as banks, reporting losses may expose a commercial weakness and threaten their business model, which raises clear conflicts between the private vs. public justice interest with regard to cybercrimes (Wall 2008: 53–54).

For many victims, the consequences of being victimised are not immediately apparent, for example, computer integrity cybercrimes, such as hacking or identity theft, are often precursors for more serious offending. The information gathered may later be used against the owner, or crackers may use remote administration Trojans to control the computers of others. Similarly, computer-related cybercrimes, such as internet scams, may seem individually minor in impact to each victim, but serious by nature of their sheer volume. Finally, computer content crime may seem less significant because it is informational, but it may nevertheless be extremely personal or politically offensive, or could even subsequently contribute to the incitement of violence or prejudicial actions.

Victimisation surveys provide much more reliable methods of measuring levels of victimisation than do statistics representing reported or recorded crimes, and such victimisation surveys do exist. The findings between different types of victim survey can, however, tend to show some marked contrasts because they canvass different victim groups. Surveys of business victims, for example, such as the BIS (formerly BERR, DTI) *Information Security Breaches Survey*, a bi-annual survey in the UK (BERR 2008), and the annual CSI (CSI 2008) survey in the USA, plus other occasional surveys such as the US Bureau of Justice 2005 survey (Rantala 2008), report high rates of business victimisation. Because of the confidential way in which the data is collected, these surveys identify types of victimisation that do not normally tend to get reported to the police because of the commercial sensitivity of their losses and the corporate victim's preference to deal with the matter themselves. In contrast, the few national surveys of personal or individual victimisation that have carried cybercrime questions, including the British Crime Survey (Allen et al. 2005; Wilson et al. 2006), found comparatively low levels of overall victimisation that individuals consider serious enough to warrant action, which is consistent with the observations noted earlier. Although dropped from the survey a few years back, a range of revised cybercrime-related questions have been reinstated in forthcoming British Crime Surveys. Generally speaking, it is very important to delineate between personal, business/organisational and national victimisation when researching cybercrimes because of the different personal meanings of victimisation and reporting behaviours in each case.

Low levels of offender profiles. Because so few cybercrimes are actually reported, relatively little is therefore known about the profiles of offenders, especially those who commit the small-impact, bulk-impact victimisations. Although these profiles are gradually being compiled as more offenders are identified and apprehended each year and a body of knowledge accrues.

Jurisdictional disparities in terms of (a) definitions of cybercrime and (b) levels of cooperation between police. Disparities exist in legislation across jurisdictions which can make legal definitions of cybercrime differ and can also frustrate law enforcement efforts, despite attempts by the likes of the Council of Europe Cybercrime Convention to harmonise laws. Pan-jurisdictional idiosyncrasies in legal process can also interfere with levels of inter-jurisdictional police cooperation.

The above-mentioned tensions in the production of knowledge about cybercrime outline some of the obstacles that researchers have to overcome in this particular field of study. The bottom line is that researchers cannot expect a common understanding of different types of cybercrime and may therefore have to include additional research techniques to enable them to understand how respondent perspectives have been constructed.

NEW METHODOLOGICAL AND ETHICAL ISSUES

The three ways, highlighted in previous sections, that research into crime and justice has been transformed – in the ways that we collect data, conduct research and also the behaviours being researched – are, on the one hand, a criminological researcher's dream because they provide new research tools with handy access to new data. Plus they also generate interesting new research topics. On the other hand, they can be a research nightmare because the new social (and criminal) relationships emerging as a focus of research interest generate some important methodological and ethical challenges. Some of these challenges will be familiar because they simply involve reconciling the longstanding research missions to produce generalisable and replicable data (positivist tradition) or constructed accounts of contextualised naturalistic experiences (interpretivist tradition) with the extension to the researcher's capabilities that new technologies facilitate. Others are entirely new and cause hitherto unforeseen problems.

A key methodological challenge in relation to the positivist tradition is the statistical integrity of the large amounts of asymmetrical data (e.g. one researcher to many – a potentially infinite number – networked respondents) about online activities that are now potentially available to researchers. Traditionally symmetrical (e.g. one researcher to one or two respondents) research imposed physical restrictions on data collection because one researcher could only interact with one respondent at a time. In contrast, digital online research survey software now enables researchers to conduct asymmetrical research – they can interact with many respondents at one moment in time. However, data sets created in this way can be so large that one minor error in definition can be magnified many fold to distort a problem out of proportion. While these large data sets represent the behaviour of large numbers of individuals, they can be statistically skewed, so researchers have to take care to avoid bias, for example, by statistically weighting the data (see earlier note on sampling online populations). The meaning of the data also has to be accurate in case the wrong conclusions are drawn. For example, because of the short time frame involved between collection and processing, researchers have to be vigilant in order to correct any sampling errors. This is especially the case as contemporary research environments are more volatile than they once were and research needs have to be satisfied more quickly. In such a fast-moving world, methodologies of the present are now required which enable researchers to know what is happening almost when it happens.

A further methodological challenge is to develop new, or adapt existing, techniques for processing and analysing the large volumes of diverse digital data that are now available to us. In addition to the data generated from online surveys (see *Survey Monkey* earlier), there is also the massive volume of large digital data sets of transaction data that are currently owned by ISPs (internet service providers) and other network providers that can be 'data-mined'. These large sets of automatically generated network data can be analysed in real time or after the event to reveal 'social' relationships. New methodologies and rules of method need to be developed to interrogate these databases in order to observe meaningful relationships. In addition to the large sets of internet-based relationships is the sheer volume of processed information on the internet. New rules and methods are also required to employ appropriate combinations of keywords in order to utilise the maximum potential of powerful internet search engines such as *Google, Bing,*

Yahoo and the many others, so that researchers can find relevant information and data posted on the internet.

A knock-on effect of all the new research possibilities outlined earlier and the methodological challenges outlined above are a range of new ethical issues. There is an increasing need today to respond to instant informational needs and a much shorter research time frame, whereas, traditionally, there was a longer time delay between the collection and processing of primary and secondary data. When combined with the large amounts of personal data, this gives rise to a number of ethical concerns.

The first concern is to ensure that the *privacy of respondents and research subjects is preserved*. While the surveillant qualities of digital technologies can generate considerable amounts of data, they can also unwittingly erode the privacy of the target population. Online discussion forums can offer online researchers predefined research populations and rich 'ready made' data sets. Such forums are considered by the novice online researcher as a goldmine of data that can efficiently reduce the data collection to a simple process of 'harvesting' the relevant textual extracts. However, such practices contravene long-established ethical and moral principles of social research. While it remains an established understanding that most online interactions are intended for public consumption, the emerging recognition that these spaces are being used for private discourse calls into question the usability and accessibility of this medium for research purposes. Furthermore, researchers also have to be keenly aware of currently data protection laws and take care not to break them if, for example, data located in one jurisdiction is moved to another with different data protection laws.

The second concern is to ensure that *mission creep is minimised*. Mission creep occurs when research objectives, intentionally or unintentionally, shift away from the researcher's original focus. In such data-rich environments, researchers have to resist the temptation to explore what they *could* do with the technology rather than what they *should* be doing with it in order to answer the original research questions.

The third concern is to prevent the *digital Hawthorn effect* from occurring by avoiding the researchers shaping the research environment. Digital technologies can enable researchers to quickly disseminate research findings, but in so doing may unwittingly (or in some cases intentionally) change the research environment by influencing respondents and relationships.

The fourth concern is to retain *sensitivity to cultural diversity online*. Ethical considerations in online research must take account of both the codes of conduct relating to behaviour in computer-mediated communities and also the codes of conduct relating to the practice of social research. Comprehensive reviews of the ongoing development of ethical guidelines for online research are available elsewhere (see, for example, Association of Internet Researchers 2002; Johns et al. 2004). The acceptable behaviour of internet users is governed in practice by a combination of internet service providers' acceptable use policies (AUPs), ethical codes of conduct and various data protection laws. Acceptable use policies are contractual agreements between users and service providers that define how the user can use the network. Informal codes of conduct, developed naturally by online communities, outline standard practices for the various services available over the internet (email, newsgroups, Internet Relay Chat, etc.) and define what is, and what is not acceptable behaviour. These codes are known as netiquette and should be required reading for anyone new to the internet.

While the methodological and ethical challenges are considerable, they are not insurmountable and their negative effects can be countered by appropriate tactics during the research planning phase. It is, however, important for researchers to leave some room for contingencies during the research process because rapid changes in the capacities of digital technologies can often create new opportunities for enhancing the research mission during the progress of the research.

SUMMARY

Never before has research into criminal justice been simultaneously so simple and yet so complicated. Today we can press a few keys on our networked computers and perform by ourselves what not so long ago might have required a large team of researchers. Internet and related networked digital technologies have transformed both the research process and the research environment. They are force multipliers of grand proportions and enable researchers to command a whole research process in ways never previously imagined. They create new globalised and networked information flows that can assist primary, secondary and tertiary data collection. They also create entirely new criminal environments and transform criminal behaviour. In so doing, they generate a range of new methodological and ethical issues or challenges. Yet, despite these changes, the basic principles of such research remain more or less unchanged. Internet research still performs the same function as social scientific research always has, that is to produce reliable knowledge from research findings that are, in the positivist tradition, generalisable and replicable or, in the interpretivist tradition, constructions of contextualised, naturalistic experience and meaning.

■ Study Questions/Activities for Students ■■■■■■■■■■

1 Is conducting research via the internet a viable way of undertaking quality criminological research or is it simply a gimmick for lazy people?

2 How is primary data (both qualitative and quantitative) collected online any different from data collected offline (consider authenticity, quality and analysis issues)?

3 Is it possible to conduct online research ethically (consider issues such as informed consent and methods such as online participant observation)?

4 Think about a small research project that you would like to do and answer the following questions:

(Continued)

- What are the main keywords that you could explore to access information? (NB: watch out for differences in US and UK spellings – this could affect your information yield)
- What quantitative and qualitative data about your topic can be found online?
- Where is this data likely to be found?
- Who are the main authors or reference points on your topic?
- How could you use online research tools to generate primary qualitative and quantitative data for your research?

5 **Online research into offline criminological environments.** You would like to conduct some research into the specific targeting of old people by burglars to see if this form of offending is any different from other types of house burglary. Your resources are limited, but you have an internet connection. How far can you use the internet to conduct this research?

Consider the following questions:

- What are the main keyword(s) used when this form of crime is discussed and which could help you find information?
- What quantitative and qualitative data is available online?
- Who is likely to have these data?
- Who are the main authors/experts in the field whose work is a reference point and from where you could begin your own research?
- How could you use online research tools to create primary qualitative and quantitative data to inform your research?

6 **Online research into online criminological environments**. You would like to conduct some research into the vandalisation of online environments (including all types of social networking site) to explore how online communities are victimised, the impact of that victimisation, and how they respond to it. You have limited resources, but you do have an internet connection.

Consider the following questions:

- What are the main keyword(s) used when this form of crime or harmful behaviour is discussed and which could help you find information about available literature and events or occurrences that you could follow up?
- What quantitative and qualitative data is available online?
- Who is likely to have these data?
- Who are the main authors/experts in the field whose work is a reference point and from where you could begin your own research?
- How could you use online research tools to create primary qualitative and quantitative data to inform your research?

RESOURCES

Association of Internet Researchers (AoIR) (2002) *Ethical Decision Making and Internet Research: Recommendations from the AoIR Ethics Working Committee*, www.aoir.org/reports/ethics.pdf

Gatson, S.N. and Zweerink, A. (2004) 'Ethnography online: "natives" practicing and inscribing community', *Qualitative Research*, 4(2): 179–200

Jones, J. (ed.) (1999) *Doing Internet Research*, London: Sage

Stewart, K. and Williams, M. (2007) 'Researching online populations: the use of online focus groups for social research', *Qualitative Research*, 5(4): 395–416

Williams, M. (2006) 'Avatar watching: participant observation in graphical online environments', *Qualitative Research*, 7(1): 5–24

REFERENCES

Allen, J., Forrest, S., Levi, M., Roy, H. and Sutton, M. (2005) 'Fraud and technology crimes: findings from the 2002/03 British Crime Survey and 2003 Offending, Crime and Justice Survey', *Home Office Online Report 34/05*, www.homeoffice.gov.uk/rds/pdfs05/rdsolr 3405.pdf [accessed 17/09/10]

Association of Internet Researchers (AoIR) (2002) *Ethical Decision Making and Internet Research: Recommendations from the AoIR Ethics Working Committee*, www.aoir.org/ reports/ethics.pdf [accessed 17/19/10]

Baym, N. (1995a) 'The emergence of community in computer-mediated communication', in S. Jones (ed.), *CyberSociety*, Newbury Park, CA: Sage. pp 138–163

Baym, N. (1995b) 'The performance of humor in computer-mediated communication', *Journal of Computer-Mediated Communication*, 1(2), www.ascusc.org/jcmc/vol1/issue2/baym. html [accessed 03/04/98]

BERR (2008) *Information Security Breaches Survey 2008*, Department of Business, Enterprise and Regulatory Reform (BERR), conducted by PricewaterhouseCoopers, www.pwc.co.uk/ eng/publications/berr_information_security_breaches_survey_2008.html [accessed 17/04/10]

Bloor, M., Frankland, J., Thomas, M. and Robson, K. (2001) *Focus Groups in Social Research*, London: Sage

CSI (2008) *Computer Crime and Security Survey 2008*, San Francisco: Computer Security Institute

Correll, S. (1995) 'The ethnography of an electronic bar: the Lesbian Café', *The Journal of Contemporary Ethnography*, 24(3): 485–496

Denscombe, M. (2003) *The Good Research Guide* (2nd edition), Milton Keynes: Open University Press

Fielding, N. and Macintyre, M. (2006) 'Access grid nodes in field research', *Sociological Research Online*, 11(2)

Gatson, S.N. and Zweerink, A. (2004) 'Ethnography online: "natives" practicing and inscribing community', *Qualitative Research*, 4(2): 179–200

Hine, C. (2000) *Virtual Ethnography*, London: Sage

Johns, M.D, Chen, S.L. and Hall, G.J. (eds) (2004) *Online Social Research*, New York: Peter Lang

Lash, S. (2001) 'Technological forms of life', *Theory, Culture and Society*, 18(1): 105–120

Leander, K.M. and Mckim, K.K. (2003) 'Tracing the everyday "sitings" of adolescents on the internet: a strategic adaptation of ethnography across online and offline spaces', *Education, Communication & Information*, 3(2): 211–240

Mann, C. and Stewart, F. (2000) *Internet Communications and Qualitative Research*, London: Sage

Markham, A. (1998) *Life Online: Researching Real Experience in Virtual Space*, Newbury Park, CA: Sage

Murray, P. (1997) 'Using virtual focus groups in qualitative health research', *Qualitative Health Research*, 7(4): 542–549

Rantala, R. (2008) *Cybercrime against Businesses: 2005 Findings from the National Computer Security Survey*, Washington, DC: Bureau of Justice Statistics

Rheingold, H. (1993) *The Virtual Community: Homesteading on the Electronic Frontier*, New York: Harper Collins

Robson, K. (1999) 'Employment experiences of ulcerative colitis and Crohn's disease sufferers', Unpublished PhD thesis, University of Wales, Cardiff

Sambrook, R. (2006) 'How the net is transforming news', *BBC News Online*, 20 January, news. bbc.co.uk/1/hi/technology/4630890.stm

Stewart, K. and Williams, M. (2007) 'Researching online populations: the use of online focus groups for social research', *Qualitative Research*, 5(4): 395–416

Stewart, F., Eckermann, E. and Zhou, K. (1998) 'Using the internet in qualitative public heath research: a comparison of Chinese and Australian young women's perceptions of tobacco use', *Internet Journal of Health Promotion*, www.monash.edu.au/heath/IJHP/1998/12

Wall, D.S. (2007) *Cybercrime: The Transformation of Crime in the Information Age*, Cambridge: Polity Press

Wall, D.S. (2008) 'Cybercrime, media and insecurity: the shaping of public perceptions of cybercrime', *International Review of Law, Computers and Technology*, 22(1–2): 45–63

Wall, D.S. and Williams, M. (2007) 'Policing diversity in the digital age: maintaining order in virtual communities', *Criminology and Criminal Justice*, 7(4): 391–415

Williams, M. (2006a) *Virtually Criminal: Crime, Deviance and Regulation Online*, London: Routledge

Williams, M. (2006b) 'Avatar watching: participant observation in graphical online environments', *Qualitative Research*, 7(1): 5–24

Wilson, D., Patterson, A., Powell, G. and Hembury, R. (2006) 'Fraud and technology crimes: findings from the 2003/04 British Crime Survey, the 2004 Offending, Crime and Justice Survey and administrative sources', *Home Office Online Report 09/06*, www.homeoffice. gov.uk/rds/pdfs06/rdsolr0906.pdf

Witmer, D.F., Colman, R.W. and Katzman, S.L. (1999) 'From paper-and-pencil to screen-and-keyboard', in S. Jones (ed.), *Doing Internet Research*, London: Sage. pp. 145–162.

PART THREE

REFLECTING ON CRIMINOLOGICAL RESEARCH

PAMELA DAVIES AND PETER FRANCIS

Part Contents

THE IMPORTANCE OF REFLEXIVITY

Reflection on the decisions which have been taken in research and on the problems which have been encountered is an essential element of doing research. In fact, it is often the case that a reflexive account is published as part of a research report or a book. Typically, such an account covers all phases and aspects of the research process. For example, it will outline and discuss how a research problem came to take the shape that it did, how and why certain cases were selected for study and not others, the difficulties faced in data collection and the various influences on the formulation of conclusions and their publication. Reflexive accounts should not be solely descriptive, but should also be analytical and evaluative. Reflexivity is not a self-indulgent exercise akin to showing photographs to others to illustrate the 'highs' and 'lows' of a recent holiday. Rather, it is a vital part of demonstrating the factors which have contributed to the social production of knowledge.

Research findings and conclusions are not 'things' that are lying around waiting to be picked up by an investigator; they are the outcome of research decisions that are taken at different stages and of the factors that influence these, including factors external to and out of the control of the investigator. **Research design** is an exercise in compromise, whereby the investigator seeks to trade off the strengths and weaknesses of different methods. But it is not possible to escape the reality that even the best laid plans and designs have to be actualized in social, institutional and political contexts which can have a profound effect on the outcome of research. Giving recognition to this is important on two counts: first, it allows some assessment to be made of the likely validity of conclusions; second, it encourages us to reflect critically on what comes to pass as 'knowledge', how and why. This latter aspect is one hallmark of critical social research. The contribution of reflexivity to assessment of validity and also to critical social research will be discussed later.

Three assumptions underpin the concern of this part with experiencing criminological research: research as a social activity; research and politics; and research and ethics.

RESEARCH AS A SOCIAL ACTIVITY

The first is that research is a social activity. Criminology is not like those physical sciences in which researchers study and engage inanimate objects. In the main, social researchers are concerned with individuals – although not always at first hand – and these are people with feelings, opinions, motives, likes and dislikes. What is more, typically, social research is a form of interaction. Criminologists should easily recognize this because one influential theoretical approach within the discipline – interactionism – emphasizes that what comes to be recognized as 'criminal' can be the outcome of interactions in the processes of the criminal justice system. Therefore it should come as no surprise that what comes to pass as 'knowledge' can be the outcome of interactions in the research process.

RESEARCH AND POLITICS

The second assumption is that criminological research is not just a social activity; it is also a political activity, as Gordon Hughes in Chapter 14 points out. It involves some form of relationship between the subjects of research and the investigators, but there are also others who have an interest. The range of stakeholders typically includes sponsors of research, gatekeepers who control access to sources of data and the various audiences of research findings. These audiences include the media, policy-makers, professionals working in the criminal justice system, politicians and academics. Gatekeepers may have a formal role and legal powers to restrict access (for example, a prison governor) or they may be able to deny access by informal means (for example, by continually cancelling appointments). Sponsors of research include government departments, especially the Home Office, institutions of criminal justice, such as the police or the legal profession, and pressure groups such as the Howard League or Prison Reform Trust. Each of these stakeholders has interests to promote and interests to protect. Also, each has differential levels of power with which to promote and protect such interests. The exercise of such power is ingrained in the research process from the formulation of problems through to the publication of results.

Research and politics connect in differing ways. For example, politics can have an impact on the course that research takes and also on its outcome. The kind of research which is funded and the ways in which research problems and questions are framed are very much influenced by sponsors. Often they are interested in policy relevance (in their terms) and insist on a formal customer–contractor relationship, in which 'deliverables' are clearly specified. How research activity takes place is also dependent on the willingness of subjects to take part and on whether gate-keepers give access to subjects – or other data sources – in the first place.

A second way in which politics and research connect is in the differing ways in which the activity of research and its outputs contribute to politics. One important way in which this occurs in criminology is in the conduct of **policy-related research**. Such research can take a variety of forms but one which has contributed substantially to the formulation and implementation of criminal justice policy is **evaluation** research. Sometimes this kind of work is known as administrative criminology because of its contribution to the administration and management of the criminal justice system. However, criminologists who represent a critical approach see such work not solely as contributing to policy, but, more importantly, as justifying policy. In this sense they look upon policy-related research as playing a political role in mechanisms of social control and not as benign, **value-free** contributions to administration and management. In Chapter 15, Barbara Hudson outlines some of the major strands within critical social science. These include the analysis of ideologies which underpin social structures (such as law and order ideologies) and the challenging of these ideologies with the aim of replacing them. In this way, criminology becomes a political activity.

RESEARCH AND ETHICS

The final assumption is that research is not just a social and political activity, but also an ethical activity, as Azrini Wahidin and Linda Moore in Chapter 13 point out. In fact, it is *because* it is a social and political activity that it is an ethical activity. Ethics is about the standards to be adopted towards others in carrying out research. Sometimes these standards are mandatory to the practice of research, for example in the conduct of certain kinds of medical research, whereas in other contexts and disciplines they are merely guidelines. Sometimes they are formally expressed in professional codes of conduct, such as in the ethical code of the British Society of Criminology, the British Sociological Association and the British Psychological Society, whereas in other disciplines there is a much less formal body of custom and practice.

One ethical principle which is often expressed in social research is that of informed consent. This can be rather elastic but basically it refers to the principle that the subjects of research should be informed of their participation in research, which may be taken to include giving information about possible consequences of participation. Further, it includes the belief that subjects should give their consent to participation, and its possible consequences, prior to their inclusion. Another principle which is sometimes put forward is that no person should be harmed by research: for example, that the introduction of 'experimental treatment' in some styles of research should not cause physical or psychological damage to subjects or, perhaps, disadvantage some individuals in comparison with others.

Matters of ethics interact with the pursuit of validity and also with the political dimensions of research. If the principle of informed consent is applied in full and in such a way that subjects are aware of all aspects of research, including its purpose, it is highly likely that they will behave or react in ways in which they would not normally do. Such reactivity on the part of subjects is a threat to the validity of findings. Further, the challenging of the ideological positions of certain groups in society – perhaps with a view to replacing them with others – is a central aim of some forms of research, especially critical research. However, this inevitably involves doing harm to the interests of such groups. In this way, the fundamental aims of critical research can come face to face with the ethical principle that research should not harm or damage individuals or groups of individuals.

THE CASE FOR REFLEXIVITY

It has been emphasized that reflexivity on the part of a researcher is a vital part of criminological research. This is because criminological research is a social, political and ethical activity. There are several roles that reflexivity can play in research, two of which can be noted here. The first concerns the assessment of validity. Validity is the extent to which conclusions drawn from a study are plausible and credible and the extent to which they can be generalized to other contexts and to other people. Validity is always relative, being dependent on the decisions which have had to be taken in the planning and conduct of research. Making such decisions explicit and, more importantly, assessing the probable effect on validity is the main purpose of a reflexive account (which is sometimes published alongside conclusions).

Second, reflection can be a form of research in its own right. This is especially the case in the critical social scientific tradition, in which reflecting upon, analyzing and challenging dominant ideological positions in society is central. For this reason, Chapter 15, in which Barbara Hudson engages in critical reflection on types of penal policy, could easily have been placed in Part II of this volume, which is about *doing* research.

CONCLUSION

It has been stressed throughout this book that the conduct of research can be expressed in terms of decision-making. Such decision-making inevitably involves trade-offs, for example trading off the weaknesses of one course of action against the strengths of another. Some decisions have to be taken about the minutiae of research, say in deciding whether to have a sample of 100 or of 120. Such technical issues matter, but so do the fundamental principles of criminological inquiry. These include validity (the pursuit of credible and plausible knowledge), politics (whose side am I on, if any?), and ethics (what standards should I adopt and in relation to what?). Unfortunately, as noted earlier, the pursuit of one principle may inhibit the pursuit of another. So the most fundamental decision an investigator must take is how to position her/himself in relation to the validity, the politics and the ethics of research and the trade-offs which may have to be made between these.

■ Study Questions/Activities for Students

1 As you read the following chapters, write down the differing ways in which politics intrudes into social research.

2 Reflect upon the chapters in this section and describe what are the main ethical issues facing criminological research.

3 What are the ways in which people can be harmed by criminological research? Are there some categories of people (e.g. corrupt police officers) who should not be protected against the harmful effects of criminological research?

4 What distinguishes critical research from policy-related research, if anything?

5 Write down the issues which you think should be addressed in a reflexive account.

THIRTEEN
ETHICS AND CRIMINOLOGICAL RESEARCH

AZRINI WAHIDIN AND LINDA MOORE

Chapter Contents

KEY POINTS

This chapter:

- Highlights the importance of an ethical approach to research in prisons
- Explains that the research should avoid harm and minimise risks to participants
- Acknowledges the importance of informed consent and confidentiality
- Outlines a range of guidelines that are available

INTRODUCTION

Our aim in this chapter is to demonstrate how ethical frameworks have been applied to the prison using overt methods. We aim to demonstrate the practical value of thinking seriously and systematically about the purpose of applying an ethical framework in the doing of criminological research. We will discuss how and why current regulatory regimes emerged and how the outcome of these discussions leads to an understanding about those practices that have contributed to the adversarial relationships between researchers and regulators. In this chapter, we outline why social scientists do, and should, take ethics seriously.

Both writers in their work aim to construct a picture of prison life in which the participants interviewed can recognise their own voices, subjectivities and priorities – that is, their own acts of communication with the outside world. The construction of such a picture is inevitably, and rightly, a dialogic transition, the product of which owes much to, but is also transformative of, the categories and modes of thought or feeling contributed by each party. In this chapter, Azrini Wahidin's contribution owes much to the two schools of thought broadly classifiable as **feminist** and **Foucauldian**, while Linda Moore's contribution derives from a **critical criminological perspective**, tracing its roots back to the ideas of Karl Marx, and also globalisation.

ETHICS AND PRISON RESEARCH

Ethics is commonly defined as the 'practical science of the morality of human acts' (Oxford English Dictionary, 2009). It is a 'science' because it is a collection of organised, systematised, and coherent ideas that explain or rationalise the morality of human acts. It is a 'practical' science because it is a body of knowledge that pertains to how we conduct ourselves through our *actions*. It is this definition that leads to questions about how research can be conducted following ethical guidelines set down by governing bodies. Ethics, in the words of Beauchamp and Childress (1994: 4), is 'a generic term for various ways of understanding and examining moral life'. It is concerned, in essence, with perspectives on right and proper conduct. The ethical perspective has been linked to a methodological approach. Thus, the central ethical criteria were (a) whether the outcome of the research would be broadly consistent with the political aim of redressing the marginalisation of women and other subordinate social groups, and (b) whether the methods employed are consistent with such an aim, i.e. able to undermine the knower/known relation of traditional epistemology and engage in truly collaborative knowledge production.

In an ideal world these two criteria would be inseparable. However, the real-life setting of the prison, and the practical necessity of abiding by the organisational rules of the prison mean that a fully collaborative procedure was not possible. The ethical issue thus becomes one of whether the potential benefit to the participants outweighs the limitation, once everything possible has been done to ensure the participants' welfare.

There are three broad positions discernable from the literature on *ethics*: the *legalistic*, the *antinomian* and the *situational*. The *legalists*, at one extreme, argue for the adherence to a professional code of conduct (British Society of Criminology, www.britsoccrim.org/ethical.htm; British Sociological Association, www.britsoc. co.uk) as a solution to the problem of ethical **decision-making**. Primacy is given to the doctrine of informed consent, respect for privacy, ensuring anonymity and confidentiality, and open and non-deceitful forms of research, which will be discussed in this chapter.

At one end of the spectrum, the *antinomians* or *conflict* methodologists, as Punch has termed them (1986), reject all such strictures. The pursuit of all knowledge, they argue, is an end in itself and must not be hampered by ethical codes and restrictions, which, for the main part, had been erected by the powerful to protect themselves rather than the weak. Between these polarised positions there are an increasing number of accounts from practising fieldworkers which stress the complexity of ethical decisions faced by the researcher (Fielding, 1982; Holdaway, 1983; see Punch, 1986). Collectively, these researchers have opted for a *situational* view of ethics. Following Fletcher (1966: 17), they argue that:

> the situationalist enters into every decision-making situation fully armed with the ethical maxims of his/her community and its heritage and treats them with respect as illuminators of his problem. Just the same as he is prepared in any situation to compromise them or set them aside in the situation....

Thus when conducting research, the researcher has to constantly address the following ethical considerations:

1 Does it undermine the principle of informed consent?
2 Does it cause direct harm to the research subjects?
3 Does it break the promise of anonymity?
4 Does it involve manipulating the data?
5 Does it potentially spoil the field for other researchers?

It is important and beneficial that from the outset, researchers interrogate and assess what may arise in the unfolding of the research process that may affect persons involved (Homan, 1991; Patai, 1991; Renzetti and Lee, 1993; Sieber, 1982, 1992). This process alerted and sensitised Wahidin in her research on women in prison to issues that perhaps she would not normally have considered. It was these questions that determined the approaches she used:

1 How would she ensure that the research remained true to where it came from?
2 How would she explain the lives of others without violating their reality?
3 How would she ensure that during and after the research process she was minimising the harm that may occur, due to the issues raised, without creating a situation of dependency?

It was vital from the outset that she informed the participants about the nature of the research, the process, the potential value of the research and its dissemination, thereby avoiding deception and preventing the exploitation of the participants. After discussing the nature of the research, the participants were then able to sign an 'informed consent' form, which stipulated that they could withdraw at any time. She felt that without full informed consent, the **validity** of the information collected would always be suspect. Of course, the question is how one can ensure that this goal is achieved? It has been argued that this quest results from 'the bewildered and disorientated self [who] finds itself alone in the face of moral dilemmas without good (let alone obvious) choices, unresolved moral conflicts and the excruciating difficulty of being moral' (Bauman, 1992: 249). We would argue that ethical standards guided and informed by a feminist orientation were imperative for this study. If ethical guidelines were abandoned altogether, then obligations to the research participants, the prison estate and the research community would inevitably be exploited.

A HISTORY OF ETHICAL CONCERNS IN PRISON RESEARCH

In order to understand how current guidelines were arrived at, and to fully comprehend why ethics principles are necessary in criminological research, it is important to develop knowledge of the historical and social context of research on, and involving, prisoners.

The eighteenth-century prison reformer John Howard travelled extensively throughout Europe reporting on prison conditions and campaigning tirelessly for a prison system based on the ideals of reform and respect for human dignity. The research carried out by reformers such as *John Howard, Elizabeth Fry* and *Sir Walton Crofton* can be viewed as predecessor of both modern prisons inspectorates and of the monitoring work carried out by non-governmental campaigning groups.

The history of prison research has not always been so altruistic and has involved grave breaches of the rights of those researched: the 'human subjects'. Researchers adopting a **positivist perspective** in the nineteenth century viewed prisoners as fruitful material for scientific study. Thus, it was while carrying out an autopsy on the well-known brigand Giuseppe Villella that the Italian physician, Cesare Lombroso, came to his 'revelation' of criminality as an atavistic throwback to early humanity. As director of several 'insane asylums', Lombroso had a ready source of human subjects among his mentally disabled and ill patients. Photographs of convicted criminals, autopsies of executed individuals and studies of the tattoos and body shape of prisoners in Turin penitentiary all provided primary material for Lombroso's researches (Gibson, 2006). Pieces of the tattooed skin of prisoners remain on display in the Turin museum dedicated to Lombroso (Becker and Wetzell, 2006).

The use by criminologists of the bodies of incarcerated individuals as objects for study continued into the twentieth century. Charles Goring's (1913) study of the physiology of English prisoners and William Sheldon's (1949) research on the criminal body-type, based on photographs of institutionalised young male 'delinquents', represented attempts to determine the physical characteristics of criminality through studies of the 'criminal body'. In neither Lombroso's nor Sheldon's research was consent sought or given by those studied, and in Sheldon's case complaints of an ethical nature were later raised by students who had been the unwitting subjects of his invasive research (Vertinsky, 2007). Early positivist research on prisoners was entangled with issues of gender, 'race' and class. The knowledge produced by social scientists was used to justify the unequal organisation of society, scientific findings being used in some contexts to legitimise racist and **eugenicist** policies. Nazi experiments on detainees in prisoner of war and concentration camps provided a stark reminder of the direction science can be taken in when 'a deep commitment to ethics seems to be lacking' (Arboleda-Flórez, 1991: 3). Experiments included conducting unnecessary surgery, causing severe pain through exposure to heat and cold and deliberately exposing people to infection. Children were among those experimented on in damaging and cruel ways.

Following the end of the Second World War, a series of international human rights instruments were developed aimed at ensuring that research with human subjects was conduced ethically and protecting the rights of prisoners involved in medical and other research. At Nuremburg, physicians who had conducted experiments without consent on concentration camp detainees were prosecuted and the Nuremburg Code (1947) established ten principles to be adhered to by researchers conducting experiments on human subjects. Although specifically addressing medical experimentation, the Code's principles are also of relevance to social science research. It requires that voluntary and informed consent be gained from research participants, that the benefits to humanity of the study outweigh any potential risks to participants, and that unnecessary pain and suffering be avoided. The Universal Declaration of Human Rights (1948) confirmed in international law the principle of informed consent. The Declaration of Helsinki in 1964 established further requirements for ethical research with human subjects and has been subject to subsequent amendment. Confirming the key principles of Nuremburg, the Declaration added to these a requirement for independent review of research protocols and that research be conducted by appropriately qualified individuals.

Despite Nuremburg, medical experimentation with prisoners in the following decades continued to breach ethical and human rights principles, some of the most notable abuses occurring in American prisons. For example, in Holmesburg Prison from the 1950s through to the 1970s, in return for a few dollars, prisoners were used to test products from cosmetics to chemical war agents (Hornblum, 1998).

It is not only the methods of conducting research with prisoners but also the subject matter and purpose of the research which raise ethical questions. Karl Marx wrote that 'Philosophers have only interpreted the world in different ways. The point is, however, to change it' (1845: thesis XI). Critical criminologists have continued to view research not as an abstract occupation but as a contribution to understanding *and* transforming the world. Concerned that social scientists were being used to conduct research on terms defined by the powerful in society, C. Wright Mills advised social researchers not to allow 'public issues as they are officially formulated' or 'troubles as they are privately felt' to determine the problems to be investigated, nor to give up their 'moral and political autonomy' (1959: 226).

The development of *labelling and interactionist perspectives* in criminology in the 1960s, a period characterised by social change and political protest, continued to challenge the nature and subject matter of traditional criminological research, raising ethical issues in the process. Howard Becker's *Outsiders* (1963) redirected the focus from the study of 'the criminal' to the process of criminalisation.

Feminist research has since sought to make women visible in criminology and studies have focused on the processes of criminalisation and women's experiences of the criminal justice system, including imprisonment. Pat Carlen's (1983) study of women in Cornton Vale women's prison in Scotland was the forerunner in this approach in its focus on the gendered punishments and responses to women. Loraine Gelsthorpe (1990) raises three key tenets of feminist research, each with ethical implications. First, feminist scholars are concerned to do research which will contribute to the elimination of women's oppression. Second, **qualitative** methods are preferred as they better allow women's voices to be heard. Third, feminist research seeks to adopt interactive methodologies which reduce the power hierarchy between researcher and interviewee. Feminist researchers have largely rejected the notion of '**value free**' research and favoured acknowledgement of personal perspective. Feminist scholarship includes research carried out *by* and *with* prisoners and ex-prisoners, attempting to further reduce power relations between researcher and researched and to facilitate incarcerated women in speaking for themselves rather than through the medium of an interviewer (see, for example, Neve and Pate, 2005). However, as Laura Piacentini (2007: 154) observes, 'there has been very little "methods" scholarship on how prisoners experience the process of being engaged in research'.

Phil Scraton describes critical social analysis as having an 'oppositional agenda' which 'seeks out, records and champions the "view from below" ensuring that the voices and experiences of those marginalised by institutionalised state practices are heard and represented' (2004: 180). For **critical theorists**, it is only through accessing the experiences of prisoners that a holistic understanding of regimes can be achieved. The ethical dimension of prison research includes its role in encouraging greater transparency, thus preventing or at least reducing human rights abuses: 'the greater the ability of excluded groups to partake in a discursive citizenship, the lesser the risk of institutional abuse occurring or of continuing unabated' (Brown 2008: 229). For critical researchers, the publication of research is not the end of the exercise, but rather research findings provide a tool to campaign for social change. As Bree Carlton (2006: 32) states, the 'challenges and responsibilities faced by critical researchers to confront and make visible the arbitrary and abusive exercise of power are greater than ever'.

The human rights requirement that the benefits of research outweigh potential risk continues to cause dilemmas for researchers. This is particularly important given the well-documented vulnerability of prisoners, both in terms of the fact of their incarceration and also because of the typically high rates of mental illness and experience of trauma, bereavement and abuse. This vulnerability requires that researchers adopt sensitivity in interviews and Gelsthorpe recalls that when interviewing prisoners, 'we frequently abandoned formal **interviews** altogether in the face of someone's distress or concern to express a particular point' (1990: 98).

Arditti (2002), writing about her experience of running a research project at a local jail in the USA, ponders whether the benefits of the research for prisoners' families was outweighed by the high emotional cost of involvement: 'entering the setting, only to depart soon thereafter seems now in retrospect like rubbing salt in the wound'. For Arditti, it is important that researchers develop an emotional response to families and prisoners. However, she concludes that the high level of emotional response tended to be reduced following completion of the study, perhaps a necessary protection for the researcher but potentially lessening the potency of the research in bringing about change.

A further ethical consideration is that researchers all too frequently come under pressure, explicit and implicit, to 'tone down' their findings, or hide problems in return for access granted. James B. Waldam (1998: 239), in his anthropological research with Aboriginal (American) prisoners, concluded that due to prison officials' scepticism about his work, and given their gatekeeping role regarding access, it was necessary to 'balance the perceived needs and goals of prisoners and prison officials' and avoid making too many demands on officials or expressing ideas that may potentially alienate them. However, Waldron chose not to wear a security device, which 'operates as a symbol of distrust', and accepted invitations to enter the prisoners' rooms in breach of security rules as both a 'declaration of trust' in prisoners and 'an acknowledged act of resistance' (1998: 241).

The dominance of ***administrative criminology***, and **policy-related** research and the pull of government funding for researchers and their institutions, has placed serious ethical demands on researchers. Piacentini (2007: 154) comments that 'the principal question prison researchers confront … is whether government-funded research is "strings-attached" research'. Scraton (2007: 237) observes that administrative criminology, with its ties to police and penal institutions, has become a lucrative business for university departments and as funding tends to be denied to critical work, 'pressure is exerted on departments, universities, learned societies and independent research bodies to reconfigure their work' (2007: 11). Issues about commissioning and autonomy raise fundamental ethical questions for researchers, especially where the independence of research is threatened by restrictions on method, the writing up of findings or dissemination of the work.

It is disturbing and more than a little ironic that regulators and social scientists find themselves faced with the above tension to comply with the needs of the funding bodies and that of the research creating a situation of division, suspicion and mistrust. After all, we each start from a point, as this chapter shows, where ethics matter.

The following section examines the role of ethical guidelines and the professionalisation of ethics by professional bodies and addresses how to resolve generic ethical dilemmas. Throughout this section the authors, by drawing on their work in prisons, address some of the ethical issues they faced.

ETHICAL GUIDELINES AND ETHICAL REVIEWING

Our individual research endeavours form part of interconnected local, national and international networks of activity. Poor practices affect not only our personal and professional reputations, but also the veracity and **reliability** of our individual and collective works. In response, universities, funding agencies, employers and professional societies all seek to protect themselves from the unethical actions of an employee, member or representative. However, the pressures on academic and professional bodies' integrity are growing.

Thus the Code of Practice and Ethical Framework of the British Society of Criminology is intended to promote and support good practice and establish benchmarks for ethical research and/or provide a research governance framework to adhere to. Members of professional organisations such as the British Sociological Association and the British Criminology Society are advised to read the Code in the light of any other Professional Ethical Guidelines or Codes of Practice to which they are subject, including those issued by individual academic institutions, relevant governance frameworks and by the Economic Social Research Council. The Economic Social Research Council Research Ethics Framework, which sets out the ESRC's expectations for research work, is asked to fund what it sees as 'good practice for all social science research' (2005: 1). In the words of Beauchamp and Childress (1994: 4), ethics is 'a generic term for various ways of understanding and examining the moral life'.

The aim of the guidelines is to provide a framework of principles to assist the choices and decisions which have to be made also with regard to the principles, values and interests of all those involved in a particular situation. The British Society of Criminology's general principle is that researchers should ensure that research is undertaken to the highest possible methodological standard and the highest quality in order that the maximum possible knowledge and benefits accrue to society. There are four key areas that one has to consider when conducting research in criminology and cognate disciplines (for further details go to www. britsoccrim.org/ethical.htm):

1 Responsibilities of researchers towards the discipline of criminology
2 Researchers' responsibilities towards research participants
3 Researchers' responsibilities to colleagues
4 Relationships with sponsors

In relation to the above, you, the reader, will have to consider the role of the ethics committee, and in doing so, how to address some of the ethical issues as an outcome of your research. Box 13.1 identifies some of the issues you may want to address when dealing with ethics committees.

BOX 13.1

STRATEGIES FOR DEALING WITH ETHICS COMMITTEES

- Consider the ethical aspects of your study from the very beginning
- Identify the regulations that govern your work
- Find out how your local research ethics committee works
- Seek advice from colleagues and examples of successful applications
- Answer the committee's questions in a simple and straightforward manner
- Be prepared to educate your committee
- Talk to your local committee
- Be prepared for delays
- Be prepared to adapt your work
- Contribute to reform

Adapted from Israel and Hersh (2006)

PERSONAL REFLEXIVITY

The importance of theory in the research process cannot be overstated. Cain (1986) argued that it is crucial at the beginning of the research process to 'confess' one's theory. Theoretical organisation, Willis (1980: 90) argues:

> ...concerns attitudes towards the social world in which the research takes place, a particular view of the social relationships within it and its fundamental determination and a notion of the analytic procedures which will be used to provide the final account. It would also explain why certain topics have been chosen in the first place.

It is, as Willis argues, by stating one's theoretical leanings and one's own contribution to and experience by which knowledge is produced, that this process becomes inseparable from that knowledge. This approach is far less dangerous or 'biased' than one in which 'theoretical assumptions exist in an unrecognised way' (1980: 91). Given that a major contribution of feminist criticism has been precisely to problematise previously unrecognised theoretical assumptions in social research, it can be argued that the epistemological demands of feminist theories include interrogating the role of the researcher in constructing the research process (Harding, 1987; Knorr Cetina and Circourel, 1981; Reinharz, 1986; Stanley, 1990; Stanley and Wise, 1993). This has enabled an awareness of the processual nature of research. It is by exploring the role of the research and the possible effects the research may have on participants that one can minimise the harm to an already vulnerable group (see Box 13.2). By constantly interrogating the research practice with the issues in Box 13.2, the researcher is actively reflecting on the research process, minimising the possible harm that research participants might be subject to.

STEPS TO RESOLVING ETHICAL DILEMMAS:

1 Identify the issues, identify the parties
2 Identify options
3 Consider the consequences
4 Analyse the options in terms of moral principles
5 Make your own decision and act with commitment
6 Evaluate the system
7 Evaluate yourself

Adapted from Bebeau et al. (1995); Joyce et al. (1996); Stark-Adam and Pettifor (1995)

We argue throughout this chapter that what is relevant throughout the research process is that the researcher acknowledges and reflects upon how diversity, differences and similarities can be shared and negotiated, and upon the implications of age, class, argot, gender, ethnicity and sexuality for the research process. For example, in Wahidin's work, the participants came from experiences, social backgrounds, historical moments which, in terms of past time, she cannot claim to share. It is cogently stated that 'prejudice' is the ontological condition of human existence in society and thus 'no researcher comes to her research a *tabula rasa*' (Roseneil, 1993: 179). Inherent in the research process, then, is the subjectivity of the 'researched', the subjectivity of the researcher and the intersubjectivity of the research process, which cannot be eliminated or ignored but has to be accounted for and reflected upon (Renzetti and Lee, 1993; Stanley, 1990; Stanley and Wise, 1993).

ETHICS IN CONDUCTING QUALITATIVE PRISON RESEARCH

As researchers, we have shown throughout this chapter the need to be reflexive in conducting research. It is by drawing on our own research in prison and in a juvenile justice centre that we have highlighted the dilemmas.

Case study 1: research with children in custody

The observations in this section relate to the ethical issues faced by Linda Moore when carrying out research with incarcerated children. Imprisoned children and young people constitute a vulnerable group in terms of research on several levels. As Goldson (2006: 454) describes, child prisoners are 'routinely drawn from some of the most damaged and distressed families, neighbourhoods and communities'. Their detention exacerbates their vulnerability. The research was carried out with Dr Una Convery in Northern Ireland's Juvenile Justice Centre (JJC or the Centre) for the

Northern Ireland Human Rights Commission (Convery and Moore, 2006). Here Moore reflects on the ethical considerations posed during the research process, some particular to conducting research with children, and others relevant to research with all incarcerated people.[1]

At the time of research, the Juvenile Justice Centre situated in Bangor, Co Down, had facilities to accommodate up to 48 boys and girls aged 10–17 remanded or sentenced to custody. The Commission had already conducted an investigation into the protection of children's rights in custody (Kilkelly et al., 2002) and decided in 2004 to conduct follow-up work to assess the extent to which its previous recommendations had been acted on. The Human Rights Commission in Northern Ireland at the time of the research had the legislative power to conduct investigations, but not to compel cooperation or production of documentation (legislation has now been amended to give the Commission more expansive powers).

Access immediately became an issue. The researchers met the Director of the Centre and agreed arrangements for starting the research. Before fieldwork could begin, however, the Northern Ireland Office (NIO) made contact to deny access. Lengthy legal proceedings followed and towards the end of 2004, the then Secretary of State, Paul Murphy MP, announced that the Commission would in future legislation be granted a right of access to places of detention and the power to compel evidence and witnesses. Probably as a consequence of this announcement, in February 2005, the NIO agreed to grant access and fieldwork finally began that spring. This was not the first or last time the Commission was denied access, with similar situations arising in relation to its research on women in prison (see Scraton and Moore, 2005, 2007). Before research could begin we were both required to go through official checks under child protection requirements to ensure that neither of us had any previous convictions that would potentially represent a danger to children. This was crucial as we would require unsupervised access to children to conduct the research.

The methodology used was a combination of semi-structured interviews with boys and girls, staff, management and other professionals; analysis of documentation; and observation of the regime. Staff members were advised by management that given the statutory status of the Human Rights Commission, they were expected to cooperate with the research but we preferred that all interviews be conducted on the basis of informed consent. Young people and staff were provided with written information in advance to enable them to take an informed decision about whether to participate. Consent was obtained verbally by discussing with the children whether they wished to take part and the issues associated with this, and recording the agreement at the start of the taped interview. Roberts and Indermaur (2003) argue that written consent forms may be inappropriate for use in some penal settings, as, among other reasons, participants may mistrust the use of written forms, and may be afraid of institutional reprisals should the authorities know that they were taking part in research. It was agreed that as the children were all over age 14 they were able to understand the process and were capable of taking an informed decision about participation. Care staff considered one child too vulnerable to be interviewed, and we accepted their

---

[1] These are Moore's personal reflections and not attributable to the Commission.

decision: this happened, in the case of a girl who was very distressed and had been crying since being received into the Centre a couple of days previously. Where there are doubts about a prisoner's capability to give informed consent, professionals, including healthcare professionals, can be consulted.

Interviews were conducted on the basis of confidentiality, with respondents referred to in the report only in terms of broad categories. However, there were some limitations to confidentiality which we alerted interviewees to. For some interviewees, for example the dentist or psychologist, the fact that there was only one person carrying out this role meant that their contribution would be identifiable. We were careful to ensure that staff in this situation understood the limits on confidentiality and asked them to make clear if they would prefer any comments to be anonymised in the report. For some children, this was also an issue. For example, it was important to document the experience and views of girls, but there were only two girls in the Centre at the time and one was too vulnerable to be interviewed. Again, this meant explaining to the sole girl interviewee that some of what she said may be identifiable and checking that she understood and gave consent for this, as well as using our own judgement about where it would be appropriate to disguise the source.

Before interviews began, we explained to the children that there were some situations where we would have to breach confidences and pass information to the appropriate person, most importantly where child protection issues were raised. In the event, one child did tell us that he had witnessed another child being assaulted and this allegation was duly reported through the Centre's child protection procedures. Sometimes, however, it is not straightforward what constitutes a child protection matter. If children intimate that they have witnessed or experienced an assault by another child or member of staff, then it is clear that this needs to be reported. Similarly, if a child suggests that they may be thinking of harming themselves, then staff must be informed. What is the situation, however, if a child has been held in isolation, handcuffed until his wrists are reddened, physically restrained in a way that was frightening to him, or (as occurred not in this project but in other research we were involved in) where children reported humiliation and distress at having been strip-searched? Examples below of children's comments demonstrate their distress at 'routine' procedures such as physical restraint:

They nearly broke my wrists [putting handcuffs on]. I had cuts and everything there they were pulling that hard.

When I first saw someone else getting restrained, I felt like helping the other wee lad instead of helping staff. This wee lad, a wee small thing, not even five foot and these men about six foot, and he was just getting jumped over ... it looked like they nearly killed him; he couldn't breathe or nothing; he's going 'I can't breathe, I can't breathe', and staff didn't see it.

It's not fair ... shouldn't take six people to hold a wee boy down. They got a shield and made his nose bleed. Bent his fingers back. It's supposed to calm you down, but it makes you more angry.

All of these are features of custodial regimes, and yet from a children's rights perspective may constitute physical or emotional abuse. As Goldson (2006: 457) comments, 'despite the use of euphemistic language and sanitised descriptions, approved "control" techniques would almost certainly be described as child abuse in any other context'. Researchers need to consider whether breach of children's rights is involved and, if so, whether it would be appropriate to inform relevant external authorities.

Often it can be difficult for a child to recount an upsetting or emotional experience and this is where the researcher needs to ask themselves whether the benefits of the research will outweigh potential risks. The quotations from children below demonstrate the sensitive nature of discussions:

> When you're in your bedroom, in your room, you can think about things. You can think about strange things so you can ... like hanging yourself or something. Thought about it a few times.

> I don't really like visits. Just do without them. Seen my ma and dad once, but they leave and you don't. I don't like when you're sitting here and they go. You'd like to be going back out.

> My dad died when I was 11 ... I just get this big thing inside me and it's coming out bit by bit ... you know I've actually seen two of my friends die. And then watching one when he was getting knee-capped, getting shot, punishment beat and whatever.

All of these young people had experienced trauma and some had experienced recent bereavement. In these situations it would have been highly unethical to ask them to recount painful experiences unless there was good reason. It is important never to leave a child in a distressed or angry state and crucial to try as far as possible to ensure that children have support, and know where to get independent advice if appropriate. In the case of the Juvenile Justice Centre, there were many sympathetic and qualified staff with whom concerns could be raised, but this is not always the case in custodial research.

We asked children questions about their experiences of the regime, as this was the focus of study, and did not ask anything about the offences or alleged offences which had led to them coming into custody. It is vital in respecting the privacy of participants that only relevant questions are asked and participants' privacy is respected. We were interested in whether custody had been used as a last resort, but explored this through questions to staff which avoided asking for details of individuals' offences.

Researchers granted access to prison and custodial regimes will witness events and situations which leave them feeling distinctly uncomfortable and compromised. Decisions have to be made on a case-by-case basis as to whether to withdraw from a situation or continue to observe. During fieldwork, we did not witness physical restraint but we did observe a child being threatened with restraint for refusing to go to bed as he wanted to get a cup of juice. This incident followed an interview with us which had kept him up beyond bedtime. Feeling some responsibility for the situation, we protested to staff that it was the child's participation in the research which had kept him up past bedtime and that he had worked hard during the interview. We felt anxious and to an extent compromised by this situation, which thankfully was resolved without restraint being carried out.

A further area of ethical consideration is whether participants or the institution should be granted access to the report or findings prior to publication. We asked children if they would like a copy of their interview to be sent to them but none requested this. The Juvenile Justice Centre management and the Youth Justice Board were provided with a draft report and invited to make comments on factual accuracy, which they did. We were clear that this was not an opportunity to influence the findings and in this case our independence was accepted.

Case study 2: research with women in custody

The following section is based on Azrini Wahidin's experience of addressing issues of confidentiality and informed consent. Following the discussions Wahidin had with the prison ethics board, preliminary discussions with potential participants and study of the literature on research ethics, she was able to draw up a letter to the women outlining the research and stating the extent and limits of confidentiality that could be guaranteed. In terms of the validity and scope of the interview material obtained, the ideal situation would have been to have offered complete confidentiality, thus providing complete immunity from social or official sanctions. Confidentiality is also desirable from the point of view of the psychological implication of revealing personal, often emotionally-charged, information: the women in this study have to contend daily with the erosion of self which results from being under constant scrutiny and constantly vulnerable to the judgements of others; and rather than the research creating a re-enactment of these intrusions, the ideal was for it to provide some personal space where they could reflect freely in an atmosphere of respect for personal boundaries.

Nevertheless, as researchers we had a responsibility to adhere to prison rules/ organisation rules as a precondition for being allowed to carry out the research, and both professional and personal integrity dictate that this commitment is taken seriously. Thus, for example, if a woman told Wahidin of a breach of prison security, such as a planned escape or an attack upon another prisoner or officer, she would be obliged to break confidentiality, although her policy would be to try to discuss this with the informant first and, if possible, persuade her to talk to an officer herself. As with any other professionals whose work involves hearing confidential information (e.g. doctors, social workers), there is a recognition that a breach of confidence is justified if there appears to be a risk of serious harm to the respondent, or another person, and also that there will be an element of personal judgement involved in assessing the seriousness of the risk, the veracity of the information and the balance of ethical principles involved.

In these circumstances, there would be general agreement that the best course is to offer *limited assurances of confidentiality* based on a principle of confidentiality with all exceptions and limitations clearly stated, so that respondents are in a position to make an informed choice about what information to share. In practical terms, confidentiality means that the individual will not be discussed outside the interview room, except for purposes strictly relevant to the preparation and publication of the research report, when the key principle is the protection of the respondent's identity (and that of anyone else to whom they refer). Thus, the letter to the women explained that all names and other potentially identifying details (places, dates, etc.) would be changed, that all transcribing would be done solely by Wahidin and that all tapes would be destroyed once the analysis was completed.

One potential situation which could, but would not necessarily, necessitate a breach of confidentiality would be if a respondent alleged professional misconduct by a prison officer. The best policy was to be aware of the complaints procedure, and of organisations which supported women in prison in order to be able to inform the women of the various channels available to them. If the respondent did not wish to make a complaint but Wahidin thought it should be addressed, she would discuss the situation with the woman and ask her permission for her to take independent action.

It appears from the above discussion that it is not morally justifiable to guarantee total confidentiality nor possible to make participants *fully aware* of *all* the potential harmful effects that could result from participating in the research. As researchers in our separate studies, we answered honestly any of the questions that the respondents had about the research and the possible publications that may result from it. The process of engaging in the informal discussions with the prison authorities, the women themselves and the ethical review boards has brought to our attention the potential implications of the research.

INFORMED CONSENT

The principle of informed consent requires that participants' engagement with the research is based on: 'a voluntary, un-coerced decision, made by a sufficiently competent or autonomous person on the basis of adequate information and deliberation, to accept rather than reject some proposed course of action that will affect her' (Butler, 1990: 165). Consent, however, operates at many levels and must be negotiated as such. A certain minimum standard of informed consent can be guaranteed by providing respondents with standardised explanations of the nature and purpose of the research, where and how it will be used, and the conditions of their participation (of which the most important will be around confidentiality anonymity). As the opportunity to ask questions and to comment upon and criticise the research are built into the research design, the negotiation of informed consent was probably more thorough and realistic than in many other studies where obtaining informed consent is seen as a necessary formality. Adherence to the principle of informed consent implies that two major conditions are met: first, that the research subjects are made aware of and understand the nature and purposes of the research; second, that from a position of knowledge, they can freely give their consent to participating in the research. The explanations which one constructs for one's research are always conditional upon the audience one is addressing. This is especially true when carrying out an **ethnographic** study where one has a vague sense of what one is looking for.

Thus, the practice of **participant observation** is, inevitably, interactionally deceitful. Researchers have to cultivate informants and lessen the distance between themselves and those they are studying. In this sense, one's aims are to make the research role invisible in the field and to emphasise similarity at the expense of difference. As Punch has rightly questioned (1986: 72): 'if the latent aim of the field worker is to create trust, then what is the aim of that trust?' The concept of trust implies mutuality of interest and an equality of dependency. To a major degree, this is inherently absent in the fieldwork role and, therefore, has to be manufactured.

However, one has to remember that consent in social research is often contingent and all probabilities cannot be covered by the consent form. Indeed, some research involves a semi-covert element where there is no obvious source of consent. As Israel (2004) succinctly argues, the medical model of a research ethics framework is applied in research governance which discourages covert research. Concerns have also been raised about the ethicality of the ethics committee (Hammersley, 2000) that manage the consent form design and process. Bourgois (1995) poses some nuanced questions about what you could characterise as the 'situated fieldwork condition': 'How can we reconcile effective participant observation with truly informed consent? Is **rapport** building a covert way of "encouraging people to forget that you are constantly observing them and registering everything they are saying and doing?"' (Bourgois, 1995: 296–297).

In this chapter, we demonstrate the nuanced and complexity of issues that are raised when doing prison research and it is in the doing of prison research, or in general terms, that the problem of field research is not just about negotiating access, getting in, staying in, surviving, and then getting out more or less intact. There is also the requirement to carry the narrative 'back home', refashioning the fieldwork experience in a textual form which, while it is accessible to a different audience (its academic readership), remains true to where it came from. It is a problem of multiple identities: '*Being There*' and '*Being Here*' in Geertz's (1974) words.

What is required of an ethnographer is neither full membership nor competence, but the ability to give voice to that experience, and to bridge between the experiences of actors and audiences, 'authenticity' and 'distance'. This process can be likened to a game of hockey where a knowledgeable spectator learns the rules of the game without ever learning how to play or just as a boxing commentator does not need to slug it out over twelve rounds to bring a fight to life, so the ethnographer must remain content 'to talk a good fight'.

SUMMARY

Some research has made important contributions to social change and improved regimes for prisoners while other research has created only misery and degradation for, often unwilling, participants. Now firmly established principles for conducting research in prison include the maxim 'do no harm'; that the benefit of the research to humanity should outweigh any potential risk; that informed consent must be gained from all participants; and that confidentiality must be maintained where appropriate (and breached only in a few situations such as where child protection or safety concerns are raised). Where vulnerable adults or children are involved in research, then particular care must be taken, and researchers must ensure that they are aware of legal and organisational responsibilities, for example, child protection procedures.

Even taking these principles onboard, it is evident from the discussion of our own research experiences that not every eventuality can be foreseen and that within a prison environment moral dilemmas will crop up on a case-by-case basis. It is easier to deal with these when more than one researcher is involved: the benefits of having another committed individual with whom to tease out dilemmas cannot be over-stated, and having someone onsite is infinitely better than having to wait until a supervision session. Unfortunately, funding and other constraints mean that researchers will often have to face difficult ethical situations alone. It is vital that in every case, adequate effective support and opportunity for 'debriefing' are available.

■ Study Questions/Activities for Students ▬▬▬▬

1   Write down the reasons why prisoners are considered a 'vulnerable' population in the context of research ethics.

2   You are planning to conduct interviews in a young offender institution. Think about the steps you will need to take to secure the informed consent of the young people who are potential participants in your research. Consider what information they will need to take an informed decision, how you would like to convey the information about the research to them, whether you will use written consent forms and, if not, how you will record their consent.

3   You are interviewing an imprisoned woman about her experience of health provision in prison. During the interview she mentions that she has been very low in mood and feels that she may harm herself. As an independent researcher do you consider yourself to have any responsibility to report this to the prison authorities or to anyone else? What (if any) action do you think you should take?

RESOURCES

The following websites provide information, advice and support on ethics frameworks used by the British Sociological Association, the British Society of Criminology, the Economic Social Research Council and the Higher Education Academy. In Northern Ireland the key governing boards are:

British Sociological Association – www.britsoc.co.uk/equality/

British Society of Criminology – www.britsoccrim.org/ethical.htm/

The Economic Social Research Council – www.esrcsocietytoday.ac.uk/ research_ethics_ framework2/

The Higher Education Academy – www.heacademy.ac.uk/

Office for Research Ethics Committee Northern Ireland – www.orecni.org.uk

The Socio-Legal Studies Association – www.slsa.ac.uk/

The Social Research Association – www.the-sra.org.uk/

Bachman, R. and Schutt, R.K. (2007) *The Practice of Research in Criminology and Criminal Justice*. New York: Sage.

Israel, M. and Hay, I. (2006) *Research Ethics for Social Scientists*. London: Sage.

King, R. and Wincup, E. (2007) *Doing Research on Crime and Criminal Justice* (2nd edition). Oxford: Oxford University Press.

Wincup, E. (2009) 'Researching crime and criminal justice', in C. Hale, K. Hayward, A. Wahidin and E. Wincup (eds), *Criminology* (2nd edition). Oxford: Oxford University Press.

REFERENCES

Arboleda-Flórez, J. (1991) 'Ethical issues regarding research on prisoners', *International Journal of Therapy and Comparative Criminology* 35(1): 1–5.

Arditti, J. (2002) 'Doing family research at the jail: reflections of a prison widow', *The Qualitative Report* 7(4), December. Available at: www.nova.edu/sss/QR/QR7-4/arditti.html.

Bachman, R. and Schutt, R.K. (2007) *The Practice of Research in Criminology and Criminal Justice*. New York: Sage.

Bauman, Z. (1992) *Intimations of Post Modernity*. London: Routledge.

Beauchamp, T.L. and Childress, J.F. (1994) *Principles of Biomedical Ethics* (4th edition). New York: Oxford University Press.

Bebeau, M.J., Pimple, K.D., Muskavitch, K.M.T., Borden, S.L. and Smith, D.H. (eds) (1995) *Moral Reasoning in Scientific Research: Cases for Teaching and Assessment*, Proceedings of a workshop at Indiana University, Poynter Centre for the Study of Ethics and American institutions, Indiana University, Bloomington.

Becker, H. (1963) *Outsiders: Studies in the Sociology of Deviance*. New York: Free Press.

Becker, H. (1967) 'Whose side are we on?', *Social Problems* 14(3): 239–47.

Becker, P. and Wetzell, R.F. (eds) (2006) *Criminals and Their Scientists: The History of Criminology in International Perspective*. Washington, DC and Cambridge: Cambridge University Press and German Historical Institute.

Belmont Report (1979) *Ethical Principles and Guidelines for the Protection of Human Subjects of Research*. National Commission for the Protection of Human Subjects of Biomedical and Behavioural Research.

Bourgois, P. (1995) *In Search of Respect: Selling Crack in El Barrio*. Cambridge: Cambridge University Press.

Brown, P. (2008) 'Giving voice: the prisoner and discursive citizenship', in T. Anthony and C. Cunneen (eds), *The Critical Criminology Companion*. Sydney: Hawkins Press.

Butler, J. (1990) *Gender Trouble*. New York: Routledge.

Cain, M. (1986) 'Realism, feminism, methodology and the law', *The International Journal of Sociology of Law* 14.

Carlen, P. (1983) *Women's Imprisonment: A Study in Social Control*. London: Routledge and Kegan Paul.

Carlton, B. (2006) 'From H. Division to Abu Ghraib: regimes of justification and the historical proliferation of state-inflicted terror and violence in maximum-security', *Social Justice* 33(4): 15–36.

Convery, U. and Moore, L. (2006) *Still in Our Care: Protecting Children's Rights in Northern Ireland*. Belfast: Northern Ireland Human Rights Commission.

ESRC (Economic and Social Research Council, United Kingdom) (2005) *Research Ethics Framework*. Swindon: Economic and Social Research Council.

Fielding, N. (1982) 'Observational research on the National Front', in M. Bulmer (ed.), *Social Research Ethics: An Examination of the Merits of Covert Participant Observation*. London: Macmillan.

Fletcher, J. (1966) *Situational Ethics*. London: SCM Press.

Geertz, C. (ed.) (1974) *Myth, Symbol and Culture*. New York: Norton.

Gelsthorpe, L. (1990) 'Feminist methodologies in criminology: a new approach or old wine in new bottles?', in L. Gelsthope and A. Morris (eds), *Feminist Perspectives in Criminology*. Milton Keynes: Open University Press.

Gibson, M.S. (2006) 'Cesare Lombroso and Italian criminology: theory and politics', in P. Becker and R.F. Wetzell (eds), *Criminals and Their Scientists: The History of Criminology in International Perspective*. Washington, DC and Cambridge: Cambridge University Press and German Historical Institute.

Goldson, B. (2006) 'Damage, harm and death in child prisons in England and Wales: questions of abuse and accountability', *Howard Journal* 45(5): 449–67.

Goring, C. (1913) *The English Convict*. London: Methuen.

Hammersley, M. (2000) *Taking Sides in Social Research*. London: Routledge.

Harding, S. (ed.) (1987) *Feminism and Methodology Social Science Issues.* Bloomington, IN: Indiana University Press.

Hobbs, D. and May, T. (1993) *Interpreting the Field: Accounts of Ethnography*. Oxford: Oxford University Press.

Holdaway, S. (1983) 'An inside job: a case study of covert research on the police', in M. Blumer (ed.), *Social Research Ethics*. London: Macmillan. pp. 57–79.

Homan, R. (1991) *The Ethics of Social Research*. London: Longman.

Hornblum, A.M. (1998) *Acres of Skin: Human Experiments at Holmesburg Prison*. New York: Routledge.

Israel, M. (2004) 'Strictly confidential? Integrity and the disclosure of criminological and socio-legal research', *British Journal of Criminology* 33(1): 1–20.

Israel, M. and Hay, I. (2006) *Research Ethics for Social Scientists*. London: Sage.

Israel, M. and Hersh, D. (2006) 'Ethics', in N. Gilbert (ed.), *The Postgraduate Guidebook: Essential Skills for a Career in the Social Sciences*. London: Sage. pp. 43–58.

Joyce, B., Weil, M. and Showers, B. (1996) *Models of Teaching* (4th edition). Boston, MA: Allyn and Bacon.

Kilkelly, U., Moore, L. and Convery, U. (2002) *In Our Care: Promoting the Rights of Children in Custody*. Belfast: Northern Ireland Human Rights Commission.

Knorr Cetina, K. and Circourel, A. (eds) (1981) *Advances in Social Theory and Methodology*. London: Routledge and Kegan Paul.

Marx, K. (1845) 'Theses on Feuerbach', in K. Marx and F. Engels, *The German Ideology*.

Neve, L. and Pate, K. (2005) 'Challenging the criminalization of women who resist', in J. Sudbury (ed.), *Global Lockdown: Race, Gender, and the Prison-Industrial Complex*. New York: Routledge.

Patai, D. (1991) 'US academics and Third World women: is ethical research possible?', in S.B. Gluck and D. Patai (eds), *Women's Words: The Feminist Practice of Oral History*. New York: Routledge.

Piacentini, L. (2007) 'Researching Russian prisons: a consideration of new and established methodologies in prison research', in Y. Jewkes (ed.), *Handbook on Prisons*. Cullompton: Willan Publishing.

Punch, M. (1986) *The Politics and Ethics of Fieldwork*. Newbury Park, CA: Sage.

Reinharz, S. (1986) 'Friends or foes: gerontological and feminist theory', *Women Studies International* 9(5): 503–14.

Renzetti, C. and Lee, R. (eds) (1993) *Researching Sensitive Topics.* London: Sage.

Roberts, L. and Indermaur, D. (2003) 'Signed consent forms in criminological research: protection for researchers and ethics committees but a threat to research participants?' Paper presented at the Evaluation in Crime and Justice: Trends and Methods Conference, Australian Institute for Criminology and Australian Bureau of Statistics, Canberra, 24–25 March.

Roseneil, S. (1993) 'Greenham revisited: researching myself and my sisters', in D. Hobbs and T. May (eds), *Interpreting the Field*. Oxford: Oxford University Press. pp. 177–208.

Scraton, P. (2004) 'Speaking truth to power: experiencing critical research', in M. Smyth and E. Williamson (eds), *Ethics, Power, Knowledge and Consent: Researchers and Their Subjects*. Bristol: The Policy Press.

Scraton, P. (2007) *Power, Conflict and Criminalisation.* Abingdon: Routledge.

Scraton, P. and Moore, L. (2005) *The Hurt Inside: The Imprisonment of Women and Girls in Northern Ireland*. Belfast: Northern Ireland Human Rights Commission.

Scraton, P. and Moore, L. (2007) *The Prison Within: The Imprisonment of Women at Hydebank Wood 2004–2006*. Belfast: Northern Ireland Human Rights Commission.

Sheldon, W.H. (1949) *Varieties of Delinquent Youth*. London: Harper.

Sieber, J.E. (1982) *The Ethics of Social Research: Surveys and Experiments*. Springer-Verlag: New York.

Sieber, J.E. (1992) *Planning Ethically Responsible Research: A Guide for Students and Internal Review Boards*. Newbury Park, CA: Sage.

Stanley, L. (ed.) (1990) *Feminist Praxis: Research, Theory and Epistemology in Feminist Sociology*. London: Routledge.

Stanley, L. and Wise, S. (1993) *Breaking Out Again: Feminist Ontology and Epistemology*. London: Routledge and Kegan Paul.

Stark-Adam, C. and Pettifor, J. (1995) *Ethical Decision Making for Practising Social Scientists: Putting Values into Practice*. Ottawa: Social Science Federation of Canada.

Sudbury, J. (ed.) (2005) *Global Lockdown: Race, Gender, and the Prison-Industrial Complex*. New York: Routledge.

Vertinsky, P. (2007) 'Physique as destiny: William H. Sheldon, Barbara Honeyman Heath and the struggle for hegemony in the science of somatotyping', *Canadian Bulletin of Medical History* 24(2): 291–316.

Waldron, J.B. (1998) 'Negotiating consent and accountability with a "captured population"', *Human Organization* 57(2).

Willis, P. (1980) 'The importance of theory', in Guruvitch et al. (eds), *Culture, Society and the Media.* London: Methuen.

Wincup, E. (2009) 'Researching crime and criminal justice', in C. Hale, K. Hayward, A. Wahidin and E. Wincup (eds), *Criminology* (2nd edition). Oxford: Oxford University Press.

Wright Mills, C. (1959) *The Sociological Imagination*. New York: Oxford University Press.

FOURTEEN
THE POLITICS OF CRIMINOLOGICAL RESEARCH

GORDON HUGHES

Chapter Contents

KEY POINTS

This chapter:

- Explains the different forms of political forces at work on criminological research

- Demarcates the relationship between scientific and political intentions in research on crime and control

- Explores the ways in which political and normative issues necessarily affect the stages of criminological research form inception to completion of the research process

- Raises some of the key challenges and opportunities opened up by undertaking applied research in criminology, particularly with regard to worlds of crime control policy and practice

INTRODUCTION

All too often research publications fail to tell us about the hidden difficulties, constraints and limitations – not least the play of power relations and politics in the broadest sense of the word – underneath the apparently smooth and detached surface appearance of the criminological research process. To redress this balance, the main aim of this chapter is to provide a comprehensive overview of the varying political contexts and related ethical dilemmas which not only have an impact on contemporary criminological research, but are in fact intrinsic to all criminological research. The chapter is organised as follows. Following an initial discussion of why an understanding of the politics in criminological research is of great importance rather than of mere marginal interest to you as students of and researchers in criminology, the chapter then takes the reader on a journey through the key stages of the research process, from inception to eventual ending of the process, focusing on and illustrating how **political** and **normative** issues are intrinsic throughout each stage. Throughout this chapter our discussion is not just about extreme cases (for example, involving deliberate deceit and disguise by the researcher, or intentional censorship and manipulation from 'the powers that be', and so on), although such examples need to be explored. Rather, for the most part our discussion will be focused on the more mundane and intrinsic political issues and normative concerns which constitute necessary aspects of all social scientific research on sensitive issues like crime and victimisation and control and criminalisation.

SCIENCE AND POLITICS IN CRIMINOLOGY

Defining the political

From the outset it is valuable to distinguish what we may term extended and restricted definitions of the term 'political'.

The broad and extended definition of the term 'political' is 'the working through of power and contests over its exercise' (Bryman, 2004/2008: 517). When viewed in this way, all social scientific work has a political dimension in the non-party political sense of the term.

All aspects of research involve the researcher in both the analysis and practice of power, and, in turn, have the potential to generate conflicts of interest between a whole host of interested parties from:

- individual victims
- offenders
- crime controllers and their agencies
- major social institutions like families, schools and industries
- neighbourhoods, communities and nations

It will become clear that the social scientific study of people and institutions will inevitably and necessarily intrude on at times, and may even subvert and criticise, deeply held moral beliefs and practices, and may uncover unwelcome truths for some groups that are very welcome truths for others. No criminological research takes place in a political and normative vacuum.

There is a second, more restricted meaning of the word 'political': the processes relating to the work and influence of explicit political ideologies, political parties, and the legitimate, organised, coercive institutional power of the modern nation state.

Alongside the extended definition previously discussed, this second sense of the word 'political' is at times also of crucial importance for 'live' research in criminology, given that so much criminological investigation is in fact the study of both legitimate and authoritative but also coercive and violent state power in its most overt form. This is the case whether one is studying the riot control measures of the state's police force out on the streets, the interrogation strategies of suspect offenders or the nature and experience of the imprisonment of offenders. While much of the mainstream work of the criminological researcher both challenges and subverts dominant and commonsensical assumptions about the world of crime and its control, nonetheless, criminological knowledge may also at times be used to lend 'scientific' credibility to prevailing dominant ideological assumptions and institutional practices.

Science and questions of detachment

Criminologists face the same challenges as all social researchers looking for empirical and falsifiable truths or the nearest approximations to shared truths that we are able to uncover in the academic study of human action and the meanings behind such actions. This is the case whether such work is directed at the much debated escalation in the number of young men involved in lethal gun-related violence in UK cities in the 2000s (Hallsworth and Silverstone, 2009) or the behaviour and views of police officers, youth workers, community safety partnerships and such like tasked with trying to manage and control such processes on the streets (Roberts and Innes, 2009). In such research, the complex relationship of trying to be scientific, and thus detached, and objective while studying such a highly politicised and morally charged area and 'hot' media issue as crime and law and order is at the very core of the shared vocation of and challenges facing us all as students of criminology.

It will be argued here that the balance between the scientific and the political in criminological research is inevitably a complex and tense one. If criminological research does not take place in a political and moral vacuum, it is *necessarily* part of a deeply *political* process in the broad and extended sense of the word defined above. Furthermore, some criminological research is also political in the more restricted and extrinsic definition of the word 'political'. Such research may be deliberately partial and driven by either the researcher's own deeply held political views or the views and ends of the powerful sponsors of research, such as government bodies or private corporations. Nevertheless, it is vital not to collapse these two very different meanings of the term 'political'.

Taking sides? Questions of involvement and detachment

The eminent sociologist of deviance, Howard Becker (1967), famously asked 'Whose side are we [sociologists] on?' when undertaking research. This question was prompted by Becker's correct belief that much sociological research was, and still is, directed at the study of 'the underdog' (the poor, the negatively labelled and stigmatised groups) rather than 'the overdog' (the rich, powerful, dominant definers of normality and laws). In turn, Becker sought to undermine the extreme claims for scientific detachment and total removal from any political and moral influences in much **positivist** criminology in the USA. Becker's conclusion from this was that social researchers should be explicit about which groups in the 'power game' they sided with. The influence of such thinking has led some camps in criminology, such as standpoint **feminist** researchers and critical criminologists, to argue for **conscious partiality** (Bryman, 2004/2008) (see Box 14.1).

In this chapter it is argued that the two extreme positions may be discerned at opposite ends of the detachment–involvement spectrum, namely:

1   Criminological research is untouched by political forces, as is evident in crude forms of positivism such as 'crime science' and experimental criminology (Sherman, 2009; and his critics, Hope, 2009; Tilley, 2009; Carr, 2010).

2   All criminological research is political in nature and partial in character, as is evident in social constructionist, critical criminology (see Hillyard, 2005; and their critics, Hughes, 2007; Edwards and Hughes, 2009).

The argument put forward here is that both extreme positions ('it's all politics and no science' vs. 'it's all science and no politics') are flawed. Instead, it is suggested that the tension between scientific labour and political influences, both extrinsic and intrinsic, needs to be recognised and accepted and struggled with (for a full discussion, see Edwards and Hughes, 2009).

BOX 14.1

CRIMINOLOGICAL RESEARCH AS EXPLICITLY POLITICAL: CONSCIOUS PARTIALITY AND FEMINIST RESEARCH

According to the argument of some feminist criminologists, this conscious partiality is celebrated since to attempt to do research on women in an objective, value-neutral way would be undesirable and incompatible with the political and normative values of feminism. Rather, much feminist criminological research argues for a stance that extols the virtues of a commitment to women and to exposing the conditions of their disadvantage and oppression in the fields of both victimisation and criminalisation. In turn, such research is explicitly driven by political intentions, previously defined as the restricted definition of political, being concerned to change the situation of women as well as to heighten our understanding of the oppression and disadvantage from which they suffer (Bryman, 2004/2008; see also Worrall, 1990).

THE PLAY OF POWER AND POLITICS IN THE KEY STAGES OF THE RESEARCH PROCESS

The main focus of this chapter is on the intrinsic politics – defined, you will recall, as the working through and contests over its exercise – which play a key part in social scientific research on questions of crime and control. This deeply political process paradoxically often remains hidden in the published products of research, such as books. At best, there may be a chapter or an appendix on the awkward realities of research. However, more often it is in the brief preface to the book that the reader gets a hint, for example, of the sponsor and the important contacts that underpin the research project. In the following subsections, the key stages of the research process are examined. For the sake of analytical clarity, the following six stages in the research journey may be distinguished (in reality it is not possible to separate these out so neatly from each other):

1 Getting started
2 Gaining support and sponsorship
3 Gaining access
4 Collecting the data
5 Publishing the results
6 Utilising the research

Getting started

All research involves the asking of questions about a particular problem and even at this initial point of departure for criminological inquiry it is impossible to avoid politics. There are instances when we may not be allowed to ask certain questions, as in a situation defined as involving 'national security'. Thus, the role of the British Forces' Special Air Service (SAS) in Northern Ireland, and its possible links to criminal assassinations of suspect terrorists (the so-called 'shoot to kill' policy in the 1970s and 1980s), was potentially an important criminological research proposal which would have been extremely difficult and dangerous to try to investigate. More recently, similar problems would be associated with trying to research the role of Special Forces or security services in the tracking, capture and interrogation of suspect terrorists associated with Muslim *jihad* extremism. There is little doubt that the UK or US governments, past and present, would have explicitly vetoed any such proposal. Of course, the influence of state power is not always so transparent. Power is often most effective when decisions are not explicit but when influence over others is hidden. Political influence may thus be most telling when no overt decision to say 'no' has been made. In the context of criminological research, the influence of dominant ideologies and institutional practices may be most evident when researchers do not even think to ask 'awkward' questions, for example, about the nature of new developments in crime control and the new security regimes, post-9/11 and the Iraq and Afghanistan wars.

You will be aware that the very formulation of a **research question** is surrounded by the types of political constraint noted above as well as the obverse of this, namely political opportunities. Political currents and counter-currents in any given socio-historical context do not just wash over a research culture but instead help construct its agenda. Feminism is an example of a political current which has drastically reshaped the research agenda in recent criminology (Heidensohn and Gelsthorpe, 2007). Where not so long ago criminology was largely 'gender-blind', it is now widely acknowledged that gender differences in both the processes of criminalisation and victimisation are crucial to mainstream criminological analysis rather than confined to the 'critical' margins. In turn, the concern with women and girls as victims of violence is firmly embedded in the crime prevention strategies of local community safety partnerships in every local authority area as well as in the cross-government national strategy in England and Wales launched in 2009, as detailed in the Press Release in Box 14.2.

BOX 14.2

ENDING VIOLENCE AGAINST WOMEN AND GIRLS: YOUR VOICE COUNTS (9 MARCH 2009 HOME OFFICE PRESS RELEASE)

The largest ever cross-government public consultation to tackle violence against women and girls was launched today by Home Secretary Jacqui Smith.

It includes a review into police powers for dealing with serial perpetrators of domestic violence and a review of the sexualisation of teenage girls.

The Together We Can End Violence Against Women And Girls consultation sets out action the government has taken to tackle all forms of violence against women and girls. It looks at what more can be done to challenge the attitudes that may uphold it in order to help women and girls feel safer.

A new opinion poll conducted by Ipsos Mori shows that more than one third of respondents know a woman who has been the victim of violence from a man she knows. Furthermore, just over two in five respondents believe that a woman should be held either partly or fully responsible for being sexually assaulted or raped if she has been flirting heavily with a man. The consultation will include public and stakeholder events in 40 towns and cities across England over the next nine weeks. Today, the Home Secretary outlined plans to consult the public and key stakeholders on a wide range of issues including:

- tackling persistent perpetrators, including a review into what additional powers police and courts may need to control violent perpetrators – particularly serial offenders who move between relationships – led by Chief Constable Brian Moore, Association of Chief Police Officers (ACPO), leading on domestic violence

- helping women feel safer when they travel, including a new website, enabling the public to report where they feel safe or unsafe and why; and the expansion of the Park Mark safer car parks scheme

- a fact-finding review into the increasing sexualisation of teenage girls
- a new advisory group with a specific focus on how schools can prevent violence against women

Such developments as the increasing 'feminisation' of both criminology as an academic discipline and of aspects of official policy and practice in crime control should not lead us to exaggerate the extent of the radical opening up of criminology's research agenda. Any optimism needs to be tempered by an awareness of the political constraints which continue to hinder criminological research. For example, research on knife- and gun-related crimes committed by members of the so-called 'underclass' or members of poor street populations today across many cities is much more likely to be looked upon favourably by official sponsors than research on state-related misdemeanours and harms, such as the abuse of human rights for suspect terrorists by politicians and officials at the higher echelons of government and the state apparatus. The example of undertaking research on the police in the 'old' apartheid South Africa graphically illustrates the difficulty of starting research in the face of opposition from the state. Commenting on the lack of research on the South African police and their own reliance on secondary data from the media, Brogden and Shearing (1993) showed the immense influence of state power on the nature of the research process in the decades preceding the new democracy in this country. Brogden and Shearing note that in the 'old' South Africa most state practices were defined as beyond legitimate public concern and, thus, beyond academic inquiry. They then go on to note that there was a methodological impasse with regard to obtaining reliable data on the South African police: 'It was no fault of critical South African academics that research on policing in South Africa was notable for its relative barrenness. ... Parliamentary debates indicated that the line between criticizing the police and subverting the "national interest" has been a very thin one' (Brogden and Shearing, 1993: 192). As a result, Brogden and Shearing had to rely largely on newspaper reports as a major source of illustrative material in putting together their analysis of the rationale for, and operations of, the 'old' South African police force.

It is rare for most routine criminological research in contemporary democracies to encounter such obvious barriers as political censorship. Nonetheless, extreme examples or *causes célèbres* are significant in highlighting the limits of 'open government' in the criminal justice system. A classic example of less extreme state control and censorship of research into the criminal justice system in the UK remains Cohen and Taylor's (1972) study of life-sentence prisoners at Durham Prison in the 1970s, which is discussed further below.

Gaining support and sponsorship

Different theoretical approaches in criminology look to different 'sponsors' for support. Research agendas, in particular in applied or policy-relevant criminology, at times emerge as the by-product of a set of preferences by commissioners of and sponsors for research of a particular character. Such preferences generally include a concern for 'relevance' or utility to the policy process; explanations focused on the immediate, 'situational' or psychological factors at play rather than those focused on the more intractable and long-term structural forces at the deeper level in social structures; and finally, **quantitative** findings which have a seemingly 'hard' scientific basis, as in the current Home Office preference for before and after experiments and the technique of the randomised control trial (see, for example, the debate and dialogue articles on arguments for and against Lawrence Sherman's call for experimental criminology in the volumes of the journal, *Criminology and Criminal Justice* in 2009 and 2010).

Given the principle of academic autonomy, researchers do not always 'supply' their sponsors with what they may wish to hear. Not all publicly sponsored research is necessarily uncritical of the status quo or subservient to the interests of the sponsor. For example, the major research programme of the government-funded Economic and Social Research Council (ESRC) on criminal justice in the 1980s produced critical and systematically sceptical findings on government and Home Office criminal justice policy in virtually all its projects, ranging from studies of penal policy to those of community consultation and policing (Downes, 1992). One illustrative example from the programme – produced by King and McDermott – clearly highlights the critical possibilities opened up even by state-funded research. In their study 'Control, security and humane containment in the penal system in England and Wales' (1992), they investigated five representative prisons in the Midlands in order to compare current conditions with those in the 1970s. Drawing on such indicators as length of time spent in a cell and amount of time available for work, training and education, the study painted a depressing picture of deterioration in conditions: 'In every comparison much less time was spent in work or similar activities today than had been the case fifteen or more years ago' (King and McDermott, 1992: 104). Their recommendations were critical of government policy on sentencing and penal policy. They recommended:

- a 'minimum-use-of-custody' principle for government and the courts which would bring the prison population into line with existing resources;
- a 'minimum-use-of-security' principle to alleviate the deterioration of conditions within prison; and,
- finally, legally enforceable standards of custody to ensure that resources were maintained at levels appropriate for the tasks of the Prison Service.

This example illustrates the relative autonomy of academic-sponsored research from the political and ideological preoccupations of the dominant authorities. However, it is quite another thing to argue that such well-informed, research-based recommendations will have any noticeable effect on government policy on law and order. Indeed, the dominant 'prison works' credo still prevails in the late 2000s in Britain, with the highest rates of incarceration per head of the population in western Europe and despite decades of criminological research pointing to the failure of imprisonment on a mass scale in deterring offenders and reducing re-offending (Morgan and Liebling, 2007).

Having noted the important qualification about academic autonomy and critique, let us now explore how the different means of gaining support may involve different political constraints and opportunities for the researcher. The typical sponsors for criminological research range from:

- direct national state sponsorship (for example, the Home Office of the British government, the Welsh Assembly government, etc.) to
- relatively autonomous government research councils (for example, the ESRC) through to
- local government support,
- private charitable organisations (for example, the Joseph Rowntree Foundation),
- university departments and employer organisations.

Each of these sponsors brings different political agendas to the researcher–sponsor relationship.

Most criminological research may be defined as '**sensitive**' **research** in that it has potentially serious consequences for all participants (Lee, 1993). Much criminological research may also be surrounded by political and moral controversy in that it 'illuminates the dark corners of society' (Lee, 1993: 2). Not least among our society's 'dark corners' are the institutions of the criminal justice system itself, which are often closed and secretive.

One of the most famous examples of criminological research in the UK to come under the withering gaze of this 'secret state' is the previously mentioned research of Cohen and Taylor on life-sentence prisoners in Durham Prison's E Wing (Cohen and Taylor, 1972). This much-discussed project illustrates the highly charged political climate in which penal research at times has to operate. The research project – as a form of **qualitative** 'action' research – focused on life-sentence prisoners' 'talk' about how they coped with long-term imprisonment and it clearly departed from the dominant positivist work previously carried out. Cohen and Taylor's research pointed to the brutalising and dehumanising effects of institutionalisation, which are compounded by the tyranny of a sense of endless time, unbroken by the escape routes available to most of us 'outside' the walls of the prison. For the Home Office, such a project was flawed, biased and 'unscientific', given its qualitative methodology, its small sample and its subjective approach. It was also suggested by the Home Office that the research ignored the fact that conditions in prisons were improving (Cohen and Taylor, 1977). At the end of their 'battle' with the Home Office, Cohen and Taylor offered an analysis of the latter's political power. Five sources of power are distinguished by the authors:

1 Centralisation of power in the prison department
2 Legalisation of secrecy, particularly through the Official Secrets Act
3 Standardisation of research
4 Mystification of the decision-making structure, given the impenetrability of civil service decision-making
5 Appeal to public interest

The power of the Home Office and, more recently, the Ministry of Justice in Britain to set limiting criteria in the form of a customer–contractor basis for deciding on the agenda of research to be funded was famously questioned by Radzinowicz (1994), one of the founding 'fathers' of mainstream criminology in post-Second World War Britain in the 1990s and has continued to sour relations between the academic criminological community and the ministries of the Home Office and Justice in England and Wales throughout the 2000s (Morgan and Hough, 2007). According to Radzinowicz (1994: 101), this development of a customer–contractor relationship:

> can lead to the agenda for research being set in relation to the administrators' (and ultimately the Minister's) conception of what kind of knowledge is needed. Moreover, it will also lead to a preference for short-term inquiries on matters of immediate concern which are regarded as politically or administratively urgent.

The dangers to criminology of this institutional pressure for '**policy-relevant**' research are multifold, but, most pressingly, they may lead to a dissolution of genuine analytical questions and the production of complex and often uncertain evidential claims due to the political pressure of delivering what the 'customer' narrowly defines as relevant and narrowly helpful to the government in the over-heated context of populist law and order politics. For all the talk of 'evidence-based policy' under the Labour governments of the 1990s and 2000s in Britain, in reality the outcome is often that of 'policy-based evidence', namely the selective use of evidence to support the preferred policy choices made by politicians and policy advisers!

This noted, it would nonetheless be inaccurate to stress the closed nature of the criminal justice system in the UK. For example, in the early 1990s there was some evidence of the Home Office's willingness to have elements of the system monitored. In part, this was due to the legal requirements of the Criminal Justice Act of 1991 whereby race and gender monitoring of the criminal justice system was required to be published annually, and this partial opening up of the system to research also arose out of a concern for the legitimacy which external 'audits' (to use the language of 'managerialism') offered public services. It is debatable how influential independent studies are on actual policy and practice in the Prison Service, but the partial opening up of the system to research or audit does show that the Home Office, and now Ministry of Justice too, like other state departments, are not monolithic bastions whose every gate is forever closed to public and academic scrutiny.

Gaining access

In order to carry out social scientific research, it is often necessary to get into an institution or an informal grouping to make first-hand contact with the subjects of study. The problem of access does not end, however, once you are 'in' through the door. Gaining access is an ongoing process of negotiation and renegotiation. In particular, a crucial role is played by key individuals (termed 'gatekeepers' in the academic literature). Furthermore, such gatekeepers are not necessarily formally 'in charge of' a given institution or group. As with many sites of research, there are often multiple points of entry into an institution or social setting. For example, any research into the existence of an informal subculture among police officers would need to have access to the rank-and-file 'canteen cowboys' rather than the formal policy statements of senior police managers if it is to explore the issue in an adequate fashion (Smith and Gray, 1983; Holdaway, 1984).

Let's take two examples of starkly different phenomena. Compare the ease of access to information about the incidence of possible criminality among London's youthful street populations as against that of the possible unreported crimes of City financiers. **'Studying down'** (that is, studying vulnerable minority groups) is much easier and commonplace in criminology than is **'studying up'** of powerful elites, even in the current recession and the exposure of the scandals over financial malpractice and corporate crimes across the globe. The criminal practices of 'violent, anti-social youth' is subject to much more public scrutiny than the harms and crimes associated with City financiers. City financiers possess a great many resources for maintaining their privacy and freedom from intrusion from researchers who may wish to study such crime as unreported fraud and illegal dealing. Closed doors, many gatekeepers and a privileged culture of privacy will confront any researcher who wishes to study business-suite crime. Undercover 'covert' ethnographic research would be possible but very difficult given the technical knowledge required of any researcher who hopes to overcome the problem of 'passing' as a financier (see Box 14.3).

The gaining of access may be either highly procedurised or personalised (Lee, 1993: 124). An example of a highly procedurised relationship is the conditional access associated with conditions laid down by the Official Secrets Act in the UK. Much of the research undertaken for the Home Office in Britain, for example, would fall into this category of procedurised access, with the Home Office maintaining the right to examine, modify or block any material to be published. In

---

BOX 14.3

COMPARING 'STUDYING DOWN' AND 'STUDYING UP'

Studying down	**Studying up**
Vulnerable minority groups/poor street populations	Powerful elites
Crimes and harms occur in accessible public domains	Crimes and harms occur in inaccessible private domains
Few resources to draw on to insulate from research	Many resources to draw on to insulate from research
Officially defined social problem/irrespectable 'underdog'	Members of respectable society/'overdog'

contrast, a more personalised mode of access often involves a designated 'chaper-one' to escort the researcher down the 'corridors' of the research process. Such access may also be very restricted in that despite this apparent openness, in reality the researcher is sent down wrong corridors into a cul-de-sac or the personalised chaperone may seek to control the nature of the information gathered.

There is often likely to be an imbalance of power between the 'insider' gate-keeper and the 'outsider' researcher which will lead to bargaining between the two parties: the so-called research bargain. If research is viewed as potentially threaten-ing, the process may generate what is often termed 'the politics of distrust', whereby each side is suspicious and secretive about the activities of the other. Perhaps unsurprisingly, gatekeepers tend to prefer methods which are thought to deliver 'hard facts' and which, as a result, offer the gatekeeper some scope for scrutiny and control. This explains the attraction for gatekeepers and sponsors of quantitative surveys and questionnaires rather than qualitative observation and interviews. This is illustrated by one example of an evaluation research project I led into a renowned multi-agency diversion and crime prevention unit in Northamptonshire in the mid-1990s (Hughes et al., 1998). This research involved quite sensitive and strained negotiations and bargaining about the balance of detailed qualitative interviews and observation to explore the (hidden) history of the unit in question (one of the research team's main intellectual interests) and the senior management of the unit's wish to get seemingly 'hard' quantitative data showing the 'success' of the Diversion Unit in reducing re-offending. It is also important to note that there is also a hierarchy of consent and differences in power between members in all formal organisations. It would be very dangerous for researchers to assume that 'superiors' (that is, formal gatekeepers) have the right to allow 'subordinates' (in organisational terms) to be investigated. In reality it is not uncommon for researchers to get formal physical access without the accom-panying informal social access. This may be termed 'the micro-politics of research'. This situation should alert you to the significance of informal gatekeepers who may erect unofficial barriers to the research process (see Box 14.4).

Examples from police research studies more generally illustrate that it is very difficult to negotiate successful access to the routine operation of the criminal justice system and its practitioners (McLaughlin, 2007). Nevertheless, the growing body of research on the rank-and-file police officer has uncovered some key find-ings with regard to such phenomena as the role of discretion in routine police decision-making and the importance of the informal occupational 'cop culture' in moulding rank-and-file attitudes and behaviour. However, very little remains known of the life of the men and the (few) women at the top of the police force and other criminal justice agencies. Access to elites in the criminal justice system is rare for researchers, but see Jones and Newburn (2007) as a rare example of elite **ethnography**. Another exception to this rule is Robert Reiner's study of chief con-stables in England and Wales (Reiner, 1991). It would be a salutary lesson for any budding 'elite studies' researcher to read Reiner's frank reflections on the attenu-ated process of negotiating access to the chief constables which accompanied his **research proposal** (see Reiner, 1991: Chapter 3).

BOX 14.4

PROCEDURISED AND PERSONALISED ACCESS: FORMAL AND INFORMAL GATEKEEPERS

It is not uncommon for researchers to get formal physical access without the accompanying informal social access. One illustrative example exemplifies these complex negotiations.

In Magee and Brewer's ethnographic research on the then Royal Ulster Constabulary (RUC) (Brewer and Magee, 1991), access to the force was granted eventually by senior officers. Allowing such research to take place during the troubles was deemed to be a good public relations exercise and would show that the often secretive and closed police force was open to public scrutiny. There was thus a pay-off for senior echelons of the RUC in terms of their professional ethos and legitimacy. However, it was likely that the research would be less popular with the rank-and-file police officers, who ran the risks of answering awkward questions and being observed doing their often 'messy' work. Having successfully jumped the first gate of the senior 'gatekeepers', Magee had a much more difficult task gaining 'social' access through the informal gate of the rank-and-file police officers and their occupational culture. Gaining the trust of this group was to prove a long-drawn-out process, in Brewer's words 'a result of a progressive series of negotiations ... continually negotiated' (Brewer and Magee, 1991: 19).

Apart from the rarity of 'studying up' on the elites of the crime control institutions, it is also highly probable that researchers are 'checked out' by information-gathering institutions such as the police in terms of their previous work and ideological-political leaning. Quite often the researcher's reputation will precede him or her. This may create complex problems for the researcher in 'passing over' as a legitimate person. There is the likelihood that as a researcher you will be tested and face unofficial 'rites of passage'. As a researcher, it is not uncommon to hear stories from the researched about the character and outcomes of previous research and researchers. One example from research I undertook in the early 1990s on the development of community safety partnerships involved comments from senior police officers with regard to a previous (now eminent) researcher who was studying victims' and offenders' treatment by the police they encountered. This researcher had subsequently become commonly known in this particular police force as the 'study and snitch' researcher since she seemed to them to be friendly during the research and then produced what they thought was a damning written report and book. Whatever the rights and wrongs of this case, it is a useful illustration of the type of informal barriers to access that may be erected by institutions following earlier research experiences.

Collecting the data

The above example of a sense of betrayal felt by the researched leads to the next stage of the research process, namely the gathering of data, and also to the issue of the extent to which 'informed consent' is required for ethically sound research (see Wahidin and Moore, this volume). You will now be aware that the collection of data is far from a purely technical exercise, but is itself a form of political activity. Most research, as we have noted, is carried out on the relatively powerless. Exposé research of dominant elites and institutions is the exception rather than the rule, but it is alive and well in critical criminology. For example, Hudson argues that one of the defining characteristics of critical social science is that it works 'on behalf of those on the downside of power relations' (Hudson, 1993: 7). Worrall's (1990) research on the regulatory discourses surrounding female lawbreakers also deliberately avoided asking such questions as 'why certain women offend', since this might perpetuate dominant practices and ideologies with regard to what Worrall argues are oppressed women. Instead of re-treading the traditional path of searching for causation and aetiology, Worrall, in collecting her data, sought to 'examine the ways in which the authorization of professionals and experts to define certain women as being the type of woman who requires treatment, management, control, or punishment serves to perpetuate the oppression of all women' (Worrall, 1990: 4). This was done by studying 15 female lawbreakers, together with 'experts' such as magistrates, solicitors, psychiatrists and probation officers.

In contrast to such critical research, but in other ways similarly potentially 'partisan' and involved, is research which is fully supported by the agency being investigated. Waddington's (1991) research into armed weapons training and public order policing policies of the Metropolitan Police offers an interesting illustration of what some would see as 'criminology from above'. In discussing his data collection, Waddington, himself an ex-police officer, appears to be very much an 'insider' with easy access to the normally hidden world, receiving, as he notes, 'the fullest co-operation from ... all ranks of the Metropolitan Police' (Waddington, 1991: 271). There is much to recommend in this study 'from the inside' of changing police policy and practice, given its privileged access to gathering data rarely available to the outside researcher. At the same time, questions may be raised as to the detachment and objectivity of a researcher who becomes very closely involved with, and possibly on the side of, the research participants. In the course of his overt **participant observational** research, Waddington arrives at the conclusion that there are distinct advantages both for the police and citizens in the existence of a professional and specialised paramilitary policing strategy.

That an individual should be informed of the nature of research in which he or she is a subject, and its likely dissemination, may seem an undeniable right to which any human is entitled. Indeed, in most of the social sciences there are codes of practice which seek to establish this entitlement as part of the working philosophy of researchers (see Wahidin and Moore, this volume). The value of such guidelines is that they acknowledge explicitly the power relations between researcher and researched. They are particularly helpful in protecting the vulnerable from exploitation by researchers. Furthermore, they have the ethically powerful appeal of being open and honest about the actions and outcomes of the work undertaken by the researcher. It is likely that research conducted along these lines will maintain a reasonable level of public trust. However, critics of such guidelines point to the danger that research organised on the basis of informed consent may not uncover important data since the cooperation of the research participants should be sought and those with things to hide may be unwilling to allow research to be undertaken! This would limit the capacity for critical exposé research of the powerful. More generally, it might be argued that life itself involves lies and distrust and, as a consequence, such codes are a denial of reality.

Clearly not all research in criminology has been characterised by openness and informed consent in the manner of its data collection. Covert or undercover research negates the principle of informed consent, as those being researched cannot refuse involvement. Controversially, it may be argued that certain types of research of necessity need to be covert and lacking informed consent. This claim applies in particular to research on the powerful and the privileged. Overt research, according to this argument, favours the rich and the powerful. As Benyon has remarked: 'Historically the rich and powerful have encouraged hagiography, not critical investigation' (quoted in Lee, 1993: 8).

Where research is threatening, the relationship between the researcher and the researched is likely to become hedged about with mistrust, concealment and dissimulation (Lee, 1993: 2). This viewpoint is relevant to studying not just the very powerful, but any group with vested interests, for example bakery workers and their illicit 'perks of the job' studied by Ditton in the 1970s. Ditton is not concerned by the accusation of subterfuge with regard to his own undercover gathering of data on the routine fiddling in the 'Wellbread' bakery: 'Without reliance on some subterfuge the practices of subterfuge will not be opened to analysis' (Ditton, 1977: 10). However, other commentators *are* concerned about the ethics of such deceitful research. Criminologists are thus faced with a difficult balancing act between the quest for greater human knowledge and harm done to individuals in the pursuit of this goal. But there is a powerful argument that researchers need to compromise. Such compromises may involve the criminological researcher in complicity in wrongdoing – for example, the witnessing of malpractice among the police, witnessing illegalities while being a participant observer of young offenders or being a non-participant observer of drug dealing. Some accommodation to, and appreciation of, the world of the deviant/wrongdoer may be necessary for the successful gathering of data in some criminological research.

Publishing the results

When research findings are published, criminologists enter another political arena in which the researcher has to take account of a variety of audiences, including:

- research participants
- sponsors and funders
- the public or various publics
- other academics

It is highly probable that all these audiences will have distinct, differing and possibly conflicting expectations, and that there will be people who feel damaged and threatened by the publication of criminological research findings. On occasions, criminological researchers themselves may be threatened as a result of their conclusions and policy recommendations which question certain vested interests. For example, Walters' (1997) research on gun control in New Zealand resulted in him receiving hate mail and telephone calls from members of the pro-gun lobby in that country.

It has already been noted that criminological research may be subject to state censorship. In the past, research has occasionally been subject to legal writs regarding defamation. In the British context, Baldwin and McConville's (1977) research into plea-bargaining remains one of the most famous examples of research which met pressure for censorship of its findings. Baldwin and McConville's research uncovered worryingly high rates of informal bargaining and negotiation as to the plea despite the formal denial in law that such practices existed at that time in England's adversarial system of justice. Evidence was found of defendants being persuaded to change their plea from innocent to guilty as a result of pressure, often from their own legal representatives. The project unearthed evidence that due process and adversarial justice were routinely undermined in practice in the Crown Courts. There thus appeared to be a gulf between what is often called the 'law in books' and the 'law in action'.

Baldwin and McConville's *Negotiated Justice* (1977) remains an instructive if extreme exemplar of the politics of publishing. Prior to its publication, the authors were confronted with a public controversy emanating from the Senate of the Inns of Court and representatives of the legal profession's elite, the Bar. The legal establishment in England was set against the publication of the study. Only after a prolonged series of negotiations, in which external academic consultants were commissioned to check the **validity** of the research findings, did the research get the go-ahead for publication from the university to which the researchers belonged. In the longer term, it is worth pointing out the undeniable value of the work in opening up the criminal justice system to critical scrutiny and more open accountability.

Utilising the research

Traditionally, in the UK the highest profile utilisation (and non-utilisation) of criminological research has been that associated with government departments like the Home Office, alongside high-profile though rare royal commissions and inquiries. Routinely, commissions collect evidence, analyse the problem, report publicly and make recommendations for governmental action. For example, in arriving at their conclusions, Royal Commissions on Criminal Justice have drawn on criminological research evidence, although the extent of academic research influence is a matter of some controversy. It is often argued that the possibility of a political or ideological consensus at times appears to be a more important factor than the most accurate explanation of events. There is a long history of political neglect of research-based policy recommendations. The 1993 Royal Commission on Criminal Justice (RCCJ) or the Runciman Commission, so named after its chair, is a useful illustration of this point (see Box 14.5).

BOX 14.5

CALLING CRIMINAL JUSTICE TO ACCOUNT? ACADEMIC RESEARCH AND THE ROYAL COMMISSION ON CRIMINAL JUSTICE 1993

Let's begin by placing this Commission in its political context. The Home Secretary announced the establishment of a RCCJ in 1991 on the day when the 'Birmingham Six' (six individuals wrongly convicted for terrorist bombings) were released after 16 years of imprisonment. The brief of the Commission seemed to be to address the many problems associated with unsafe convictions and there is little doubt that its setting up was an exercise in addressing a widely perceived crisis of legitimacy in the criminal justice system. When eventually established, the terms of reference of the Commission were to examine the workings of the system from the stage at which police investigations of alleged criminal offences occur right through to the point at which the defendant has exhausted his or her rights of appeal. Furthermore, the emphasis moved from that of wrongful convictions to encompass effectiveness in securing convictions and the efficient use of resources (Field and Thomas, 1994: 2).

To assist the Commission in its work, a programme of academic research was commissioned and organised by the Home Office Research and Statistics Department. When the Commission came to make its 352 recommendations, the response from much of the academic community was anger and disappointment at the neglect of its research. Viewed critically, the RCCJ has been termed a Commission, which 'normalizes injustice' (Bridges, 1994). In order to understand the controversy over the apparent non-utilisation of academic research by the RCCJ, some of its key recommendations need to be outlined.

The RCCJ rejected most of the academic suggestions put to it that were aimed at reducing the likelihood that the innocent would be convicted. That noted, the RCCJ did make some important recommendations with regard to the 'efficiency' of the criminal justice system such as that, in cases of either way offences, the defendant should no longer have a right to trial by jury. Pre-trial disclosure of defence evidence was extended and plea-bargaining was more overtly accepted with a higher discount for an early plea. More scope for procedures which clarified issues before trial was also recommended. As two leading legal scholars, Field and Thomas (1994: 4) conclude, the Commission's most radical proposals went in the opposite direction, of greater safeguards against miscarriages of justice because of its focus on greater efficiency. Higher standards for both police and defence lawyers were recommended and an end to the right to silence was rejected.

Following the publication of its report, the utilisation by the government of the RCCJ's recommendations was highly selective and this illustrates the complex ways in which research and its policy recommendations are liable to be refracted, if not ignored, by dominant political

(Continued)

(Continued)

discourses. Addressing the Conservative Party Conference on 6 October 1993, the Home Secretary, Michael Howard, announced the unveiling of a dramatic and draconian 'law and order package'. As Field and Thomas (1994: 7) again note:

All the penal lessons that had been painfully learnt in the early 80s were lost in a scramble for a law and order rhetoric with popular appeal. Inconvenient evidence was simply ignored. In this process, the Runciman Commission was cannibalized: anything that could be presented as a contribution to cost-effective crime control became an urgent political priority. Other issues could wait. Some of the announced changes follow the Runciman Report closely; others flatly reject the majority view or simply cut across the Commission's assumptions.

The broad message seems to be that governments are able to pick and choose which pieces of informed recommendations to accept and which to banish from the populist 'law and order' discourse, or discreetly shelve.

From the above outline of the history of the 1993 RCCJ, it should be clear that politics plays a central and determining role in the ways in which research will be utilised, or not, as the case may be, in policy-making. During this same period of Michael Howard's tenure as Home Secretary, it appeared that ministers were preventing publication of evaluation research from within the Home Office which contradicted Howard's proclaimed 'law and order crackdown' and 'prisons work' credo (*The Guardian*, 4 July 1994). However, it is not only governments who will be selective in their use and political manipulation of evidence. It is evident that other political actors, including pressure groups, in the 'crime control industry' also use research findings selectively. Accordingly, NACRO (National Association for the Care and Rehabilitation of Offenders), formerly a radical, left-of-centre pressure group, together with the Audit Commission (1996), has used research on multi-agency crime prevention in a selective manner in order to make its case for reparation and multi-agency crime prevention partnerships to government as an alternative to more traditional approaches to dealing with offending. For example, in an article entitled 'Diversion tactics', in *The Guardian* (Society section) of 26 August 1998, a NACRO spokesperson painted a simplified message of one of this author's own research study's tentative and very qualified findings on the effects of this Diversion Unit in reducing re-offending (see Hughes et al., 1998). Selective use of research findings is therefore not the preserve of party politicians, but instead characterises much of the policy-making politics in the crime control 'business' across the ideological spectrum.

SUMMARY

This chapter has explored the realities of doing criminological research in what is the highly politicised world of studying human conflicts and exchanges between actors in different positions of power and influence which make up the worlds of crimes and controls. It is evident that criminological research does not occur in a metaphorical germ-free, antiseptic zone for all the discipline's vital claims to degrees of (social) scientific expertise. In particular, you will now be aware of the influence of politics at all six key stages of the research process from 'getting started' to 'utilising the research'. We need to be especially wary of the talk of the end of politics and rise of non-political technical fixes for research. Such talk is likely to usher in very restrictive research agendas for criminology. Furthermore, it is impossible to envisage a time when criminological research will not generate the types of political controversy and dilemma discussed in this chapter. However, the importance of the long-term influence of criminological research on both the policy and political process should not be lost. Indeed, criminological research over time, and as a result of its capacity to generate organised controversy as well as systematic, rigorous and falsifiable evidence for truth claims, has helped in its modest way to redraw the frameworks employed in the often over-heated political discourses on law and order and tackling the problem of crime.

■ Study Questions/Activities for Students

1   What are the major ethical and political issues, broadly defined, which are associated with your own research project at university?

2   Imagine you have been asked to undertake ethnographic research on a group of young people suspected of engaging in anti-social behaviour in your locality. What major obstacles are you likely to face in trying to undertake this sensitive research at the six key stages distinguished in this chapter?

3   Following on from question 2, think through the challenges you would face in trying to research from 'the inside' the misdemeanours and possible crimes of city bankers, with whom you have been granted a six-month placement. What major obstacles are you likely to face in trying to undertake this sensitive research at the six key stages distinguished in this chapter?

4   Ask your lecturers in criminology and PhD students at your university about their own experiences of the 'play of power and politics' in some of their own research, past and present. Do the issues raised by criminological researchers in your own institution correspond to some of the issues in this chapter?

RESOURCES

The most comprehensive and authoritative text on social research methods, covering the range of issues from epistemology, research strategy and design right through the key techniques and skills is Alan Bryman's *Social Research Methods* (2004/2008). This text also has a brief but useful Chapter 25 on normative and political aspects of social research. The section on political aspects draws extensively on my chapter in the first edition of this book (Hughes, 2000).

In terms of criminology methods, the following are very useful source texts:

Jupp, V. (1989) *Methods of Criminological Research.* London: Routledge. This book has some valuable discussion throughout of the political contexts and institutional constraints within which much criminological research is undertaken.

King, M. and Wincup, E. (2007) *Researching Crime and Justice.* Oxford: Oxford University Press. See especially Chapter 2 by Morgan and Hough on 'The politics of criminological research' and Parts 3 and 4 for vivid accounts of real-life research on criminals and victims and crime control agencies.

REFERENCES

Audit Commission (1996) *Misspent Youth.* London: Audit Commission.

Baldwin, J. and McConville, M. (1977) *Negotiated Justice.* Oxford: Martin Robertson.

Becker, H. (1967) 'Whose side are we on?', *Criminology and Criminal Justice*, 9 (3): 359–78.

Brewer, J. and Magee, K. (1991) *Inside the RUC: Routine Policing in a Divided Society.* Oxford: Oxford University Press.

Bridges, L. (1994) 'Normalizing injustice', *Journal and Society*, 21 (1): 20–34.

Brogden, M. and Shearing, C. (1993) *Policing for a New South Africa.* London: Routledge.

Bryman, A. (2004/2008) *Social Research Methods.* Oxford: Oxford University Press.

Carr, P. (2010) 'The problem with experimental criminology: a response to Sherman's "Evidence and Liberty"', *Criminology and Criminal Justice*, 10 (1): 3–10.

Cohen, S. and Taylor, L. (1972) *Psychological Survival.* Harmondsworth: Penguin.

Cohen, S. and Taylor, L. (1977) 'Talking about prison blues', in C. Bell and H. Newby (eds), *Doing Sociological Research.* London: Allen and Unwin.

Downes, D. (ed.) (1992) *Unravelling Criminal Justice: Eleven British Studies*. Basingstoke: Macmillan.

Edwards, A. and Hughes, G. (2009) 'Crime, science and politics', European Society of Criminology conference paper, Lubijyana: European Society of Criminology.

Field, S. and Thomas, P. (1994) 'Justice and efficiency? The Royal Commission on Criminal Justice', *Journal of Law and Society* 21 (1): 1–19.

Hallsworth, S. and Silverstone, D. (2009) 'That's life innit: a British perspective on guns, crime and social order', *Criminology and Criminal Justice*, 9 (3): 359–78.

Heidensohn, F. and Gelsthorpe, L. (2007) 'Gender and crime', in M. Maguire et al. (eds), *Oxford Handbook of Criminology*. Oxford: Oxford University Press.

Hudson, B. (1993) *Penal Policy and Social Justice.* London: Macmillan.

Hughes, G. (1998) *Understanding Crime Prevention: Social Control, Risk and Late Modernity*. Buckingham: Open University Press.

Hughes, G. (2007) *The Politics of Crime and Community*. Basingstoke: Palgrave.

Hughes, G., Leisten, R. and Pilkington, A. (1998) 'Diversion in a culture of severity', *Howard Journal of Criminal Justice*, 37 (1): 16–33.

Jones, T. and Newburn, T. (2007) *Policy Transfer and Criminal Justice.* Buckingham: Open University Press.

King, M. and McDermott, K. (1992) 'Control, security and humane containment in the penal system in England and Wales', in D. Downes (ed.), *Unravelling Criminal Justice: Eleven British Studies.* Basingstoke: Macmillan.

Lee, R.M. (1993) *Doing Research on Sensitive Topics*. London: Sage.

McLaughlin, E. (2007) *The New Policing*. London: Sage.

Morgan, R. and Hough, M. (2007) 'The politics of criminological research', in M. King and E. Wincup (eds), *Researching Crime and Justice*. Oxford: Oxford University Press.

Morgan, R. and Liebling, A. (2007) 'Imprisonment: an expanding scene', in M. Maguire et al. (eds), *Oxford Handbook of Criminology*. Oxford: Oxford University Press.

Radzinowicz, L. (1994) 'Reflections on the state of criminology', *British Journal of Criminology*, 34 (2): 99–104.

Reiner, R. (1991) *Chief Constables.* Oxford: Oxford University Press.

Roberts, C. and Innes, M. (2009) 'The death of Dixon?', *Criminology and Criminal Justice*, 9(2)3: 125–34.

Smith, D. and Gray, J. (1983) *The Police and the People in London.* London: Policy Studies Institute.

Waddington, P. (1991) *The Strong Arm of the Law.* Oxford: Clarendon Press.

Walters, R. (1997) 'Gun control in New Zealand'. Paper delivered at Australian and New Zealand Criminology Conference, Wellington, July.

Worrall, A. (1990) *Offending Women: Female Lawbreakers and the Criminal Justice System.* London: Routledge.

FIFTEEN
CRITICAL REFLECTION AS RESEARCH METHODOLOGY

BARBARA HUDSON

Chapter Contents

KEY POINTS

This chapter:

- Offers personal critical reflection on being an academic researcher
- Explores the contours of critical reflection
- Reflexively examines research strategy
- Introduces the key elements of critical criminology
- Traces the stages that critical criminology goes through
- Explores the stages of doing critical criminological analysis

---

INTRODUCTION

My chapter in the first edition of *Doing Criminological Research* drew mainly on my own experiences of doing research during the 1980s and 1990s. For most of the 1980s, I had worked as a researcher looking at criminal justice alongside, or as a member of, criminal justice agencies. The topics I carried forward as an academic researcher were drawn from the concerns of the agencies I worked with and for: youth crime from 1981 to 1985, and then from 1985 to 1989, sentencing patterns, and race and criminal justice.

Moving to the University of Northumbria in 1989, my interest was in putting these research interests into a criminological/social context, moving from showing probation officers and social workers what was happening, to seeking explanations of why they were happening. *Penal Policy and Social Justice* (Hudson, 1993) represented my work in finding explanations for questions raised by developments in penal policy and practice in the 1980s. Two general threads bound my various **research questions** together: why had the crime and punishment framework become so dominant over alternative frames, for example health and welfare?; and what was the impact of criminal justice on powerless or minority groups? These concerns led me to the works of criminologists and socio-legal writers who were asking questions about race, about the treatment of female offenders, about the difference between crimes which were serious in terms of the harm they caused and crimes which were taken seriously by politicians and the media, and about why the use of imprisonment persisted in spite of its obvious failure in terms of re-offending rates and in deterring crime. I was drawn to writers, including Pat Carlen, Stanley Cohen, Paul Gilroy, Richard Sparks, Jonathan Simon and others who were asking what seemed to me the important questions and who looked for answers in wider social theory rather than the narrow confines of so-called 'administrative criminology' and **policy-related research**. In other words, I discovered '**critical criminology**'.

In this chapter for the second edition, I am drawing on my own research in the 2000s, and on the methodological issues that have arisen regularly with my research students, whether working on PhD, Masters by research, or undergraduate projects or dissertations. Although there has been a shift in my topics – from sentencing to immigration and terrorism, which reflects developments in policy and in the events which have prompted policy – the essential concern has been the same, to look at questions affecting the poor, the marginalised and the excluded. This chapter looks at work I have done since the publication of *Justice in the Risk Society* (Hudson, 2003a). That book ended with questions of human rights, and of justice for strangers, those with whom we feel no sense of community. My work since then has investigated different aspects of 'doing justice to strangers'.

My research students look at a wide range of topics: women's imprisonment; human rights in prisons; gendered violence in minority communities; the legal response to women who kill abusive husbands; policies and penalties for drug crime; religious freedom and human rights; immigration; diversity and policing; and detention under mental health legislation. They do, however, all tend to be students with critical perspectives and passionate concerns for justice. Although their topics may differ, the research students I supervise tend to have similar approaches and similar methodological issues. Their starting point is often some perceived injustice or ineffectiveness in criminal justice policy which they have encountered perhaps in their own employment or personal lives, or through their studies. They are concerned not only to contribute to academic understanding of the issues, but to produce evidence and insights which can contribute to reform of policies and practices.

Another thing my students tend to have in common is that they dread writing their methodology chapter or section. Partly this is impatience – they want to be working on the issues that drew them to the subject, not methodology. More, though, it is because they find it difficult to think of much of their work in terms of methodology. Many methodology courses and texts concentrate primarily on research with people – interviews, questionnaires, focus groups and so on – or with material such as media reports, so that much of what these students are doing does not seem like 'real research' but background reading. Critical reflection, however, involves analysing literature, law and policy, statistics, proposals by reformers and other documentary material, and may not involve research with live subjects at all, or if it does, there will probably be only a small amount of live subject research, with most of the work being analysis of texts and other documentary material.

This chapter, then, is about research *strategy*: choosing what to examine; adopting a standpoint from which to ask questions; generating questions; selecting a theory or perspective from which to critique theories, policies and practices. The methods used will typically be a mix of content analysis, interpretation of statistics, semi-structured interviews, comparing literature on the topic coming from different criminological traditions, so that the researcher will need to draw on the methodology literature on the different kinds of data to be collected (many of these research techniques are dealt with in this volume). Different research techniques may be needed for different sections of the research, what will provide coherence to the work are its aims and objectives, the questions asked, and the critical standpoint adopted. While there will almost always be a literature survey which is part of the background reading rather than being data generated in the course of the research, the other materials need to be analysed by addressing the research questions to them, rather than presenting them in a purely descriptive or summarising way.

WHAT IS 'CRITICAL' ABOUT 'CRITICAL CRIMINOLOGY'?

More years ago than I care to admit, one of the essays I wrote for the social philosophy option on my MA degree concerned the concept 'critical'. What, the essay question asked, was the meaning of 'critical' in philosophy? Enlightenment philosopher Immanuel Kant had distinguished critical concepts from metaphysical concepts. Critical concepts were concepts that were aware of their range of application, their limitations, and their contexts. In the twentieth century, and in social science rather than philosophy, 'metaphysical' came to be replaced by the term 'ideological', but the difference was the same: ideological/metaphysical concepts are presented as limitless in their application, and somehow without precise origin or construction. They are, as critical theorists say, unaware of their *conditions of possibility*. Ideological terms that are familiar to most of us include precepts such as 'markets must decide': but why must they decide, what must they decide, who says that markets must decide and in whose interests must they be left to decide?

'Critical Theory' is associated first with a group of scholars attached to the Frankfurt Institute of Social Science in Germany who were publishing work across a range of disciplines in the 1930s. During the Second World War some of them moved to the USA, but some remained in Germany. Among the first generation of Frankfurt writers, probably the best known are Theodor Adorno, Walter Benjamin, Max Horkheimer and Herbert Marcuse. As (mainly) Jewish scholars, they not surprisingly undertook a series of investigations of the rise of the Fascist state. They analysed the development of the authoritarian personality (Adorno), the displacement of a liberal aesthetic in culture (Benjamin) and the rise of a politics of repression (Marcuse). Their overall quest was to investigate the conditions of possibility of the rise of Fascism in Germany, formerly the model of a liberal, tolerant, cultured society.[1]

In its early phase, before the rise of Nazism, the critical theorists of the Frankfurt School had become known for their opposition to **positivism**. Leaders of the first wave of Critical Theory – Adorno and Horkheimer – wrote incisive critiques about the application of the positivist methodology of the natural sciences to social sciences, arguing against the idea that one methodological approach is best for all possible disciplines and themes. The critique of positivism also contested the possibility of **value-free knowledge**, insisting that all knowledge is interest and value-bound. I encountered this debate during my MA studies, and had no difficulty in choosing which side I was on!

As well as insisting on the centrality of values and interests in, for example, choosing topics of inquiry, in the questions the researcher chooses to ask and in the means by which knowledge is sought, critical theory has drawn attention to the interpretation of information. Critical theory is known as a 'dialectical' perspective (Jay, 1973). The basic dialectic is that between experience and our already-existing ideas and categories, ideas and categories which are constantly formulated and reformulated through conventional understandings ('common sense'), through political and cultural ideas, and of course through the theories we encounter as students and researchers. All our acts of interpretation, according to critical theorist Gadamer, come about through a 'fusion of horizons' of what we experience or investigate, and what we already bring with us (Palmer, 1969: 194–217).

Critical theory urges us not to disguise our values and our pre-existing knowledge and interpretations in order to pass off our research as 'objective', but to be open about them. The goal of the Frankfurt School scholars was *emancipation*; their investigations were to contribute to the emancipation of the poor and downtrodden, of those who were trapped by hegemonic ideas and who were cut off from the means of their own emancipation through poverty, marginalisation, and lack of access to ideas that challenge dominant modes of thinking. Oppression

---

[1] The themes of the Frankfurt School are explained and analysed in Jay (1973) and a selection of readings is provided in Connerton (1976: Part 3).

through politics, tradition, and also through culture, the hegemony of ideas that were specific to one class and yet promoted as though they were relevant to all sections of society, and the way people came to accept political, economic and social arrangements that were not in their interest, were the targets of much of their work. These were themes in Marxist analysis, and so for these Frankfurt critical theorists, the horizon of value and of conceptualisation that they brought to their encounters and investigations was that of Marxism. Although there were differences between members of the School, and with different streams of Marxist thought, critical theory retained and reworked the principal ideas of Marxist analysis of capitalist society. Critical theory has also drawn on Freud and other psychoanalytic theorists.

The most well-known of the second generation of critical theorists is probably Jürgen Habermas. His theory of communicative ethics has been influential with contemporary social theorists. It has two themes in particular. First, his idea of restricted and distorted speech, which carries on the emancipatory goal through identifying barriers to inclusion of certain groups to the dominant discourses of modern states. His second is the trend for moral and political concerns to be displaced from discourse, with only economic and instrumental aspects of issues considered. His ideas have been taken up by contemporary social theorists such as Iris Young (1990) and Nancy Fraser (1992), who are concerned with the inclusion of marginalised groups in democratic deliberations.

CRITICAL THEORY AND CRITICAL CRIMINOLOGY

'If Critical Theory was a creation of the early thirties, it was also a discovery of the late sixties' (Connerton, 1976: 12). There are clearly strong affinities between Frankfurt School themes, its opposition to positivism, its emancipatory objectives, and critical criminology. One Frankfurt scholar well known to those interested in prisons and punishment is Otto Kirchheimer, who with Georg Rusche wrote the first 'revisionist' history of the use of imprisonment. *Punishment and Social Structure* (1968 [1939]) broke from the tradition of seeing the rise of the prison as the primary form of punishment as an unbroken humanitarian advance, seeing it rather as a penal form particularly compatible with capitalist social-economic structure, and linking imprisonment rates and conditions with the value of and demand for labour. This groundbreaking book was first published in the 1930s and 'rediscovered' and republished in the late 1960s (Rusche and Kirchheimer, 1968 [1939]). By the 1980s, looking at imprisonment in relation to the labour market had become well established (Melossi and Pavarini, 1981; Box, 1987, *inter alia*).

The themes of authoritarianism, displacement of liberal tolerance, and the politics of repression have obvious relevance to more contemporary criminological and criminal justice themes, such as the rise of authoritarian populist penal politics; changing images of offenders from the deprived to the depraved; racism and repression of the powerless. Research investigating ideologies in crime and punishment using conceptual frameworks owing much to Frankfurt School approaches appeared in works in the 1980s by Stuart Hall, Paul Gilroy and others at the Centre for Contemporary Studies (Gilroy, 1982; Hall et al., 1978), and by Phil Scraton (1987) and colleagues. Hall, Gilroy and their colleagues investigated the criminalisation of black youth, showing how the perception of black communities as revealed in successive editions of police training manuals and in press reports, showed a move from police and politicians regarding black communities much like any others – law-abiding communities with a small minority of troublemakers – to seeing whole communities as law-less and hostile, as 'no-go areas' where police could expect little or no cooperation. Scraton (1987) and Hall (1980) and their co-authors looked at aspects of the 'authoritarian state', recording the rise of repression and the clamp-down on the poor and the unconventional; in Hall's terms the drift into a 'law-and-order society'.

These critical analysts of authoritarianism have drawn extensively on writers in the Marxist tradition of ideology critique. Gramsci's idea of hegemony, the dominance of world views that serve the interests of a particular class, is especially prominent. These were 'critical' investigations, exposing the politics and practices of law and order, punishment and repression as ideologies.

The investigations of the rise of Nazism in the 1930s and its effects over a wide range of social spheres has its counterpart in contemporary criminology in looking at the rise of social authoritarianism, exclusionary and repressive penalities in the era of what has come to be known as neo-liberalism, in which one of the primary and most pernicious of ideological concepts was that markets must be left to operate freely. Under this neo-liberal ideology of the untouchability of markets, governments were not allowed to intervene in the economic field. This posed a clear dilemma for countries such as the UK where weak governments are deplored, so that governments needed to demonstrate sovereignty and strength through some other field (Gamble, 1988). Dramatising crime served the purposes of neo-liberal governments well: crime called for ever-increased government activism (Simon, 2007). Best of all for those in power, dramatising crime shifts the blame for social problems away from government policies, factors such as structural unemployment, and central values of capitalism such as competitive individualism, and on to the poor and powerless themselves (Young, J., 1997).

Like the Frankfurt School analysts, critical criminology has also been strongly opposed to positivism. Critical criminology has not set itself to be a predictive science, or to be concerned with formulating causal laws. David Matza's critique of positivism as a mode of doing criminology, rather than of individual positivist theories, has been taken up by authors of, for example, *The New Criminology* (Taylor et al., 1973).

Critical criminology generally shares the emancipatory ideals of Critical Theory. Critical criminologists take seriously Howard Becker's question of 'whose side are we on?', and their answer is, usually, the side of the powerless, the marginalised and the excluded. In different contexts, 'the powerless, the marginalised and the excluded' may mean women, children, race/ethnic/cultural minorities, sexual minorities, non-citizens, prisoners, victims, but critical criminology is always on the side of those on the downside of power.

CRITICAL THEORY AND CRITICAL CRIMINOLOGY

Rejection of positivism

- Denial of the possibility of value free-knowledge
- Acknowledgement of value-base – on the side of the powerless

Critique of ideology

- Interest in discourse/ideology/conditions of possibility of cultural and political ideas and beliefs, and of policies and practices deriving from them

An example – race, crime and justice

- A critical approach focuses on why certain ethnic minorities are associated with crime, and are under-protected and over-penalised by criminal justice

- *Critical questions* – how do certain crimes, e.g. mugging, come to be seen as 'black crimes'? Why do police think of Afro-Caribbean or Muslim communities as no-go areas? And how do police–minority interactions reinforce negative stereotypes of each other? How is it that certain groups, especially black males, are readily seen as likely offenders but less readily recognised as victims? Why are black women less likely than white women to be credible as victims of rape? Why are black women less likely to receive community penalties than white women?

- *Critical concepts* – criminalisation, moral panics, suspect communities, ideal victims and suitable enemies

MICHEL FOUCAULT AND CRITICAL CRIMINOLOGY

Contemporary critical criminologists often draw on the work of Michel Foucault. Foucault's analysis of power: his power/knowledge linkage; the discursive workings of power through constructions of the sane/insane, healthy/sick, normal/deviant; the regulation of sexuality through discursive power; the objectives and mentalities of governance, are among the Foucauldian themes that have come into contemporary critical criminology (Hudson, 2003b). From the late 1970s, criminologists drew on Foucault's ideas of the 'disciplinary' nature of modern penality and the diffusion of the power to punish. Cohen, in particular, documented the spread of the disciplinary mode of the panopticon prison, with its arrangement of mirrors so that guards can see into the cells but prisoners cannot see when they are being watched so must assume they are under observation all the time, through the institutions of social control in the community as well as inside the prison, blurring the boundaries between 'inside' and 'outside' the institution (Cohen, 1979). Recent criminological concern with the spread of surveillance also draws on Foucault: the 'punitive city' is now part of the 'surveillance society', with the CCTV camera rather than the mirrors and prisms of the prison wings the all-seeing panopticon device (Lyon, 1994).

Foucault's ideas have also influenced criminological writings looking at the growing concern with risk and security, at devolving control functions from central government to local agencies and to groups based on coalitions of interest, for example, partnerships of local authorities, businesses and private security providers to ensure 'safe shopping' (Crawford, 1997; Garland, 2001; O'Malley, 1992, 2001). Decentralisation of power and the shift of concern from morality and individual responsibility for crime to an 'actuarial' concern with prevention of future crime and disorder are central concerns of the 'new penology' perspective (Cohen, 1985; Feeley and Simon, 1992). These themes are linked to Foucault's central point in his work on governmentality (Burchell et al., 1991), that the defining task of governments in modern societies is not to demonstrate power through acts such as the torture and death of Damien portrayed at the beginning of *Discipline and Punish* (Foucault, 1977), but to use their power to provide security for their populations. They pursue their aims not by centralising power to themselves but by 'rolling back the state' (Rose, 1996) through a dispersed network of local control (Cohen, 1979; Crawford, 1997).

Critical studies have used Foucault's insights and methods to develop rich understandings of the workings of power in the penal realm. What Foucault does not provide, however, is a critical theory, a world view that plays the same role as Marxism in the Frankfurt School. For researchers with emancipatory objectives, those of us who want our analyses to contribute in however small a way to the promotion of social justice, Foucauldian analysis needs something else: it needs to be complemented by critique from a *standpoint*.

Critical analyses of punishment, critical analyses of the surveillance state, critical analyses of disciplinary penalisation of women and non-hegemonic sexual identities, for example, ally understandings of penality, which may well use concepts and methods derived from Foucault, with a critical standpoint. Human rights, feminism, critical race theory and abolitionism are examples of perspectives which are linked to the standpoint of powerless or marginalised groups, and are used to provide critique of the workings of power revealed by Foucauldian methods and insights. Sim (1990, 2009), for example, draws on Foucault to lay bare the working of power in prisons, but his analysis is anchored in the abolitionist critical perspective. Scott (2006) also uses Foucault's notion of discourse, but shares Sim's abolitionist standpoint and it is this that informs his critique of the lack of a penal culture firmly committed to respecting prisoners' human rights.

DOING CRITICAL RESEARCH: DISCOURSE AND CRITIQUE

Critical criminology research is typically concerned with exposing areas of injustice. The injustice may be a failure to give the protection of law to social groups – women, children, ethnic, religious and sexual minorities suffering gendered violence, hate crimes and abuse; it may be excessive penalisation of some groups;

it may be overuse of imprisonment; it may be failure to take corporate crimes seriously; it may be exposure of crimes of the state such as torture; it may be policies about drug use which lead to more crime and to the devastation of neighbourhoods; it may be discriminatory crime prevention strategies. The research will often involve analysis of policy and practice (policy documents, legislation, use of provisions provided by legislation, reports written by criminal justice workers, policing tactics, for example). Research may study media accounts, reform campaigns, or political rhetoric; it may include a case study of affected groups such as prisoners, victims, residents, campaigners, prison officers, probation officers.

An issue that comes up regularly with research students is that they draft their proposals clearly stating that they are going to collect and interrogate these different types of material, but when they begin to write their methodology chapter, and to analyse their research data, material such as legislation, sentencing statistics, policy documents, campaign literature is not dealt with adequately in the description of methodology or in the analyses. The status of these forms of data becomes blurred as they hover between the literature review, the findings and the discussion. If they do appear in the methodology section or subsequent analytic sections, they tend not to be described in methodological terms and they are not analysed systematically and rigorously. Although most students usually find it easy to say what the purposes of looking at these materials are when describing the objectives of their research, they often struggle to treat them as 'empirical research' as they structure and write the draft dissertation or thesis.

It is in this regard that Foucault's idea of *discourse* is extremely useful. With most of his studies, Foucault's purpose is to interrogate the exercise of power by looking at everything that is said in relation to a particular sphere: madness, delinquency, sexuality, for example. His method is to examine elements of discourse from the point of view of what is said/produced, and from what positions it is said. Who can and does say what? From what position will what is said be given credence? Who has discursive power? On whom is power exercised, and with what effect? How does what is said, and from what positions, come to be constructed as 'truth' or 'reality'? Foucault's idea of discourse clearly directs us to see the different forms of material we look at as part of the research rather than the background to the research. Foucault's analysis of the connections between elements of discourse leads us to look at the context and meaning of discursive products, such as laws, theory, political positions, policies and practices proposed and carried out by different actors, seeing how they fit together, influence each other, how they reveal the social, political and economic contexts and pressures under which they are produced, and disclose the power relations of the speakers and the spoken about.

A critical criminological interest in a topic will yield a research plan to interrogate different elements of discourse, and to critique them, first, in their own terms, and then to critique them from a standpoint which will include a value perspective (ethnic minorities should not be excessively penalised, for example) and a view that a particular theoretical perspective (post-colonial theory, for example) is most likely to yield understandings which could contribute to a reduction of discriminatory criminal justice treatment. Foucault's conception of discourse helps us deal with our material as research by prompting questions about the different discursive elements. The first layer of critical analysis will generate questions suggested by the data itself. For example:

- What are the main principles expressed in this law or policy?
- Who were its promoters; who were its opponents?
- What do statistics tell us about the extent to which new provisions were used by the courts or by the relevant professionals?
- Do outputs (for example, police recording of racially correlated incidents, practice guidelines for dealing with reported rapes, or probation pre-sentence reports) show changes in response to the new legislation or policy?
- Has there been any demonstrable effect on crime rates or re-offending rates?
- Has there been any increase in victim reporting or use of services? For example, has there been an increase in numbers of women from minority communities seeking assistance from statutory or voluntary organisations because of violence or other forms of abuse?

Other forms of discourse, for example media representations or political rhetoric, will yield their own questions, about, for example, changing themes, changing definitions of 'the problem', changing representations of groups. Addressing material in this way clearly marks it as 'research' rather than 'background', because research questions are being asked. Asking questions of the data also means that what is being produced is 'critical analysis', moving on from description which may have been provided in the introduction to the thesis or dissertation, or at the beginning of the sections on the various materials.

This first layer of analysis is a form of critique that is often described as **immanent critique**. Immanent critique is a critique where the questions arise from the material itself; it is not critique which arises from another standpoint. 'Immanent' is a term connected to critique of principles and concepts in the tradition of Kant's critique of metaphysics, and continued in the Frankfurt School ideological critiques. For criminology and socio-legal studies, and for research concerned with materials such as laws, policies, reports, statistics, newspaper reporting, television programmes, etc., rather than philosophical or theoretical concepts, a simpler and probably more accurate term is **internal critique** rather than immanent critique (Lacey, 1993).

The end of this first phase may well be a conclusion that the principles and concepts underlying the policies or laws being studied lead to a closure, a limit to reform, or a brake on effectiveness. The term 'internal' critique can encompass both questions of effects in practice, and the interrogation of principles and concepts. What defines internal critique is that the questions are those generated by the material itself. They are not being asked from an exteral standpoint.

Internal critique, then, takes the objectives of law or policy at face value. One of my research students is concerned with defences and mitigations for women who kill abusive partners.[2] She has analysed cases where self-defence or provocation has been put forward as defence or partial defence, and where it has not. She has looked at circumstances of cases where such defences and arguments have been successful and where they have not, and has also analysed proposals for legislative reform, and the arguments and views of legal professionals and legal academics. While there has been much feminist critique of the failure of mitigations and partial defences in these cases by feminist campaigners, criminologists and socio-legal scholars, this researcher's careful internal critique is bringing into focus the closures inherent in legal constructions of homicide and reasonable fear of death or serious injury, for example. The effect of such closures is often that even the most sympathetic of legal minds appear unable to support or introduce changes in law and interpretation radical enough to afford substantive justice to abused women who kill.

Another research student is working on sexualised violence in Black and Minority Ethnic communities.[3] Again, her analysis of laws, procedures, policies and proposals for change has shown how sincere, well-intentioned policy-makers and professionals can still fail to put in place resources and procedures which encourage women to come forward for help. She demonstrates how lack of attention to some of the specifics of abuse and its effects on Black and Minority Ethnic women, and thinking in over-general or loose categories such as 'women' or 'domestic violence' or slipping into cultural stereotypes, can restrict adequate and appropriate responses to those suffering violence.

Internal critique, then, commonly leads to a point of closure: a point where the definitions, conceptions and underlying assumptions of legal categories, of professional roles and ethics, of social roles and characteristics of social groups, for example, mean that change reaches its limits. In regard to criminological topics concerning women, for instance, this closure is reflected in Celia Wells's (2004) observation that looking at the topics that are the subject of legal concern may give the impression that law has been considerably influenced by feminist arguments, but looking at outcomes shows the same old presumptions and prejudices about women's nature and women's roles.

If internal critique leads to a point of closure, if the presumptions and prejudices involved in classification of crimes, in laws, policies and practices, prove to be the limit or the obstacle to desired change, then the researcher is prompted to move to **external critique**. External critique is the use of a theory or perspective which incorporates the value-stance of the researcher and/or which expresses a counter-standpoint to that exposed by the internal critique. Juxtaposing external critique, the external standpoint, to internal critique is the dialectic of critical theory. The objective of external critique is to raise issues, and to propose values and understandings, that do not arise in internal critique.

While critical criminology continues to show the influence of Marxist analysis – seeing the criminal justice system as being the system that deals with wrongdoings of the poor, while affluent misdeeds are usually dealt with by administrative

---

[2] I am grateful to Susan Evans for allowing me to refer to her research project.
[3] I am also grateful to Helen Monk for allowing me to refer to her research.

regulatory systems, for example – other theoretical perspectives are also drawn on as external critical standpoints. Feminist theory, post-colonial theory, and human rights theory are among the most influential critical perspectives in contemporary criminology.

So far, discussion of internal and external critique has focused on documentary materials – legislation, policy documents, media reports – but what about **interviews**? Criminology research projects often include interviews or discussions with professionals, and with victims, offenders or others affected by the issues that are

---

BOX 15.2

DOING CRITICAL ANALYSIS

The research materials

- Decide on the material to be collected: for example, legislation, policy documents, statistics, media, cases, interviews, etc.
- Decide key points: for example, how far back in time to include documentary materials, who to interview

Internal critique

- Analyse material in its own terms: what are the stated aims and objectives of policy and legislation? What changes or advances are claimed over previous approaches? What principles and criteria are stated? What are the objectives of campaigners, professionals? What are the perspectives and themes of media representations?
- Are the stated objectives achieved, as indicated by statistics, cases, commentaries by media or by professionals?
- Are there any failures or difficulties revealed by official statistics, opinions of professionals or campaigners, media, victims, etc.?

Closures and limits

- Does the material (including interviews and other assessments of the laws, policies, procedures) show any limits to effectiveness or to desired objectives or changes that can be attributed to the ways of thinking about the field being researched and the constructs/ concepts embedded in the materials analysed in the internal critique?

External critique

- From your own chosen perspective/theory/standpoint, how do the assumptions, conceptualisation, existing theoretical and political/professional constructions impede desirable progress?
- What are the limits and problems of existing ways of thinking and acting, and what insights are yielded by your external critique?
- What recommendations for change or development (in theory and practice) emerge from your critique?

---

the topic of the research. Typically in research degree projects, there will be a fairly small number of interview subjects (one prison, one women's refuge, one probation or police area, one estate or neighbourhood, for example) so that this phase of the project is very much a case study rather than a large-scale survey.

Critical criminologists are usually concerned to conduct any interviews or discussions so as to allow their subjects to tell their own stories and raise their own concerns (see Chapters 7 and 13) but will nonetheless want to include questions that will illuminate the central research questions. Interviews will often be semi-structured, to allow for both interviewer and interviewee to raise issues, or sometimes they may take the form of a **life history**, allowing the subject to give her own story, picking out the events that are significant to her.

In analysing interview or group discussion data, the researcher will be concerned both to give the interviewee her voice, so that the things she chooses to say are not lost in analysis and interpretation, but will also want to link the material to the other sections of the research. The progression from internal to external critique is again relevant here. This means that there will be two levels of analysis, the first looking at answers in relation to internal critique: Are the offenders, victims or communities those targeted by the policy, legislation or practices being investigated? What do the professionals, campaigners or those affected say about its effects? Why are respondents using or not using services provided? These are among the sorts of questions addressed of interview material by internal critique. The second layer of analysis is, of course, external critique: Do the interviewees raise questions or issues that go beyond the closures of current ways of thinking or acting? Does the external critical perspective preferred by the researcher make it easier for those questions to be addressed? Would policies drawing on the insights of the critical perspective have led to better outcomes?

CHOOSING AND USING EXTERNAL CRITIQUE

So far, my references to standpoints and theories drawn on for external critique have been very general: feminism, human rights theory, for example. These are value standpoints, and theoretical orientations, but within these general frames of reference, choices have to be made. Examples are: Which feminism? Which approach to human rights? Researchers usually come to their projects already more impressed by one strand of theory than another, but the topic will also point to choices within the wider framework. The researcher working on violence against Black and Minority Ethnic women, for example, and my own contribution to a journal special edition on restorative justice and indigenous women, point to intersectionality and critical race feminism (Hudson, 2006). For these topics, it is important to consider both gender and race, without allowing one to be the primary concept that obscures the other. Similarly, in much work in criminology and criminal justice, gender, race/ethnicity and poverty need to be held together.

In two recent works, I have used human rights as external critique (Hudson, 2007, 2009). I have had to make choices within the wider human rights paradigm:

Am I concerned with human rights law or with human rights as an ideal, human rights as privileges of citizenship or human rights as a universal entitlement? My interest in human rights as universal has led me to **cosmopolitan justice**. The idea of cosmopolitanism in social theory and in everyday usage tends to suggest a cosmopolitan identity, a pick-and-mix identity exemplified by the professional elite, speaking several languages, enjoying the music and cuisine of many countries, at ease in the international hotels which are reassuringly the same the world over, the Danish businessman encountered on a flight described by Beck (2006). Cosmopolitan justice, however, invokes an older meaning of cosmopolitanism, the Greek-derived sense of *all the people of all the world*. Everyone, everywhere, from this viewpoint, is entitled to those human rights regarded as fundamental, simply because of being human: rights do not depend on citizenship; rights do not have to be deserved or earned.

Although I would agree with Beck (2006) and Gilroy (2004) that cosmopolitanism in their methodological sense avoids the shortcomings of single dimension approaches to race and gender which tend to exaggerate differences between social groups and gloss over or miss differences within groups, my main interest is in this idea of all the people of all the world. For cosmopolitan justice proponents such as Derrida (2001) and Appiah (2006), the important principle is that all the people of all the world are owed justice, and an important principle of justice (drawn from Kant's essay *On Perpetual Peace*, first published in 1783–94) is that of hospitality, which Kant defined as the right of the stranger to be received without violence.

Writing about migration, and then the war on terror, I have used this cosmopolitan stance on human rights as external critique. In 'The rights of strangers' (Hudson, 2007) I looked at issues of immigration and emigration first through laws and policy, using internal critique of legal scholars and commentators. I also looked at John Rawls' *The Law of Peoples* (2001). Rawls is a philosopher of justice who has had considerable influence on UK and US legal scholarship and legal institutions. Although a philosopher, he is an 'insider'. His book distinguishes well-ordered and non-well-ordered states, and suggests what the former owe to the latter. Well-ordered states owe less fortunate ones, he says, assistance in becoming better ordered (more democratic, more economically stable), but this does not imply a duty to admit all those individuals who wish to move to the well-ordered states. Rawls provides an analysis which is centred on the nation-state: his 'peoples' means nations, not persons.

The external critique is that of human rights as belonging to individuals. The state-centred approach predicated on the right of states to control their own populations and so determine their own immigration policies, is contrasted with the cosmopolitan approach exemplified by Moellendorf (2002). From a cosmopolitan perspective, if rights to life, to freedom, and to human flourishing are due to all the people of all the world, then there are strict limits to a nation-state's rights to set quotas and restrict numbers. Cosmopolitan theorists, when thinking about migration, argue that only open borders would prompt richer nations to give meaningful kinds and levels of aid to poorer nations, and they suggest that international organisations are needed to reduce inequalities between nations.

In 'Justice in a time of terror' (Hudson, 2009) I again began with legal analysis: Were the invasions and occupations of Iraq and Afghanistan legal? Has torture been used illegally, and has it been used systematically as a matter of policy rather than just by some 'bad apple' personnel? I worked through the arguments that would justify techniques that are unacceptable in 'normal' circumstances, arguments such as the use of a lesser evil to prevent a greater evil, and those that have been put against occupation and torture by 'insider' critics, such as the unreliability of information obtained under torture, the likelihood that resentment will lead to more terrorist actions, and the degradation of democratic values. Finally, I come to the 'all the people in all the world' questions: Are only the innocent deserving of rights? Are only the rights of our own citizens those that we should protect? On this account, the emphasis on innocence (or at least lack of any proven guilt) in notorious cases of torture and rendition is questioned. Further, the question about the shooting of Jean Charles de Menezes should not be 'was enough care taken to establish his identity?', but 'should a shoot-to-kill policy be allowed under any circumstance?'[4] For cosmopolitans, even those who perpetrate the most incomprehensible of actions and who appear the most dangerous and undeserving of humans nonetheless deserve justice and have rights which must be respected.

SUMMARY

Critical criminology research goes through the following stages:

- Define and introduce the research topic and questions
- Decide on a research strategy, specifying what kinds of material are to be investigated (e.g. law, policy, professional practice, persons affected)
- Review the existing literature on the topic generally and on the different elements to be studied
- Place the research in relation to the literature (to fill a gap, to investigate a topic about which there has been significant change in law/policy, levels of concern, to illuminate an area where there have been contradictory findings, etc.)
- Explain one's preferred theoretical perspective
- Describe the methodology (content analysis, semi-structured interview, focus groups, etc.), and introduce internal and external critique as levels of analysis
- Analyse each element through internal and external critique
- Derive conclusions and recommendations

For those of us who see criminology as inevitably involved in political and moral areas, critical criminology appeals. This chapter has suggested a strategy for critical research that helps the researcher to work through a range of materials and provide rigorous and constructive critique, pointing towards better outcomes for the powerless, excluded or marginalised.

---

[4] Jean Charles de Menezes was a young Brazilian electrician who was shot by police on a London Underground train on 22 July 2005 after being wrongly identified as a terrorist suspect.

Study Questions/Activities for Students

1. Propose a topic for research and identify the kinds of data that you will gather and analyse.

2. Identify questions for internal critique.

3. Identify your value stance and preferred theoretical perspective.

4. What advantages do you expect from using this perspective for external critique?

5. Identify questions likely to be raised by external critique.

RESOURCES

British Journal of Criminology (2001) Special issue on Criminology and Social Theory, 40(2)

Melossi, D. (2008) *Controlling Crime, Controlling Society*, Cambridge: Polity Press, especially Introduction and Chapter 8

Van Swaaningen, R. (1997) *Critical Criminology: Visions from Europe*, London: Sage

REFERENCES

Appiah, K.A. (2006) *Cosmopolitanism: Ethics in a World of Strangers*, London: Allen Lane

Beck, U. (2006) *Cosmopolitan Vision*, Cambridge: Polity Press

Box, S. (1987) *Recession, Crime and Punishment*, Basingstoke: Macmillan

Burchell, G., Gordon, C. and Miller, P. (eds) (1991) *The Foucault Effect: Studies in Govern-mentality*, Chicago: University of Chicago Press

Cohen, S. (1979) 'The punitive city: notes on the dispersal of social control', *Contemporary Crises*, 3: 339–63

Cohen, S. (1985) *Visions of Social Control: Crime, Punishment and Classification*, Cambridge: Polity Press

Connerton, P. (1976) *Critical Sociology*, Harmondsworth: Penguin

Crawford, A. (1997) *The Local Governance of Crime*, Oxford: Clarendon Press

Derrida, J. (2001) 'Cosmopolitanism', in *Cosmopolitanism and Forgiveness* (trans. M. Dooley and M. Hughes), London: Routledge

Feeley, M.M. and Simon, J. (1992) 'The new penology: notes on the emerging strategy of corrections and its implications', *Criminology*, 30: 449–74

Foucault, M. (1977) *Discipline and Punish: The Birth of the Prison*, London: Allen Lane

Fraser, N. (1992) 'Rethinking the public sphere: a contribution to the critique of actually existing societies', in C. Calhoun (ed.), *Habermas and the Public Sphere*, Cambridge, MA: MIT Press

Gamble, A. (1988) *The Free Economy and the Strong State: The Politics of Thatcherism*, Basingstoke: Macmillan

Garland, D. (2001) *The Culture of Control*, Oxford: Oxford University Press

Gilroy, P. (1982) 'Police and thieves', in Centre for Contemporary Cultural Studies, *The Empire Strikes Back*, London: Hutchinson

Gilroy, P. (2004) *Between Camps: Nations, Cultures and the Allure of Race*, London: Routledge

Hall, S. (1980) *Drifting into a Law and Order Society*, London: Cobden Trust

Hall, S., Crichter, C., Clarke, J., Jefferson, T. and Roberts, B. (1978) *Policing the Crisis*, London: Macmillan

Hudson, B. (1993) *Penal Policy and Social Justice*, Basingstoke: Macmillan

Hudson, B. (2003a) *Justice in the Risk Society*, London: Sage

Hudson, B. (2003b) *Understanding Justice*, Milton Keynes: Open University Press

Hudson, B. (2006) 'Beyond white man's justice: race, gender and justice in late modernity', *Theoretical Criminology*, 10(1): 29–47

Hudson, B. (2007) 'The rights of strangers: policies, theories, philosophies' in M. Lee (ed.), *Human Trafficking*, Cullompton: Willan Publishing

Hudson, B. (2009) 'Justice in a time of terror', *British Journal of Criminology*, 49(5): 702–17

Jay, M. (1973) *The Dialectical Imagination*, London: Heinemann

Lacey, N. (1993) 'Closure and critique in feminist jurisprudence: transcending the dichotomy, or a foot in both camps', in A. Norrie (ed.), *Closure and Critique: New Directions in Legal Theory*, Edinburgh: Edinburgh University Press

Lyon, D. (1994) *The Electronic Eye: The Rise of the Surveillance Society*, Cambridge: Polity Press

Melossi, D. and Pavarini, M. (1981) *The Prison and the Factory*, London: Macmillan

Moellendorf, D. (2002) *Cosmopolitan Justice*, Boulder, CO, and Oxford: Westview Press

O'Malley, P. (1992) 'Risk, power and crime prevention', *Economy and Society*, 21: 252–75

O'Malley, P. (2001) 'Risk, crime and prudentialism revisited', in K. Stenson and R.R. Sullivan (eds), *Crime, Risk and Justice*, Cullompton: Willan Publishing

Palmer, R.E. (1969) *Hermeneutics*, Evanston, IL: Northwestern University Press

Rawls, J. (2001) *The Law of Peoples*, Cambridge, MA: Harvard University Press

Rose, N. (1996) 'The death of the social? Refiguring the territory of government', *Economy and Society*, 25(3): 327–56

Rusche, G. and Kirchheimer, O. (1968 [1939]) *Punishment and Social Structure*, New York: Russell and Russell

Scott, D. (2006) 'Ghosts beyond our realm: a neo-abolitionist analysis of prisoner human rights and prison officer occupational culture', unpublished PhD thesis, University of Central Lancashire, Preston

Scraton, P. (1987) *Law, Order and the Authoritarian State*, Milton Keynes: Open University Press

Sim, J. (1990) *Medical Power in Prisons*, Buckingham: Open University Press

Sim, J. (2009) *Punishment and Prisons: Power and the Carceral State*, London: Sage

Simon, J. (2007) *Governing through Crime: How the War on Crime Transformed American Democracy and Created a Culture of Fear*, New York: Oxford University Press

Taylor, I., Walton, P. and Young, J. (1973) *The New Criminology*, London: Routledge

Wells, C. (2004) 'The impact of feminist thinking on criminal law and justice: contradiction, complexity, conviction and connection', *Criminal Law Review*, July: 503–15

Young, I.M. (1990) *Justice and the Politics of Difference*, Princeton, NJ: Princeton University Press

Young, J. (1997) 'Left realist criminology: radical in its analysis, realist in its policy', in M. Maguire, R. Morgan and R. Reiner (eds), *The Oxford Handbook of Crimiology* (2nd edition), Oxford: Oxford University Press, 473–99

GLOSSARY

ANNOTATED BIBLIOGRAPHY – a set of descriptive summaries of published work which focuses on one source at a time. Each source or annotation will include as a minimum the full bibliographic citation, a content summary and a short analysis.

BIOGRAPHICAL INTERVIEWS – qualitative interviews that have a prime interest in understanding an individual's life as it has unfolded from the perspective of the interviewee. Close attention is paid to the sequence and meaning of events and experiences and their consequences for a person's life course.

CASE STUDY – an approach that uses in-depth investigation of a single 'case' or several 'cases'. Data may derive from individuals, social activities, groups or organizations.

CATEGORY SATURATION – in qualitative analysis, the point at which your interviews/observations add nothing to what you already know about a category, its properties, and its relationship to the core category. When this occurs you cease coding for that category.

CLASSICAL CRIMINOLOGY – classicism is based on the idea that human beings respond rationally to punishment, and that the justice system must be logical and consistent and operate in accordance with due process. Classical criminology is associated with the late eighteenth-century writings of Cesare Beccaria in Italy and Jeremy Bentham in Britain.

CONSCIOUS PARTIALITY – a methodological standpoint which extols the virtues of an ethical and political position of commitment in the research process and at least partial identification with the research objects as oppressed groups. Those adopting a stance of conscious partiality are concerned to expose and critique the conditions of their oppression by means of their research and advocacy.

CONTENT ANALYSIS – a process of analysis which focuses on the words and/or pictures contained in documents. Data can be quantitative (e.g. the number of times a word is used) or qualitative (the nature of language or style of picture). Examples include the analysis of crime reporting in national newspapers and the analysis of policy documents. Qualitative and quantitative content analysis can be usefully combined in one project.

COSMOPOLITAN JUSTICE – a cosmopolitan stance on human rights contends that everyone, everywhere – *all the people of all the world* – are entitled to those human rights regarded as fundamental, simply because of being human.

CRIME/VICTIM SURVEY – originally referred to as a crime survey but more latterly referred to as a victim survey, these terms are often used interchangeably. Such surveys are specifically designed to collect data about the incidence, patterning and experiences of victimization. Typically, individuals (usually a sample) are asked if they have been victims of crime, whether or not they reported it to the police and if not, why not.

CRITICAL CRIMINOLOGICAL RESEARCH – a form of conflict criminology which sees ideas about crime as located in class society and which highlights the ways in which poverty, racism, sexism and other discriminations contribute to the criminalization of oppressed groups within society. It is typically concerned with exposing areas of injustice. It is both theoretical and policy related. It draws upon abstract concepts, such as ideology, power and discourse. In addition, it often addresses criminal justice policies but in a critical vein rather than as a form of evaluative research which will act as an aid to management.

CRITICAL THEORY – draws attention to our acts of interpretation. It is a dialectical perspective where the basic dialectic is that between experience and our already existing ideas and categories, which are likewise constantly being reformulated. Critical theory has emancipatory objectives, is opposed to positivism and urges us not to disguise our values and our pre-existing knowledge and interpretations.

CROSS-SECTIONAL RESEARCH – such studies involve the collection of data during one specific point in time (e.g. a survey). Because cross-sectional research provides a snapshot of a situation, it is vulnerable to claims of non-generalizability and criticisms of a lack of spatial-temporal perspective.

DATA-MINING – the interrogation of large (usually) online databases to extract informational patterns that reflect online behaviour. Such behaviour could include fraud, spending patterns, movements. The speed of data collection can mean that the data-mining can identify behaviour almost as it happens.

DECISION-MAKING – the process of adjudicating between alternative courses of action and of making choices based upon such adjudication. One way of viewing the research process is as a series of decisions taken about the topic of research, the way in which research problems are formulated, the form of case selection, data collection and data analysis. The validity of research conclusions is the outcome of such decisions.

DESCRIPTIVE RESEARCH – the aim of this research strategy is to provide information about the unit of analysis at the centre of the research question. The research can be qualitative (e.g. the physical layout of a courtroom) or quantitative (e.g. the number of offences recorded by the police across police force areas). Although the aim of the research is not to look for causal relationships (*see* **Explanatory research**), it is possible for descriptive research to be deeply analytic.

DIGITAL DIVIDE – the gap between those who have access to networked computer facilities and those who do not. It is increasingly being used to refer to those who have 'meaningful' access because factors such as levels of technical knowledge can influence access.

DIGITAL TECHNOLOGIES – technologies that use digital data comprised of discrete values (numbers, letters or icons). Digital technologies contrast with analogue technologies of non-discrete continuous values (images, sounds or other continuous forms of measurement).

ETHNOGRAPHIC CONVERSATIONS – arise from the ongoing daily interaction of the researchers with members of the group being studied. Often they start out as a means through which rapport and trust can be developed between the researcher and the researched, but soon become more focused and the challenge for the researcher is to develop them in a systematic way.

ETHNOGRAPHY – a qualitative approach to research in which the researcher immerses him/herself overtly or covertly into the social setting under study or the daily lives of those being studied. This form of research involves a variety of methods that share the assumption that personal engagement with the subject is the key to understanding. The emphasis is on describing and understanding the social processes that are observed and experienced. Ethnography will often combine **participant observation**, **ethnographic conversations** and **interviews** before a period of distance in order to develop an informed assessment. It is heavily time- and resource-intensive (*see also* **Participant observation**).

EUGENICS – the supposed science of human races, which demanded that 'undesirables' and 'defectives' (including criminal types) be isolated and sterilized. Selective breeding was viewed as the key to the production of healthy populations and improving the quality of the human race. The movement had an impact in some versions of biological criminology in the early to mid-twentieth century.

EVALUATION – a research strategy in which the researcher seeks to assess the ways in which initiatives, programmes or criminal justice policies work. Often, the aim is to test out the effectiveness of an intervention before it is implemented on a wider scale.

EXPLANATORY RESEARCH – the aim of this research strategy is to look for patterns and relationships between variables, thus providing a causal explanation for a phenomenon.

FEMINIST APPROACHES – although there are a variety of different types of feminism, they all tend to challenge the empiricist orthodoxy that social science research should strive for objectivity and be value-free, questioning the role of power between the researcher and the participant. The subjectivity of the researcher is acknowledged as significant to the research process and is a salient methodological principle in feminist research.

FOCUS GROUPS – a form of group interview in which the researcher focuses on the nature of the interactions between people as well as what is actually said. This enables the researcher to get closer to the to-and-fro social exchanges that take place in everyday life, thus getting a more dynamic picture of the topic.

(THE) GRID – an 'enhanced' internet used mainly for research purposes in the sciences. Also used in social science contexts where many computer resources are combined towards achieving a common task (such as real-time visual data analysis across geographically dispersed research teams).

GROUNDED THEORY – associated originally with Glaser and Strauss (1967), this is an inductive approach which starts with data collection, and as data emerge, constant comparisons are made between data and theory.

GROUP INTERVIEWS – a way of doing interviews with more than one person at a time. The interview usually follows a semi-structured approach, allowing all members of the group time to speak. The researcher collects all the responses of the individuals involved for analysis.

HARD-TO-REACH GROUPS – groups that are difficult to access for any reason. In research terms, they represent those who are not readily available or able or willing to be 'the researched' and so have traditionally been under-represented.

HYPOTHESIS – a logical conjecture about the possible relationship between two or more variables expressed in the form of a testable statement.

IMMANENT CRITIQUE – a form of critique common to critical criminological research where the research questions arise from and are generated by the material itself and not from an external standpoint.

INDUCTIVISM – an orientation to research inquiry that involves reasoning from evidence or 'inference' and often involves generalizing from something that has been studied or observed to other cases that have not.

INSIDER RESEARCH – research undertaken on a social group or issue (e.g. a youth subculture) by someone who can claim membership of that group or special, previous knowledge of that issue. Insider research is said to bring advantages of access, understanding and insight (e.g. a researcher might be more easily accepted into the Goth youth culture for qualitative research if he/she carries elements of Goth identity). Less commonly referred to are the potential disadvantages of insider research (e.g. there may be a tendency for the researcher and researched to presume that knowledge about the subculture is already taken for granted – and shared assumptions go unquestioned).

INTERNAL CRITIQUE – similar to **immanent critique** and a form of critique common to critical criminological research where the research questions arise from and are generated by the material itself and not from an external standpoint.

INTERNET SEARCH ENGINE (OR WEB BROWSER SUCH AS GOOGLE) – a program that mines online databases to locate information about web sources.

INTERPRETIVISM – the opposite of **positivism**. Interpretivists believe that it is necessary to study a phenomenon in its natural state, undisturbed by the researcher. So they adopt a more flexible research design, selecting whatever method best suits the specific circumstances. The focus is on extracting the meaning of people's actions. **Ethnography** is a good example of interpretivistic research.

INTERVENTION-BASED RESEARCH – this is very close to policy research as it is often concerned with evaluating the effectiveness or otherwise of interventions in producing intended outcomes. This form of research is sometimes also known as **evaluation** research.

INTERVIEWS – a method of data collection, information or opinion gathering that specifically involves asking a series of questions.

KEYWORD SEARCH – using combinations of keywords entered into a web browser or internet search engine to locate online information.

LABELLING PERSPECTIVE – emerging in the 1960s and particularly identified with the ideas of American sociologist, Howard Becker, labelling theory challenged the idea of crime as a given reality. In his seminal text *Outsiders* (1963), Becker argued that crime is a social construct that changes according to historical context and is determined by the 'powerful definers' in society.

LIFE HISTORY – a form of criminological research, consistent with **critical criminological research** and linked to critical ethnography, oral history and narrative interviewing, which gather stories of a life and allow subjects to give their own stories.

LITERATURE REVIEW – an evaluative overview, synthesis or survey of the main published work in a given topic or field. It provides an overview of the state of academic knowledge on a research topic and is increasingly known as a **narrative literature review**.

LONGITUDINAL RESEARCH — longitudinal research typically seeks to investigate phenomena by including the same participants over different points in time so as to focus on processes of social change and continuity. Often, these are called cohort studies. Most frequently, longitudinal social research is quantitative in nature, drawing upon panel surveys of samples over regular intervals. Qualitative longitudinal research is less common, partly because of the problems of retaining sufficient numbers of necessarily smaller samples over time. Longitudinal studies are difficult to administer because people tend to drop out of the research study for various reasons.

META-ANALYSIS — a statistical synthesis of the findings of several previous studies on the same topic.

MIXED METHODS — refer to the use of more than one method in social research.

NARRATIVE ANALYSIS — an overarching term for methods that are concerned with the detailed analysis of a media text. Many of these methods involve breaking the narrative structure of a text into units of analysis, which are then closely scrutinized.

NARRATIVE LITERATURE REVIEW (*SEE* LITERATURE REVIEW)

NETWORKED TECHNOLOGIES — the digital technologies that use the internet to create or encourage the formation of networks.

NEWS VALUES — the informal codes used by news professionals in the selection and construction of news stories across media forms.

NORMATIVE — a term used to describe the expression of value judgements as contrasted with stating (scientific) facts. Accordingly, the term 'normative' concerns those expressive value judgements ('should', 'ought', 'must', etc.) rather than the claims associated with the stating of (scientific) facts ('is', etc.).

ONLINE FIELD-SITE — a term that describes a specific online research environment.

OPERATIONAL RULES — link abstract concepts to observations. Such observations are sometimes also known as indicators.

OPERATIONALIZATION — refers to the laying down of rules which stipulate when instances of a concept have occurred. Operational rules link abstract concepts to observations. Such observations are sometimes also known as indicators. The extent to which observations are truly indicating instances of a concept is the extent to which an operationalization has measurement validity.

OUTCOME-ORIENTED EVALUATION – an approach to evaluation that adheres to a strict experimental model to assess whether an intervention results in specific outcomes. The experiment involves the construction of equivalent experimental and control groups. The intervention is then applied to the experimental group only and comparisons of the changes that have taken place in the experimental and control groups are used as a method of finding out what effect the intervention has had.

PARTICIPANT OBSERVATION – the research technique *par excellence* of classic ethnography (and social anthropology). It involves immersion in the life worlds and cultures under study by the researcher, who will participate in and observe phenomena so as to gain understanding from an insider perspective using this as the basis of the social scientific analysis. True participant observation is fraught with epistemological and methodological challenges and is consequently quite rare. More common are less grand and demanding attempts at some level of participation and/or observation of social phenomena.

PILOT STUDY – an exploratory investigation that attempts to outline the area of study prior to the development of questionnaires. 'If the main study is going to employ mainly closed questions, open questions can be asked in the pilot to generate the fixed-choice answers' (Bryman, 2008: 247).

PILOTING – a term used to describe the process of 'trying out' or practising the proposed research instruments (interview/questionnaire) on a population that matches the target population. Piloting reveals which parts of an interview/questionnaire work and which don't. Research tools can then be adjusted accordingly.

POLICE CULTURE – a broad term used throughout the literature to refer to the collectively understood and often taken-for-granted occupational norms and values of police officers which informs both what they do and how they operate. It is sometimes referred to in the literature as 'cop culture', canteen culture or the police occupational culture.

POLICY-RELATED RESEARCH – the collection of data and the presentation of conclusions and arguments as aids to the formulation of social policies.

POLITICAL – there are both restricted and broad definitions of the term used in this book. The restricted definition refers to processes relating to the work and influence of explicit political ideologies, political parties and the legitimate, organized, coercive institutional power of the modern nation-state. The broad, extended definition is used in the non-party political sense to convey the working through of power and the contests over its exercise.

POSITIVISM/POSITIVIST METHODOLOGY – an approach to criminological research which is underpinned by the empirical methods of the natural sciences. Scientific inquiry relies on observations and measurements, survey research and experimental approaches. Positivism requires the researcher to control and manipulate the variables in order to test hypotheses and find causal relationships. There is a heavy emphasis on standardizing the measurement tools so that the study can be replicated. Survey-based research is a good example of positivistic research.

PRIMARY RESEARCH/ANALYSIS – refers to a form of inquiry and analysis based entirely on pre-existing data sources. It can be distinguished from primary research and analysis whereby an investigator collects the data first hand.

PROSPECTIVE RESEARCH – applicable where research subjects are going through a process (e.g. a court case or a rehabilitation course). Prospective studies involve waiting for subjects to enter the process and studying them throughout their journey. These studies tend to be time-consuming and resource-intensive but give the researcher a great deal of control over the data collection process.

QUALITATIVE RESEARCH – research that investigates aspects of social life which are not amenable to quantitative measurement. Associated with a variety of theoretical perspectives, qualitative research uses a range of methods to focus on the meanings and interpretation of social phenomena and social processes in the particular contexts in which they occur (Sumner, 2006). Qualitative data includes words, sounds and images.

QUANTITATIVE RESEARCH – the collection of data in numerical form for quantitative analysis. The numerical data can be durations, scores, counts of incidents, ratings or scales. Quantitative data can be collected in either controlled or naturalistic environments, in laboratories or field studies, from special populations or from samples of the general population. The defining factor is that numbers result from the process, whether the initial data collection produced numerical values or whether non-numerical values were subsequently converted to numbers as part of the analysis process, as in content analysis (Garwood, 2006).

RAPPORT – the feeling of trust and openness between the researcher and researched. Greater empathy between the interviewer and interviewee is said to generate greater levels of insight and understanding.

REALISTIC EVALUATION – advocates of realistic evaluation doubt whether outcome-oriented evaluation is a good way of finding out whether interventions are successful or not because they assume that interventions will have the same impact in all situations. In realistic evaluation, measures are expected to vary in impact depending on the circumstances in which they are introduced. The key question is 'What works for whom in what circumstances?' In order to answer this, the research must measure contexts (the conditions needed to trigger mechanisms), mechanisms (what causes the intervention to have an impact) and outcomes (the practical effects of the mechanisms).

RELIABILITY – the extent to which concepts and measures are well defined, consistent and repeatable.

REPLICABILITY – the extent to which the research is well planned and well explained so that the study can be replicated and the findings confirmed.

RESEARCH DESIGN – a detailed plan of the procedures for data collection and analysis.

RESEARCH OBJECTIVES – the purposes for which the research is being carried out. They can be basic (couched in terms of exploration, description, understanding, explanation or prediction) or they can be of an applied nature (e.g. to change, to evaluate or to assess social impacts).

RESEARCH PROPOSAL – a written document which describes the proposed research, including what it aims to do, how it will be undertaken, and the anticipated outcome(s). A proposal also outlines why the proposed research is important and justifies the research design, including how it connects research questions to data.

RESEARCH QUESTION – the overarching question that defines the scope, scale and conduct of a research project. It is an initial statement of the territory to be examined in the research inquiry.

RESEARCH STRATEGY – a strategic framework adopted at the start of the research process which helps to shape the research design. The choice of framework depends on the overall purpose of the research, the nature of the conclusion that is to be reached and the theoretical underpinnings of the research. The three main types of strategy are: descriptive, explanatory or exploratory strategies.

RETROSPECTIVE RESEARCH – research that analyzes data relating to events that have already occurred (e.g. at the end of a court case process or a rehabilitation course). They are usually fairly quick and easy to conduct, but the researcher must make do with the data that is available (usually collected by the administrators of the process under study). Retrospective research contrasts with real-time research techniques that observe the unfolding of the present and prospective research and seeks to draw upon past trends to predict future scenarios as a basis for policy or regulation.

SAMPLING – there are different ways of and approaches to constructing samples in social and criminological research. Sometimes it is not possible, simple or necessary to generate a statistically representative sample (e.g. of all young adults living in a particular locality). Convenience sampling refers to the process of constructing a sample in a way that is convenient to the researcher, given lack of resources such as time (e.g. interviewing relatively easily accessible young adults in a particular locality, such as those attending local colleges). Theoretical sampling refers to the way that a sample is generated that reflects the theoretical concerns and research questions of the study. Random samples are intended to be representative of the population from which they are drawn and therefore the characteristics of the sample are assumed to be generalizable across the whole population. Members of the sample are drawn randomly using a sampling frame and everyone in the population stands the same chance of being included in the sample. Probability sampling is another name given to random sampling. Purposive samples are not intended to be generalizable to the population as a whole. Instead, they are used to focus on specific groups or categories and select units based on predefined characteristics (such as gender or victim status). They are particularly useful for populations that are hard to reach. Non-probability sampling is another name given to purposive sampling.

SAMPLING ERROR – the level of statistical error that arises when a sample is observed rather than a complete population. It helps researchers assess the reliability of their data and the findings that arise from the data for the purposes of generalizability.

SECONDARY RESEARCH/ANALYSIS – research that is based upon existing sources of information which have been collected by someone other than the researcher and with some purpose other than the current research problem in mind. It can be distinguished from primary research and analysis whereby an investigator collects the data at first hand. Examples of secondary sources include census data and the recorded crime statistics.

SEMIOTICS/SEMIOTIC ANALYSIS – literally, the 'science of signs'. Semiotic analysis is concerned with the analysis of media texts to elicit manifest and latent meanings and to decode the signs in the narrative structure and the technical composition of a text.

SENSITIVE RESEARCH/TOPICS – should be understood as research 'which potentially poses a substantial threat to those who are or have been involved in it' (Lee, 1993: 4). Included within this is any research that includes private, stressful, controversial or stigmatizing topics. For instance, questions asked of respondents may be of a personal, intimate nature (e.g. to do with emotions and feelings about family life or relationships) or concerned with topics that might show respondents in a bad light (e.g. to with wrong-doing or illegality).

SNOWBALL SAMPLING – the process of constructing a sample of research participants from the recommendations and suggestions of other research participants (i.e. an 'early' interviewee suggests to the researcher other likely interviewees). It is a valuable method when clear sampling frames (e.g. official lists of a potential sample) are difficult to obtain and when the social group under study might be relatively 'hidden' or '**hard-to-reach groups**'.

STUDYING UP/DOWN – this distinction points to the different types of research challenges when the focus is on those people and institutions which are associated with positions of established power and privilege ('studying up') as against the more common tendency in mainstream criminology to focus on the people and groups most commonly criminalized and marginalized as outsiders ('studying down'). Historically, in criminology, as the social sciences more generally, 'studying down' (i.e. studying vulnerable minority groups) has been much easier, has had greater institutional backing from the state and is much more commonplace in criminology than is the 'studying up' of powerful elites.

SURVEY RESEARCH – the systematic collection of data, by means of questionnaires and/ or **interviews**, from a sample of a target population.

SYSTEMATIC REVIEW – a formulaic and prescriptive form of review that employs transparent and systematic criteria for searching the literature, evaluating the suitability and findings of each source and synthesizing results. Such reviews are favoured for feeding into policy-making as they bring together the most directly relevant and rigorous evaluations on a particular topic.

THEORETICAL RESEARCH – the emphasis is on understanding and explaining human behaviour and social action, the workings of social institutions and how all of these connect with the different dimensions of social structure. The primary aim is knowledge accumulation.

TRIANGULATION – the use of different research methods or sources of data to examine the same problem.

UNDERCLASS – this contentious term suggests that there is a group or class of people in society set below the established working-class as a consequence of socio-economic change and/or patterns of cultural behaviour.

VALIDITY – the extent to which one can rely upon and trust the findings and conclusions of a research study. This involves an evaluation of the methodological objections that can be raised. This means looking at internal validity (can we be sure that a causal relationship exists?), external validity (can the results be generalized?) and ecological validity (are the conclusions applicable to everyday situations or have they been drawn from unnatural or unique conditions?). In addition, construct or measurement validity is concerned with whether a measure accurately reflects the concept it is designed to measure.

VALUE-FREE KNOWLEDGE – research that is impartial and dispassionate, stripped of the researcher's own beliefs, values, prejudices and opinions.

WEB 1.0/2.0/3.0 – web versions are used to denote enhancements in collaborative and immersive technologies. For example, Web 2.0 technologies differ from Web 1.0 because they allow interactive information-sharing, interoperability (enabling diverse systems and organizations to interoperate or work together) and various forms of collaboration in the production and consumption of www information.

REFERENCES

Becker, H. (1963) *Outsiders: Studies in the Sociology of Deviance*. New York: Free Press.

Bryman, A. (2001) *Social Research Methods*. Oxford: Oxford University Press.

Garwood, J. (2006:250–251) 'Quantitative Research', Dictionary entry in V. Jupp (ed.) *The Sage Dictionary of Social Research*. London: Sage.

Glaser, A. and Strauss, A. (1967) *The Discovery of Grounded Theory*. Chicago: IL: Aldine.

Lee, R. M. (1993) *Doing Research on Sensitive Topics*. London: Sage.

Sumner, M. (2006:248–250) 'Qualitative Research', Dictionary entry in V. Jupp (ed.) *The Sage Dictionary of Social Research*. London: Sage.

INDEX

Page references in *italics* indicate boxes, those in **bold** indicate tables, and those in ***bold italics*** indicate figures.

data-mining
  defined 346
  online sources of information and 265
Davies, B. 23
Davies, M.D. 19
Davies, P. 18, 64
decision-making
  defined 346
  research design and 10–11
  research objectives and conclusions and 9
  research problems and 7
  research questions and 8, 43–45, *44*
  research strategies and 10–11, *75*
Declaration of Helsinki (1964) 291
deductivism
  vs. inductivism 38–39
  literature reviews and 81
Denscombe, M. 200–201
Derrida, J. 341
descriptive research
  defined *56–57*, 347
  fixed vs. flexible research designs 59
  research questions and 39, *39*, 49
  on young adult offenders *57*
descriptive statistics 143–144
Dickinson, R. 259
digital divide
  defined 347
  research and 268
digital Hawthorn effect 276
digital technologies 347
disaggregated data 114
discourse analysis 248–249, 251
  See also narrative analysis; semiotics/semiotic
    analysis
dissertations
  data collection methods and 22–27, *24*, *25*
  ethical considerations and 27
  literature reviews and 16–17, *17*,
    21–22, 82
  primary research/analysis and 16–17, *17*,
    22–23
  quantitative vs. qualitative research and
    23–25, *28*
  research proposals and 29–31, *31*, *32*
  research questions and 19–20, *20*
  resources *18*
  secondary research/analysis and 22–23
  supervision and peer support 32–33
  time management and 27–29, **29**
  topics 17–20, *20*
Ditton, J. 247, 321
Dixon of Dock Green (BBC series) 235
Doing a Literature Review (Hart) 97
domestic violence 145–147, *146*
Duffy, B. 227, *227*, 247
Durham prison 313, 315

ecological validity 355
Economic and Social Research Council (ESRC)
    167, 294, 314
economic crimes *42*, 165, 165–166
Ely, M. 213
EndNote (bibliographic software) 22, 92
epistemology 80
Ericson, R. 255
ethics
  defined 288
  anonymity 153, 168
  children and *141*, 154, 296–300
  dilemmas *296*
  dissertations and 27
  guidelines and reviewing 294, *295*, 303
  Internet and 276–277
  interviews and 166–168, 175–176
  politics and 283–284
  prison research and 167, 288–294, 296–301
  privacy 276
  qualitative research and 296–301
  reflexivity and 295–296
  research design and 73
  See also confidentiality; informed consent
ethnographic conversations
  defined 347
  rapport and 213
ethnography
  defined 2, 70, 200–201, 347
  drug dealers and *58*
  methodology and 105
  myths of 201, *202*
  note-taking and 213–214
  online environments and 266, 268–269
  police culture and 203–206, *205*
  research questions and 42
  See also appreciative ethnography; participant
    observation
eugenics 291, 347
evaluation
  defined 347
  research questions and 41
evaluation research
  See intervention-based research
Evans, S. 338n2
explanatory research
  defined *57*, 348
  fixed vs. flexible research designs 59
  reintegrative shaming theory and *57*
  research questions and 39, *39*, 49–50
external critique 338, *339*, 340–342
external validity 355

Farrington, D.P. 85–87, *86*
feminist approaches
  defined 348
  conscious partiality and 310, *310*